LAKE ERIE COLLEGE

A GIFT IN MEMORY OF
LAVINIA ELIZABETH STOCKWELL DAY
WHO WAS BORN IN PAINESVILLE OHIO
8 DECEMBER 1852

Ruth

———

VOLUME 7D

THE ANCHOR YALE BIBLE is a project of international and interfaith scope in which Protestant, Catholic, and Jewish scholars from many countries contribute individual volumes. The project is not sponsored by any ecclesiastical organization and is not intended to reflect any particular theological doctrine.

THE ANCHOR YALE BIBLE is committed to producing commentaries in the tradition established half a century ago by the founders of the series, William Foxwell Albright and David Noel Freedman. It aims to present the best contemporary scholarship in a way that is accessible not only to scholars, but also to the educated nonspecialist. Its approach is grounded in exact translation of the ancient languages and an appreciation of the historical and cultural contexts in which the biblical books were written, supplemented by insights from modern methods, such as sociological and literary criticism.

John J. Collins
General Editor

THE ANCHOR YALE BIBLE

Ruth

A New Translation with
Introduction and Commentary

JEREMY SCHIPPER

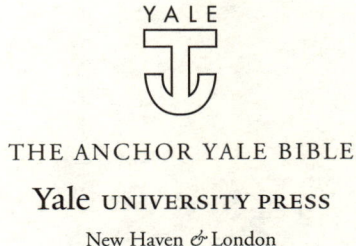

THE ANCHOR YALE BIBLE
Yale UNIVERSITY PRESS
New Haven & London

"Anchor Yale Bible" and the Anchor Yale logo are registered trademarks of Yale University.

Copyright © 2016 by Yale University.
All rights reserved.
This book may not be reproduced, in whole or in part, including illustrations, in any form (beyond that copying permitted by Sections 107 and 108 of the U.S. Copyright Law and except by reviewers for the public press), without written permission from the publishers.

Yale University Press books may be purchased in quantity for educational, business, or promotional use. For information, please e-mail sales.press@yale.edu (U.S. office) or sales@yaleup.co.uk (U.K. office).

Set in Adobe Garamond and Centennial types by Newgen North America.
Printed in the United States of America.

Library of Congress Control Number: 2015942781
ISBN: 978-0-300-19215-5

A catalogue record for this book is available from the British Library.

This paper meets the requirements of ANSI/NISO Z39.48–1992 (Permanence of Paper).

10 9 8 7 6 5 4 3 2 1

For my teacher Dennis T. Olson,
from whom I learned to read a biblical narrative

Contents

Preface, xi
Acknowledgments, xiii
List of Abbreviations, xv

INTRODUCTION, 1

I. This Commentary's Translation of Ruth	3
A. The Text for This Commentary's Translation	3
B. The Structure of This Commentary's Translation	4
C. The Diction of the Hebrew in Ruth	7
D. The Diction of This Commentary's Translation	9
II. Literary Contexts and Genre(s) for Ruth	10
A. Canonical Placements	10
B. Ruth and Ancient Israelite Literary Traditions	13
C. Genre(s) in Ruth	16
III. Ruth's Authorship and Date of Composition	18
A. The Authorship of Ruth	18
B. The Date of Ruth's Composition	20

IV. The Narrator and Narrative Style	23
A. Selective Representation and Narrative Ambiguity	24
B. Characterization	26
1. Speech	26
2. Actions, Events, and Consequences	27
V. The Commentator and the Focus of This Commentary	28
A. Divine Activity and Acts of *ḥesed* in Ruth	29
B. Sexual Desire in Ruth	35
C. Exogamy and Ethnicity	38
1. Judahite and Moabite Marriages	39
2. Moabites as Descendants of Lot	40
3. Moabites as Kin in Ruth	43
D. Household Organization	44
1. Household and Clan Statuses of Ruth's Characters	46
2. Gender, Patriarchy, and the Household	49

BIBLIOGRAPHY, 53

TRANSLATION, 69

NOTES AND COMMENTS, 77

Residing in Moab (1:1–7a)	79
Notes	79
Comments	86
On the Road (1:7b–19a)	90
Notes	91
Comments	101
Arriving in Bethlehem (1:19b–22a)	106
Notes	106
Comments	109

Ruth and Naomi's Conversation (1:22b–2:2)	111
Notes	111
Comments	114
In the Field Held by Boaz (2:3–17)	116
Notes	117
Comments	128
Ruth and Naomi's Conversation (2:18–23)	132
Notes	132
Comments	138
Naomi's Instructions (3:1–5)	141
Notes	141
Comments	144
On the Threshing Floor (3:6–15)	147
Notes	147
Comments	153
Ruth and Naomi's Conversation (3:16–18)	158
Notes	158
Comments	160
At the Gate (4:1–12)	162
Notes	163
Comments	172
The Birth of Obed (4:13–17)	178
Notes	178
Comments	182
The Generations of Perez (4:18–22)	185
Notes	185
Comments	186

Index of Subjects, 189
Index of Modern Authors, 195
Index of Ancient Sources, 199

Preface

This is the second commentary on Ruth in the Anchor Yale Bible series. The first one, by Edward Campbell, was published forty years ago. Obviously, the breadth and scope of Ruth scholarship, as well as biblical studies in general, have grown tremendously since then. Nonetheless, out of respect for my predecessor, I have tried to preserve the aspects of his commentary that I found most helpful, especially his attention to the versions. I do not intend this commentary to either replace or supplement Campbell's work. Rather, I hope that it is received and evaluated independently as its own small contribution to a larger conversation that his work has helped to shape for numerous students of Ruth over the past four decades.

As this volume is part of a series, I have tried to write a commentary that reflects the current state of the field while maintaining an emphasis on the traditional strengths and approaches of the Anchor Yale Bible that are explained in the series statement. This means that not all methods of scholarship receive equal attention in this volume. No one work can account for every aspect of Ruth scholarship sufficiently, and some important areas of critical inquiry are better covered in other commentaries or by other genres of scholarship. For example, other monographs or commentaries may provide more coverage of Ruth's reception history, which is discussed only in piecemeal fashion in the present volume. I view the limits of this commentary as a reflection of the richness and diversity of Ruth scholarship in the early twenty-first century. In this respect, my goal is not to write the definitive word on the book of Ruth that forecloses all other exegetical possibilities. Rather, I aim to provide detailed discussions of the text in order to assist readers in asking whatever questions they may have about the book and its contents more precisely, including the many important questions that I have not anticipated. While I offer interpretive options that are shaped by my own questions about Ruth, I hope that my NOTES and COMMENTS sections make it especially apparent that I do not intend to dictate how the book must be understood. I tend to agree with Tod Linafelt when he writes in the preface to his influential commentary on Ruth that "the task of the commentator is to enable the reader to apprehend and negotiate the uncertainties of the text."

A critical commentary is not the appropriate genre for a comprehensive literature review. Also, considering the vibrant state of Ruth scholarship, a thorough review would require many more words than the publisher has allotted for this entire commentary. Thus, rather than providing a more general bibliography, I have limited my list of secondary sources to works that I cite in the commentary, with an emphasis on works published since Campbell's commentary in 1975. Unfortunately, this means that I do not reference all of the sources that informed my thoughts on Ruth and deserve to be noted. Nonetheless, while my citations are not exhaustive, I hope that they responsibly represent the range of scholars who make up the current state of the field.

Acknowledgments

My favorite line in all of Campbell's commentary on Ruth is in the preface. In regard to his many colleagues, he writes: "I have no intention of giving such people the usual exoneration from responsibility for errors that remain. They should have corrected me!" Nevertheless, my commentary was greatly improved by many talented colleagues. I thank John J. Collins, the general editor of the Anchor Yale Bible series. Although I had never worked on Ruth previously, he invited and persuaded me to write this commentary. I also thank the other members of the editorial board, especially Susan Ackerman for her excellent editorial work on this volume. Many others patiently answered my half-baked questions, generously shared resources (even lending me some of their books!), read drafts, offered timely encouragement, or became my writing partners who met with me as I wrote this book in various coffee shops around Philadelphia and occasionally Washington, D.C. They include Samuel L. Adams, Rebecca Alpert, Joel Baden, Simeon Chavel, Stephen L. Cook, Blake Couey, Andrew R. Davis, Chip Dobbs-Allsopp, Danna Nolan Fewell, Maxine Grossman, Jo Ann Hackett, Christopher B. Hays, Robert Holmstedt, Jeremy Hutton, Bernard Jackson, Robert Kawashima, Jennifer Koosed, Jacqueline Lapsley, Tracy Lemos, Mark Leuchter, Tod Linafelt, Naphtali Meshel, Robert Miller, Candida Moss, Saul Olyan, Gary Rendsburg, Stephen Russell, Sarah Shectman, Mark S. Smith, Jeffrey Stackert, Brent Strawn, Matthew Suriano, and Bruce Wells, to name a few. I especially thank all my students in my spring 2013 graduate seminar on the book of Ruth. They participated in a series of helpful discussions throughout the semester that greatly influenced my thinking about the interpretation of this book. I thank my student Vincent Moulton for his careful preparation of the indexes and our many conversations about the commentary's content. The faculty and staff in Temple University's Department of Religion continue to provide a wonderful working environment. I deeply appreciate the commitment to collegiality that they have fostered. Research for this commentary was supported by a 2013 Faculty Research Award from Temple University and a 2013–2014 Bridwell Library Fellowship from Perkins School of Theology at Southern Methodist University. I am grateful to the librarians at both schools and at the Catholic University of America for all of their assistance.

Authors of Ruth commentaries often refer to their partners as women or men of worth (Ruth 2:1; 3:11). Rather than settling for such a hackneyed reference, I will simply say that anything of worth in this commentary comes from my partner in all things, academic or otherwise, Nyasha Junior. While I was working on this commentary, Nyasha and I celebrated our engagement, our marriage, and our first and second anniversaries. In his book *God: A Biography,* Jack Miles wrote that "Ruth can clearly enough be read as a book about the difficulties of marriage." I don't know whether writing a critical commentary has ever made a marriage easier, and we are looking forward to the day when Ruth is no longer part of ours. Nonetheless, writing this commentary was easier because I am married to the finest scholar that I will ever know. Everything that might be considered a blessing in my life would involve proclaiming her name. Every day.

I am happy to dedicate this commentary to Dennis T. Olson. A decade has passed since he directed my dissertation at Princeton Theological Seminary, and I have said on countless occasions that Dennis is one of the seminary's best-kept secrets. The fact that colleagues are often surprised to learn that I studied with him is evidence of his value as a mentor. In a field that is so often driven by ego and force of personality, it is rare to find teachers who do not try to replicate themselves and their own interests in their students. Dennis's concern was never to shape me into his own image, but to make me into the best scholar I could be. As I have graduate students of my own now, I have become increasingly aware of how difficult it is to train students to get out of your shadow. The field would be vastly improved if there were more teachers like Dennis.

Abbreviations

AB	Anchor Bible
AcT	*Actatheologica*
ANES	*Ancient Near Eastern Studies*
ANET	*Ancient Near Eastern Texts Relating to the Old Testament.* Edited by James B. Pritchard. 3rd ed. Princeton: Princeton University Press, 1969.
AOTC	Abingdon Old Testament Commentaries
AYB	Anchor Yale Bible
BASOR	*Bulletin of the American Schools of Oriental Research*
BHQ	*Biblia Hebraica Quinta: Fascicle 18: General Introduction and Megilloth.* Edited by A. Schenker. Stuttgart: Deutsche Bibelgesellschaft, 2004.
BHS	*Biblia Hebraica Stuttgartensia.* Edited by K. Elliger and W. Rudolph. Stuttgart: Deutsche Bibelgesellschaft, 1983.
BibInt	*Biblical Interpretation: A Journal of Contemporary Approaches*
BKAT	Biblischer Kommentar, Altes Testament
BZAR	Beiheftezur Zeitschrift für Altorientalische und Biblische Rechtsgeschichte
BZAW	Beiheftezur Zeitschrift für die alttestamentliche Wissenschaft
CAD	*The Assyrian Dictionary of the Oriental Institute of the University of Chicago.* Edited by Martha Roth. Chicago: University of Chicago Press, 1956–2011.
CBQ	*Catholic Biblical Quarterly*

COS	*The Context of Scripture.* Edited by William H. Hallo. 3 vols. Leiden: Brill, 1997–.
DJD	Discoveries in the Judean Desert
FAT	Forschungen zum Alten Testament
GKC	*Gesenius' Hebrew Grammar.* Edited by Emil Kautzsch. Translated by A. E. Cowley. 2nd ed. Oxford: Clarendon, 1910.
HALOT	*The Hebrew and Aramaic Lexicon of the Old Testament.* Edited by Ludwig Koehler, Walter Baumgartner, and Jakob Stamm. Translated and edited under the supervision of M. E. J. Richardson. 5 vols. Leiden: Brill, 1994–2000.
HAT	Handbuch zum Alten Testament
HS	*Hebrew Studies*
HSM	Harvard Semitic Monographs
HSS	Harvard Semitic Studies
HTKAT	Herders theologischer Kommentar zum Alten Testament
HTR	*Harvard Theological Review*
HUCA	*Hebrew Union College Annual*
IEJ	*Israel Exploration Journal*
IOS	*Israel Oriental Studies*
JAAR	*Journal of the American Academy of Religion*
JAOS	*Journal of the American Oriental Society*
JBL	*Journal of Biblical Literature*
JHS	*Journal of Hebrew Scriptures*
JM	Joüon, Paul, and T. Muraoka. *A Grammar of Biblical Hebrew.* Subsidia Biblica 27. Roma: Editrice Pontificio Istituto Biblico, 2006.
JNSL	*Journal of Northwest Semitic Languages*
JSOT	*Journal for the Study of the Old Testament*
JSOTSup	Journal for the Study of the Old Testament: Supplement Series
JSS	*Journal of Semitic Studies*
KAI	*Kanaanäische und aramäische Inscriften.* H. Donner and W. Röllig. 5th ed. Wiesbaden: Harrassowitz Verlag, 2002.
LBH	Late Biblical Hebrew
LHBOTS	Library of the Hebrew Bible/Old Testament Series
LXX^A	Codex Alexandrinus
LXX^B	Codex Vaticanus

LXX^L	Major Lucianus manuscripts
LXX^M	Codex Coislinianus
LXX^N	Codex Basiliano-Vaticanus
MT	Masoretic Text
MT^A	Apello Codex
MT^L	Leningrad Codex
MT^Y	Cambridge University Add. Ms. 1753
NAC	The New American Commentary
NCBC	New Cambridge Biblical Commentary
NICOT	The New International Commentary on the Old Testament
OTL	Old Testament Library
OTS	Old Testament Studies
RB	*Revue biblique*
SBH	Standard Biblical Hebrew
SJOT	*Scandinavian Journal of the Old Testament*
Syr.	Syraic
TDOT	*Theological Dictionary of the Old Testament*. Edited by G. Johannes Botterweck and Helmer Ringgren. Translated by J. T. Willis, G. W. Bromiley, and D. E. Green. 15 vols. Grand Rapids, MI: William B. Eerdmans, 1974–2006.
TZ	*Theologische Zeitschrift*
VT	*Vetus Testamentum*
VTSup	Vetus Testamentum Supplemental Series
Vulg.	Vulgate
WBC	Word Biblical Commentary
WO	Waltke, Bruce K., and Michael Patrick O'Connor. *An Introduction to Biblical Hebrew Syntax*. Winona Lake, IN: Eisenbrauns, 1990.
ZAH	*Zeitschrift für Althebräistik*
ZAW	*Zeitschrift für die alttestamentliche Wissenschaft*

INTRODUCTION

I.
This Commentary's Translation of Ruth

As explained in the series statement, the Anchor Yale Bible commentaries are "grounded in exact translation." As the present volume follows in this tradition, I begin by addressing what exactly I am translating as "Ruth," how I am structuring my translation, the diction of the Hebrew in Ruth, and the reasons for the diction of my translation.

A. The Text for This Commentary's Translation

As with all biblical books, Ruth exists in many versions, forms, and contexts, whether oral, visual, or even cinematic. There are also many written versions, both ancient and modern. For example, multiple versions of the book exist in Hebrew, Greek, Latin, English, German, French, Spanish, and so on. This commentary translates Ruth from folios 421r–423r of manuscript EBP I B 19a of the Leningrad Codex (MT^L) as they appear in *BHQ* and Sanders. For texts of versions aside from MT^L, I consulted Quast, who was especially helpful for the Greek witnesses, and the critical editions listed in *BHQ*, 5*–7*. I also routinely consulted Jan de Waard's commentary on the critical apparatus for Ruth in *BHQ*, 51*–56*.

Overall, the evidence from the other ancient versions suggests that the text is much better preserved in Ruth MT^L than in some other books in MT^L. For example, unlike Samuel MT^L, Ruth MT^L does not require much textual reconstruction. It has only a handful of spelling errors (e.g., NOTES *go after them* on 2:9, *who are you?* on 3:9, and *at his feet* on 3:14). Also, there is only one case of textual corruption (NOTE *But if you do not want to redeem* on 4:4). While the present commentary's translation occasionally reads with the *qere* provided in MT^L (e.g., NOTE *at his feet* on 3:14 or *to me* on 3:17), the NOTES endorse reading with another version against MT^L only once (NOTE *also Ruth* on 4:5).

Given the general reliability of Ruth MT^L, in this commentary I translate from an extant witness rather than relying on my own textual reconstruction of a hypothetical urtext. To be clear, one should not mistake my use of Ruth MT^L as the basis for this commentary's translation as an endorsement of the inherent textual superiority of the MT among the ancient versions. Instead, it reflects my choice to translate and interpret a Hebrew text that existed before the publication of this commentary. In other words, this translation does not reflect a composite or eclectic text. I did not create or reconstruct the Hebrew text that I am translating and interpreting in this commentary, as might be necessary if this were a critical commentary on Samuel.

Although Ruth MT^L has relatively few textual difficulties, it poses many translation difficulties. Thus, as with every volume in the Anchor Yale Bible series, this commentary supplements its translation with NOTES sections. Many of the NOTES include my analysis of the syntax and grammar of MT^L and detailed, but not exhaustive, discussions of the versions of Ruth from antiquity. The NOTES also include discussions of some of the literary effects and nuances of Ruth's diction, as well as comparisons with other ancient Israelite or cognate literature that uses similar idioms, cognates, technical terminology, and references (consult "Ruth and Ancient Israelite Literary Traditions," below). The NOTES call attention to these factors because of their influence on my translation.

As this commentary translates from MT^L, the information about other versions is intended to help to explain various choices in my translation by comparing the differences and similarities of MT^L with other versions. At certain points, some versions may support a particular way of interpreting the sense of the Hebrew in MT^L. For example, in 2:14, my translation interprets the clause "at the time of the meal" as part of the narrator's discourse rather than as Boaz's speech even though the latter option remains a viable reading of MT^L. My interpretation of the Hebrew syntax finds support in LXX^L, the Targum, Syr., and Vulg. Discussions of these versions contribute to the plausibility of this commentary's translation. In this regard, the versions play an important role in explaining my translation of Ruth.

Regarding the other versions, the material from Qumran (2QRuth^a, 2QRuth^b, 4QRuth^a, 4QRuth^b, and a few fragments) does not provide a complete text of Ruth, and the accents and vowels in MT^L do not occur in the extant portions of Ruth from Qumran. Although the MT^L and Qumran material diverge at a few points, such cases are relatively minor (e.g., NOTE *at his feet* on 3:14 or *whose are you* on 3:16). The Old Greek tends to reflect a Hebrew *Vorlage* close to MT^L. One may explain most differences as interpretative, including harmonization, use of Greek idioms, or chronological or contextual concerns (*BHQ*, 6*). Although the Syr. frequently supports the Old Greek, it does not rely on it in a consistent fashion and includes more interpretative material than the Old Greek (Beattie, 10–17; Gerleman, 3–4). The manuscript evidence for the Old Latin is relatively late, although Latin references to the book of Ruth occur in some patristic texts. In general, the Vulg. supports MT^L, but its divergences often support the Old Greek and Syr. The Targum seems to reflect a Hebrew text close to MT^L, although it has a great deal of additional material that makes it much longer than MT^L.

B. The Structure of This Commentary's Translation

MT^L includes all eighty-five verses of Ruth, although many scholars argue that 4:18–22 is secondary (consult COMMENTS on 4:18–22). The traditional division of the text into eighty-five verses reflects the use of *sôph pasûq* in MT^L, although MT^L does not number these divisions. The traditional division of Ruth into four chapters is credited to the Archbishop of Canterbury Stephen Langton's chapter divisions of an edition of the Vulg. in the thirteenth century C.E., roughly two hundred years after MT[L]. The only larger section division in MT[L] occurs after 4:17, where a *parašâ pĕtûḥâ* separates the genealogy of Perez (4:18–22) from the rest of the book. If one follows this section division, it would translate into two chapters (1:1–80 and 2:1–5). Nevertheless, in order to make my translation more user friendly, especially for those who use this commentary as a reference work, I have divided it into four chapters and numbered the verses according to the format in most critical editions of Ruth.

Most critical commentaries, including the present one, provide a more detailed structure for Ruth than Langton's four chapter divisions. In 2001, Marjo Korpel surveyed no fewer than twenty different scholars' proposals for the book's structure and concluded that "opinions with regard to the structure of the Book of Ruth reveal a bewildering variety of opinion" (29). For example, scholars differ significantly on whether the first unit of chapter 1 ends with v. 5 (e.g., Bertman; Campbell; Fentress-Williams; Hubbard; LaCocque; Linafelt, 1999; Pressler; Sakenfeld, 1999; Zenger) or v. 6 (e.g., Bush; Porten, 1978; Sasson; Zakovitch). For reasons explained below, the present commentary ends the first unit at v. 7a.

Often, scholars use their proposed structures as evidence for their interpretation of the narrative. This may serve to structure their arguments about Ruth as much as the text itself. For example, some argue that the narrative is organized according to chiastic frameworks and *inclusios* (e.g., Bertman; Gow; Nielsen; Porten, 1978). Tod Linafelt uses his chiastic structure to draw connections to other biblical texts, such as 2 Sam 5:13–8:18, which he suggests follow a similar pattern (1999, xxi–xxiv). Others find structural patterns through comparisons to narratives involving Abraham, Lot, and Judah (Gen 13; 18–19; 38; e.g., Fisch). Some scholars describe Ruth as a "comedy" because they find a movement in the plot from harmony to chaos to resolution (e.g., Trible, 195; Fentress-Williams, 17–18, 134–36; Melissa Jackson, 180–97). Others structure Ruth around a progression of loss and a progression of gain or from death to life (e.g., Karlin-Neumann; Matthews, 219; Dubin).

Regarding references to God in Ruth, Jack Sasson notes that they are "mostly set in formulaic contexts [such as blessings and oaths] . . . Thus, of the twenty-four references to a divine figure, only two [1:6 and 4:13] could be considered as contributing to the development of the tale . . . [but these two references] occur at the tale's extremities" (221). Sasson implies that the divine actions in 1:6 and 4:13 are of peripheral importance, in part because he argues that Ruth follows the pattern of a folktale (197–216). Other scholars stress the importance of these divine actions toward the beginning and ending of the book to argue that Ruth is a salvation history (e.g., Hals; Campbell). Assuming that the genealogy in 4:18–22 is secondary, they argue that the placement of these actions provides evidence of a *Heilsgeschichte* pattern that culminates with the reference to David in 4:17 (consult "Divine Activity and Acts of *ḥesed* in Ruth," below). Daniel I. Block's outline moves from crisis to rescue, allowing him to focus on what he understands as "the narrator's central theme—the providential hand of God in the preservation of Israel's royal line during the dark days of the judges" (620).

To a certain extent, how one structures the text is very much related to one's exegetical interests and interpretations of the text. Scholars do not always explain the rationale behind their proposed structures, nor is the rationale always obvious. This may create the impression that their readings, including my own throughout this commentary, follow a structure that is an objective property of the text rather than one that they use as a means of making sense out of the text. Structuring the text provides an efficient way for scholars to organize the textual evidence in order to trace whichever themes or issues are of interest to them. Following a particular structure will promote certain interpretative possibilities and foreclose others. Yet, intentionally or not, the ways that scholars discuss structures may create the impression that they, including myself, are describing a feature of the narrative rather than making an argument about how the story is narrated. Thus, I will explain how I structure the book because my structure is an act of interpretation that allows me to organize the textual data.

I have divided my translation into smaller units at points that reflect a change in location within the narrative (thus 1:1–7a, 7b–19a, 19b–22a; 1:22b–2:2, 3–17, 18–23; 3:1–5, 6–15, 16–18; 4:1–12, 13–17, 18–22). These divisions help to call attention to a standard feature of biblical narrative poetics rather than to trace or provide evidence for a particular theme over the course of the book. As Shimon Bar-Efrat notes: "In biblical narratives space is shaped primarily through the movement of characters and references to places . . . The characters act, and within the framework of their actions they leave or reach a certain place. The scene of the events moves from one spot to another" (185, 187). Changes in places within the story, rather than particular themes, dictate the structure for the translation in this commentary.

Also, as with the inclusion of the chapter and verse divisions in the translation, I intend the smaller units to make this commentary more user-friendly. These divisions serve heuristic instead of thematic purposes. As with most commentaries, many, if not most, readers will not read this volume from cover to cover. I imagine that they will consult it to locate textual information about the versions or interpretative proposals for particular verses or passages. Thus, my division of the translation into smaller sections aims to help readers locate such details efficiently. Although it is somewhat repetitive, each Notes and Comments section includes my translation of the corresponding verses to facilitate further the user-friendly quality of the commentary. Also, to conform to the guidelines for the Anchor Yale Bible, I have included titles for each unit of text to help readers locate them more easily. For the most part, these titles reflect the various locations where the particular unit occurs (e.g., Moab, the road, Bethlehem, the field, etc.). I have tried as much as possible to create titles that do not dictate to the reader how to interpret the content of a particular unit.

Finally, I have formatted my translation in a way that deviates significantly from the format of MT^L. MT^L formats certain biblical passages differently to mark them as poetry as opposed to prose (e.g., the offset lines in Exod 15:1–18; Judg 5:1–30) but does not mark any verses in Ruth as poetry. Nevertheless, the characters speak in poetry in 1:16b–17a, 20–21 (consult "Speech," below). Thus, following a standard convention in many English translations of the Bible, I have offset my translation of these verses to mark them as poetry.

C. The Diction of the Hebrew in Ruth

One could ask many questions about the diction in Ruth. For example, as discussed later, one could try to provide historical context by analyzing the vocabulary for evidence of Ruth's date of composition on the basis of historical linguistics or intertextual references to other extant texts. One could discuss the historical etymology of certain words or phrases or whether the narrator uses them with a particular technical legal sense or cultic nuance. As explained in the NOTE *about an ephah* on 2:17, scholars debate the precise unit of measurement that the word "ephah" (*'êpāh*) conveys. Yet, one cannot be certain whether Ruth's unknown author used ephah as an estimated unit of measurement or for literary effect, since the word *'êpāh* creates alliteration with *'êpoh* ("where") in 2:19. Likewise, when Ruth refers to herself as a *šipḥâ* ("maidservant") in 2:13 or a *nākriyyâ* ("foreign woman") in 2:10, these titles may carry technical nuances (e.g., the discussions of *'āmāh* and *šipḥâ* in Sasson, 53–54). At the same time, Ruth's reference to herself as Boaz's maidservant (*šipḥâ*) rhymes with the narrator's report that Boaz is actually part of her clan (*mišpāḥâ*; 2:20; NOTE *clan* on 2:1). Regarding *nākriyyâ*, many scholars note that Ruth's use of this word in 2:10 contributes to the assonance and rhyme in her phrase *lĕhakkîrēnî wĕ'ānōkî nākriyyâ* (NOTE *a foreign woman* on 2:10).

Regarding the names of characters and geographic locations in the narrative, critical commentaries, including the present one, often provide information about possible etymologies of these names based on cognates in Hebrew or related Semitic languages. Nevertheless, there is no hard evidence that Ruth's author was aware of the etymological origins or significance of the names that she or he used, especially if the etymology reflects an Ugaritic cognate and the author lived during the early Persian period, as I tentatively argue (consult "Ruth's Authorship and Date of Composition," below). For example, even if one were to explain the origins of the name Bethlehem as "house of Laḥmu [a Canaanite deity]" on the basis of Ugaritic cognates known to contemporary scholars, one does not know whether Ruth's author was familiar with this cognate or other possible Ugaritic cognates that I discuss throughout the NOTES. One can be certain, however, that the author of Ruth knew the Hebrew words *bêt* ("house of") and *leḥem* ("food") since forms of these words occur throughout the book. One could translate the name "Bethlehem" as "house of food" (*bêt leḥem*) on the basis of this popular rather than historical etymology. This creates a play on words in that there is a famine in the house of food (1:1; consult COMMENTS on 1:1–7a).

Unlike speculations about the author's knowledge of historical etymologies, there is hard evidence that Ruth's narrative contains puns, alliteration, assonance, rhyme, and so on. To be clear, one cannot verify whether these literary effects reflect authorial intent or whether the author was even aware of them. Thus, I do not endorse Campbell's claim that the literary crafting of the book reflects the fact that the author "was a genius" (10). Instead, since other scholars have noted many, if not all, of the literary effects that I discuss, I only claim that my translation has benefited from the ingenious analyses of Ruth by many scholars before me, including Campbell. Nevertheless, there is at least hard evidence that the narrative style creates a number of these literary effects for the commentator to exploit.

Although not historically verifiable, it seems more historically plausible that the names of characters and geographic locations in Ruth probably reflect "popular etymologies" based on literary associations rather than linguistic considerations (Barr, 109; Garsiel, 17–18; Saxegaard, 23–25). Considering the amount of puns, rhyme, alliteration, and assonance that occurs throughout the narrative, a focus on how certain proper names create these literary effects may provide a more compelling explanation of the names than a focus on their semantic nuances and the etymological or technical precision that they may convey.

Naomi creates an explicit pun on her name, which means "kindness of Yahweh" (NOTE *Naomi* on 1:2). In 1:20, she says to call her Mara, meaning "bitterness," instead of Naomi (cf. 1:13). In 1:21b, she creates a rhyme with her name: "Why should you call me *Naomi?* Yahweh has *testified against me* [*'ānâ bî*]; Shaddai has *brought disaster upon me* [*hēra' lî*]" (emphasis added). While not as explicit as the pun involving Naomi's name, the rhyming names of Naomi's sons, Mahlon and Kilyon, carry associations with sickness, sterility, and the annihilation of a linage. Even if the name Kilyon is etymologically related to an Ugaritic name, the popular etymology of this name aptly describes Kilyon's experience in Moab. After introducing the brothers by name in 1:2, the narrator reports in vv. 4–5 that they both were married for ten years without indicating that they had any children and then they both died (cf. 1:8; 2:20; 4:5, 10). Along similar lines, if the name Ruth derives from the root *rwy* ("refreshment"), there is a possible pun in the phrase "she [Ruth] was satisfied [*śb'*]" (2:14; cf. 2:18; NOTE *Ruth* on 1:4).

In 2:19–20, the name Boaz (*b'z*) forms a consonantal anagram with the word "abandon" (*'zb*). Like the name Boaz, the word "abandon" occurs repeatedly throughout the book (1:16; 2:11, 16, 20; NOTE *Boaz* on 2:1). In 4:4, the word *'eglê* in the clause *'eglê 'ozěnkā* ("I would uncover your ear") forms a consonantal anagram with the word *haggō'ēl* ("the kindred redeemer"; 4:1, 6, 8), creates alliteration with the various verbal forms of the root *g'l* ("to redeem") that occur five times in 4:4 (NOTE *I thought I would uncover your ear* on 4:4), and seems to play off of Ruth's "uncovering" (*glh*) herself at Boaz's feet (3:4, 7). As with *gō'ēl* ("kindred redeemer"), the rarely attested word *těmûrâ* ("substitution"; 4:7) can function as technical legal terminology (cf. Lev 27:10, 33) but also creates assonance with the proper name Tamar (*tāmār*) in 4:12.

At certain points, the use of uncommon Hebrew forms creates these literary effects. In 1:8, Naomi references the rarely used term "the mother's household" rather than the much more common term "house of the father" (NOTE *her mother's household* on 1:8; "Household Organization"). Often, scholars cite this reference in discussions of gendered roles in ancient Israel or as evidence of the book's female authorship. At the same time, the use of "her mother's household" (*'immāh*) results in rhyme, assonance, and alliteration with the term "under [Naomi's] authority" (*'immāh;* 1:7a). In 1:19, the infrequently attested feminine suffix *-nâ* on the end of the words *bō'ānâ* ("entered"), *kěbō'ānâ* ("entered"), and *wattēlaknâ* ("traveled") results in rhyme and assonance. In 2:14, the verb *wayyiṣěbbāṭ* ("heaped together") is a hapax legomenon that creates alliteration with the noun *haṣṣěbāṭîm* ("the heaps") in 2:16. In 4:13, the use of the rare nominal form *hērāyôn* ("conception"), rather than the more common verbal form *wattahar* ("and she conceived"), creates a rhyme with several of the proper names elsewhere in Ruth 4 (Mahlon, Kilyon, Hezron, Nahshon, Salmon). The fact that these examples of alliteration, assonance, and rhyme result from the use of uncommon Hebrew forms may account for certain linguistic peculiarities in MT^L. Also, although scholars often cite uncommon Hebrew forms as evidence for the date of Ruth's composition, one could account for them as a means of characterization.

The literary effects that result from the diction of the Hebrew may account for some of Boaz's unprecedented legal maneuvers. For example, scholars debate whether Boaz's land redemption occurs preemptively or after the fact, since he uses a *qal* perfect form for the verb "to sell" (*mākĕrâ*) which could mean that Naomi has sold or that Naomi is now selling the field. These legal considerations notwithstanding, the verb form *mākĕrâ* with "the portion of the field" (*ḥelqat haśśādeh*) as its object creates alliteration with the only other occurrence of the same object in the book. In 2:3, Ruth first meets Boaz because, to translate woodenly, "her chance [*miqrehā*] chanced upon the portion of the field [*ḥelqat haśśādeh*] held by Boaz" (NOTE *she chanced upon* on 2:3).

Many scholars note that the legal situation in Ruth differs from any other biblical representations of marriage to the wife of a dead man, although Ruth's narrator uses terminology and legal idioms that occur in texts that describe levirate customs regarding such marriages (e.g., "until he grows/they grew," Gen 38:11 and Ruth 1:13; "to establish a name," Deut 25:7 and Ruth 4:5, 10; "wife of the dead man," only in Deut 25:5 and Ruth 4:5). As Simeon Chavel correctly notes, the levirate marriage custom in Genesis 38 and Deuteronomy 25 addresses the concern that a dead relative's lineage continue but never explicitly addresses the issues of inheritance despite the fact that many scholars connect this custom to inheritance in these texts. Yet, without known legal precedent, Boaz uses this custom to ensure inheritance rites when he states, "Ruth the Moabite, the wife of Mahlon, I now acquire for myself as a wife to establish the name of the dead man upon his inheritance" (4:10a; cf. 4:5).

To be sure, one could explain this difference by noting that Genesis 38 and Deuteronomy 25 may not provide a comprehensive account of the situations in which this custom was applicable, or that Boaz creates a legal fiction that conflates this custom with various property laws (e.g., Lev 25; Num 27, 36; Jer 32; e.g., Baruch Levine; Berlin, 2010; Chavel). At the same time, one could also explain the reference to inheritance as creating a pun with the name Mahlon (*maḥlôn*) and the word "inheritance" (*naḥălātô;* cf. Garsiel, 252; Porten, 1978, 46; Sasson, 19). Through this pun, a name associated with sickness and death in Moab (1:5) becomes associated with the survival of a household in Bethlehem. One finds a similar pun in Isa 17:11 when a harvest results not in an inheritance, but "in a day of sickness" (*bĕyôm naḥălâ*).

Whether they are a product of authorial intention or not, puns, rhyme, alliteration, and assonance occur throughout Ruth's narrative. Other explanations notwithstanding, these literary effects account for many aspects of the Hebrew diction, including, but not limited to, the use of certain personal and place names as well as uncommon Hebrew forms and legal maneuvers.

D. The Diction of This Commentary's Translation

As with most biblical narrative, the vocabulary in Ruth is very repetitive. Thus, I have tried to translate words deriving from the same or similar roots consistently, especially when they occur only a few times in the book (e.g., "children/child" in 1:5; 4:16; "kindly/

kindness" in 1:8; 2:20; 3:10; "rest" in 1:9; 3:10; "bitter[ness]" in 1:13, 20; "abandon" in 1:16; 2:11, 16, 20; "lodge" in 1:16; 3:13; "empty" in 1:21; 3:17; "skirt[s]" in 2:12; 3:9; "worth/worthily" in 2:1; 3:11; 4:11; "close to us/closer than I" in 2:20; 3:12). In other cases, they occur several times in the span of a few verses (e.g., "return[s]/returned" in 1:6, 7, 8, 10, 11, 12, 15 [two times], 16, 21, 22 [two times]; 2:6; 4:3, 15; "know[s]/known" in 2:1, 11; 3:3, 4, 11, 14, 18; 4:4; cf. "relative" in 2:1; 3:2; "redeem/kindred redeemer[s]" in 2:20; 3:9, 12 [two times], 13 [four times]; 4:1, 3, 4 [five times], 6 [four times], 8, 14; cf. "redemption" in 4:6, 7; "lay/lies/lay down/lying" in 3:4 [three times], 7 [two times], 8, 13, 14). When I do not translate words from the same root consistently, I often note the common root in the corresponding NOTES (e.g., "clung to/stick/stuck with" in 1:14; 2:8, 21, 23; "attack/pressure" in 1:16; 2:22; "foreign woman/the one who paid attention" in 2:10, 19; "undress[ed]/uncover" in 3:4, 7; 4:4).

Although such repetitions do not in themselves endorse any particular literary effect, be it a pattern, theme, play on words, etc., my translation aims to make these repetitions available to readers should they decide to use them as evidence of a particular interpretation. Nevertheless, the translation alone captures only a very limited number of the literary effects that I perceive in the Hebrew of MT^L. Thus, the Introduction, NOTES, and COMMENTS that supplement my translation detail many of these literary effects.

II.
Literary Contexts and Genre(s) for Ruth

This section addresses the literary context and genres that influence my translation and commentary. I interpret Ruth within the context of ancient Israelite literary traditions rather than a canonical context. Although the literature belonging to these two categories largely overlaps, the categories themselves are not interchangeable. Some canons that include Ruth also include the literature in the New Testament although it is not ancient Israelite literature. Moreover, numerous ancient Hebrew inscriptions provide extant examples of ancient Israelite literature that is not canonical literature. Also, additional ancient Israelite literature may have existed at some point, such as the supposed Book of Jashar (Josh 10:13; 2 Sam 1:18) or the Book of the Acts of Solomon (1 Kgs 11:41). The Hebrew Bible contains the largest collection of extant ancient Israelite literature, but it is not an exhaustive collection.

A. Canonical Placements

If one reads Ruth as canonical literature, the book's position within a particular Jewish or Christian canon provides its literary context. Certainly, some scholars offer profitable readings of Ruth within a particular canonical context (e.g., Childs, 560–68); however, nothing in Ruth's narrative necessitates an interpretation of the book according to its placement within a biblical canon. In fact, Ruth's canonical placement differs depending on which version or edition one consults. In editions of the MT, it appears within the Writings among the five scrolls, which also include Song of Songs, Qoheleth, Lamentations, and Esther. Each of these books is connected to a different point in the liturgical season, with Ruth being read on Shavuot, sometimes referred to as the Feast of Weeks, which commemorates the giving of the Torah at Sinai (Eskenazi and Frymer-Kensky, xxvi; cf. Exod 34:22–23; Deut 16:9–10, 16; *Ruth Zuta* 1.1). The sequence of the five books, however, differs depending on which edition of the Hebrew Bible one consults (e.g., various printings of *Miqra'ot Gĕdolot, BHS, BHQ,* etc.; cf. Tov, 3–4).

In editions of the Septuagint, Ruth appears among the Former Prophets between Judges and 1 Samuel. This order may reflect a chronological rather than liturgical interest, since Ruth begins with a reference to the period of the chieftains, traditionally translated as "judges" (1:1), and ends with references to David (4:17, 22). In this sense, it provides a chronological bridge between the contents of Judges and 1 Samuel. Rather than the sequence of events, a Talmudic reference lists certain biblical books according to the chronology of the authors to whom the books are attributed by tradition. Thus, among the Writings, Psalms and then Proverbs follow Ruth as they are attributed to Samuel, David, and Solomon, respectively (*b. B. Bat.* 14b). In short, one should not simply assume the priority of one particular canonical context over another.

Internal textual evidence from Ruth does not endorse its placement according to any particular canonical ordering. Reading Ruth within its canonical-historical context, Michael Moore finds some thoughtful parallels between the "chaos" in Judges 17–21 and in Ruth 1:1–5 (2000, 294–96). Nonetheless, Ruth contains no undisputable references to the material in Judges. Some scholars suggest that a later, possibly Deuteronomistic, editor appended Ruth onto the end of Judges on the basis of supposed verbal correspondences and thematic continuities and contrasts between Ruth and Judges 19–21 (Campbell, 35–36; Linafelt, 1999, xix). If this were the case, however, it does not demonstrate an internal connection to Judges within Ruth's narrative. Instead, it is a claim about Ruth's possible redaction and placement by a later editor. Moreover, the distribution across biblical literature of the supposed verbal correspondences between Ruth and Judges 19–21 shows that these features are not unique to either of these texts. Also, the supposed correspondences do not use these words and phrases in a technical sense. For example, certain words in Ruth reflect a technical usage similar to their use in Priestly and Deuteronomic legislation, as I discuss shortly. Yet, the correspondences with Judges 19–21 are based on widely distributed, nontechnical words and phrases or simply words that are grammatically appropriate in both contexts (e.g., the independent use of the negative *'al* in Judg 19:23 and Ruth 1:13; consult Holmstedt, 83–84).

The clearest example of a clause shared with Judges occurs in Ruth 1:1 (cf. Judg 17:7–9). Yet, this clause could just as easily allude to 1 Sam 17:12 since it also occurs there (NOTE *a man from Bethlehem of Judah went* on 1:1). In fact, whereas 1 Sam 17:12 and Ruth 1:2 refer to Ephrathites from Bethlehem of Judah, Judg 17:7–9 refer to a Levite from Bethlehem of Judah. "Ephrathite" and "Levite" are not always interchangeable terms. Likewise, the blessing formula "blessed is *X* to Yahweh" occurs in Judg 17:2

and Ruth 2:20; 3:10 (NOTE *Blessed is he to Yahweh* on 2:20). Yet, this formula also occurs in 1 Sam 15:13; 23:21; 2 Sam 2:5; and Ps 115:15.

The reference in Ruth 1:1 to the time period when chieftains (*šōpeṭîm*) ruled prompts many scholars to read the book against the backdrop of Judges even if they are not prioritizing a specific canonical placement. According to Nielsen, this reference leads readers "into a network of stories to which Ruth also belongs, namely the narratives found in Judges" (40; cf. Jobling, 1993). Some scholars contrast the constant warfare in Judges with the more peaceful description of the same time period in Ruth (e.g., Eskenazi and Frymer-Kensky, xxiv, 4; Sakenfeld, 1999, 17–18). The only references to "the chieftain(s)" that do not denote a specific individual in the book of Judges occur in 2:16–18. This passage associates the chieftains with military deliverance (cf. 2 Sam 7:10–11; 1 Chr 17:9–10). Among the individually named chieftains, Deborah is the only one not involved in warfare (Judg 4:4–5). The placement of Ruth immediately after Judges in editions of the Septuagint may have encouraged early interpreters to draw such a contrast.

Nevertheless, the portrayal of the chieftains in Judges does not reflect their portrayal throughout the Hebrew Bible. Outside of the book of Judges, biblical references to chieftains, especially in Deuteronomy, tend to associate them with local legal proceedings, as with Deborah, rather than with warfare (e.g., Deut 1:16–17; 16:18; 17:9, 12; 19:17–18; 21:2; 25:2; 1 Sam 8:1–2; 2 Chr 19:5–6). Ruth's portrayal of "the days when the chieftains ruled" is in keeping with this portrayal of chieftain authority, especially as presented in Deuteronomy. Like the book of Judges, portions of Deuteronomy also imagine Israelite life during a period when chieftains ruled. These texts set protocols for localized governance in the Cisjordan (Deut 6:10–12; 7:1; 11:31–32).

Ruth and Deuteronomy use words and phrases with similar technical senses. For example, the chieftains are among those appointed "in the gate" in Deuteronomy (16:18; cf. 21:19; 22:15–16; 25:7). Boaz consults this type of assembly, namely those in "the gate," when settling legal matters (Ruth 4:1, 10–11, 18–19; cf. 3:11). More specifically, Boaz discusses his case before "the elders of the town" (*ziqnê hāʿîr*), a technical term that occurs mostly in Deuteronomy (19:12; 21:3, 4, 6, 19, 20; cf. Josh 20:4; Judg 8:16; 1 Sam 16:4). This term refers to a governing body that presides over legal cases, including ones involving marriage (Deut 22:15, 17, 18; 25:8; cf. Ezra 10:14). Also, both Ruth and Deuteronomy use the *hiphil* infinitive "to establish" (*lĕhāqîm;* Deut 25:7; Ruth 4:5, 10) and the term "wife of the dead man" (occurring only in Deut 25:5 and in Ruth 4:5; NOTE *the wife of the dead man* on 4:5) as technical language associated with different customs involving marriages to wives of dead men (consult Steinberg; COMMENTS on 4:1–12). Also, Ruth's characters engage in blessings throughout the book (2:4, 19, 20; 3:10; 4:14; cf. the blessing formulas in 1:8–9a; 4:11–12). Although Judges rarely discusses blessings (13:27; 17:2) outside of the poem in Judges 5 (vv. 2, 9, 24), Deuteronomy discusses blessings consistently when describing life under Cisjordanian chieftain authority, especially in the context of progeny and food (consult 1:11; 7:13–14; 8:10; 12:7; 14:29; 16:15; 24:19; 26:15; 28:3–5, etc.). Prioritizing texts from Deuteronomy (or Genesis, Leviticus, Jeremiah, Chronicles, etc.) for one's interpretation of Ruth, however, requires one to read Ruth within a literary context that is not determined by its canonical placement.

One could find verbal correspondences with the books that surround Ruth in its placement in MT[L]. Proverbs comes immediately before and Song of Songs comes immediately after Ruth. The final chapter of Proverbs praises at length a figure described as a "woman of worth" (*ēšet ḥayil;* Prov 31:10). Boaz uses this same rare phrase, which occurs elsewhere only in Prov 12:4, to describe Ruth (Ruth 3:11). Proverbs 31 also describes the unnamed woman of worth's management of "her house" (vv. 21, 27). Similarly, Naomi encourages each of her daughters-in-law to return to "her mother's household" in Ruth's opening chapter (1:8). This rare reference to the mother's household occurs twice in Song of Songs (3:4; 8:2), which immediately follows Ruth in MT[L]. Ultimately, arguments for Ruth's canonical placement on the basis of correspondences in vocabulary do not provide decisive evidence because one could find such correspondences with the end of either Judges or Proverbs as well as with texts in the books of Samuel or Song of Songs. Reading Ruth within a particular canonical context reflects a commentator's interpretive preference rather than anything mandated by the text.

B. Ruth and Ancient Israelite Literary Traditions

One could interpret the book of Ruth as an example of ancient Israelite literature apart from any specific collection of literature, such as a Jewish or Christian Bible, just as one could interpret the novel *The Color Purple* as American literature apart from any specific collection of American literature. The book of Ruth is ancient Israelite literature in that it assumes many figures, idioms, and customs from ancient Israel's written and/or possibly oral traditions. How accurately these traditions reflect the historical realia of ancient Israel remains uncertain. My decision to read Ruth within the context of ancient Israelite literary traditions rather than a context based on its canonical placement shapes many of my interpretative choices. Yet these choices are not intended to foreclose all other reading strategies for Ruth that other scholars offer. Rather, I aim to provide interpretations that make sense within the literary context in which I have chosen to place the book.

Ruth reflects a number of the literary traditions that are also reflected in ancient Israelite texts outside of the book. For example, 4:11–12 contains references to several figures from Israel's ancestral traditions (Rachel, Leah, Israel/Jacob, Tamar, Judah, Perez). As these figures appear nowhere else in Ruth, aside from Perez in 4:18, one cannot account for these verses by reading Ruth in isolation. Instead, one must explain them as reflecting ancient Israelite ancestral traditions. Even if one avoids arguments for intentional authorial allusion to specific extant texts outside of Ruth (consult "The Authorship of Ruth" and "The Narrator and Narrative Style," below), one could situate Ruth within the context of the literary traditions of ancient Israel by appealing to similar references to characters, customs, and idioms in other biblical texts.

Regardless of whether other extant ancient Israelite texts contain the source material for Ruth or vice versa, at the very least such texts contain comparative materials that are helpful for understanding Ruth's references and idioms. Comparisons can reveal aspects of a text that may not be as readily apparent when the text is studied in isolation (Strawn, 2009, 117). To be precise, comparability is not an inherent quality of the texts. Rather, as the commentator, I am using two or more texts as data to address my questions about Ruth's references and idioms through comparisons (Jonathan Z. Smith, 52; "The Commentator and the Focus of This Commentary"). For this commentary's purposes, the utility of comparisons between texts is not limited to the provision of evidence of source material or authorially intended allusions.

Comparisons can help to explain idioms even when the literary relationship between the texts under comparison remains uncertain. For example, the narrator in Gen 29:30–30:24 refers to Rachel's husband as "Jacob" (cf. Jub 28:9–24), whereas Ruth's narrator refers to him as "Israel" (Ruth 4:11), which may reflect the source material also used by 1 Chronicles rather than Genesis (consult "Judahite and Moabite Marriages," below). Yet, the comparison of Ruth to Rachel and Leah in 4:11 uses the same idiom as Rachel uses in Gen 30:3 ("to build" a household through procreation). Sarai also uses this idiom in 16:2. Regardless of whether or not Ruth's unknown author used these texts in Genesis as source material, this comparison helps to explain an idiom ("to build a household") that occurs in Ruth.

Similarly, the statements that Ruth "clung" to Naomi (1:14) and "abandoned [her] father and [her] mother" (2:11) may reflect Gen 2:24, or they could reflect a popular proverb that also appears in Gen 2:24. Either way, a comparison of these two texts helps one account for the idiomatic use of the term "cling" in Ruth 1:14 (NOTE *clung* on that verse). Likewise, my translation of the preposition *'im* as "under X's authority" in 1:7, 11, 22; 2:6, 19 finds support in similar idiomatic uses of this preposition elsewhere (Gen 29:14, 25, 30; 31:31, 38; 32:5; 32:15; Deut 15:12, 16; 2 Sam 3:15, etc.; NOTE *under her authority* on 1:7a). Also, one could translate Ruth 1:1b as "a man from Bethlehem of Judah went" or as "a man went from Bethlehem of Judah." The uses of a similar phrase in Judg 17:7, 8, 9; 19:1; and 1 Sam 17:12 support the case for the former translation on the basis of how the phrase is used in these other examples from outside of Ruth.

Comparisons may also help produce evidence that is relevant for a particular exegetical issue. For example, the first verse of Ruth contains the introductory formula "there was a famine in the land" (1:1). Genesis 12:10 and 26:1 use the exact same formula to introduce the stories of Abram and Isaac's temporary residences as aliens in Egypt and the Philistine city of Gerar, respectively. Likewise, a Shunammite woman and her household follow Elisha's instructions and reside as aliens in Philistine land during a famine (2 Kgs 8:1–2). Elsewhere, the Egyptians, Philistines, and Moabites are each portrayed as Israel's enemies (e.g., Exod 1; 1 Sam 17; 2 Kgs 3, respectively). Yet, as with the Moabites in Ruth, Genesis 12, 26, and 2 Kings 8 do not present the Egyptians and Philistines as enemies. Comparisons with other stories of Israelite ancestors introduced with this formula could help to explain the portrayal of Moab in Ruth ("Exogamy and Ethnicity"; COMMENTS on 1:1–7a).

Ruth's references to legal ideas and uses of technical legal terminology can seem unclear when read in isolation. For example, in 4:3, Boaz's grammar does not clarify whether he means that Naomi "has sold" or "now offers for sale" the field that Elimelech held (NOTES *Naomi . . . offers for sale* on 4:3 and *acquire for yourself* on 4:8). Comparisons with other texts that discuss and redemption may help clarify his meaning. Leviticus 25:23–55 discusses scenarios in which land redemption occurs after the land is sold. This passage frequently uses the words "redeem" or "kindred redeemer(s)" with a similar technical sense as Ruth does (cf. NOTE *under her authority* on 1:7a). Moreover, both texts discuss redemption performed by a "close" (*qrb*) relative (NOTE *the man is close to us* on 2:20). Yet, discussions of preemptive land redemption occur in Jer 32:6–15, where the root *gʾl* is used with the same technical sense as in Ruth and Leviticus 25. In fact, the exact same phrase for land acquisition occurs only in Ruth 4:8 and Jeremiah 32 ("acquire for yourself"; *qĕnê-lāk*). Comparisons with the language that Leviticus 25 and Jeremiah 32 use when applying a legal idea can inform both one's understanding of how the idea is applied in Ruth and one's translation of Boaz's statement in 4:3.

The occurrence of a particular word or phrase in both Ruth and another text is not necessarily evidence of literary dependence between the texts. For example, in 2:16, Boaz instructs his servants to "abandon" (*ʿzb*) some of what they harvest so that Ruth may glean it. Although Ruth's gleaning is often compared to the gleaning law in Deut 24:19, the verb "abandon" occurs in the laws concerning gleaning in Lev 19:9–10 and 23:22, but not in Deut 24:19. While various forms of the root *lqṭ* ("glean") occur in these verses from Leviticus and throughout Ruth (Lev 19:9 [two times], 10; Ruth 2:2, 3, 7, 8, 15 [two times], 16, 17 [two times], 18, 19, 23), this root never occurs in Deuteronomy. At the same time, Boaz's use of the word "abandon" may not necessarily indicate that Ruth uses the gleaning laws in Holiness legislation from Leviticus over Deuteronomy as a source text. (To complicate matters, it is quite possible that the Holiness legislation used Deuteronomic material as a source text for these laws; consult Stackert.) Instead, Boaz's word choice could just as easily reflect a theme developed through the repeated use of this word elsewhere in Ruth (1:16; 2:11, 20) and a play on the name "Boaz" (*bʿz*; NOTE *Boaz* on 2:1). In other words, it could be a byproduct of Ruth's narrative style rather than an indication of the book's source texts.

On the other hand, textual differences do not necessarily indicate that texts are unrelated. Biblical or other ancient Near Eastern texts often modified material from their source texts for a variety of reasons (Stackert, 25–27, 141–64). If, for the sake of argument, certain Pentateuchal legal texts served as Ruth's source material, Ruth's unparalleled use of a word with a technical legal definition may result from a stylistic tendency in Ruth. For example, some of Ruth's legal jargon creates puns, rhymes, alliteration, and assonance even if it does not conform precisely to the use of the same jargon in their Pentateuchal source text (e.g., consult the discussion of the word "inheritance" [*naḥălâ*] under "The Diction of the Hebrew in Ruth"). In such cases, Ruth's narrative style may explain some of the differences in the uses of the technical legal terminology in Ruth and in the Pentateuch. Such differences do not provide decisive evidence of Ruth's literary independence from these texts. Moreover, even if a particular extant legal text served as source material for Ruth's author, the precise application of legal ideas in Ruth may still differ from its source text because individual biblical texts do not usually contain a comprehensive account of a given law. Details mentioned in one legal text but not in another do not mean that the texts contradict each other but simply that neither text represents a comprehensive account of the possible applications of that particular legal idea (Westbrook, 71; for this reason, one should not assume that texts involving marriages to wives of dead men [Gen 38; Deut 25:5–10; Ruth 4] reflect the historical development of levirate marriage customs [contra Davies, 266–67; Thompson and Thompson]).

Reading Ruth within the context of ancient Israelite literary traditions does not require one to demonstrate Ruth's literary dependence on or independence from other ancient Israelite texts definitely. Also, it does not require any assumption regarding

Ruth's historical accuracy. In fact, it remains uncertain whether the legal ideas in Ruth reflect actual legal practices in ancient Israel. Instead, my approach requires that my interpretations are informed by ideas, traditions, customs, and idioms reflected elsewhere in extant ancient Israelite literature, even if Ruth applies them differently from the way other texts do. Thus, my interpretive proposals throughout this commentary still make extensive use of comparisons with biblical and other related ancient Near Eastern texts, even if I remain agnostic about Ruth's precise literary relationship to other extant texts. Later in this introduction, I use comparisons as evidence for my interpretations of exogamy, ethnicity, household organization, and issues related to status, gender, and patriarchal systems within the household. The utility of these comparisons for understanding Ruth within an ancient Israelite literary context does not depend on determining its author's historical relationship to other literary products of or lived practices in ancient Israel.

C. Genre(s) in Ruth

Ruth reflects not only the literary traditions of ancient Israel but also its literary genres. The study of these genres often helps scholars to identify the social origins or cultural settings (*Sitz im Leben*), whether real or imagined, that a text reflects. For example, Hermann Gunkel described Ruth as a "novella" that developed out of popular "folktales and saga." He thought the saga focused on the acquisition of a son to continue the family line. Gunkel identified this theme in Egyptian fables (*Märchen*), as well as in biblical texts such as Genesis 38 (1913, 85). Campbell refers to Ruth as a "historical short story" because he found the term "novella" to be too broad to serve as a meaningful formal category of Israelite literature, although he thought the use of the term could be defended (3–4). Other scholars have raised serious questions about whether the generic features of Ruth necessarily indicate that it originated in oral form (for an overview of such critiques, consult Bush, 35). Sasson refers to Ruth as "folkloristic," meaning that it originated as a written composition that was modeled after orally transmitted "folktales" (214–15). Nonetheless, with various modifications, many scholars have adopted the terms "novella" or "short story" to identify the genre of Ruth (e.g., Bush, 30–47; Eskenazi and Frymer-Kensky, xix–xx; Hubbard, 47–48; LaCocque, 9; Nielsen, 5–8; Pressler, 261; Zenger, 22–25; for a detailed overview of scholarly assessments of Ruth's genre, consult Witzenrath, 362–58).

A short story or novella may include a mixture of third-person narration and narrated dialogue as well as prose and poetry as modes of narration (e.g., Jonah, Tobit, Judith). While the subject matter of these stories varies greatly, scholars have profitably compared Ruth to book-length short stories from the Second Temple period such as Jonah, Esther, Tobit, and Judith. Also, the description of the stories as "short" is relative since some examples are significantly longer than Ruth (Esther, Tobit, Judith) and others are significantly shorter (Gen 38; Lev 24:10–23; Num 9:6–14; 15:32–37; 27:1–11; 2 Sam 14:5b–7; Susanna, among others). As a matter of convenience rather than technical or generic precision, I refer to Ruth as a short story.

Increasingly, scholars have used the generic labels "novella" or "short story," as well as others such as "tale" or "legend," to describe the content of the story rather than to identify the supposed cultural setting or social origins that the story reflects.

Even Gunkel echoes this tendency when he describes Ruth as an "idyll" (1930, 4:2181; cf. Würthwein, 3–4; Zakovitch, 11). This description is attributed to Goethe, who referred to Ruth as "the loveliest little epic and idyllic entity" (quoted in Fischer, 2007, 140). Regardless of whether Gunkel assumed that the book's idyllic quality reflected its social origins in what he called folktales, this quality describes the book's contents or perceived atmosphere rather than its formal generic features. Although other scholars have criticized this description (e.g., Levinson, 24–35; Fischer, 2007; Zenger, 22–25), whether Ruth is an "idyll" is a debate over how best to describe the book's subject matter rather than its formal properties.

Regarding the book's contents, Humphreys distinguishes a short story as a genre that "*reveals* the nature of a character or situation" from a novella as a genre that "*develops* characters or situations" (84 [emphasis in original]; cf. Bush, 41). Yet, when applied to Ruth, this distinction describes the narrative poetics rather than the genre of the book. Any number of narrative genres may reveal or develop characters or situations, but that is a matter of what one is able to communicate when one uses a particular genre rather than the identification of the genre itself. Although often unacknowledged, such discussions of genre in Ruth scholarship typically involve questions about how a genre helps to provide a particular rhetorical orientation to the text rather than questions about the genre's formal features reflected in the text.

Along these lines, whether verbal or written, genres provide a culturally contextualized means of communication. They may provide an audience with the means of classifying or framing their perception of a speech or text. Genre helps both parties, whether speaker and audience or writer and reader, to structure communication (Schipper, 2009, 7–10). This approach is somewhat related to the emphasis on the social origins of a genre. As Carol A. Newsom explains, "rather than referring to texts [only] as belonging to genres one might think of texts as participating in them, invoking them, gesturing to them, playing in and out of them, and in so doing, continually changing them" (2007, 21). For Newsom, genres are "modes of perception that conceptualize aspects of reality in distinctive ways . . . [as a] means of grasping or perceiving reality" (2003, 12, 82; cf. Lapsley, 102–3). In this regard, the narrator or characters in Ruth may invoke a number of different genres that provide various rhetorical orientations depending on the communicative needs at a particular point in the story.

For example, the narrator presents Ruth and Boaz's marriage through a legislative novelty without exact precedent elsewhere in the Hebrew Bible. One may ask why this legislative novelty is presented as part of a short story, or what Bernard Levinson refers to as a "legal narrative" (45). What narrative resources become more readily available with the use of a short story rather than some other genre? In theory, the narrator could have presented this novel legislation in the form of highly specific case law (as in Deut 24:1–4) or as a report of a vision (as in Ezek 47:22–23). The narrator could have had Boaz cite and clarify previous legislation and its contemporary application, as Nehemiah does (Neh 8:8; 13:1). Ruth is not the only short story in the Hebrew Bible that involves a very specific legal case regarding marriage or inheritance (Gen 38; Num 27:1–11). As noted below ("Moabites as Descendants of Lot"), scholars have identified a number of internal similarities between Ruth and Genesis 38. Also, Ruth and Num 27:11 use the same technical terminology for a close relative (NOTES *the man is close to us* on Ruth 2:20 and *closer than I* on 3:12). These texts involve numerous mitigating factors, including the lack of male descendants, which would complicate a straightforward application of any biblical law to the situations described. As with Ruth, some short stories address situations that highlight various categories of difference, such as ethnicity (Lev 24:10, 22), place of origin (Num 9:14), or gender (Num 27:1–11) within the Israelite community. Despite their differing lengths and subject matters, such short stories allow one to account for such mitigating factors with greater nuance than another genre, such as a case law or a vision report, might.

Instead of discussing *the* single genre of the book of Ruth, one could also analyze its use of multiple genres, just as one could for most biblical books. Genres invoked in Ruth's narrative include, among others, oath formulas (1:17b; 3:13) and blessings (1:8b–9a; 2:20; 4:11). The invoked genre may provide particular rhetorical orientations to a speaker's words. For example, certain characters may use oath formulas to intensify their promises to commit to a particular action. These oaths seem to help convince Naomi of Ruth's determination (1:18) and to persuade Ruth to stay with Boaz until morning (3:14). Naomi's aborted blessing (1:9) signals a dramatic shift in tone midway through the verse and contributes to the effect of her speech (Schipper, 2012). The blessing formula in 4:11 is appropriate for a wedding (e.g., Gen 24:60 or El's blessing at Kirta and Huraya's wedding; consult Parker) and may reinforce the community's endorsement of the marriage. In these examples, invoking various genres suits a variety of communicative needs. Although this approach may not always help us to reconstruct a cultural setting for the origins of a genre that is reflected in the text, it highlights the use of various culturally conditioned forms of communication that influence this commentary's translation and interpretation of the speech of certain characters (e.g., NOTE *May Yahweh give to you . . . [Oh, forget it!]* on 1:9 and the corresponding COMMENTS).

III.
Ruth's Authorship and Date of Composition

In this commentary, "the author" refers to the unknown historical figure or figures responsible for the book of Ruth as a written composition. Although I discuss theories regarding the date of Ruth's composition and authorship together, the dating of the book's composition provides little information about its author other than a general idea of when she or he may have lived.

A. The Authorship of Ruth

A general scholarly consensus holds that Ruth is mostly the product of a single author, although a few contemporary scholars make more detailed redactional proposals (e.g., Korpel, 219–21; Zenger, 9–18), and significant debate remains about whether 4:7, 18–22 are later redactions. Source analysis has not had a significant effect on recent Ruth scholarship, although occasional attempts exist (Brenner, 1993b; Glanzmann). Although the author of Ruth never identifies herself or himself, a number of theories about the author's gender, ethnicity, social status, political investments, and so on have flourished within Ruth scholarship.

A Talmudic tradition attributes Ruth's authorship to the prophet Samuel (*b. B. Bat.* 14b–15a), but Shlomo Dov Goitein suggested in 1957 (1988) that it was composed by a wise, older woman. Other scholars have suggested tentatively that the book was transmitted orally by women, including female storytellers in the tradition of the "wise women" (cf. 2 Sam 14:2; 20:16), before its written composition (Campbell, 18–23; Van Dijk-Hemmes, 136). Some make the more qualified claim that, regardless of the author's gender, she or he "woman-identified," meaning that the author identified with "women's interests and took them seriously" (Fischer, 1999, 34; cf. Meyers, 1993, 88–91). Still others have argued that the book emerged from royal scribes (Hubbard, 23–24) or wisdom circles (Gordis, 243, and the scholars he cites) or was written by a Northern Israelite (Block, 597) or a Moabite (Miles, 342). Theories about the author's identity and her or his reasons for writing the book help some scholars create a back story that carries explanatory force for an otherwise tersely written narrative. For example, one could imagine the author as concerned with providing a defense of the Davidic dynasty (e.g., Gow; Gerleman; Nielsen) or a response to the perceived xenophobia reflected in Ezra, Nehemiah, and other biblical texts (e.g., Fischer, 2001; Köhlmoos; LaCocque; Lau), among other possible agendas.

Nevertheless, the author's supposed gender or ethnicity does not imbue her or him with a particular perspective or set of concerns and intentions. The diverse evidence from extant ancient Israelite literature does not support such ethnic or gender essentialism. For example, if one places Ruth's composition within the Second Temple period, one may find that literature from this period reflects a variety of positions on several of the possible themes and issues in Ruth (consult "Exogamy and Ethnicity," below; Knoppers, 2001). Ruth's author may or may not have endorsed any one of these positions. One cannot determine an author's ideological perspective about a particular issue within her or his social context on the basis of when and where she or he lived. While the author had a reason or reasons for writing the book of Ruth, claims about her or his intentions remain largely speculative.

Moreover, it is doubtful that the author wrote any other extant literature, biblical or otherwise. Thus, one has no comparative material on which to construct a historical profile of Ruth's author's life. Since we lack personal details or biographical information about whoever wrote Ruth, we have very little, if any, clues as to why she or he may have written the book or her or his agenda(s). The various theories rely mostly on internal evidence from the text itself, such as particular words, types of speech, perceived themes, political or theological positions, and subject matters. Although the author composed a written version of Ruth at some point in time, the only evidence of her or his historical existence is the book itself. All that the text indicates for certain about the author historically is that she or he was literate, knew Hebrew, and seemed familiar with certain ancient Israelite traditions since the book includes explicit references to characters found elsewhere in ancient Israelite literature (4:11–12, 17b–22). Beyond these facts, any profile of the historical figure who produced the book remains mostly the product of one's analysis of the book.

The use of allusion in Ruth has received a great deal of scholarly attention in recent years (for an overview, consult Berger; Köhlmoos; Nielsen; Yavin; Zakovitch; on the distinction between allusions that are intended by Ruth's author and intertextual connections perceived by readers in Ruth scholarship, consult Callaham, 2012, 186–95; von Wolde, 1997, 8–12). Yet, it is difficult to identify authorially intended allusions in the book with certainty because, unlike other ancient Israelite literature, it contains no direct acknowledgment of other texts, through either a citation (contrast Josh 8:31; Neh 13:1) or a reference (contrast 1 Kgs 14:19, 29). Thus, I cannot deny or verify whether connections that I make between a text in Ruth and another text, whether inside or outside of Ruth, represent allusions intended by the book's author. This difficulty does not mean that one cannot make compelling cases for Ruth's connections with other texts. It only means that even the most obvious connections are made by the commentator interpreting the text and not the text itself. For example, the phrase *'ăšer lō'-'āzar ḥasdô* occurs in both Ruth 2:20 and Gen 24:27; yet, although this phrase occurs in Ruth 2:20, the connection of this phrase to Gen 24:27 is not specified in Ruth 2:20 (again, contrast Josh 8:31; Neh 13:1).

B. The Date of Ruth's Composition

Scholars have assigned a wide range of possible dates for the written composition of the book of Ruth, from the time of the united monarchy in the tenth to ninth centuries B.C.E. to the late Persian period or early Greek period (for surveys of scholarly opinions, consult Bush, 18–30; David, 55–59; Gow, 183–206; Hubbard, 23–35; Sasson, 240–52; Lau, 45–53; Vesco; Zakovitch, 62–64). Three approaches have considerably influenced scholarly proposals for a general date of Ruth's written composition (regardless of whatever oral history the story may or may not have had): (1) possible literary dependence on Pentateuchal texts and not simply traditions common to those texts, (2) analyses of certain linguistic features of the book, and (3) the supposed ideological or theological themes or "message(s)" that scholars find in their readings.

The recent scholarly interest in authorial allusion in Ruth has some effect on the dating of the book's composition, especially for scholars comfortable with claiming that the author alludes to specific Pentateuchal *texts* rather than simply invoking traditions that are also invoked in those texts. For example, if Ruth's author alludes to specific texts from Deuteronomic or Holiness legislation, then one may assign a relative date for Ruth's composition sometime in the postmonarchic period or at least after the reign of Josiah according to a general scholarly consensus for the composition dates of these legal texts. More precisely, Ruth uses vocabulary for gleaning that occurs in Holiness legislation but not in its Deuteronomic counterparts (consult the discussion of the words "abandon" and "glean" in "Ruth and Ancient Israelite Literary Traditions"). Thus, if Ruth shows literary dependence on Holiness legislation, one might propose the early Persian period as a relative date of composition.

Utilizing a number of studies on the development of Biblical Hebrew (e.g., Hurvitz, 1982; Polzin), Fredric Bush provides a detailed summary of both Standard Biblical Hebrew (SBH) and Late Biblical Hebrew (LBH) linguistic features in Ruth (22–30).

He concludes that Ruth's "transitional" Hebrew includes features of both SBH and LBH and tentatively dates the book's composition to the early postexilic period. Bush's analysis has widely influenced subsequent scholarship on Ruth (e.g., Eskenazi and Frymer-Kensky, xvii–xviii; Linafelt, 1999, xx; Matthews, 209, n. 8; Pressler, 262; Sakenfeld, 1999, 2–3; for a differing opinion, consult Lau, 52). Other scholars have refined the linguistic analysis for dating Ruth's composition (Holmstedt, 17–39; Zevit, 575, 592–94). Such reevaluations of the linguistic evidence suggest that Ruth contains no clear evidence of archaic Hebrew and fewer clear indicators of SBH and LBH than Bush suggests. Considering the small amount of such features, the evidence for transitional Hebrew is suggestive but not decisive.

Moreover, it is not always clear whether a particular linguistic feature that patterns after archaic Hebrew, SBH, or LBH indicates that the book was composed during a period when that type of Hebrew was linguistically dominant. Some scholars have considered how unusual linguistic features in a character's dialogue may characterize that character as foreign or "foreign sounding" or may seem contextually appropriate for addressing a non-Israelite (consult the discussions of "style-shifting" and "addressee-shifting" in Greenstein; Holmstedt, 46–49; Rendsburg, 1995). Characters speak in fifty-nine of the book's eighty-five verses (fifty-nine of eighty verses if one brackets the genealogy in 4:18–22). This proportionally large amount of dialogue presents a difficulty for using linguistic features to determine a date of composition. A character's speech pattern in Ruth may depict her or him as sounding younger or older or having a higher or lower social status and so on (Humbert, 92; cf. Campbell, 25). Considering the amount of dialogue in the book, a particular linguistic feature could simply distinguish a character's speech pattern as a means of characterization rather than provide reliable evidence for the date of the book's composition.

I do not have space to exhaustively catalogue or evaluate every potential SBH or LBH indicator in Ruth, but, beginning with the book's first verse, the NOTES address several cases when they occur (e.g., NOTE *ruled* on 1:1). Nevertheless, a thorough mapping of the idiolects in Ruth would require much more space than this commentary affords. Idiolects consist of a number of different linguistic features that may be dated differently and may reflect geographic variation. One should examine them on the phrase or clause level rather than assuming a single idiolect or "style" for the book as a whole. Yet, if one analyzes them at these smaller levels, one should consider the possibility that Ruth's author adopts a particular linguistic feature that patterns after LBH relatively early in its usage (e.g., the possible use of *nś'* in an idiom for taking a wife in Judg 21:23; NOTE *They took . . . wives* on Ruth 1:4) but could also employ another linguistic feature long after its usage was established (possibly the use of the *-tî* suffix on second feminine singular verbs; e.g., NOTE *go down* on 3:3).

Isolating a particular ideological or theological perspective encoded in the text does not provide reliable evidence for its date of composition. Nevertheless, scholars have used the theological or ideological themes that they identify in their readings of Ruth as evidence for a wide variety of composition dates. For example, Nielsen endorses "much current scholarship [that] regards the defense of the Davidic dynasty as the key to understanding the book's purpose, and thus a means to dating it" (29). Informed by Gerhard von Rad, Ronald Hals interprets Ruth's supposed interest in mundane human events orchestrated by a hidden deity as a product of a "Solomonic Enlightenment" in the tenth century B.C.E. (65–75; cf. Beattie, 252; von Rad, 48–56). Such interpretative strategies assume that a certain theological or ideological position would be especially appropriate for a particular period and the controversies of that time. A few representative examples may be sufficient to show the problems with dating the book on the basis of ideology or theology.

Following Hals, Campbell argues for a similar date because "the theological perspective of the book fits well into the early monarchic period" (24; but consult "Divine Activity and Acts of *ḥesed* in Ruth," below). Yet, other scholars have used the same types of argumentation to assign the book to the postexilic period. Susan Niditch notes that a similar theological perspective as Hals found in Ruth is often attributed to Esther in support of a Persian period date of composition for Ruth. Niditch concludes that Ruth's supposed theology cannot settle the question of its date (454). Nonetheless, André LaCocque writes that the book "cannot have been composed during any other era than when such a tension [between 'Law and commandment'] was the expression of an existential problem: the legalistic period of Ezra and Nehemiah" (30).

Benjamin D. Sommer helpfully articulates the methodological problem with assigning a date of composition on the basis of theology or ideology. He questions "the assumption that if an idea or text is especially relevant to a particular historical period, then the idea or text must have originated in the period. . . . When scholars claim that a text is obviously appropriate for a particular moment in history, they are often correct, but they fail to acknowledge that the idea or text is equally appropriate for some other moment as well" (94). To Sommer's point, many of the theological perspectives attributed to Ruth, such as divine control over mundane events, seem equally appropriate to several moments in Israel's history. Likewise, a certain political agenda could seem necessary at several moments. For example, propaganda for the Davidic dynasty could have served Hezekian and Josianic as well as Solomonic interests (Gow, 201–2; Sasson, 250–52). In fact, during the postmonarchic period, it even could have served Zerubbabal's interests as a descendant of David (1 Chr 3:19). Similarly, an ideological openness to non-Israelites within the community is not simply a product of postmonarchic conditions but emerges in texts from throughout Israel's history (Zevit, 574). Even if we knew when Ruth's author lived, the date of the book's composition does not provide any evidence for the ideological perspectives of that author.

No single piece of evidence definitively determines the date of Ruth's composition. In my opinion, one could make a reasonable but still extremely tentative argument for the early Persian period on the basis of the cumulative evidence. While arguments that the book's ideologies are uniquely fitted with a particular time period remain inconclusive, if one allows for literary dependence on Holiness texts and the possibility that certain linguistic features in Ruth reflect later developments in Hebrew that had already been adopted widely at the time of the book's composition, one could place its date of composition in at least the early Persian period.

IV. The Narrator and Narrative Style

For the purposes of this commentary, I distinguish between the author, narrator, and commentator (on the commentator, consult "The Commentator and the Focus of This Commentary," below). Unlike my references to the author, my references to the narrator of Ruth do not refer to any historical figure who composed a version of Ruth in either oral or written form. The story is presented through anonymous third-person narration, which includes reported speech or quotations of the characters. For example, the narrator reports that "Naomi said," "Ruth said," "Boaz said," "she said," "he said," and so on. Scholars attribute this anonymous narration to a literary construct called the "narrator." As an analytic tool rather than a historical figure, the narrator has no identity markers although one could imagine the narrator with a particular ethnicity or gender (e.g., Brenner and Van Dijk-Hemmes, 108–9). One might say that Ruth's author *composed* the book's narrative whereas its narrator *presents* the book's narrative.

Some scholars occasionally attribute certain interpretative connections to Ruth's narrator. For example, Kirsten Nielsen, among others, explains the skirt imagery in 3:9 through a very plausible connection with the similar imagery in 2:12: "The narrator is here trying to create a connection between Boaz's first meeting with Ruth and this second one" (74; cf. 44). Yet, while the narrator of Ruth may use the same or similar words repeatedly, the narrator does not "create a connection" with a previous verse as other biblical narrators do (e.g., the explicit reference in 1 Kgs 16:12 to 16:1–4 or the reference in 2 Kgs 9:36 to 9:10). Instead, Nielsen, as a commentator, is responsible for this connection between Ruth 2:12 and 3:9. She is stating her own interpretive proposals but attributing them to the narrator. Ruth's narrator is one of the products rather than the source of interpretations of the book. One may claim that Ruth's narrator does or does not describe particular details about certain events or characters. For example, one may claim that the narrator introduces Orpah and Ruth by name (1:4). One should not claim, however, to know Ruth's narrator's reasons for including or not including any particular details. Although a given scholar may not be the first to make a particular textual connection in Ruth, the scholar rather than the author, the narrator, or the text of Ruth makes the connection discussed in the scholar's interpretation.

Disguising one's interpretative choices as descriptions of the goals of Ruth's author or narrator distances the commentator from her or his own interpretive agency. It may provide an illusion of interpretive objectivity or of an external endorsement of one's own interpretations by the unknown author or constructed narrator. Thus, to be clear, this commentary's focus on relationships in Ruth and the interpretative proposals offered to flesh out this focus are my own (consult "The Commentator and the Focus of This Commentary"). This does not mean that I am the first scholar to offer any of these proposals.

(In fact, it is historically possible but unverifiable that Ruth's author would have endorsed them.) Rather, it means that I am responsible for the interpretations offered in this commentary instead of describing the interpretive activity of another party.

Regarding the style of narration in Ruth, space does not allow for a full exploration of the poetics of Ruth's narrative in MT^L. Nevertheless, the following sections offer some limited observations on this topic in order to explain the interpretative approach that this commentary takes toward the text. I address my approach to narrative ambiguity as well as characterization in relation to speech and actions, and their consequences.

A. Selective Representation and Narrative Ambiguity

As with most biblical prose, Ruth's narrator provides a very selective representation of the setting, timing, characters, and events depicted in the book (Berlin, 1983, 97). None of these elements is developed fully. There are gaps in any narrator's representation since it includes or foregrounds a few essential details, but many details remain in the unexpressed background (Auerbach, 3–23). For example, in MT^L, after Naomi's sons die (1:5), the next narrated event is the beginning of her journey back to Bethlehem because she heard that the famine had ended there (1:6). The narrator does not specify whether she heard about the famine's end before or after her sons died. Nor does the narrator specify whether YHWH ended the famine after ten years had elapsed (1:4) or ten years had elapsed before the report of this alleged divine intervention reached Naomi. The narrator does not indicate the timing of either of these events. The scope, length, and cause of the famine are not represented in the narrative. Similarly, the causes of Naomi's husband and sons' deaths are not included in the narrative (1:3, 5). One could imagine their deaths resulting from a number of causes, including, but not limited to, disease, accident, human violence, or divine punishment. Yet, such causes remain outside the narrative's selective representation.

The narrator of MT^L occasionally indicates the selectivity of the events narrated with references to certain events that are not narrated in the text but take place "offstage." In 2:11, Boaz claims that Ruth's personal history "has been completely reported to me." Before this verse, however, the book contains no record of this report reaching Boaz unless one assumes that the statement in 1:19 that "the whole town was abuzz" over Naomi and Ruth explains how he acquired this information. Alternatively, considering that his male servant told him only about Ruth's place of origin and relationship to Naomi (2:6), it is possible that Boaz lies about or exaggerates how much he knows about Ruth. Whether Boaz refers to a report that is not narrated in MT^L or he is lying depends on how one chooses to interpret his character (consult "Characterization," below).

Some scholars offer proposals to fill in the gaps in information produced by the narrator's selective representation. As Fewell and Gunn explain: "To understand the story we will have to be constantly filling gaps . . . [that] lead us to construe what is missing in terms of what information we do have. . . . Careful and imaginative 'gap filling' enriches the reading experience" (1990, 16; on "gaps" in biblical narrative, consult Sternberg, 186–90). To be precise, Fewell and Gunn's project aims to understand and (re)construct the *story* of Ruth on the basis of information derived from extant versions rather than interpreting a specific *version* of Ruth such as the one found in MT^L. In contrast, this commentary focuses on interpretative proposals which address ambiguities that result from the narrator's description of events, dialogue, or characters in MT[L] rather than on proposals that fill in the gaps in our information.

The gaps in information that result from the narrator's selective representation differ from the ambiguity that results from the narrator's description of characters or events. For example, the descriptions of the famine and deaths in 1:1–5 are terse but not ambiguous. The narrator conveys essential facts about these events clearly (namely, that there was a famine and that certain characters died) even if the details concerning these events, such as their causes, are provided only selectively. The narrator may not give much information about these events, but the little the narrator does give is not in itself ambiguous.

By contrast, the report that Mahlon and Kilyon married Moabite women is not only terse but also ambiguous. The ambiguity about these marriages does not result from the lack of detail, but from how the details are narrated. The narrator does not confirm the identities of each man's spouse (1:4). Genesis 11:29 lists Abram and his brother Nahor followed by the names of their respective wives: Sarai and Milcah. Yet, Ruth 1:2–5 may create the false impression that Mahlon married Orpah and Kilyon married Ruth because the name Mahlon appears before Kilyon and the name Orpah appears before Ruth. The actual identity of Ruth's husband is not revealed until Boaz's statement in 4:10. For most of the book, the audience does not know to whom she "belongs" (consult Boaz's and Naomi's respective questions in 2:5 and 3:16). Her relationship to Naomi's people remains a topic of conversation (1:10, 15, 16; 2:11). In chapter 3, the narrative describes what happens on the threshing room floor too vaguely to confirm what exactly Boaz and Ruth did that night (3:7, 14a; for further discussion, consult COMMENTS on 3:6–15). In 3:16, the narrator states only *that* Ruth told Naomi what happened that night but does not include as part of the narrative *what* Ruth told Naomi.

Ruth's opinion about Orpah's decision to return to Moab is not addressed in the narrative. This does not mean that Ruth, as a character, would not have the capacity for such an opinion based on her statements elsewhere in the book (cf. 1:16–17; 2:10). Indeed, scholars have asked a variety of thoughtful questions about Ruth's or Orpah's unexpressed opinions or emotions (e.g., Brenner, 2004, 99–119; Dube, 1999; Fewell and Gunn, 1990, 29–40, 52–56; Whitman). Nevertheless, one may distinguish a character's thoughts, opinions, and emotions that are unexpressed in the narrative and thus unknown from those that are ambiguous and require interpretation or clarification because of how they are expressed in the narrative. For example, in 1:16, when Ruth says "Your people, my people / Your ancestors, my ancestors," her syntax does not clarify whether she means Naomi's people and ancestors will be or will remain Ruth's people and ancestors since she is already a member of Naomi's household and under her authority as her daughter-in-law (consult NOTE *Your people, my people / Your ancestors, my ancestors* on 1:16). Also, in 1:18, Naomi infers Ruth's resolve to stay with her on the basis of Ruth's speech in 1:16–17. After Boaz speaks in 2:11–12, Ruth infers Boaz's opinion when she concludes, "I must have found favor in the eyes of my lord because you comfort me and because you speak to the heart of your maidservant" (2:13). In these examples, Ruth's and Boaz's respective intentions or opinions require interpretation not because they are unexpressed, but because of how they are expressed. Their speech does not necessarily provide direct or unambiguous access to their internal opinions or emotions. Unlike Gen 37:4, which states that Joseph's brothers hated him (cf. 37:5, 8, 11),

Ruth's narrator does not provide direct indications of the characters' opinions and few external clues, such as their tones of voice or body language.

B. Characterization

Frequently, scholars use Ruth to discuss methods of characterization in biblical narrative (e.g., Alter, 58–60; Berlin, 1983 83–110; Fewell and Gunn, 1993, 83–85; Saxegaard). After distinguishing references and characters, my discussion of characterization focuses on narrative techniques that provide access into various characters' thoughts, emotions, or opinions. References are simply proper names mentioned in the book (e.g., Leah, Rachel, Perez, Tamar, and the names in the genealogies in 4:17–22; Berlin, 1983, 86). As already discussed, one must appeal to literary traditions outside of Ruth in order to understand these references since they appear only once or twice in Ruth ("Ruth and Ancient Israelite Literary Traditions"). Unlike references, characters perform some action, including but not limited to speech, in the narrative. My working assumption is that all of the characters in Ruth, whether named or unnamed, have the capacity for an emotional or interior life even though it remains largely opaque within the narrative. Even Orpah, whose interiority remains almost entirely opaque, expresses some emotion when she, along with Naomi and Ruth, lifts her voice and weeps (1:9). Her motives for weeping may be open to interpretation, and the weeping may simply be a stock feature of a ritualized farewell that helps the narrative progress; nevertheless, her weeping implies an inner life even if it is unexplored by the narrator. The characters are not simply representations of a particular moral position or flat character types but are "a mass of conflicting desires and vested interests ... presented as complex manifestations of humanity" (Linafelt, 1999, xv, xvi; cf. Davis, 513, n. 59; Sharp, 240–47).

Moreover, Ruth's characters are not simply functionaries of the plot. They have the capacity to do or say more than what is necessary for the plot to progress. For example, in 3:17, Ruth quotes a statement that she attributes to Boaz. Yet, the narrator provides no previous record of Boaz ever making this statement. This could serve as evidence of the narrator's selective representation or suggest that Ruth's character has the capacity to embellish if not lie (compare the servant's quotation of Ruth in 2:7a). As already noted, one could ask a similar question about Boaz's claim regarding his knowledge of Ruth's personal history (2:11) or his claim about Naomi's otherwise unattested involvement in a land transaction (4:3).

I. SPEECH

One should distinguish modes of discourse within the dialogue portions of Ruth. While the characters in Ruth speak in prose for the majority of the book, Ruth and Naomi each speak in poetry at one point (1:16–17, 20–21, respectively; NOTE *Do not pressure me to abandon you . . . And there I will be buried* on 1:16–17). In fact, poetry occurs only in these verses despite Jacob Myers's claim based on meter that thirty-three verses include poetry or Eduard Sievers's metrical study of Ruth 1 (378–79). A thorough overview of the distinguishing markers of biblical Hebrew poetry remains beyond the scope of this commentary, but I provide a brief discussion in NOTES *Do not pressure me to abandon you . . . And there I will be buried* on 1:16–17 and *Do not call me Naomi . . . Shaddai has brought disaster upon me* on 1:20–21.

Prose and poetry represent different modes of discourse and, like all modes of discourse, offer different literary resources (consult "Genre[s] in Ruth"). For example, a story narrated in the third person may allow access to multiple characters' inner thoughts more easily than a story narrated in the first person. Conversely, first-person narration may allow for a greater sense of intimacy between the narrator and the audience. Regarding the literary resources afforded by either Hebrew prose or poetry, Linafelt argues that biblical prose provides extremely limited access to characters' inner lives (cf. Auerbach) and tends to register emotions that are publicly available, such as the hatred that Esau wears on his sleeve, so to speak, for his brother Jacob (Gen 27:41). Biblical poetry, however, allows for "eloquent expression" of a range of interior emotions and thoughts. In fact, such emotional expression characterizes much of biblical poetry (e.g., Psalms, Song of Songs, Job 3:1–42:6) (Linafelt, 2010, 127). Although not all poetry conveys a sense of interiority, in many respects, poetry is the usual, though not exclusive, discourse of choice for conveying a speaker's interiority in biblical Hebrew (Davis and Linafelt, 635, n. 26). Thus, although Ruth and Naomi speak in prose most of the time, for the particular moments narrated in 1:16–17, 20–21, they switch to poetry, which can convey the appropriate emotional intensity. In these verses, both characters use a mode of discourse associated more with access into a person's interiority. In fact, Ruth's poetic speech, along with her use of an oath formula (1:17b), seems to provide a sense of her inner thoughts effectively since it allows Naomi to finally understand Ruth's determination. Although Ruth and Orpah had wailed and protested against the idea of abandoning Naomi earlier (1:9–10, 14), it is only after Ruth's poetic speech that Naomi understands the depths of Ruth's resolve. In 1:18, the narrator indicates as much immediately after Ruth's speech: "When she saw that she was resolved to travel with her, she ceased to speak to her."

This does not mean that a character's emotional state cannot be conveyed when the narrator has the character speak in prose rather than poetry. The syntax of certain characters' prose speech may reflect a particular emotional state even if the syntax itself does not endorse or condemn any particular interpretation of the characters' emotional states. For example, while the narrator does not explicitly address the inner life of Boaz's male servant in 2:5–7, the way that I translate his speech reflects my interpretations of his emotional state (e.g., NOTE *this . . . her sitting . . . the house . . . a little* on 2:7). The same holds true for my translation of Naomi's aborted blessing of her daughters-in-law (NOTE *May Yahweh give to you . . . [Oh, forget it!]* on 1:9). In prose speech, intense emotions can sometimes be conveyed through unusual or difficult syntax (cf. Moses' ultimatum in Exod 32:32). The gloss offered in my translation on 1:9 reflects my interpretation of the narrative context and Naomi's mindset. My proposals for translating the prose of MT^L require occasional discussion of characters' emotional states even if a (re)construction of the characters' opinions about issues that are unaddressed in that narrative is not a primary aim of this commentary.

2. ACTIONS, EVENTS, AND CONSEQUENCES

Although dialogue dominates the book of Ruth, one does not need to infer a character's interiority from the dialogue alone. In 1:6, the narrator does not quote Naomi's dialogue when conveying the thought process behind her decision to leave Moab. In 1:18, the narrator uses a similar technique to explain why Naomi did not continue to debate Ruth. In 3:14a, the narrator uses an internal monologue to convey Boaz's thoughts (NOTE *he thought* on 3:14). To be sure, narration of a character's thoughts is not the same as clarification of those thoughts. The inclusion of Boaz's thoughts in this verse does not explain why he is concerned that Ruth not be seen, and scholars have speculated about the reasons for his concern (consult COMMENTS on 3:6–15). Nevertheless, this verse assumes a difference between dialogue spoken to others and an internal monologue or thought process. One's access to certain characters' thoughts (3:14) or thought processes (1:6, 18) is not entirely limited to spoken dialogue alone.

Yet, unlike Naomi's actions in 1:6, 18, the narrator does not provide motivations for the vast majority of the characters' actions in the book. With few exceptions, the narrator's selective representation focuses on the effect or consequences of events instead of on their causes. For example, Ruth's narrator describes the effect that the deaths in Moab have on Naomi rather than the reasons that these characters died. Immediately after Naomi's sons died, the narrator states that Naomi "was left without her two children or her husband" (1:5b; cf. 1:3). Following the death of her sons, Naomi is the subject of every verb during the description of the rest of the stay in Moab (1:5b–7a). As with these deaths, the consequences of the famine are represented in the narrative whereas its cause or causes are not. The narrator foregrounds the effect of the famine on Naomi's family. The famine inspires them to leave Bethlehem in 1:1, and a rumor of its end inspires the surviving family members to return to Bethlehem in v. 6.

V.

The Commentator and the Focus of This Commentary

As already explained, Ruth's author composed the narrative and the narrator presents it. It is the commentator, however, who interprets the narrative. Or, to be precise, the commentator offers possible interpretations of it. One should not necessarily attribute a commentator's interests, interpretative proposals, or textual connections to Ruth's author or narrator. The author or narrator does not explain the narrative beyond the statements in 1:6b and 4:7 (and even these verses require further explanation!). Aside from these two verses, any explanation of the narrative comes from a secondary commentator. As the commentator in this particular volume, I am responsible for the commentary's focus, any interpretive proposals offered or endorsed in it, and any connections drawn between two or more texts, whether inside or outside of Ruth.

As a general rule, the volumes in the Anchor Yale Bible series are not thesis-driven commentaries. Nonetheless, a representative sampling from the jackets of various volumes suggests that each one tends to have a focus. For example, the three-part Leviticus commentary "provides an authoritative and comprehensive explanation of the ethical values concealed in Israel's rituals." In P. Kyle McCarter's two-part commentary on Samuel, "A key issue for McCarter is accounting for the historical circumstances that led to the composition of the books of Samuel." The commentary on 1 Chronicles 1–9 "reveals how the Chronicler's unique introduction to the people of Israel redefines Israel itself and how [the Chronicler] applies this understanding to the realities of his own age." The earlier volume on Ruth for this series "shows that God is not only present throughout [the book], but is indeed the moving force behind all the developments of the story." In short, the Anchor Yale Bible commentaries tend to "explain" or "account for" or "reveal" or "show" how particular issues relate to most of the content of the biblical book under discussion.

In keeping with this tradition, this commentary has a particular focus. It concentrates on the nature of relationships in Ruth. Among other things, a focus on relationships foregrounds the negotiations throughout the book of ability, asymmetrical authority, blessings and their absence, divine activity, ethnicity, exogamy, gender, *ḥesed*, household structures, human desires, impoverishment, labor, patriarchy, religious expression, responsibilities of the clan, sexuality, and status, among other topics.

What a given commentary focuses on, however, is not necessarily what the corresponding biblical book is about. For example, the books of Samuel are not about the historical circumstances that led to their composition even if that is the focus of McCarter's commentary. Likewise, Leviticus is not about Israel's ethical values even if its rituals reflect such values as Milgrom claims. Compositional or ethical issues may provide a profitable tool for analyzing the contents of biblical books, but they are not the subjects of the books. A chosen focus is not an objective description of the meaning or meanings that an author may have intended but a means of organizing commentators' interpretations of the book.

The following sections focus on relationships in order to offer my interpretations of how the word *ḥesed* describes the nature of particular relationships in Ruth, including that of God to humans and humans to each other; the role that sexual desire plays; and the organization of the household. My interpretations of these issues will help to provide some of the context for my focus on relationships in the NOTES and COMMENTS on specific texts throughout the commentary.

A. Divine Activity and Acts of *ḥesed* in Ruth

Scholars often note that God never speaks, no one speaks to God directly, and God does not perform any supernatural activities in the book of Ruth. Characters mention God a number of times, but the narrator mentions God only twice. In 1:6, the narrator acknowledges but does not verify the report that YHWH gave food to the people. In 4:13, the narrator explicitly credits YHWH as the one who gave conception to Ruth. Nevertheless, scholars have greatly expanded the scope of YHWH's alleged activity in relation to many other events and actions in the book. By contrast, while Ruth has diverse roles and actions throughout the book (consult "Gender, Patriarchy, and the Household," below), scholars have often reductively focused on issues related to marriage and fertility although she herself never expresses any desire for a child or interest in maternity (Twersky Reimer, 104). These contrasting scholarly foci in relation to the characters of YHWH and Ruth may relate to how certain gender expectations may influence one's interpretation of the textual and historical evidence.

Although anticipated by a number of scholars (Hertzberg; Humbert; Rudolph), Ronald M. Hals presents the fullest and arguably the most influential argument for a theological reading of Ruth. He argues that the writer of Ruth wants "to stress one particular aspect of God's providence, namely its hiddenness . . . the writer portrays God's guiding hand as totally hidden in normal causality" (16, 18). Hals contends that the "complete sovereignty of God" emerges in the structure of the book. According to Hals, the two passages that mention God's actions explicitly "constitute a kind of frame for the book, since they come one at the beginning and one at the end. . . . [The] writer trace[s] a chain of events whose beginning (1:6) and ending (4:13) are found in God's all-causality" (4–5, 11–12).

For Hals, this "chain of events" consists of a series of human prayers and blessings that are all fulfilled or granted later in the book (1:8–9; 2:12, 20; 3:10; 4:11–12, 14). These and other examples serve as evidence of a hidden God operating behind the scenes of mundane events. The two actions that the narrator mentions in 1:6 and 4:13 serve as bookends that begin and end a chain of divinely inspired events culminating in the birth of Obed, the grandfather of David, in 4:13. Hals uses this "interpretative framework," as he calls it, to argue that the book of Ruth is in fact a salvation history in that its structure retrospectively reveals God's salvific plan. Hals declares that, by the end of chapter 4, "it becomes clear that this has all been *Heilsgeschichte!*" (17 [emphasis in original]).

Over the past several decades, Hals's proposal has influenced many subsequent discussions of the book's portrayal of God (e.g., Beattie; Bush; Campbell; Childs; Gerleman; Hubbard; LaCocque; Nielsen; Sakenfeld, 1999; Trible). Yet, his interpretations of specific texts are far from definitive because each text could and has been interpreted as something other than evidence of divine providence (e.g., NOTE *she chanced upon* on 2:3). For example, instead of interpreting Ruth's use of skirt imagery as evidence of divine causation, as Hals does (8), one could interpret it as Ruth urging Boaz to back up his pious words (2:12) with his own actions because of the absence of divine intervention. According to Fewell and Gunn, in 3:9, "Boaz is challenged [by Ruth] to make good with action his earlier profession of pious well-wishing" (1990, 89). As Linafelt notes "one reader's sense of hidden providential workings is another reader's sense of God's absence" (1999, xvii). To a certain extent, the presence or the lack of divine providence in the book of Ruth lies in the eye of the beholder.

Nevertheless, Hals traces a divine plan and reads the book as *Heilsgeschichte* because of the structure that he maps onto the book of Ruth. He does not link the divine actions in 1:6 and 4:13 on the basis of the types of actions credited to God, namely, the divine "giving" of food (agricultural fecundity) and the divine "giving" of conception (human fertility). Rather, he interprets these two divine actions in terms of their placement within and contribution to the overall structure or pattern that he discerns in the narrative. Indeed, mapping a structure, framework, or outline onto the text is a common method for discovering a theology of Ruth (consult "The Structure of This Commentary's Translation"). For example, Korpel uses his proposed structure and a series of intertextual links as evidence for his argument that theodicy represents the central theme of the book (227–28). To a certain extent, asking how well the actions credited to YHWH in 1:6 and 4:13 fit into any proposed structure for the book of Ruth depends on how one outlines the book.

The narrator provides little evidence to support Hals's analysis of God's role in Ruth. Rather, the narrator explicitly attributes to God only things that are beyond human control. It is not that the narrator hides God behind human activities or that Ruth's pregnancy is the culmination of a chain of events guided by divine providence, but that the narrator does not credit God with activities that humans can control on their own. Intercourse does not always result in pregnancy, and agricultural work does not guarantee a sufficient harvest. God is needed to fulfill these basics, according to many biblical texts. Thus, only human and agricultural fertility fall under divine control rather than human causality. Rather than focusing on efforts to map an overall framework onto the book to analyze divine activity in Ruth, one could consider the quality of the actions credited to God in 1:6 and 4:13.

The characters associate YHWH with fertility in the Cisjordan throughout the book (1:20–21; 4:11–14; cf. 1:8; 2:4). The narrator indicates that the characters credited YHWH with ending the famine in the Cisjordan (1:6). From their perspective, God's actions involving fertility are hardly hidden, even if God and humans do not communicate directly and God does not perform any supernatural activities in the book. In fact, the report of YHWH's action involving agricultural fertility is so widespread that it eventually reaches Naomi in Moab. In short, multiple characters associate YHWH with fertility in a very open and obvious manner. Throughout the book, divine associations with fertility are rarely subtle or hidden. YHWH's activity is self-evident for the narrator and characters, even if it is limited to the provision of only those needs that are beyond human control, namely, fertility. Commenting on the nature of the divine activities in 1:6 and 4:13, Sakenfeld writes: "These two interventions, the giving of food and of pregnancy, represent areas of life over which ancient Israelites experienced little sense of human control. Elsewhere, the direction of the story of Ruth could be and indeed was determined largely by human decision" (1999, 14; cf. Clark, 267; Sakenfeld, 1978, 107).

One may ask why scholars, unlike the narrator or characters, so often characterize YHWH's actions as hidden in Ruth. It may be because not many actions are explicitly attributed to divine causation in the book. Yet, just because a relatively short book does not attribute many actions to God does not mean that those actions are hidden. The portrayal of divine activity in Ruth comes through in the quality of divine actions, not the quantity. The quantity of YHWH's actions in Ruth artificially increases only if one posits hidden divine activity as the motivating or causative force behind mundane actions in the cases where the narrator does not address the causes or motivations behind such actions.

This can help provide nuance to a commonplace understanding of divine acts of *ḥesed*, the meanings of which I discuss shortly, in the book. Only one verse associates YHWH explicitly with *ḥesed* in the entire book. In 2:20, Naomi associates YHWH with *ḥesed* after she sees tangible evidence that YHWH had given abundant food to the people (cf. 1:6). Often, scholars claim that YHWH's *ḥesed* manifests itself through human actions (e.g., Eskenazi and Frymer-Kensky, l; Fewell and Gunn, 1990, 104; Hubbard, 66–74). Yet, the narrator does not hide divine actions behind any of the other human actions explicitly referred to as acts of *ḥesed* (1:8; 3:10). In the first use of the word in the book (1:8), Naomi does not suggest in any way that Orpah and Ruth's *ḥesed* toward Naomi and her family is a veiled expression of divine *ḥesed*. In fact, her daughters-in-law's acts of *ḥesed* provide a "model" for YHWH or, at the very least, a compelling reason for YHWH to act with *ḥesed* toward Orpah and Ruth (Trible, 170; followed by, among others, Fewell and Gunn, 1990, 71; Lapsley, 92; Sakenfeld, 1999, 25). Likewise, Boaz does not imply YHWH's involvement in Ruth's acts of *ḥesed* in 3:10. Just because the narrator spends more time on human actions than divine actions does not mean that the divine acts of *ḥesed* are somehow hidden behind human acts of *ḥesed*. To assume that the examples of *ḥesed* credited to humans in Ruth are a reflection of hidden providence confuses the nature of the divine actions depicted in the book and artificially increases their amount.

Although the word *ḥesed* occurs only three times in Ruth (1:8; 2:20; 3:10), readers have noted the central role that it plays in the story since very early in the history of the book's interpretation. A complicating issue, however, is that *ḥesed* has a broad semantic range within Biblical Hebrew, as documented in book-length studies of the term (Glueck; Sakenfeld, 1978; Clark). When commenting on *ḥesed* in Ruth, contemporary scholars frequently cite postbiblical rabbinic texts (e.g., the citations of *b. B. Qam.* 103b, *Ruth Rab.* 2:14, and Maimonides in Eskenazi and Fryer-Kensky, xlix–l; LaCocque, 28–29) or appeal to a survey of biblical texts that use the term (e.g., Anderson; cf. Lau, 107). Yet, given the wide semantic range of the term *ḥesed*, I do not ask what it usually means in biblical or rabbinic literature and then apply a general definition of *ḥesed* to its uses in Ruth. Rather, I consider how Ruth's narrator uses the term even if it is used differently in many other biblical texts.

Often, scholars debate whether acts of *ḥesed* are motivated by obligation, loyalty, merit, duty, generosity, justice, excessive kindness, and so on. Yet, in keeping with the tendency of Ruth's narrator to describe the consequences or effect of actions and events rather than their motives or causes, the narrator does not indicate what motivates divine or human acts of *ḥesed*. For example, the narrator never explains why Orpah or Ruth acted with *ḥesed* toward Naomi and her family (1:8). As the word *ḥesed* in Ruth describes an action rather than its motivation or the quality of a character (contrast "man/woman of worth" in 2:1; 3:11), I have preferred to translate *ḥesed* as "kindness" or "kindly" rather than as "loving-kindness" or "covenant-loyalty," among other options.

In addition to more altruistic reasons, an act of kindness could just as easily be motivated by self-interest or a desire for praise and recognition. Regarding YHWH's role in 1:6 and 4:13, Koosed writes: "God's actions are after extended periods of inaction, extended periods that lead to hardship in the lives of the characters. At best these actions of God point to God's fickleness not to God's steadfast love" (79–80). As already noted, the narration in 1:6 does not specify whether the famine in Judah lasted the entire time Naomi was in Moab or Naomi heard of its end only after ten years. Nevertheless, even if one were to interpret YHWH's character more generously, Koosed's comment serves as a reminder that an act of kindness, whether human or divine, is not necessarily evidence of its motivation or of a defining inner quality of the character who performs the act. One should also consider the timing of the action and other contextual factors or mitigating circumstances. One should not overstate what these acts reveal about YHWH's motivations or character in Ruth. In fact, YHWH never expresses an opinion or emotion in the book. YHWH does not show disfavor with anyone in the book of Ruth (contrast Onan and YHWH in Gen 38:6–10). The narrator leaves YHWH's interiority completely opaque.

As with other actions or events that the narrator describes, such as the deaths of Naomi's husband and sons, the narrator emphasizes the effect or consequences of acts of *ḥesed*. Throughout the book, acts of *ḥesed*, whether performed by God or humans, result in blessings. In 1:8b, Orpah's and Ruth's acts of *ḥesed* inspire Naomi's blessing of them with the hope that YHWH will deal with them kindly (*ḥesed*). In 2:20, the kindness of YHWH, or less likely of Boaz, inspires Naomi to bless Boaz. In 3:10, Boaz blesses Ruth because of the kindness that she performed. If the divine granting of conception in 4:13 qualifies as an act of *ḥesed*, even YHWH receives a blessing for this action. In 4:14, the women identify the baby as a kindred redeemer for Naomi and declare, "Blessed be YHWH who has not removed a kindred redeemer for you today" (cf. Gen 24:27).

I do not mean to dismiss the importance of YHWH's role in Ruth or divine acts of *ḥesed* by limiting that role to the provision of fertility. Human reproductive capabilities were not taken for granted in the ancient Near East. Certain Mesopotamian texts imply that some humans were created infertile (e.g., Epic of Atra-Hasis, *COS* 1.130: 452; Enki and Ninmah, *COS* 1.159: 518). Although much ancient Israelite literature seems to imply that most, but not all, humans were created with the capacity to conceive within the appropriate age range, this does not mean that successful reproduction was guaranteed. Rather, the assumption was that all humans still depended on divine action to have children.

Multiple texts depict successful reproduction under any circumstance as a divine blessing. Even if one has the capacity to conceive, it still requires a divine blessing to ensure successful reproduction. For example, although both Eve and Leah had given birth previously and thus their reproductive potential was not in question, they acknowledge YHWH's continued aid in their ability to reproduce (cf. Gen 4:25; 29:33, respectively). Other texts assume that, if not for an extremely unusual divine blessing, at least some fertile women will miscarry under normal circumstances (Exod 23:26; Deut 7:13; 28:11; Ps 127:3). Rather than interpreting infertility as a punishment or a curse that deviated from the supposed norm, more often than not it is more accurate to interpret fertility as a blessing and infertility as a nonblessing (Baden and Moss). The fact that reproduction happened frequently does not mean that it was not considered a divine blessing or that its absence represented a divine curse.

Likewise, very little textual evidence in Ruth suggests that successful reproduction was considered the default norm unless stated otherwise. Instead, it is the result of divine blessing, as the narrator makes clear in 4:13. The attribution of conception to a divine blessing in Ruth is in keeping with other ancient Near Eastern texts. In a text from Ugarit, the god El blesses Kirta and promises that his bride will bear eight sons (Parker, 26). In Gen 24:60, when Rebekah leaves home to become Isaac's wife, her mother and brother bless her with a prayer that she will have thousands of descendants. The following chapter attributes her conception to divine intervention after Isaac prays for her (25:21). Similarly, Ruth has a child only after an explicit divine intervention following the townspeople's appeal to God (4:11–12). Moreover, when the townspeople bless her marriage, they compare Ruth specifically to Rachel and Leah (4:11). In Genesis, God "opens" the wombs of Leah and Rachel so they can produce children (29:31; 30:22), just as God "opens" a donkey's mouth so it can speak (Num 22:28) or "opens" a rock (Ps 105:41) so that it produces water. Yet, ancient Israelites would not have considered speaking donkeys or water-producing rocks as normal (Baden, 15–17).

To be clear, Ruth's narrator never indicates directly that any character is infertile. Yet this does not mean that fertility is portrayed as the unwritten norm and infertility as a biological deviation or curse in Ruth. While this does not prove that a particular character in Ruth is portrayed as infertile any more than a queer reading proves that Ruth and Naomi were lesbians, it raises questions about whether fertility is portrayed as the unwritten norm and infertility as a deviation just as a queer reading questions heterosexual desire as the unwritten norm in Ruth. If the text does not support the assumption that fertility is normal unless indicated otherwise, one may question whether one should map fertility onto the characters. To apply an argument frequently made in critical biblical scholarship on disability (consult Melcher, Parsons, and Yong; Avalos, Melcher, and Schipper; Baden and Moss; Moss and Schipper; Schipper, 2006, 2011), the assumption that fertility in Ruth represents a normative state of existence unless the text indicates otherwise often reflects contemporary nondisabled privilege rather than textual evidence.

Outside of Ruth, infertility is often, but not always, identified with the root 'qr (Gen 11:30; 25:21; 29:31; Exod 23:26; Deut 7:14; Judg 13:2–3; 1 Sam 2:5; Isa 54:1; Job 24:21). Yet, the absence of 'qr in Ruth does not necessarily mean that one should assume that the characters are fertile by default. As discussed below ("Sexual Desire in Ruth"), although the narrator never indicates that Ruth was beautiful, her beauty is often assumed on the basis of comparisons with Sarai, Rebekah, and Rachel, all of whom are described as beautiful in Genesis. Yet, Genesis also describes all three women as infertile (*'ăqārâ;* Gen 11:30; 25:21; 29:31, respectively) before a divine intervention (Gen 21:1–2; 25:21; 30:22, respectively). If one assumes Ruth's beauty on the basis of comparisons with the descriptions of Sarai, Rebekah, and Rachel in Genesis, one could also assume her infertility before a divine intervention (Ruth 4:13) on the same basis. Yet, the widespread assumption of Ruth's beauty is not always held to the same standard for textual evidence that is often demanded of those who map infertility onto her character. Nonetheless, questions concerning Ruth's possible infertility have existed since very early in the history of interpretation. According to a rabbinic tradition, Ruth did not have a uterus until YHWH granted her conception (*Ruth Rab.* 7:14). The fertility of Ruth (as well as of Boaz) remains inconclusive before 4:13.

More significantly, several texts indicate short-term or long-term infertility without using 'qr (Gen 16:2; 20:17–18; 1 Sam 1:5–6; Isa 66:9; also possibly 2 Sam 6:23; 2 Kgs 4:14). In fact, several scholars have compared Ruth with one of these texts that describes infertility without using 'qr. According to Ruth 1:4, both Orpah and Ruth were married for "about ten years" without any indication that they had children. This text is compared to the statement in Gen 16:3 that after "ten years" Sarai gave Hagar to Abram because she claims "YHWH has prevented me from bearing children" (16:2; cf. Sasson, 21). The Mishna discusses remarriage if a couple does not have children within ten years (*m. Yeb.* 6.6). Hubbard refers to Orpah and Ruth as "infertile daughters-in law" (95), and Sakenfeld writes that Ruth is "implicitly portrayed as a barren women" (1999, 20), although the lack of children could just as easily have resulted from male sterility since other Hebrew Bible texts acknowledge both male sterility and female infertility (e.g., Gen 20:17; Deut 7:14; possibly 2 Kgs 4:14). In fact, among the named characters in Ruth, the narrator confirms only that Naomi's sons never had children. (As the narrator does not address Orpah's subsequent life after she returns to Moab, her fertility or infertility remains inconclusive.)

Although the majority of biblical characters are depicted as being fertile, several texts suggest that fertility was a divine blessing rather than a given. The notion of fertility as a divine blessing is very different from a contemporary understanding of fertility as normative and infertility as a deviation from this norm or even a divine curse. If, as an interpretive starting point, one takes infertility as a nonblessing and fertility as a blessing, then divine activity is very important in Ruth even if it is limited to the granting of fertility rather than being the hidden force behind actions or events that are not beyond human control, as Hals suggests.

B. Sexual Desire in Ruth

None of the characters in Ruth ever expresses any sexual preferences explicitly. There is little, if any, textual evidence in MT^L to endorse or preclude sexual desire, whether anachronistically understood as homosexual or heterosexual, as driving particular actions or the formation of particular relationships at points in the story where the narrator does not address the possible motives or causes. Yet, some scholars interpret human actions in the book by mapping contemporary categories of sexual desire onto the characters rather than positing divine causation as the driving force behind them. For example, Fewell and Gunn tentatively consider the possibility that Boaz inquires about Ruth in 2:5 because he is sexually attracted to her (1990, 42, 84–85, but consult their qualification on 115–16, n. 32). Linafelt develops this idea further, although he acknowledges that it is an interpretation rather than a conclusion mandated by the text (1999, 30–34; for another opinion, consult NOTE *to whom does this female servant [belong]?* on 2:5). Although speculative, it is not unusual for commentators to ask whether Boaz had "fallen in love with Ruth" (Hubbard, 178; cf. Hyman, 195; for a helpful discussion of the mapping of a romantic or erotic element onto Boaz and Ruth's relationship in scholarship and popular culture, consult Exum, 150–68). Although she maps bisexual desire onto Ruth, Celena M. Duncan comes to a similar conclusion regarding Boaz when she writes: "Boaz was clearly motivated by more than just Levirate duty . . . Boaz wanted Ruth . . . in the end, I believe, he was more interested in the lady" (98).

The notion that Boaz was attracted to Ruth may reflect the widespread assumption that Ruth was physically attractive. According to *Ruth Rab.* 4:6, Ruth was so beautiful that the mere sight of her caused men to have involuntary emissions because the word *mqnh* in 2:4, translated as "her chance" in this commentary, uses the same consonants as the word in Deut 23:11 (Eng. 23:10) for an involuntary, or "chance," nocturnal emission (*mqnh-lylh*). As already discussed, scholars often compare Ruth to the matriarchs in Genesis. In 4:11, the people and the elders compare her to Rachel explicitly, and many interpreters have made compelling comparisons to Sarai and Rebekah on the basis of intertextual evidence. In Genesis, all three matriarchs are described as physically attractive (cf. Gen 12:11, 14; 24:16; 29:17b, respectively). Moreover, the narrator in Genesis notes Jacob's attraction to Rachel immediately after mentioning her beauty (29:18a). If Ruth is interpreted against the backdrop of these matriarchal traditions, some may simply assume her attractiveness as a stock feature of these traditions.

Ruth is often portrayed as beautiful in popular culture, including artwork and film (Exum, 146–50). Scholars also make passing references to her beauty. For example, although the narrator never provides Ruth's age or a physical description, Hubbard refers to her as a "lovely young lady," which could imply her beauty (1); Hertzberg notes her "youth and beauty" (*Jugend und Schönheit;* 274); and LaCocque calls her "a pretty young lady" (97). According to *Ruth Rab.* 6:2, Ruth was still very attractive at the age of forty (on other rabbinic traditions regarding Ruth's beauty, consult Beattie, 191–92). As many scholars note, however, the book contains no physical descriptions nor provides the ages of any of the characters, including Ruth (Bronner, 161–63; Sasson, 218).

Even if arguments that sexual desire motivates certain characters' actions serve as a corrective to overreading divine activity in Ruth (consult "Divine Activity and Acts of *ḥesed* in Ruth"), queer analysis complicates such interpretations. To be clear, a queer analysis does not reduce expressions of sexual desire to particular physical acts. As Duncan, who offers a "bisexual midrash" on Ruth, writes, "the physical act of sex does not need to be the bottom line in every discussion of sexuality" (93). While acknowledging the central role that romantic or sexual love has in lesbian communities, Rebecca Alpert writes that "public vows of commitment, familial connections, female friendship, and cross-cultural and intergenerational relationships are important aspects of lesbian culture. . . . Many heterosexuals mistakenly assume that all that is different about lesbian woman is that they have sex with other women. Jewish lesbians have sought to establish that lesbian culture includes other elements, including those described above" (95). Alpert emphasizes several aspects of Ruth and Naomi's relationship that correspond with expressions of sexuality that she says are valued greatly in lesbian cultures (cf. Koosed, 103–13; West). Although other interpretive possibilities for 1:16–17 and 4:15 exist (consult the corresponding COMMENTS), Jennifer L. Koosed writes: "Ruth's only words of undying devotion are to Naomi (1:16–17) and the only person she is said to love is Naomi (4:15). In some ways a romance between Ruth and Boaz is less supported in the text itself, more dependent on the imagination of the reader, than a romance between Ruth and Naomi" (55). Nevertheless, very few, if any, scholars make exegetical arguments for Boaz's heterosexual desire or explain why they read a modern category of sexual desire back into the text. Instead, heterosexuality is often presumed without explicit justification unless another contemporarily recognized expression of sexual desire is clearly identified in the text. Some might describe this anachronistic reading strategy that assumes a natural or universal attraction of men to women and vice versa as projecting hetero-normativity back into ancient Israelite relationships.

Hetero-normativity does not imply that sexual desire between women and men did not exist in ancient Israel. Rather, as Ken Stone explains, "the point is that 'heterosexuality' as it exists in the modern West is associated with a range of specific meanings and practices that are not identical to the meanings and practices associated with opposite sex relations in other times and places" (160). Although other possibilities in Ruth have been recognized since at least the first publication of Jeannette H. Foster's *Sex Variant Women in Literature* in 1956, heterosexual desire is mapped onto the characters in Ruth more often than any other type of sexual desire. This does not mean that one cannot offer a compelling reading of Boaz or Ruth that maps heterosexual desire onto their characters. Instead, it recognizes such readings as historically privileged interpretative strategies that nonetheless must be justified with the same standard for textual evidence that is often demanded of those who map queer desires onto one or more of the characters in Ruth.

A rabbinic tradition holds that Boaz buried his previous wife on the very day that Ruth arrived in Bethlehem (*b. B. Bat.* 91a; cf. *Ruth Rab.* 1:19), but the narrator never indicates that Boaz had any women as sexual partners besides Ruth or that their sexual relationship extended beyond the occurrence described in 4:13 (for a detailed analysis of scholarly assumptions regarding Boaz's sexuality, consult Krutzsch). The fact that Boaz has sexual intercourse with Ruth does not indicate his attraction to her. Other biblical texts provide examples of men having intercourse with women to whom they are not attracted. For example, Jacob has sex repeatedly with Leah, presumably for procreation, even though the narrator indicates that he was not attracted to her (Gen 29:30–35). Two verses before Boaz and Ruth have sex, the people in the gate and the elders compare Boaz and Ruth's relationship not only to Israel's relationship with Rachel, but also to his relationship with Leah (Ruth 4:11). In other words, Boaz's sexual activity with Ruth is explicitly compared to other procreative relationships, one that involves sexual attraction and another that does not. Which relationship one chooses to prioritize as paradigmatic for understanding Boaz and Ruth's marriage remains a matter of interpretation.

Boaz's stated reason for acquiring Ruth as a wife is "to establish the name of the dead man upon his inheritance" (4:10). Nonetheless, there is a tendency to read romance or sexual desire into his marriage to Ruth, even if this reading overrides the reason that Boaz actually gives in the text. Boaz and Ruth never verbally express any love, affection, or sexual attraction toward each other. In fact, Boaz commends Ruth because she "did not go after the young men whether poor or rich" (2:10), which may imply that she could have pursued younger, more physically attractive men (cf. 1 Sam 8:16; 9:2; Ezek 23:6, 12, 23). Boaz seems to recognize that their relationship is based on factors other than sexual desire. Some scholars have suggested that it has more to do with survival (Donaldson, 132). If one translates *ṭôb* as a superlative ("that is best") in 3:13, Boaz may even imply that he would prefer that someone else marry Ruth (COMMENTS on 3:6–15). Occasionally, scholars note Boaz's reluctance to marry her, although they usually assume it relates to concerns over her ethnicity rather than a lack of sexual interest on his part (e.g., Fewell and Gunn, 1990, 87–88; Saxegaard, 170). Yet, both explanations are equally speculative as Boaz never expresses opinions about Ruth's ethnicity or his sexual preferences.

A queer reading does not mean that one is anachronistically interpreting Boaz or other characters as gay or lesbian. Rather, it suggests that there are an infinite number of constructed categories of sexuality, which include but are not limited to heterosexuality and homosexuality (Hornsby and Stone, xii). Instead of ahistorically assuming that all texts reflect one or two universally constant sexual identities, queer readings foreground how interpretative strategies may uncritically privilege certain relationships over others, be it Ruth and Naomi, Ruth and Boaz, or some other relationship (Duncan). To be clear, noting the tendency toward hetero-normative interpretations of Ruth does not mean that mapping other understandings of sexual desire onto the characters is any less presumptive. Instead, it highlights how interpretations that posit sexual desire as the motivating force behind mundane actions in Ruth tend to be hetero-normative exercises.

C. Exogamy and Ethnicity

Throughout the book of Ruth, the title character is identified repeatedly as a Moabite (1:4, 22; 2:2, 6, 21; 4:5, 10). The Hebrew Bible contains a variety of traditions about Moab and the Moabites. As a nation, Moab is depicted as Israel's enemy (Judg 3:12–30; 2 Sam 8:2; 2 Kgs 3:4–27; 13:20; 24:2; 1 Chr 18:2; the Mesha Inscription, *ANET* 320–21) and condemned in several Israelite prophetic oracles (Isa 15:1–16:14; Jer 48:1–47; Amos 2:1–3; Zeph 2:9; cf. Ps 83:6–9), although the Moabites are also listed in Dan 11:41 among those who will escape captivity.

Other texts condemn marriage and sexual relations between Israelite men and Moabite women and Israelite participation in Moab's cultic practices (Num 25:1–5 [cf. Ps 106:28]; 1 Kgs 11:1–2; Ezra 9:1–2; Neh 13:1–2), as well as the Moabites' behavior toward Israel during the wilderness period (Deut 23:4–7 [Eng. 23:3–6]; cf. Judg 11:17–18; Neh 13:1–2). Some scholars interpret Ruth's marriages to Mahlon and Boaz against the backdrop of these condemnations (e.g., Fewell and Gunn, 1990, 70; Köhlmoos, xv; Korpel, 233; LaCocque, 42; van Wolde, 1998, 132–37; Zakovitch, 38–41, 62–64; for a review of scholarly opinions, consult Fischer, 2001, 61–65, 86–93). Similarly, some rabbinic traditions explain the deaths of Mahlon and Kilyon as a punishment for marrying Moabite woman (Targum Ruth 1:4–5; *Ruth Rab.* 2:9). When 1 Chronicles notes that two of Judah's male descendants, Joash and Saraph, married into Moab (4:22), the Targum for 1 Chr 4:22 identifies Joash as Naomi's son Mahlon (meaning "sickness," consult Note *Mahlon* on 1:2) and Saraph as her son Kilyon (meaning "annihilation," consult Note *Kilyon* on 1:2).

Nevertheless, as Koosed notes, "Reading Ruth alone fails to present the negative assessment of Moabites that reading Ruth in combination with these other texts produces" (106). If one must read Ruth in combination with other texts to produce evidence that the book responds to negative assessments of Moabites, the question becomes which other texts, if any, should one choose to read in combination with Ruth? The fact that two or more otherwise unrelated texts discuss Moab does not necessitate reading them in combination any more than two otherwise unrelated texts that each discuss Moses, priests, or Egypt would necessitate a combined reading. Many of the texts that discuss Moab could produce either a unified or a conflicting opinion about Moabites when read in combination. As Ruth never addresses attitudes reflected in the texts that seem to disparage Moabites, one may ask whether Ruth's failure to assess Moabites negatively is best explained as a polemic against negative attitudes that are never referred to or addressed in the text.

One could cite texts that do and texts that do not assess Moab negatively from both monarchic and postmonarchic periods. To be clear, a nonnegative assessment is not necessarily an endorsement of Moab, but simply not a condemnation. A text does not necessarily bless Moab by default just because it does not curse Moab. Nevertheless, at a minimum, the option of assessing Moab negatively or nonnegatively existed throughout Israel's history. Whatever time period one chooses for Ruth's date of composition, the book would not be the only biblical text from that period that fails to present a negative assessment of Moab. I argue that it is easiest to account for this nonnegative presentation in Ruth as simply one of several examples of texts that fail to assess Moabites negatively. In this respect, the following sections discuss Ruth as one of several biblical texts that provide a nonnegative depiction of Moab, especially when associated with the Ephrathites, Bethlehem, the Judahites, or Abraham's relative Lot.

1. JUDAHITE AND MOABITE MARRIAGES

Ruth is not the only text to connect Ephrathites from Bethlehem of Judah with Moab. In 1 Sam 22:3–4, David's parents "dwell" (*wayyēšbû;* cf. Ruth 1:4) in Moab while David waits to know what God will do for him during a time of crisis (cf. Ruth 1:6). Although the natures of the crises are different, both Jesse, who is an "Ephrathite from Bethlehem of Judah" (1 Sam 17:12; cf. Ruth 4:22), and Elimelech's family, who are "Ephrathites from Bethlehem of Judah" (1:2), dwell in Moab during times of crisis. Neither 1 Sam 22:3–4 nor Ruth 1:1–7a explicitly censures these Ephrathites for residing in Moab. Also, Ithmah the Moabite appears on a list of David's mighty warriors (1 Chr 11:46).

Discussions of ethnicity and marriage in Ruth scholarship often focus on Ruth's Moabite ethnicity. Yet, the book identifies her husband Mahlon's ethnicity in its opening verses (1:2). Mahlon and Boaz's ethnicities are just as, if not more, significant to discussions of exogamy in Ruth in light of other traditions about Judahite marriage practices, especially in Bethlehem. The significance of the husbands' ethnicities within Israel is often underappreciated when scholars focus on marriages between Moabites and Israelites more generally. Yet, Ruth describes marriages not just between Moabites and Israelites in general, but between a Moabite and Ephrathites from Bethlehem in Judah.

Rather than reading Ruth as countering traditions that condemn Judahite exogamy (e.g., 1 Kgs 11:1–2; Ezra 9:1–2; Neh 13:1–2), one may read it as one of several texts which discuss uncensored Judahite exogamy, particularly associated with Bethlehem, that do not reflect a particular polemical agenda. For example, Ibzan, who, like Elimelech, was "from Bethlehem" (Judg 12:8; cf. Ruth 1:1–2), married his sixty children to spouses "outside (his clan)" (Judg 12:9; cf. "outside [the clan]" in Deut 25:5). In fact, a rabbinic tradition identifies Ibzan as Boaz (*b. B. Bat.* 91a). In 1 Chr 4:22, the narrator states without condemnation that Judah's descendants Joash and Saraph married into Moab and returned to Bethlehem. (In 4:22, Bethlehem is spelled "Lehem"; cf. Beth-nimrah [Num 32:3] spelled Nimrah [Num 32:36; Josh 13:27] or Beth-tappuah [Josh 15:53] spelled Tappuah [Josh 15:3].) Both Chronicles and Ruth claim that long ago Judah's descendants in Bethlehem married into Moab. Immediately after noting the marriages of Joash and Saraph, the narrator of Chronicles interjects to claim that these "records are ancient" (1 Chr 4:22b). Similarly, the genealogies at the end of Ruth imply that several generations have passed since the time in which the story took place "in the days when the chieftains ruled" (1:1; Note *formerly* on 4:7).

Elsewhere, David, the most famous Ephrathite from Bethlehem (1 Sam 17:12; cf. 16:18; 20:6), married outside of Israel repeatedly (2 Sam 3:3; 1 Chr 3:1–2). According to other biblical traditions, his sister Abigail married an Ishmaelite (1 Chr 2:17), and his son Solomon married an Egyptian (1 Kgs 3:1). The mother of Rehoboam, Solomon's only known son and his successor, was Naamah the Ammonite (1 Kgs 14:21, 31; 2 Chr

12:13), who, like Ruth the Moabite, married into the Davidic line and ensured its survival. Judahite marriages with Ruth the Moabite and Naamah the Ammonite ensure the survival of the royal lineage before and after David's reign, respectively (cf. Gen 19:30–35).

Other texts make references without censure to Judah's marriage to a Canaanite woman (Gen 38:2; 1 Chr 2:3–4). Although Ruth does not mention this Canaanite wife, it makes reference to Judah's relationship with Tamar (Ruth 4:12; cf. Gen 38; 1 Chr 2:4). Her ethnicity is uncertain, but she may be a Canaanite woman from Chezib (Gen 38:5–6), which is possibly the conquered Canaanite city "Achzib" in Judah's territory (Josh 15:44). It is also worth noting that an early Christian text claimed that Judah's descendant Salmon fathered Boaz with Rahab, a Canaanite woman (Matt 1:5; cf. Ruth 4:21).

Ruth 4:11–12, 17–22 refer to several of Israel's descendants through his son Judah and grandson Perez. The genealogies in 1 Chr 2:1–4:23 also focus on Israel's descendants through Judah's lineage. They include uncensored marriages with Moabite women (4:22) among several other uncensored examples of Judahite exogamy. They also imply uncensored marriages to Moabites by Benjaminites (8:8). The Judahite names listed in Ruth 4:17–22 are nearly identical with those in 1 Chr 2:5, 9–12, 15 (cf. Gen 46:12). Their internal similarities suggest a shared tradition (Zenger, 10; for surveys of scholarly opinions, consult Bush, 13; Sasson, 179–87). Both Ruth and 1 Chronicles refer to Judah's father as Israel rather than Jacob (NOTE *house of Israel* on 4:11). Also, Ruth 1:2 identifies Elimelech and Naomi's household as Ephrathites. First Chronicles connects them to Perez's lineage through Ephrathah, who was the wife of Perez's grandson Caleb and an ancestress of the eponymous founder of Bethlehem (1 Chr 2:19, 50–55; 4:4), although no genealogical record outside of that in 1 Chronicles supports this claim. Moreover, women play a prominent role throughout the book of Ruth and the Judahite genealogies in 1 Chronicles (1 Chr 2:4, 16–18, 21, 24, 26, 29, 34–35, 46, 48–49; 4:5, 7, 9, 18–19; Knoppers, 2003, 358–59).

Although Ruth may have been composed slightly earlier (consult "The Date of Ruth's Composition"), one finds examples of uncensored intermarriage among the literature from Elephantine (e.g., the marriage of Ananiah to an Egyptian slave named Tamut; cf. 1 Chr 2:34). Regarding literature from Yehud, Gary N. Knoppers is correct to ask, "Did the firm stance of Ezra and Nehemiah against intermarriage dominate this period, or were their positions exceptional?" (2001, 15).

If one's interpretation starts with a focus on the ethnicity of Ruth's husbands as Ephrathites from Bethlehem of Judah rather than of Ruth as a Moabite, the marriages in Ruth are not particularly exceptional among depictions of Judahite marriage practices in either First or Second Temple literature. There is no reason why one must read Ruth against the backdrop of the condemnations of Judahite marriages with Moabites. One could just as easily read it as one of several examples of texts that discuss such marriages without a clear polemic against them.

2. MOABITES AS DESCENDANTS OF LOT

If Ruth is not read as a polemic against condemnations of exogamy or against negative stereotypes of Moabites, why does the book refer to its title character's ethnicity so often?

One possibility is that Ruth reflects traditions that depict the Moabites as the descendants of Lot, the son of Abram's brother Haran (Gen 11:27). Moabites are referred to as the "children of Lot" when the Israelites are instructed not to battle Moab (Deut 2:9, 19) because the Moabites sold the Israelites food and water and let them travel through Moabite territory during the wilderness period (2:28–29; Num 21:11–20; contrast Deut 23:4–5 [Eng. 23:3–4]). According to Gen 19:37, Moab's eponymous ancestor is the son of Lot. In the Pentateuch, the few texts which claim that the Moabites are Lot's descendants do not present the Moabites negatively (contrast Ps 83:9 [Eng. 83:8] and possibly Zeph 2:9, which compares Moab's fate to the destruction of Sodom).

Although Ruth contains no mention of Lot, its portrayal of Moabites may reflect traditions that trace their ancestry through Lot. As many scholars have noted, Ruth's encounter with Boaz on the threshing floor has striking similarities in context and vocabulary with the story of Moab's birth in Gen 19:30–38. Both Ruth and Genesis 19 depict intimate encounters at night between a woman whose husband had died (Gen 19:14–16; Ruth 1:4–5) and an intoxicated man (Gen 19:33–35; Ruth 3:7–8). Zakovitch (50) notes that all of the women are referred to as "daughters" during these encounters (Gen 19:30, 36; Ruth 3:10, 11; although the nature of the respective relationships is very different). Both texts use the same term (*wattiškāb*) to depict a woman "lying" with or near a man while he is either initially or completely unaware of her presence (Gen 19:33; Ruth 3:7–8; note the rare use of the feminine imperative *šikĕbî* in Gen 19:34 and Ruth 3:13).

Some scholars read Ruth as countering Gen 19:30–38b (e.g., Braulik; Ebach; Fentress-Williams, 28–29; Goulder; Nielsen, 41). Yet, it is unclear whether Genesis 19 portrays the mother of Moab in a negative light. There is no censure of her actions, and she seems unashamed of them (Coxon, 31). In v. 31, Moab's mother explicitly states her motives for sleeping with Lot as a desire to continue Lot's lineage (his "seed," 19:32, 34; cf. Ruth 4:12) under very exceptional circumstances. This concern also occurs in the ancestral tradition about Tamar (Gen 38:12–30; cf. Ruth 4:12) and conforms to Boaz's stated rationale for his marriage to Ruth (4:5, 10). Rather than implying a condemnation of Lot's daughters' unusual actions that result in Moab's and Ammon's births, Gen 19:30–38 explicitly connects those actions with the survival of the descendants of Abram's brother Haran. One could interpret the daughters' actions as resourceful just as easily as illegitimate. Moreover, while Leviticus 18, which comes from a different Pentateuchal source than Gen 19:30–38, condemns sexual activity between close relatives (v. 6; cf. Jub 16:7–9), it does not include father-daughter sexual relations among its examples of prohibited relations. Also, it does not address Israelite-Moabite relations. All of the texts that explicitly call for the exclusion of Moabites provide rationales other than Moab's incestuous origins (e.g., Deut 23:4–7 [Eng. 23:3–6]; cf. Num 23:6–7; 24:17; Neh 13:1–2).

Scholars have also noted similarities between Ruth 1 and Genesis 13, which is the only biblical text aside from Genesis 19 in which Lot plays a major role (Lot is mentioned in 14:12, 16, but his character does not make an appearance in that story). According to Gen 13:1, when Abram left Egypt after his famine-inspired sojourn, Lot was "under his authority" (*'immô*; NOTE *under her authority* on 1:7a). The following verses, however, detail how Lot "separates" from Abram. Various forms of the root *prd* ("to separate") appear repeatedly (13:9, 11, 14) when Abram settles in Canaan while Lot settles in Sodom. In Ruth 1:7, Ruth travels "under [Naomi's] authority" (*'immāh*) back to Canaan after Naomi's time in a foreign land due to a famine. Yet, in contrast to her ancestor Lot, Ruth swears not to let anything "separate" (*prd*; 1:17b) her from Naomi. Connecting these uses of *prd*, Bezalel Porten writes: "[Ruth's] refusal to be 'separated' [*prd*] from Naomi even in death (Ru. 1:17) marks a reunion of the lines of Lot and Abraham which 'separated' earlier (Gen. 13:9, 11). Similarly, the marriages of Isaac with Rebekah and of Jacob with Rachel and Leah were unions of Abraham's descendants with those of Nahor (Gen. 24:24, 29:10)" (1976, 16; cf. Fisch; *Gen. Rab.* 41:10). For Porten, although Abram left his ancestral home in the land of Haran (Gen 11:26–12:5), his lineage is reunited with his brother Nahor's lineage through the marriages in Genesis and is reunited with his brother Haran's lineage through the marriages in Ruth. To be sure, Porten's argument would work if Ruth were an Ammonite since the Ammonites are also descendants of Lot (Gen 19:38; Deut 2:19).

If Ruth is interpreted as a descendant of Lot and his father Haran, then the book named after her recognizes the role that female descendants of both of Abram's brothers (Haran and Nahor) play in the growth of the lineage that will eventually become the Judahites. Rebekah is the granddaughter of Abram's other brother Nahor (Gen 11:26; 22:23; 24:15, 24, 47). Many scholars have noted Ruth's similarities in context and vocabulary with the story of Isaac and Rebekah's marriage (Gen 24), especially since Hermann Gunkel's work (consult "Genre[s] in Ruth"). As with Ruth and Boaz's relationship, Isaac and Rebekah's involves a "chance" (*qrh*) encounter (Gen 24:12; Ruth 2:3). When Abraham's servant and Naomi each realize the significance of these encounters, they use exactly the same words to credit YHWH (*'ăšer lō'-'āzar ḥasdô*; NOTE *who has not abandoned his kindness with the living and with the dead* on 2:20), although, unlike Gen 24:12, Ruth's narrator does not attribute Ruth's chance encounter with Boaz to YHWH (cf. NOTE *she chanced upon* on 2:3). Both stories include the only uses of the phrase "to her mother's household" (*lĕbêt 'immāh*) in the Bible (Gen 24:28; Ruth 1:8; cf. Song 3:4; 8:2; NOTE *her mother's household* on 1:8). In both cases, the finalization of the marriage arrangements is followed by a prayer for the new wife's fertility (Gen 24:60; Ruth 4:11–12; consult "Divine Activity and Acts of *ḥesed* in Ruth").

The references to the female descendants of Nahor become more explicit in 4:11–12. In these verses, the people and the elders make reference to how Rachel and Leah "built" the house of their husband Israel/Jacob (Gen 30:3) through procreation. Rachel and Leah are descendants of Nahor through their father Laban (29:5). As for Leah, she is the mother of Judah (29:35; 35:23) and the grandmother of Perez. Judah fathered Perez with Tamar (38:29), resulting in the house of Perez (Ruth 4:12, 18–22). Scholars have identified many potential textual connections between the book of Ruth and the story of Tamar and Judah in Genesis 38. The connections include, but are not limited to, instructions for a daughter-in-law to return to her birth household (Gen 38:11; Ruth 1:8) until her potential husband is grown (cf. the use of "until he grows" in Gen 38:11 with Ruth 1:13; for a summary of other connections, consult Berger, 434, n. 2; Melissa Jackson, 181). As for Rachel, she died shortly after giving birth to Israel/Jacob's last child Benjamin on the road to Ephrathah/Bethlehem (Gen 35:16–19). In 48:7, Jacob tells Joseph that Rachel "died . . . and I buried her there on the road to Ephrath, which is Bethlehem" (cf. 35:19). While on the "road" back to Judah (Ruth 1:7; specifically Bethlehem, cf. 1:19, 22), Ruth commits to "die" where Naomi dies and specifies "there I will be buried" (1:17). In Ruth 4:11, the people and the elders not only mention Bethlehem/ Ephrathah explicitly, they also compare Ruth to Rachel and Leah. With the birth of Obed, Ruth continues to build the house of Israel near the very location where Israel/ Jacob's last son was born. In this sense, Ilana Pardes argues that the book of Ruth picks up "where the story of Rachel ends" (115).

When read against the backdrop of traditions about marriages of Abram's male descendants to Nahor's female descendants, one may find significance in Ruth's ethnicity for reasons other than a polemic against prohibitions of marriages with Moabites that are otherwise unmentioned in the book.

3. MOABITES AS KIN IN RUTH

The indirect reference to Ruth and Orpah's mothers notwithstanding (1:8), there are only two Moabites in the book of Ruth. There are no Moabites in Ruth outside the Israelite clan structure (consult "Household Organization," below). While Moabites in general may be distant relatives of the Israelites going back ten generations, both of the Moabites in Ruth are members of a Judahite clan through marriage, although Orpah eventually returns to Moab. The next reference to Moabite ethnicity occurs in 1:22, which does not describe Ruth as simply a Moabite but also describes her affiliation with a Judahite clan and her status within the clan relative to Naomi's status: "Now Ruth the Moabite, her daughter-in-law, was under her authority." A similar description of Ruth occurs in 2:6. Likewise, Boaz does not refer to her as simply a Moabite but as "Ruth the Moabite, the wife of the dead man" (4:5) and "Ruth the Moabite, the wife of Mahlon" (4:10).

The narrator refers to her simply as "Ruth the Moabite" in 2:2a and 21. The first reference, however, occurs immediately after the narrator noted in the two previous verses that Naomi's husband had a relative named Boaz (2:1) and that Ruth was "her daughter in law" (1:22). Moreover, in 2:2b, Naomi refers to Ruth as "my daughter," which reflects kinship terminology for an unmarried woman in an extended family or clan (consult "Household Organization"). Ruth is not simply a Moabite when the narrator's reference in v. 2a is read in the context of the surrounding verses. In 2:21, the reference occurs immediately after Naomi tells Ruth that Boaz "is close to *us*. He is one of *our* kindred redeemers" (2:20b [emphasis added]). In vv. 2 and 21, the references to "Ruth the Moabite" occur in the context of her and Naomi's affiliation with the clan to which Boaz belongs. Noting that references to Ruth's ethnicity always occur in the context of her membership in a Judahite clan, Eunny P. Lee refers to Ruth as a "foreigner-kinswoman" (92–93).

Ruth never self-identifies as a Moabite. Instead, she refers to herself as Boaz's "maidservant" (2:13) and his "handmaid" (3:9), which describes her status within the Judahite clan relative to Boaz's status. The only possible reference that she makes to her ethnicity occurs in 2:10 when she tells Boaz that she is a "foreign woman" (*nākriyyâ*). Yet, this term can also refer to a woman who is married to another man regardless of her ethnicity (NOTE *a foreign woman* on 2:10). Since Ruth is speaking to Boaz, she could be identifying herself as either a Moabite or the wife of the Ephrathite Mahlon or both. In this sense, this self-identification fits with the qualified references to her Moabite ethnicity throughout the book. She is both a Moabite and a member of a Judahite clan through marriage. As a foreigner-kinswoman, the title character epitomizes the Moabite in the book of Ruth as not simply a foreigner but kin who has become foreign through ten generations of separation since the time of Isaac and Lot (consult COMMENTS on 4:18–22).

D. Household Organization

Kinship terminology occurs very often in Ruth. Characters are frequently described with terms such as "wife/wives" (1:1–2, 4; 4:5, 10 [two times], 13), "son(s)" (1:1–3, 5; 4:13, 17), "husband" (1:3, 5; 2:11), "daughter(s)-in-law" (1:6–8, 22; 2:20–23; 3:3, 18; 4:15), "daughter" (1:11–13; 2:2, 8, 22; 3:1, 10–11, 16, 18), "relative" (2:1; 3:2), "close (relative)" (2:20; 3:12), and "kin/brother(s)" (4:3, 10). Also, the characters use kinship terminology without referring to a specific person (e.g., husband[s] [1:11, 9, 12 (two times), 13] and sons [1:11–12; 4:15]). Such terminology positions the characters within a patrimonial "household" framework, which served as a foundational building block for social organization in ancient Israel. As J. David Schloen explains:

> In the absence of the rather abstract idea that an impersonal political constitution or universal egalitarian social contract underpins the social order, personal relationships patterned on the household served to integrate society and to legitimate the exercise of power. . . . Far from being merely banal or euphemistic, the use of [kinship terminology] expressed a basic understanding of political and social relations that was derived from familiar household relationships. This model of society was quite simple, to be sure, but it was also quite flexible and extensible to encompass personal relationships at many different levels from the affairs of the humblest family to the dealings between kings. (255, 258)

Although Schloen's study concentrates on the Bronze and Iron Ages, this model of social organization was not necessarily limited to those time periods but was used "for all manner of political and social relationships throughout the Near East in the pre-Hellenistic period" (Schloen, 255). To be sure, if one dates Ruth's composition to a later time period, as I tentatively suggest (consult "The Date of Ruth's Composition"), the integrity of the household may have broken down by that time (as I explain below). Nevertheless, the durability of household terminology provided a productive means of describing social relations even if the household model did not fit with contemporary lived experience when and where Ruth was composed. Moreover, considering that Ruth's author is imagining how life in Bethlehem was during the period of the chieftains (1:1), it would be contextually appropriate to situate the characters within this type of household framework.

Two terms for the organization of the household occur in Ruth: *bayit* (1:8, 9; 2:7; 4:11 [two times], 12 [two times]) and *mišpāḥâ* (2:1, 3). The terms are difficult to distinguish when they occur together (Gen 24:38, 40, 41; Judg 9:1; 2 Sam 16:5; McNutt, 90, n. 79). Yet, however else a *bayit* and *mišpāḥâ* were configured, both terms could describe a socioeconomically integrated unit of various sizes consisting of humans, their material goods, and their livestock. This represents how these terms, which I translate as "household" and "clan," respectively (NOTE *clan* on 2:1), are used throughout Ruth except for one use of *habbayit* to describe a physical structure (2:7). In Ruth, the term *'am,* often translated as "people," is used within the context of the household or clan. Although *'am* has a wide semantic range across biblical literature, it refers to human members of a household or clan throughout Ruth (1:10, 15, 16 [two times]; 2:11), except for 1:6 where it refers to YHWH's "people." One also finds this use of *'am* in texts outside of Ruth (e.g., 1 Sam 9:12; 2 Kgs 4:13). Leviticus 21:14 requires a priest to marry a woman "from his people" (*mē'ammâw*), meaning within his own clan. Similarly, Naomi refers to Orpah's return to her birth household, presumably with the intention to remarry, as a return to "her people" (1:10). Conversely, when Ruth refuses to return to her birth household, she says to Naomi, "your people, my people" (1:16; van der Toorn, 1996, 203–4).

In Ruth, the term *bayit* describes two types of "households," which correspond to what other texts call the "house of the father" (*bêt 'āb*) and "the house of the fathers" (*bêt 'ābôt*), although these terms do not occur in Ruth. The first type of household can be either a nuclear or an extended family. The members of Elimelech's household constitute a nuclear family consisting of a husband, a wife, and two sons living together (1:1–2). In 1:4, Orpah and Ruth join this household through marriage, and "they [the sons, their wives, and their mother/mother-in-law] dwelled there." As in v. 4, when a woman married a man, she left her birth household and resided in her husband's household (e.g., Gen 24:60–67), whereas a widowed woman without children could return to her birth household (Gen 38:11; Lev 22:13), as Orpah presumably does (Ruth 1:14) though Ruth does not (2:11). In 1:8–9, Naomi advises her daughters-in-law to return to Moab and join another household (e.g., the household of their birth or of a future husband). This implies that the family living together in Moab represented a household even though the narrator did not use *byt* in the previous verses. In its idealized form, several nuclear families made up a larger extended family. This larger socioeconomically integrated unit consisted of three or four generations. In addition to livestock and material goods, these extended families included a senior living male ("the father"), his wives, their unmarried sons and daughters, their married sons and their wives, the sons' children, and possibly other dependents such as widows, orphans, servants, people residing as aliens, or Levites (Exod 20:10; Deut 12:18; 16:11, 14; cf. Ben-Dor; Gottwald, 285–92; Lemche, 245–72; McNutt, 81–94; Schloen, 150–55; van der Toorn, 1996, 194–205; Note *clan* on 2:1; for a discussion with attention to rabbinic sources, consult Weisberg, 45–96). Usually, the extended family resided together on land that was considered its inalienable "inheritance" (*naḥălâ;* cf. Ruth 4:5, 6, 10). Individuals within the extended family could control the usufruct of various portions of this inheritance depending on the individual's status. For example, Boaz and Elimelech both hold a "portion of the [inherited] field" (*ḥelqat haśśādeh;* 2:3; 4:3, respectively).

A clan consisted of several extended families (as many as twelve, by some estimations, e.g., Schloen, 154–55) that could live and be buried together on their inherited field (Josh 24:32; cf. Gen 33:19). Thus, Boaz may associate Mahlon's inheritance (*naḥălātô*) with his ancestral burial place (Ruth 4:10; cf. 1:17–18). According to some texts, the clan represents the ancient Israelite social unit by which land was apportioned and held as an inheritance (Num 33:54; cf. 26:52–56; Josh 13:23, 28; 15:20; 16:8; 18:20, 28; 19:8, 23, 31, 39, 48). This fits the context in which the term *mišpāḥâ* is used in Ruth 2:3. The narrator explains that Boaz belonged to Elimelech's clan and held a portion of the clan's inherited field (NOTE *clan* on 2:1). While it remains unclear whether Boaz and Elimelech belonged to the same extended family, the narrator indicates that they belonged to the same "clan" (*mišpāḥâ*), which may be the Ephrathites (NOTE *Ephrathites from Bethlehem of Judah* on 1:2).

The second type of household, corresponding to the term "house of the fathers," usually describes a much larger transgenerational social grouping defined on the basis of real or fictive lines of descent as well as social and geographic considerations beyond simply bloodlines (Knoppers, 2004, 616–17; for scholarship on this social grouping, consult Collins, 105, n. 7). Although there are few references to the "house of the father" in Chronicles, Ezra, and Nehemiah, texts from postmonarchic periods include references to the "house of the fathers" (various forms of *bêt 'ābôt*) more frequently than earlier texts. As already noted, the integrity of the extended family and clan structure may have broken down by the time of Ruth's composition. The blessing in Ruth 4:11–12 seems to use the term "house of" in the sense of a *bêt 'ābôt*, and the genealogical lists in vv. 17–22 seem to reflect this idea as well. Whereas Ruth 1 raises concerns over whether the title character will remain in the extended family into which she married (a "house of the father"), Ruth 4 frames her marriage to Boaz as her incorporation into the house of his fathers. Whether Ruth's different uses of *bayit* reflect an endorsement of possible historical shifts in kinship organization during the early Persian period cannot be confirmed, but for a helpful discussion of such shifts in relation to Ruth, consult Lau, 167–74.

I. HOUSEHOLD AND CLAN STATUSES OF RUTH'S CHARACTERS

The various types of household organization described as nuclear or extended families (*bayit*) and clans (*mišpāḥâ*) help to explain the relative statuses of Ruth's characters and many of the roles that they play throughout the book. For example, members (*'am*) of a clan served several protective social functions for other members of the clan's households. These functions included, but were not limited to, the redemption of fellow members of the clan when the status quo was disrupted for any number of reasons (NOTE *kindred redeemers* on 2:20). As a member of Elimelech's clan, Boaz could serve as a kindred redeemer for the portion of the inherited field held by Elimelech when its redemption was required. In Ruth, redemption is conceptualized within the context of the clan. Yet, as discussed throughout the COMMENTS, whether the book presents an optimistic picture of how well the clan provides for its dependents is up for debate.

Authority in Ruth is conceptualized through asymmetrical relationships within the household and clan structures. After Boaz asks "to whom does this female servant [belong]?," he is informed that she is a Moabite "female servant" under Naomi's authority (2:5–6). This identifies not only Ruth's ethnicity, but also her status relative to another member of the clan. Also, although Ruth was already a member of Boaz's larger clan, the people and the elders acknowledge that she is "entering [Boaz's] household" through marriage (4:11). In this context, she is referred to again as a "female servant" (4:12). In each case, the term describes her asymmetrical relationship to a more senior member of her clan. As Boaz would be the senior member of his household, she would fall under his authority within the household system (cf. "maidservant" [2:13], "handmaid" [3:9]).

Naomi and Boaz could simultaneously have authority over Ruth. Since the extended family and clan consisted of multiple generations of parents and nonparents, servants and nonservants, married and unmarried people, siblings with different genders and places in the birth order, etc., members had varying degrees of authority depending on the nature of the relationship. An unmarried woman, often referred to as a "daughter" (e.g., Judg 21:21), would be under the authority of her father, mother, and male sibling(s). For example, Rebekah is under the authority of her father, mother, and brother (Gen 24:50–59). A mother of a married son and of an unmarried daughter would have authority over her daughter and her daughter-in-law (Mic 7:6). Members could simultaneously have authority over and be under the authority of other parties because authority was relative to the nature of the relationship. For example, one could simultaneously be a "servant" (*'ebed*) to the senior member of the extended family and still be the senior member of one's own nuclear family (e.g., Exod 21:2–3; cf. the discussion of heterarchy in Meyers, 2013, 196–99).

One's status within the clan could shift because of expected and unexpected life circumstances. Expected circumstances might include changes in marital status, the birth of a child, or changes in seniority upon the death of a senior male. Unexpected circumstances might include the death of a spouse or child (Ruth 1:3–5) or shifts in one's economic position. For example, Lev 25:23–55 discusses various scenarios in which a clan member comes under the authority of another member after becoming impoverished (Milgrom, 2001, 2205–6; Wells). This text includes a scenario in which a "resident alien" (*ger wĕtôšāb*) dwelling with the clan becomes wealthy enough to acquire as a servant a clan member who was presumably born into the clan (25:47). Both positive and negative economic changes could affect one's status and authority in relation to other members of the clan.

Kinship terminology was not limited to parties with a current marital or genetic relationship given the scope of the extended family and clan structure. Instead, this terminology described one's family or clan status relative to other living or dead members. For example, the narrator and characters of Ruth continue to use kinship terminology to describe Naomi's, Ruth's, and Orpah's statuses within the household and clan that they joined through marriage, even after their marriages end because of the deaths of their husbands. Following these deaths, neither Naomi nor Ruth is ever described as an *'almānâ*, a term often translated as "widow" but that more precisely refers to a woman outside of the protection of the household or clan into which she was married (Hiebert; cf. Steinberg). Naomi has the option to return to Bethlehem to seek support from Elimelech's clan (2:1), and her daughters-in-law could return to their birth households or join another household through marriage (1:8–9). In other words, none of these women is without a male guardian within the patriarchal structure of the clan. Instead, they are described according to their previous relationship to another clan member (e.g., "daughter[s]-in-law" [1:6–8, 22; 2:20–23; 3:3, 18; 4:15], "mother-in-law" [1:14; 2:11, 18–19, 23; 3:1, 6, 16–17], "sister-in-law" [1:15 (two times)]). Moreover, the narrator describes Naomi as still related to members of her deceased husband's clan (2:1; cf. 2:20).

Boaz uses kinship terminology to describe Ruth's status change within his clan due to the death of Mahlon when he refers to her as "the wife of the dead man" (NOTE *the wife of the dead man* on 4:5). In 2:11, Boaz tells Ruth that he knows "all that you did for your mother-in-law *after* your husband died, namely, how you abandoned your father and your mother and the land of your birth" (emphasis added). Boaz refers to Naomi as Ruth's mother-in-law not because Ruth is still married to her son, but because Ruth remained in the household into which she married after her husband's death instead of returning to her birth household (1:16). As surviving members of Elimelech's household who lived together in Moab (v. 4b), Ruth and Naomi continue to live together as a socioeconomically integrated unit upon their return to Bethlehem (2:23b). Although the narrator does not specify the location of Naomi and Ruth's residence upon their return to Bethlehem, they presumably reside on the portion of the inherited field held by Elimelech (4:3). Also, Naomi and Boaz describe Ruth's newly acquired status within this household after her husband's death when they refer to Ruth repeatedly as an "(unmarried) daughter" (1:11–13; 2:2, 8, 22; 3:1, 10–11, 16, 18).

Considering the patrilocal structure of Israel's households, Ruth's situation is unusual in that an unmarried member of a clan leaves her birthplace in Moab to reside on the inherited land of the Judahite clan into which she previously married. A comparison to the case of Jacob in Genesis may help to explain Ruth's status within this clan. According to Gen 12:4–5, Abram and Lot leave their extended family (*bêt 'āb;* 12:1) in Haran. This departure would seem to leave the extended family's inheritance in Haran to Abram's only surviving brother, Nahor, the grandfather of Rebekah (29:5), although Pentateuchal sources may differ on this point. In 27:43, Rebekah instructs her unmarried son Jacob to return to Haran. Although Jacob is born outside his clan's inherited land, he returns to it (28:10) and, like Ruth, eventually marries members of his clan there (29:21–30). The obvious differences between Jacob and Ruth notwithstanding, both characters are unmarried members of a clan who are not native residents of the clan's inherited land. One could be both an alien resident and a member of a clan within the Israelite clan structure. While in Haran, Jacob works under the authority of Laban, a wealthier member of his clan (Gen 29:14, 25, 30; 31:38; NOTE *under her authority* on 1:7a). Although Laban identifies Jacob as a kinsman, he negotiates Jacob's "wages" (*maśkōret;* 29:15; 31:7, 41). The only other biblical text in which this word occurs is Ruth 2:12, when Boaz discusses the "wages" owed to Ruth. Although Jacob is a member of Laban's clan and Haran is their clan's inherited land, Jacob describes himself as an alien in Haran working under his uncle's authority: "I have sojourned under the authority of Laban" (*'im-lāban gārětî;* 32:5). Similarly, Ruth would qualify as an alien (*gēr*) who works under the authority of a wealthier clan member for wages, although the narrator never describes her as a *gēr* explicitly. If being a woman born in Moab who married into a Judahite clan makes Ruth a "foreign kinswoman," then she becomes an "alien-kinswoman" when she resides in Bethlehem.

Whether male or female, being alien-kin is by no means a privileged status within the clan structure. Leviticus 25 discusses scenarios in which kin who become impoverished are legally considered resident aliens under the authority of a wealthier clan member (v. 35; Wells, 151). While this text prohibits charging interest to impoverished kin, they still must work under a wealthier member of the clan's authority until either the Jubilee or they are redeemed. Although Leviticus 25 insists that such impoverished wage-earning laborers are not slaves, this rhetoric does not change the status of the impoverished kin as slaves in all but name (Stackert, 162–63). Although this text considers cases involving Israelite kin rather than Moabite kin, it indicates the precarious labor status of a member of the clan who is considered an alien. In regard to Ruth, a number of scholars have argued that Boaz and Naomi benefit from her labor (e.g., Boer; Brenner, 1999b; Dube, 2001). Rather than romanticize the inclusion of Ruth in the Judahite clan structure, one should note how her status, like Jacob's status under Laban, may leave her vulnerable to exploitation.

2. GENDER, PATRIARCHY, AND THE HOUSEHOLD

In Ruth, gender expectations are conceptualized and performed within the household or clan structure. Interpreters have focused on gender in Ruth since at least the women's advocacy movements in the nineteenth century (e.g., Aguilar; Stanton), a period sometimes retrospectively referred to as first-wave feminism (Junior). Within critical biblical scholarship, gender has had a significant effect on Ruth scholarship. The field increasingly engaged second-wave feminism in the 1970s and 1980s, and this engagement has continued with the emergence of gender studies and third-wave feminism in the 1990s and into the twenty-first century. Although scholarly considerations of female authorship or at least female voices in the book is not a recent phenomenon (consult "The Authorship of Ruth"), Phyllis Trible's seminal study of Ruth in her 1978 book *God and the Rhetoric of Sexuality* is widely recognized as popularizing scholarly attention to gender in Ruth scholarship (for a small representative sample of the influence of her work, consult Brenner, 1993a, 1999a; Fischer, 1999; Kates and Twersky Reimer).

Expanding on Trible's legacy, some highlight female subjectivity and agency. Certain scholars characterize Naomi and Ruth's relationship as a friendship as they struggle to survive within a patriarchal environment (e.g., Chu; Putman; Weems, 27; consult "Sexual Desire in Ruth"). For Mieke Bal, a "collective heroism" emerges insofar as the characters resemble each other (68–88). Others interpret the characters' relationships as involving self-interest, contention, or ambivalence (e.g., especially Fewell and Gunn; cf. Davis), if not exploitation based on ethnic and class differences (e.g., Boer; Brenner, 1999b; Dube, 2001; Honig; Yee). Some suggest that the book may reinforce notions of female submission for contemporary audiences (e.g., Pa). Kwok Pui-lan argues that the book "does not challenge patriarchal or heterosexual familial structures" (141). She suggests that many white feminist readings reflect an "overemphasis on individualist female subjectivity [that] may overshadow other power dynamics at work in the story and suggest that heroic acts of the protagonist can solve all problems" (142).

In many respects, the book does not present the subjectivity of any character, whether female or male, as operating outside the power dynamics conceptualized through the patriarchal model of the household or clan (Fuchs, 2005, 225). This does not mean that this structure works to crush the subjectivity of its female members. It would be hard to argue that the book's female characters are devoid of autonomy or agency. For example, both Naomi and Boaz imply that Ruth is free to choose whom she wants to marry (1:13; 3:10, respectively; cf. Sasson, 132). Instead, as Esther Fuchs notes, under this structure, "women's collaboration is essential for the successful functioning of patriarchal authority. . . . A patriarchal system does not mean the elimination of all [female] autonomy or independence, but rather of certain kinds of social actions and symbolic expressions that may subvert patriarchal authority" (2005, 224). (Meyers presents a different understanding of patriarchy in ancient Israel when she proposes that it is unable to "acknowledge that Israelite women were not dominated in *all* aspects of Israelite society" [2014, 27, emphasis in original; cf. Meyers, 2013, 193–99].) Fuchs implies that even if one imagines the book as a positive portrayal of women and their relationships, as written by women or as reflecting women's voices, the book does not subvert patriarchal authority but can in fact reinforce it. In particular, she argues that the book reflects a patriarchal ideology in which women support "the patriarchal institution of the levirate, which insures the patrilineage of the deceased husband" (1985, 130). Regarding 4:14–15, Amy-Jill Levine writes, "It is only in the context of childbirth that these women acknowledge Ruth's value or even her existence" (90). A number of scholars have noted that Ruth disappears from the story once she gives birth to the male heir Obed (Amy-Jill Levine, but consult Koosed, 117–19).

Over the past several decades, many scholars have scrutinized gendered social organization more generally, and they have emphasized that understandings of biblical wives and mothers within the household structure should not be overly influenced by more recent models of domestic family or household life. While acknowledging "wife" and "mother" as the "two primary roles that defined most women's lives," Phyllis Bird argues that "the ancient Israelite woman contributed more substantially and more significantly to the welfare of the family and society than the modern Western woman in the same role. She was not simply a consumer but primarily a producer and manufacturer of much of the essential goods required by the household" (69, 70). Ruth has much more complex roles throughout the story. She is referred to as a Moabite, a wife (of a dead man), a daughter(-in-law), a handmaid, a maidservant, a female servant, and a woman of worth (cf. the discussion of these references in Saxegaard, 110–28). She travels, marries twice, expresses opinions verbally (unlike YHWH), clings, gleans, has intercourse, gives birth, and so on (Saxegaard, 129–42).

To be sure, Bird's characterization of the "modern Western woman" may better reflect circumstances of white, middle-class women in 1974 than it would today. Nevertheless, her comments suggest that contemporary distinctions between public and private/domestic economic contributions do not map very well onto ancient Israelite household structures. More recently, Koosed argues that Ruth integrates herself into the networks of bread production central to economic productivity in Bethlehem. The community's incorporation of Ruth does not solely depend on the stereotypically "domestic" roles of wife or mother but on her incorporation into their food systems (64–71). In Ruth, the networks of bread production involve both men and women of a certain status, as evidenced by the roles played by both male and female servants during the harvest (2:5, 6, 8, 9, 15, 21, 22, 23; 3:2).

Using comparative anthropological and social scientific evidence, Carol Meyers argues that ideological shifts during the Industrial Revolution "reinforced the reconfiguration of the family and took away the opportunity and need for women's economic productivity, except for those in the poorest sectors of society. . . . The home became 'private' and the Cult of Domesticity effectively kept women out of the 'public' sphere" (1999, 112). Meyers shows how biblical scholars often anachronistically read this dichotomy back into ancient Israel. She argues that the activity of the female inhabitants of Bethlehem (1:19; 4:17) provides evidence of women's participation in ancient Israelite sociopolitical life throughout "informal networks" that may not be formally recognized forms of community organization but were just as essential (2013, 139–40).

The stereotype of women in the home as a private sphere may also assume a high of degree of social stability that the book of Ruth does not reflect. Jon L. Berquist, followed by Anna May Say Pa and Sarojini Nadar, argues that the crises in Ruth provoke "role dedifferentiation," which includes filling gendered roles that were typically considered socially inappropriate under more stable conditions (cf. the discussion of gender in periods of "social dysfunction" [Hackett, 1985, 19] and "carnival" [Aschkenasy]). Although she does not discuss examples from Ruth, Susan Ackerman argues that standard gender conventions may be suspended in literature depicting liminal situations (71). Andrew R. Davis interprets the grammatical disagreement in gender between a pronoun and its antecedent in Ruth as a literary device that, among other things, highlights gender reversals in the book. Even at the end of the book, the townswomen refer to Naomi with a formula usually reserved for a paternal relation (NOTE *For Naomi a son has been born!* on 4:17). Nevertheless, if gender expectations become fluid in Ruth, their fluidity helps to ensure the survival of the household or clan structure. For example, if women could serve as the paterfamilias in liminal situations, Naomi's authority ensures that there is a senior member to maintain her household. Gender fluidity does not operate outside of this patriarchal structure. Rather, patriarchy shapes gender practices throughout the book.

BIBLIOGRAPHY

Ackerman, Susan. 2002. "Why Is Miriam Also Among the Prophets? (And Is Zipporah Among the Priests?)." *JBL* 121: 47–80.

Aguilar, Grace. 1945. *The Women of Israel or Characters and Sketches from Holy Scriptures and Jewish History.* London: George Routledge and Sons. First published in 1845.

Alpert, Rebecca. 1994. "Finding Our Past: A Lesbian Interpretation of the Book of Ruth." Pages 91–96 in Kates and Twersky Reimer.

Alter, Robert. 1981. *The Art of Biblical Narrative.* New York: Basic Books.

Anderson, Francis I. 1986. "Yahweh, the Kind and Sensitive God." Pages 41–88 in *God Who Is Rich in Mercy: Essays Presented to Dr. D. B. Knox.* Edited by Peter T. O'Brien and David G. Peterson. Sydney: Lancer.

Aschkenasy, Nehama. 2007. "Reading Ruth Through a Bakhtinian Lens: The Carnivalesque in a Biblical Tale." *JBL* 126: 437–53.

Auerbach, Erich. 1953. *Mimesis: The Representation of Reality in Western Literature.* Princeton, NJ: Princeton University Press.

Avalos, Hector, Sarah Melcher, and Jeremy Schipper, eds. 2007. *This Abled Body: Rethinking Disability and Biblical Studies.* Semeia Studies 55. Atlanta: Society of Biblical Literature.

Baden, Joel S. 2011. "The Nature of Barrenness in the Hebrew Bible." Pages 13–27 in Moss and Schipper.

Baden, Joel S., and Candida R. Moss. 2015. *Reconceiving Infertility: Biblical Perspectives on Procreation and Childlessness.* Princeton, NJ: Princeton University Press.

Bal, Mieke. 1987. *Lethal Love: Literary Feminist Readings of Biblical Love Stories.* Bloomington: Indiana University Press.

Bar-Asher, Elitzur Avraham. 2009. "Dual Pronouns in Semitics and an Evaluation of the Evidence for Their Existence in Biblical Hebrew." *ANES* 46: 32–49.

Bar-Efrat, Shimon. 1989. *Narrative Art in the Bible.* Sheffield: Almond.

Barr, James. 1961. *The Semantics of Biblical Language.* Oxford: Oxford University Press.

Beattie, D. R. G. 1977. *Jewish Exegesis of the Book of Ruth*. JSOTSup 2. Sheffield: Sheffield University Press.

Ben-Dor, S. 1996. *The Social Structure of Ancient Israel*. Jerusalem: Simor.

Berger, Yitzkah. 2009. "Ruth and the David-Bathsheba Story: Allusions and Contrasts." *JSOT* 33: 433–52.

Berlin, Adele. 1983. *Poetics and Interpretation of Biblical Narrative*. Sheffield: Almond.

———. 2010. "Legal Fiction: Levirate *cum* Land Redemption in Ruth." *Journal of Ancient Judaism* 1: 3–18.

Berman, Joshua. 2007. "Ancient Hermeneutics and the Legal Structure of the Book of Ruth." *ZAW* 119: 22–38.

Berquist, Jon L. 1993. "Role Decifferentiation in the Book of Ruth." *JSOT* 57: 23–37.

Bertman, Stephen. 1965. "Symmetrical Design in the Book of Ruth." *JBL* 84: 165–68.

Bird, Phyllis. 1974. "Images of Women in the Old Testament." Pages 41–88 in *Religion and Sexism: Images of Woman in the Jewish and Christian Traditions*. Edited by Rosemary Radford Ruether. New York: Simon and Schuster.

Block, Daniel I. 1999. *Judges, Ruth*. NAC 6. Nashville: B and H.

Boer, Roland. 1999. "Culture, Ethics and Identity in Reading Ruth: A Response to Donaldson, Dube, McKinlay and Brenner." Pages 163–70 in Brenner, 1999a.

Borowski, Oded. 2003. *Daily Life in Biblical Times*. Leiden: Brill.

Brady, Christian M. M. 2013. "The Conversion of Ruth in Targum Ruth." *Review of Rabbinic Judaism* 16: 133–46.

Braulik, Georg. 1999. "The Book of Ruth as Intra-Biblical Critique on the Deuteronomic Law." *AcT* 19: 1–20.

Brenner, Athalya, ed. 1993a. *A Feminist Companion to Ruth*. Sheffield: Sheffield Academic Press.

———. 1993b. "Naomi and Ruth." Pages 70–84 in Brenner, 1993a.

———, ed. 1999a. *Ruth and Esther*. A Feminist Companion to the Bible (Second Series). Sheffield: Sheffield Academic Press.

———. 1999b. "Ruth as a Foreign Worker and the Politics of Exogamy." Pages 158–62 in Brenner, 1999a.

———. 2004. *I Am . . . Biblical Women Tell Their Own Stories*. Minneapolis: Fortress.

Brenner, Athalya, and Fokkelien Van Dijk-Hemmes. 1993. *On Gendering Texts: Male and Female Voices in the Hebrew Bible*. Leiden: Brill.

Brichto, Herbert C. 1973. "Kin, Cult, Land, and Afterlife—A Biblical Complex." *HUCA* 44: 1–54.

Bridge, Edward J. 2012. "Female Slave vs Female Slave: *'āmāh* and *šipḥâ* in the HB." *JHS* 12: article 2, 1–21.

Bronner, Leila Leah. "A Thematic Approach to Ruth in Rabbinic Literature." Pages 146–69 in Brenner, 1993a.

Bruppacher, Hans. 1966. "Die Bedeutung des Namens Ruth." *TZ* 22: 12–18.

Bush, Fredric. 1996. *Ruth/Esther*. WBC 9. Nashville: Thomas Nelson.

Butting, Klara. 1993. *Die Buchstaben werden sich noch wundern: Innerbiblische Kritik als Wegweisung feministischer Hermeneutik*. Alektor-Hochschulschriften. Berlin: Alektor.

Callaham, Scott N. 2010. *Modality and the Biblical Hebrew Infinitive Absolute*. Wiesbaden: Harrassowitz.

———. 2012. "But Ruth Clung to Her: Textual Constraints on Ambiguity." *Tyndale Bulletin* 63.2: 179–98.

Camp, Claudia. 1985. *Wisdom and the Feminine in the Book of Proverbs*. Sheffield: Almond.

Campbell, Edward F. 1975. *Ruth: A New Translation with Introduction and Commentary*. AB 7. New York: Doubleday.

Carasik, Michael. 1995. "Ruth 2,7: Why the Overseer was Embarrassed." *ZAW* 107: 493–94.

Chavel, Simeon. 2012. "Law and Narrative in Ruth and the Pentateuch." Unpublished paper presented at 2012 International Meeting of the Society of Biblical Literature, Amsterdam, 22–26 July 2012.

Childs, Brevard S. 1979. *Introduction to the Old Testament as Scripture*. Philadelphia: Fortress.

Chu, Julie. 1997. "Returning Home: The Inspiration of the Role of Dedifferentiation in the Book of Ruth for Taiwanese Women." *Semeia* 78: 47–53.

Clark, Gordon R. 1993. *The Word Hesed in the Hebrew Bible*. JSOTSup 157. Sheffield: Sheffield Academic Press.

Collins, John J. 1997. "Marriage, Divorce, and the Family in Second Temple Judaism." Pages 104–62 in *Families in Ancient Israel*. Edited by Leo G. Perdue, Joseph Blenkinsopp, John J. Collins, and Carol Meyers. Louisville, KY: Westminster John Knox.

Conklin, Blane. 2011. *Oath Formulas in Biblical Hebrew*. Linguistic Studies in Ancient West Semitic 5. Winona Lake, IN: Eisenbrauns.

Couey, J. Blake. 2015. *Reading the Poetry of First Isaiah: The Most Perfect Model of the Prophetic Poetry*. New York: Oxford University Press.

Coxon, Peter W. 1989. "Was Naomi a Scold?: A Response to Fewell and Gunn." *JSOT* 14: 25–37.

David, Martin. 1941. "The Date of the Book of Ruth." *OTS* 1: 55–63.

Davies, Eryl W. 1981. "Inheritance Rights, Part 2." *VT* 31: 264–66.

Davis, Andrew R. 2013. "The Literary Effect of Gender Discord in the Book of Ruth." *JBL* 132: 495–513.

Davis, Andrew R., and Tod Linafelt. 2013. "Translating *ḥnm* in Job 1:9 and 2:3: On the Relationship Between Job's Piety and His Interiority." *VT* 63: 627–39.

Day, Linda, and Carolyn Pressler, eds. 2006. *Engaging the Bible in a Gendered World: An Introduction to Feminist Biblical Interpretation in Honor of Katherine Doob Sakenfeld*. Louisville, KY: Westminster John Knox.

Dobbs-Allsopp, F. W. 2015. *On Biblical Poetry.* New York: Oxford University Press.

Dobbs-Allsopp, F. W., J. J. M. Roberts, C. L. Seow, and R. Whitaker. 2005. *Hebrew Inscriptions: Texts from the Biblical Period of the Monarchy, with Concordance.* New Haven, CT: Yale University Press.

Donaldson, Laura E. 1999. "The Sign of Orpah: Reading Ruth Through Native Eyes." Pages 130–44 in Brenner, 1999a.

Dube, Musa W. 1999. "The Unpublished Letters of Orpah to Ruth." Pages 145–50 in Brenner, 1999a.

———. 2001. "Divining Ruth for International Relations." Pages 179–95 in *Other Ways of Reading: African Women and the Bible.* Edited by Misa W. Dube. Atlanta: Society of Biblical Literature.

Dubin, Lois C. 1994. "Fullness and Emptiness, Fertility and Loss: Meditations on Naomi's Tale in the Book of Ruth." Pages 131–44 in Kates and Twersky Reimer.

Duncan, Celena M. 2000. "The Book of Ruth: On Boundaries, Love, and Truth." Pages 92–102 in *Take Back the Word: A Queer Reading of the Bible.* Edited by Robert E. Goss and Mona West Cleveland: Pilgrim.

Ebach, Jürgen. 1985. "Fremde in Moab—Fremde aus Moab. Das Buch Rut als politische Literatur." Pages 277–304 in *Bibel und Literatur.* Edited by Jürgen Ebach and Richard Faber. Munich Fink.

Eskenazi, Tamara Cohn, and Tikva Frymer-Kensky. 2011. *Ruth: The Traditional Hebrew Text with the New JPS Translation Commentary.* Jewish Publication Society Bible Commentary. Philadelphia: Jewish Publication Society.

Exum, J. Cheryl. 1996. *Plotted, Shot, and Painted: Cultural Representations of Biblical Women.* JSOTSup 215. Sheffield: Sheffield Academic Press.

Fentress-Williams, Judy. 2012. *Ruth.* AOTC. Nashville: Abingdon.

Fewell, Danna Noel, and David M. Gunn. 1990. *Compromising Redemption: Relating Characters in the Book of Ruth.* Louisville, KY: Westminster John Knox.

———. 1993. *Narrative in the Hebrew Bible.* Oxford: Oxford University Press.

———. 1988. "Boaz, Pillar of Society: Measures of Worth in the Book of Ruth." *JSOT* 40: 99–108.

Fisch, Harold. 1982. "Ruth and the Structure of Covenant History." *VT* 32: 425–37.

Fischer, Irmtraud. 1999. "The Book of Ruth: A 'Feminist' Commentary on the Torah?" Pages 24–49 in Brenner, 1999a.

———. 2001. *Rut.* HTKAT. Freiburg: Herder.

———. 2007. "The Book of Ruth as Exegetical Literature." *European Judaism* 40.2: 140–49.

Foster, Jeannette H. 1985. *Sex Variant Women in Literature.* Tallahassee, FL: Naiad. First published, New York: Vantage, 1956.

Frevel, Christian. 1992. *Das Buch Ruth.* Neuer Stuttgarter Kommentar: Altes Testament. Stuttgart: Katholisches Bibelwerk.

Fuchs, Esther. 1985. "The Literary Presentation of Mothers and Sexual Politics in the Hebrew Bible." Pages 117–36 in *Feminist Perspectives on Biblical Scholarship*. Edited by Adela Yarbro Collins. Missoula, MT: Scholars.

———. 2005. "The History of Women in Ancient Israel: Theory, Method, and the Book of Ruth." Pages 211–31 in *Her Master's Tools? Feminist and Postcolonial Engagements of Historical-Critical Discourse*. Edited by Caroline van der Stichele and Todd Penner. Society of Biblical Literature Global Perspectives on Biblical Scholarship 9. Atlanta: Society of Biblical Literature.

Frymer-Kensky, Tikva. 2002. *Reading the Women of the Bible: A New Interpretation of Their Stories*. New York: Schocken.

Garsiel, Moshe. 1991. *Biblical Names: A Literary Study of Midrashic Derivations and Puns*. Ramat Gan: Bar-Ilan University Press.

Gerleman, Gillis. 1981. *Ruth: Das Hohelied*. 2nd ed. BKAT 18. Neukirchen-Vluyn: Neukirchener.

Glanzmann, G. 1959. "The Origin and Date of the Book of Ruth." *CBQ* 21: 201–7.

Glover, Neil. 2009. "Your People, My People: An Exploration of Ethnicity in Ruth." *JSOT* 33: 293–313.

Glueck, Nelson. 1967. *Hesed in the Bible*. Translated by Alfred Gottschalk. Cincinnati: Hebrew Union College Press.

Goitein, Shlomo Dov. 1963. "Megillat Rut." Pages 49–58 in Goitein, *Studies in the Bible*. 2nd ed. Tel Aviv: Yaveh.

———. 1988. "Women as Creators of Biblical Genres." *Prooftexts* 8: 1–33. First published in 1957.

Gordis, Robert. 1974. "Love, Marriage and Business in the Book of Ruth: A Chapter in Hebrew Customary Law." Pages 241–63 in *A Light unto My Path: Old Testament Studies in Honor of Jacob M. Myers*. Edited by Howard N. Bream, Ralph D. Heim, and Carey Moore. Philadelphia: Temple University Press.

Gottwald, Norman K. 1979. *The Tribes of Yahweh: A Sociology of the Religion of Liberated Israel, 1250–1050 B.C.E.* Maryknoll, NY: Orbis.

Goulder, Michael D. 1993. "Ruth: A Homily on Deuteronomy 22–25?" Pages 307–19 in *Of Prophets' Visions and the Wisdom of Sages: Essays in Honor of R. Norman Whybray on His Seventieth Birthday*. Edited by Heather A. McKay and David J. A. Clines. JSOTSup 162. Sheffield: Sheffield Academic Press.

Gow, Murray D. 1992. *The Book of Ruth: Its Structure, Theme, and Purpose*. Leicester: Apollos.

Gray, John. 1986. *Joshua, Judges, Ruth*. Grand Rapids, MI: Eerdmans.

Greenstein, Edward L. 2003. "The Language of Job and Its Poetic Function." *JBL* 122: 651–66.

Gunkel, Hermann. 1913. *Reden und Aufsätze*. Göttingen: Vandenhoeck and Ruprecht.

———. 1930. "Rut." Pages 4: 2180–82 in *Die Religion in Geschichte und Gegenwart*. 2nd ed. 4 vols. Tübingen: J. C. B. Mohr.

Hackett, Jo Ann. 1985. "In the Days of Jael: Reclaiming the History of Women in Ancient Israel." Pages 15–38 in *Immaculate and Powerful: The Female in Sacred Image and Social Reality*. Edited by C. W. Atkinson, C. H. Buchanan, and M. R. Miles. Boston: Beacon.

———. 2014. "Ruth's Undoing." Alexander Thompson Lecture, Princeton Theological Seminary, Princeton, NJ.

Hals, Ronald M. 1969. *The Theology of the Book of Ruth*. Facet Books 23. Philadelphia: Fortress.

Havrelock, Rachel S. 2007. "The Two Maps of Israel's Land." *JBL* 126: 649–67.

Hertzberg, Hans Wilhelm. 1969. *Die Bücher Josua, Richter, Ruth*. Das Alte Testament Deutsch 9. Göttingen: Vandenhoeck and Ruprecht.

Hiebert, Paula S. 1989. "'Whence Shall Help Come to Me?': The Biblical Widow." Pages 125–41 in *Gender and Difference in Ancient Israel*. Edited by Peggy Day. Minneapolis: Fortress.

Holmstedt, Robert D. 2010. *Ruth: A Handbook on the Hebrew Text*. Waco, TX: Baylor University Press.

Honig, Bonnie. 1999. "Ruth, the Model Emigrée: Mourning and the Symbolic Politics of Immigration." Pages 50–74 in Brenner, 1999a.

Hopkins, David C. 2007. "'All Sorts of Field Work': Agricultural Labor in Ancient Palestine." Pages 149–72 in *To Break Every Yoke: Essays in Honor of Marvin L. Chaney*. Edited by Robert B. Coote and Norman K. Gottwald. Sheffield: Phoenix.

Hornsby, Teresa J., and Ken Stone. 2011. "Already Queer: A Preface." Pages ix–xiv in *Bible Trouble: Queer Reading at the Boundaries of Biblical Scholarship*. Edited by Teresa J. Hornsby and Ken Stone. Atlanta: Society of Biblical Literature.

Hubbard, Robert L. 1988. *The Book of Ruth*. NICOT. Grand Rapids, MI: Eerdmans.

Humbert, Paul. 1958. "Art et leçon de l'histoire de Ruth." Pages 83–110 in Humbert, *Opuscules d'un hébraïsant*. Neuchâtel: Université de Neuchâtel. First published in 1938.

Humphreys, W. 1985. "Novella." Pages 82–96 in *Saga, Legend, Tale, Novella, Fable*. JSOTSup 62. Edited by George Coats. Sheffield: JSOT.

Hurvitz, Avi. 1975. "On 'Drawing off the Sandal' in the Book of Ruth." *Shnaton* 1: 45–59 [Hebrew].

———. 1982. *A Linguistic Study of the Relationship Between the Priestly Source and the Book of Ezekiel*. Paris: Gabalda.

———. 1983. "Ruth 2:7—'A Midrashic Gloss'?" *ZAW* 95: 121–23.

Hutton, Jeremy M. 2009. *The Transjordanian Palimpsest: The Overwritten Texts of Personal Exile and Transformation in the Deuteronomistic History*. BZAW 396. Berlin: Walter de Gruyter.

———. 2012. "Review of *Oath Formulas in Biblical Hebrew* by Blane Conklin. Linguistic Studies in Ancient West Semitic 5. Winona Lake, Ind.: Eisenbrauns, 2011." *JAOS* 132: 129–31.

Hyman, Robert T. 1984. "Questions and Changing Identity in the Book of Ruth." *Union Seminary Quarterly Review* 39: 189–201.

Irwin, Brian P. 2008. "Removing Ruth: tiqqune sopherim in Ruth 3:3–4?" *JSOT* 32: 331–38.

Jackson, Bernard S. 2011. "Ruth's Conversion: Then and Now." *Jewish Law Annual* 19: 53–61.

Jackson, Melissa A. 2012. *Comedy and Feminist Interpretation of the Hebrew Bible: A Subversive Collaboration.* Oxford: Oxford University Press.

Jobling, David. 1986. "'The Jordan as Boundary': Transjordan in Israel's Ideological Geography." Pages 88–133, 142–47 in *The Sense of Biblical Narrative II: Structural Analyses in the Hebrew Bible.* JSOTSup 39. Sheffield: JSOT Press.

———. 1993. "Ruth Finds a Home: Canon, Politics, Method." Pages 125–39 in *The New Literary Criticism and the Hebrew Bible.* Edited by J. Cheryl Exum and David J. A. Clines. Sheffield: JSOT Press.

Joüon, Paul. 1924. *Ruth: Commentaire philologique et exégétique.* Rome: Pontifical Biblical Institute.

Junior, Nyasha. 2015. *An Introduction to Womanist Biblical Interpretation.* Louisville, KY: Westminster John Knox.

Karlin-Neumann, Patricia. 1994. "The Journey Toward Life." Pages 125–30 in Kates and Twersky Reimer.

Kates, Judith A., and Gail Twersky Reimer, eds. 1994. *Reading Ruth: Contemporary Women Reclaim a Sacred Story.* New York: Ballantine Books.

Kawashima, Robert. 2004. *Biblical Narrative and the Death of Rhapsode.* Indiana Studies in Biblical Literature. Bloomington: University of Indiana Press.

Kidd, José E. Ramirez. 1999. *Alterity and Identity in Israel: The gr in the Old Testament.* BZAW 283. Berlin: de Gruyter.

Kim, Dong-Hyuk. 2013. *Early Biblical Hebrew, Late Biblical Hebrew, and Linguistic Variability: A Sociolinguistic Evaluation of the Linguistic Dating of Biblical Texts.* VTSup 156. Leiden: Brill.

Knoppers, Gary N. 2001. "Intermarriage, Social Complexity, and Ethnic Diversity in the Genealogy of Judah." *JBL* 120: 15–30.

———. 2003. *1 Chronicles 1–9: A New Translation with Introduction and Commentary.* AB 12A. New York: Doubleday.

———. 2004. *1 Chronicles 10–29: A New Translation with Introduction and Commentary.* AB 12B. New York: Doubleday.

Köhlmoos, Melanie. 2010. *Ruth.* Das Alte Testament Deutsch. Göttingen: Vandenhoeck and Ruprecht.

Koosed, Jennifer L. 2011. *Gleaning Ruth: A Biblical Heroine and Her Afterlives.* Columbia: University of South Carolina Press.

Korpel, Marjo C. A. 2001. *The Structure of the Book of Ruth.* Pericope: Scripture as Written and Read in Antiquity 2. Assen: Koninklijke Van Gorcum.

Kruger, Paul A. 1984. "The Hem of the Garment of Marriage: The Meaning of the Symbolic Gesture in Ruth 3:9 and Ezek 16:8." *JNSL* 12: 79–86.

Krutzsch, Brett A. Forthcoming. "Un-Straightening Boaz in Ruth Scholarship." *BibInt*.

Labuschange, C. J. 1967. "The Crux in Ruth 4:11." *ZAW* 79: 364–67.

LaCocque, André. 2004. *Ruth: A Continental Commentary*. Translated by K. C. Hanson. Minneapolis: Fortress.

Landy, Francis. 1994. "Ruth and the Romance of Realism, or Deconstructing History." *JAAR* 62: 285–317.

Lapsley, Jacqueline E. 2005. *Whispering the Word: Hearing Women's Stories in the Old Testament*. Louisville, KY: Westminster John Knox.

Lau, Peter H. W. 2010. *Identity and Ethics in the Book of Ruth: A Social Identity Approach*. BZAW 416. Berlin: de Gruyter.

Lee, Eunny P. 2006. "Ruth the Moabite: Identity, Kinship, and Otherness." Pages 89–101 in Day and Pressler.

Lemaire, André. 2007. "New Photographs and *ryt* or *hyt* in the Mesha Inscription Line 12." *IEJ* 57: 204–7.

Lemche, Niels Peter. 1985. *Early Israel: Anthropological and Historical Studies on the Israelite Society Before the Monarchy*. Leiden: E. J. Brill.

Lemos, T. M. Forthcoming. "Were Israelite Women Chattel?: Shedding New Light on an Old Question." In *Women, Worship, and War: Essays in Honor of Susan Niditch*. Edited by John J. Collins, T. M. Lemos, and Saul M. Olyan. Atlanta: Society of Biblical Literature.

Leuchter, Mark. 2013. "Genesis 38 in Social and Historical Perspective." *JBL* 132: 209–27.

Levine, Amy-Jill. 1998. "Ruth." Pages 84–90 in *Women's Bible Commentary*. Exp. ed. Edited by Carol A. Newsom and Sharon H. Ringe. Louisville, KY: Westminster John Knox.

Levine, Baruch A. 1983. "In Praise of the Israelite *Mišpahâ*: Legal Themes in the Book of Ruth." Pages 95–106 in *The Quest for the Kingdom of God: Studies in Honor of George E. Mendenhall*. Edited by Herbert B. Huffmon, Frank A. Spina, and Alberto R. W. Green. Winona Lake, IN: Eisenbrauns.

Levinson, Bernard, M. 2008. *Legal Revision and Religious Renewal in Ancient Israel*. New York: Cambridge University Press.

Lewis, Theodore J. 1989. *Cults of the Dead in Ancient Israel and Ugarit*. HSM 39. Atlanta: Scholars.

Lim, Timothy H. 2011. "How God Was Ruth's Hebrew? Linguistic 'Otherness' in the Book of Ruth." Pages 101–15 in *The "Other" in Second Temple Judaism: Essays in Honor of John J. Collins*. Edited by Daniel C. Harlow, Karina Martin Hogan, Matthew Goff, and Joel S. Kaminsky. Grand Rapids, MI: Eerdmans.

Linafelt, Tod. 1999. *Ruth*. Berit Olam. Collegeville, MN: Liturgical.

———. 2010. "Narrative and Poetic Art in the Book of Ruth." *Interpretation* 64: 117–29.

Lys, Daniel. 1971. "Résidence ou repos? Notule sur Ruth u 7." *VT* 21: 497–501.

Marsman, H. J. 2003. *Women in Ugarit and Israel: Their Social and Religious Position in the Context of the Ancient Near East.* Leiden: E. J. Brill.

Martín-Contreras, Elvira. 2012. "The Phenomenon *Qere We La' Ketib* in the Main Biblical Codices: New Data." *VT* 62: 77–87.

Matthews, Victor A. 2004. *Judges and Ruth.* NCBC. Cambridge: Cambridge University Press.

McNutt, Paula. 1999. *Reconstructing the Society of Ancient Israel.* Louisville, KY: Westminster John Knox.

Melcher, Sarah, Mikeal Parsons, and Amos Yong, eds. Forthcoming. *Disability and the Bible: A Commentary.* Waco, TX: Baylor University Press.

Meyers, Carol. 1993. "Returning Home: Ruth 1.8 and the Gendering of the Book of Ruth." Pages 85–114 in Brenner, 1993a.

———. 1999. "'Women of the Neighborhood' (Ruth 4.17): Informal Female Networks in Ancient Israel." Pages 110–27 in Brenner, 1999a.

———. 2013. *Rediscovering Eve: Ancient Israelite Women in Context.* New York: Oxford University Press.

———. 2014. "Was Ancient Israel a Patriarchal Society?" *JBL* 133: 8–27.

Miles, Jack. 1996. *God: A Biography.* New York: Random House.

Milgrom, Jacob. 1991. *Leviticus 1–16: A New Translation with Commentary and Notes.* AB 3A; New York: Doubleday.

———. 2001. *Leviticus 23–27: A New Translation with Commentary and Notes.* AB 3B. New York: Doubleday.

Miller, Cynthia L. 1996. *The Representation of Speech in Biblical Hebrew Narrative: A Linguistic Analysis.* HSM 55. Atlanta: Scholars.

Moore, Michael S. 1993. "Job's Texts of Terror." *CBQ* 55: 662–75.

———. 1997. "Two Textual Anomalies in Ruth." *CBQ* 59: 234–43.

———. 2000. "Ruth." Pages 289–373 in J. Gordon Harris, Cheryl A. Brown, and Michael Moore. *Joshua, Judges, Ruth.* Peabody, MA: Hendrickson.

Moss, Candida R., and Jeremy Schipper. 2011. *Disability Studies and Biblical Literature.* New York: Palgrave Macmillan.

Myers, Jacob M. 1955. *The Linguistic and Literary Form of the Book of Ruth.* Leiden: E. J. Brill.

Nadar, Sarojini. 2001. "A South African Indian Womanist Reading of the Character of Ruth." Pages 159–75 in *Other Ways of Reading: African Women and the Bible.* Edited by Misa W. Dube. Atlanta: Society of Biblical Literature.

Newsom, Carol A. 2003. *The Book of Job: A Contest of Moral Imaginations.* New York: Oxford University Press.

———. 2007. "Spying Out the Land: A Report from Genology." Pages 19–30 in *Bakhtin and Genre Theory in Biblical Studies.* Edited by Roland Boer. Atlanta: Society of Biblical Literature.

Niditch, Susan. 1985. "Legends of Wise Heroes and Heroines." Pages 445–63 in *The Hebrew Bible and Its Modern Interpreters*. Edited by Douglas A. Knight and Gene M. Tucker. Philadelphia: Fortress.

Nielsen, Kirsten. 1997. *Ruth: A Commentary*. OTL. Louisville, KY: Westminster John Knox.

Novick, Tzvi. 2011. "Wages from God: The Dynamics of a Biblical Metaphor." *CBQ* 73: 708–22.

Ostriker, Alicia. 2002. "The Book of Ruth and the Love of the Land." *BibInt* 10: 343–59.

Pa, Anna May Say. 2006. "Reading Ruth 3:1–15 from an Asian Woman's Perspective." Pages 47–59 in Day and Pressler.

Pardes, Ilana. 1992. *Countertraditions in the Bible: A Feminist Approach*. Cambridge, MA: Harvard University Press.

Parker, Simon B. 1976. "The Marriage Blessing in Israelite and Ugaritic Literature." *JBL* 95: 23–30.

Pfau, Julie. 2013. "'I did not have sexual relations with that woman . . .': The Scandal of Ruth 3." Unpublished manuscript.

Polzin, Robert. 1976. *Late Biblical Hebrew: Toward an Historical Typology of Biblical Hebrew Prose*. Missoula, MT: Scholars.

Porten, Bezalel. 1976. "Structure, Style, and Theme of the Scroll of Ruth." *Association for Jewish Studies Newsletter* 17: 15–16.

———. 1978. "The Scroll of Ruth: A Rhetorical Study." *Gratz College Annual of Jewish Studies* 7: 23–49.

Pressler, Carolyn. 2002. *Joshua, Judges, and Ruth*. Westminster Bible Companion. Louisville, KY: Westminster John Knox.

Propp, William. *Exodus 1–18: A New Translation with Commentary and Notes*. AB 2A. New York: Doubleday.

Pui-lan, Kwok. 2004. "Finding Ruth a Home: Gender, Sexuality and the Politics of Otherness." Pages 137–54 in *New Paradigms for Bible Study: The Bible in the Third Millennium*. Edited by Robert M. Fowler, Edith Blumhofer, and Fernando F. Segovia. New York: T and T Clark.

Putman, Ruth Anna. 1994. "Friendship." Pages 44–54 in Kates and Twersky Reimer.

Qimron, Elisha. 2008. *The Hebrew of the Dead Sea Scrolls*. HSS 29. Winona Lake, IN: Eisenbrauns.

Quast, Udo. 2006. *Ruth. Septuaginta: Vetus Testamentum Graecum*. Band 4,3. Göttingen: Vandenhoeck and Ruprecht.

Rendsburg, Gary A. 1987. "Ù-Ma and Hebrew WM." Pages 1:34–41 in *Eblaitica: Essays on the Ebla Archives and Eblaite Language*. 4 vols. Edited by C. H. Gordon, G. A. Rendsburg, and N. H. Winter. Winona Lake, IN: Eisenbrauns.

———. 1995. "Linguistic Variation and the 'Foreign' Factor in the Hebrew Bible." *IOS* 15: 177–90.

———. 1999a. "Hebrew Philological Notes (I)." *HS* 40: 27–32.

———. 1999b. "Confused Language as a Deliberate Literary Device in Biblical Hebrew Narrative." *JHS* 2: article 6, 1–20.

———. 2001. "Once More the Dual: With Replies to J. Blau and J. Blenkinsopp." *ANES* 38: 28–41.

———. 2013. "Variation in Biblical Hebrew Prose and Poetry." Pages 197–226 in *Built by Wisdom, Established by Understanding: Essays on Biblical and Near Eastern Literature in Honor of Adele Berlin*. Edited by Maxine L. Grossman. Bethesda, MD: University Press of Maryland.

Revell, E. J. 1995. "The Two Forms of First Person Singular Pronoun in Biblical Hebrew: Redundancy or Expressive Contrast?" *JSS* 43: 69–87.

Roberts, J. J. M. 1971. "The Hand of Yahweh." *VT* 21: 244–51.

Rudolph, Wilhelm. 1962. *Das Buch Ruth, Das Hohe Lied, Die Klagelieder*. Kommentar zum Alten Testament. 2nd ed. Gütersloh: Mohn.

Sakenfeld, Katharine Doob. 1978. *The Meaning of Hesed in the Hebrew Bible: A New Inquiry*. HSM 17. Missoula, MT: Scholars.

———. 1999. *Ruth*. Interpretation: A Bible Commentary for Teaching and Preaching. Louisville, KY: Westminster John Knox.

Sanders, James A., ed. 1998. *Leningrad Codex: A Facsimile Edition*. Grand Rapids, MI: William. B. Eerdmans.

Sarna, Nahum N. 1989. *Genesis: The Traditional Hebrew Text with the New JPS Translation Commentary*. Jewish Publication Society Bible Commentary. Philadelphia: Jewish Publication Society.

Sasson, Jack M. 1999. *Ruth: A New Translation with a Philological Commentary and a Formalist-Folklorist Interpretation*. 2nd ed. The Bible Seminar. Sheffield: Sheffield Academic Press.

Saxegaard, Kristin M. 2010. *Character Complexity in the Book of Ruth*. FAT II 47. Tübingen: Mohr Siebeck.

Schipper, Jeremy. 2006. *Disability Studies and the Hebrew Bible: Figuring Mephibosheth in the David Story*. LHBOTS 441. New York: T and T Clark.

———. 2009. *Parables and Conflict in the Hebrew Bible*. New York: Cambridge University Press.

———. 2011. *Disability and Isaiah's Suffering Servant*. Oxford: Oxford University Press.

———. 2012. "The Rhetoric and Syntax of Ruth 1:9a." *VT* 62: 642–45.

———. 2013. "Translating the Preposition 'm in the Book of Ruth." *VT* 63: 663–69.

Schloen, J. David. 2001. *The House of the Father in Symbol and Fact: Patrimonialism in Ugarit and the Ancient Near East*. Studies in the Archaeology and History of the Levant 2. Winona Lake, IN: Eisenbrauns.

Schmitt, Rüdiger. 2012. "Rites of Family and Household Religion." Pages 387–428 in Rainer Albertz and Rüdiger Schmitt. *Family and Household Religion in Ancient Israel and the Levant*. Winona Lake, IN: Eisenbrauns.

Shade, Aaron. 2005. "New Photographs Supporting the Reading *ryt* in Line 12 of the Mesha Inscription." *IEJ* 55: 205–8.

Sharp, Carolyn J. 2014. "Feminist Queries for Ruth and Joshua: Complex Characterization, Gapping, and the Possibility of Dissent." *SJOT* 28: 229–52.

Sievers, Eduard. 1901. *Metrische Studien I: Studien zur Hebräischen Metrik*. Leipzig: B. G. Teubner.

Siquans, Agnethe. 2009. "Foreignness and Poverty in the Book of Ruth: A Legal Way for a Poor Foreign Woman to Be Integrated into Israel." *JBL* 128: 443–52.

Sommer, Benjamin D. 2011. "Dating Pentateuchal Texts and the Perils of Pseudo-Historicism." Pages 85–108 in *The Pentateuch: International Perspectives on Current Research*. Edited by Thomas B. Dozeman, B. Konrad Schmid, and Baruch J. Schwartz. FAT 78. Tübingen: Mohr Siebeck.

Smith, Jonathan Z. 1990. *Drudgery Divine: On the Comparison of Early Christianities and the Religions of Late Antiquity.* Chicago: University of Chicago Press.

Smith, Mark S. 1991. "Converted and Unconverted Perfect and Imperfect Forms in the Literature of Qumran." *BASOR* 284: 1–16.

———. 2007. "'Your People Shall Be My People': Family and Covenant in Ruth 1:16–17." *CBQ* 69: 242–58.

Stackert, Jeffrey. 2007. *Rewriting the Torah: Literary Revision in Deuteronomy and the Holiness Legislation*. FAT 52. Tübingen: Mohr Siebeck.

Stanton, Elizabeth Cady. 1993. 'The Book of Ruth." Pages 20–25 in Brenner, 1993a. First published in 1898.

Steinberg, Naomi. 2004. "Romancing the Widow: The Economic Distinction Between the *'almānâ*, *'iššâ-'almānâ*, and the *'ēšet-hammēt*." Pages 327–46 in *God's Word for Our World, Vol. 1*. Edited by Deborah L. Ellens, Isaac Kalimi, Rolf Knierim, and J. Harold Ellens. JSOTSup 388. Sheffield: T and T Clark.

Sternberg, Meir. 1987. *The Poetics of Biblical Narrative: Ideological Literature and the Drama of Reading*. Bloomington: Indiana University Press.

Stone, Ken. 2013. "Queer Criticism." Pages 155–76 in *New Meanings for Ancient Texts: Recent Approaches to Biblical Criticisms and Their Applications*. Edited by Steven L. McKenzie and John Kaltner. Louisville, KY: Westminster John Knox.

Stone, Timothy J. 2013. "Six Measures of Barley: Seed Symbolism in Ruth." *JSOT* 38: 1989–99.

Strawn, Brent A. 2009. "Comparative Approaches: History, Theory, and the Image of God." Pages 117–42 in *Method Matters: Essays on the Interpretation of the Hebrew Bible in Honor of David L. Petersen*. Edited by Joel LeMon and Kent Richards. Atlanta: Society of Biblical Literature.

———. 2004. "*yšb* in the Kethib of Ruth 1:8: Historical, Orthographical, or Characterological?" Unpublished manuscript.

Sutskover, Talia. 2010. "The Themes of Land and Fertility in the Book of Ruth." *JSOT* 34: 283–94.

Talmon, Shemaryahu. 1964. "The New Hebrew Letter from the Seventh Century B.C. in Historical Perspective." *BASOR* 176: 29–38.

Thompson, Thomas, and Dorothy Thompson. 1968. "Some Legal Problems in the Book of Ruth." *VT* 18: 79–99.

Tov, Emanuel. 2001. *Textual Criticism of the Hebrew Bible*. 2nd ed. Minneapolis: Fortress.

Trible, Phyllis. 1978. *God and the Rhetoric of Sexuality*. Philadelphia: Fortress.

Tropper, Josef. 1992. "Dualische Personalpronomina und Verbalformen im Althebräischen." *ZAH* 5: 201–8.

Twersky Reimer, Gail. 1994. "Her Mother's House." Pages 97–105 in Kates and Twersky Reimer.

van der Toorn, Karel. 1990. "The Nature of the Biblical Teraphim in the Light of the Cuneiform Evidence." *CBQ* 52: 203–22.

———. 1996. *Family Religion in Babylonia, Syria, and Israel: Continuity and Change in Forms of Religious Life*. Leiden: E. J. Brill.

Van Dijk-Hemmes, Fokkelien. 1993. "Ruth: A Product of Women's Cultures?" Pages 134–44 in Brenner, 1993a.

Vesco, Jean-Luc. 1967. "La date du Levre de Ruth." *RB* 74: 235–47.

von Rad, Gerhard. 1962. *Old Testament Theology Volume I: The Theology of Israel's Historical Traditions*. Translated by D. M. G. Stalker. New York: HarperCollins.

von Wolde, Ellen. 1997. "Texts in Dialogue with Texts: Intertextuality in the Ruth and Tamar Narratives." *BibInt* 5: 1–28.

———. 1998. *Ruth and Naomi*. Translated by John Bowden. Macon, GA: Smyth and Helwys.

Weems, Renita J. 2005. *Just a Sister Away*. New York: Warner.

Weisberg, Dvora E. 2009. *Levirate Marriage and the Family in Ancient Judaism*. HBI Series on Jewish Women. Waltham, MA: Brandeis University Press.

Weiss, David W. 1964. "The Use of *qnh* in Connection with Marriage." *HTR* 57: 243–48.

Wells, Bruce. 2011. "The Quasi-Alien in Leviticus 25." Pages 135–55 in *The Foreigner and the Law: Perspectives from the Hebrew Bible and the Ancient Near East*. Edited by Reinhard Achenbach, Rainer Albertz, and Jakob Wöhrle. BZAR 16. Wiesbaden: Harrassowitz.

West, Mona. 2006. "Ruth." Pages 190–94 in *The Queer Bible Commentary*. Edited by Deryn Guest, Robert E. Goss, Mona West, and Thomas Bohache. London: SCM.

Westbrook, Raymond. 1991. *Property and the Family in Biblical Law*. JSOTSup 113. Sheffield: Sheffield Academic Press.

Whitman, Ruth. 1994. "Ruth's Journey." Pages 161–65 in Kates and Twersky Reimer.

Wilson, Robert R. 1977. *Genealogy and History in the Biblical World*. New Haven, CT: Yale University Press.

Witzenrath, Hagia Hildegard. 1975. *Das Buch Ruth: Eine literaturwissenschaftliche Untersuchung.* Munich: Kösel.

Wojcik, Jan. 1985. "Improvising Rules in the Book of Ruth." *Publications of the Modern Language Association of America.* 100: 145–53.

Würthwein, E. 1969. *Die Fünf Megilloth.* 2nd ed. HAT 18. Tübingen: Mohr/Siebeck.

Yavin, Zipora. 2007. "Ruth, the Fifth Mother: A Study in the Scroll of Ruth (The Semantic Field as a Ground of Confrontation Between Two Giants—The Judean Writer and the Ephraimite Writer)." *Jewish Studies* 44: 167–213 [Hebrew].

Yee, Gale. 2009. "'She Stood in Tears Amid the Alien Corn': Ruth, the Perpetual Foreigner and Model Minority" Pages 119–40 in *They Were All There in One Place?: Toward Minority Biblical Criticism.* Edited by Randall C. Bailey, Tat-siong Benny Liew, and Fernando F. Segovia. Atlanta: Society of Biblical Literature.

Young, Ian, Robert Rezetko, and Martin Ehrensvärd. 2008. *Linguistic Dating of Biblical Texts.* 2 vols. London: Equinox.

Zakovitch, Yair. 1999. *Das Buch Rut: Ein jüdischer Kommentar.* Stuttgarter Bibelstudien 177. Stuttgart: Verlag Katholisches Bibelwerk.

Zenger, Erich. 1986. *Das Buch Ruth.* Zurich: Theologischer Verlag.

Zevit, Ziony. 2005. "Dating Ruth: Legal, Linguistic, and Historical Observations." *ZAW* 117: 574–600.

Zvi, Ron. 2010. "The Genealogical List in the Book of Ruth: A Symbolic Approach." *JBQ* 38: 85–92.

TRANSLATION

Residing in Moab

1 ¹In the days when the chieftains ruled, there was a famine in the land. So a man from Bethlehem of Judah went to reside as an alien in the territory of Moab—he and his wife and his two sons. ²The name of the man was Elimelech and the name of his wife was Naomi and the names of his two sons were Mahlon and Kilyon—Ephrathites from Bethlehem of Judah. They entered the territory of Moab and stayed there. ³Yet, Elimelech, the husband of Naomi, died and she was left, she and her two sons. ⁴They took for themselves Moabite wives—the name of the first was Orpah and the name of the second was Ruth—and then dwelled there for about ten years. ⁵The two of them, Mahlon and Kilyon, also died. The woman was left without her two children or her husband. ⁶She arose, she and her daughters-in-law, and she returned from the territory of Moab because she heard in the territory of Moab that YHWH had visited his people to give to them food. ⁷ᵃShe set out from the place where she had stayed. Her two daughters-in-law were under her authority.

On the Road

⁷ᵇThey traveled along the road in order to return to the land of Judah. ⁸Naomi said to her two daughters-in-law, "Go! Return, each one to her mother's household. May YHWH deal with you kindly just as you have dealt with those who are dead and with me. ⁹May YHWH give to you . . . [Oh, forget it!] Find rest, each one in the household of her husband!" She kissed them and they lifted their voices and wept. ¹⁰They said to her, "We will certainly return with you to your people." ¹¹Naomi replied, "Return my daughters! Why should you travel under my authority? Are there still sons in my womb that could become husbands for you? ¹²Return my daughters! Go! For I am too old to belong to a man. For even if I thought, 'There is hope for me,' even if I were to belong to a man tonight and even if I bore sons, ¹³would you wait for them until they grew? Would you restrain yourselves for them by not being with a man? No, my daughters! For my bitterness is much greater than yours because the hand of YHWH has gone forth against me." ¹⁴They lifted their voices and wept again. Orpah kissed her mother-in-law, but Ruth clung to her. ¹⁵She said, "Look! Your sister-in-law has returned to her people and to her ancestors. Return after your sister-in-law." ¹⁶But Ruth said,

"Do not pressure me to abandon you
To return from after you
For to [the place] where you may travel, I will travel
And in [the place] where you may lodge, I will lodge
Your people, my people
Your ancestors, my ancestors
¹⁷In [the place] where you may die, I will die
And there I will be buried.

Thus, may YHWH do to me and thus may he add if death should separate me from you!" ¹⁸When she saw that she was resolved to travel with her, she ceased to speak to her. ¹⁹ᵃThe two of them traveled until they entered Bethlehem.

Arriving in Bethlehem

¹⁹ᵇWhen they entered Bethlehem the whole town was abuzz over them. The [women of the town] said, "Isn't this Naomi?!" ²⁰But she said to them,

"Do not call me 'Kindness of YHWH' [Naomi]
Call me 'Bitterness' [Mara]
For Shaddai has made me very bitter.
²¹I left full,
YHWH made me return empty.
Why should you call me 'Kindness of YHWH' [Naomi]?
YHWH has testified against me,
Shaddai has brought disaster upon me."

²²ᵃSo Naomi returned. Now Ruth the Moabite, her daughter-in-law, was under her authority, the one who returned from the territory of Moab.

Ruth and Naomi's Conversation

²²ᵇThey entered Bethlehem at the beginning of the barley harvest.
2 ¹Now Naomi had a relative of her husband, a mighty man of worth from the clan of Elimelech. His name was Boaz. ²Ruth the Moabite said to Naomi, "Let me go to the field so I may glean the ears of grain after anyone in whose eyes I may find favor." She said to her, "Go, my daughter."

In the Field Held by Boaz

³When she went and came and gleaned in the field behind the harvesters, she chanced upon the portion of the field held by Boaz who was from the clan of Elimelech. ⁴Look! Boaz came from Bethlehem. He said to the harvesters, "YHWH be with you," and they said to him, "May YHWH bless you." ⁵Boaz said to his male servant who was set over the harvesters, "To whom does this female servant [belong]?" ⁶The male servant who was set over the harvesters answered and said, "She is a Moabite female servant, who returned under the authority of Naomi from the territory of Moab. ⁷She said, 'Let me glean [ears of grain] please and gather [them] into bundles behind the harvesters.' She

came and stood from then, the morning until now, this . . . her sitting . . . the house . . . a little." ⁸Boaz said to Ruth, "Haven't you heard my daughter? Do not go to glean in another field. In fact, you should not leave this one so that you may stick with my female servants. ⁹Your eyes should be on the field that they harvest and you may go after them. Haven't I instructed the male servants not to assault you? So, if you become thirsty, you may go to the vessels and drink from whatever [water] the male servants may draw." ¹⁰Then she fell on her face and bowed down to the ground. She said to him, "Why have I found favor in your eyes that you have paid attention to me although I am a foreign woman?" ¹¹Boaz answered and said to her, "It has been completely reported to me—all that you did for your mother-in-law after your husband died, namely, how you abandoned your father and your mother and the land of your birth and traveled to a people that you did not know previously. ¹²May YHWH compensate your deed. May your wage be complete from YHWH, the god of Israel, whom you came to seek refuge under his skirts." ¹³She said, "I must have found favor in the eyes of my lord because you comfort me and because you speak to the heart of your maidservant, even though I am not like one of your maidservants." ¹⁴Boaz said to her at the time of the meal, "Come here and eat some of the food and dip your morsel in the vinegar." So she sat alongside the harvesters. He heaped together for her parched grain and she ate and was satisfied and left over [some of the parched grain]. ¹⁵Then she arose to glean. Boaz instructed his servants, "Even among the bundles, she may glean. Do not humiliate her! ¹⁶In fact, you should even pull out for her some of the heaps and abandon [them] so that she may glean [them]. Do not rebuke her!" ¹⁷So she gleaned in the field until evening and she beat out what she had gleaned. Now it was about an ephah of barley.

Ruth and Naomi's Conversation

¹⁸She carried [the grain] and entered the city. Her mother-in-law saw what she had gleaned. She brought out [the grain] and gave to her what she had left over because of her fullness. ¹⁹Her mother-in-law said to her, "Where did you glean today and where did you work? May the one who paid attention to you be blessed." She told her mother-in-law under whose authority she worked. She said, "The name of the man under whose authority I worked today is Boaz." ²⁰Naomi said to her daughter-in-law, "Blessed is he to YHWH, who has not abandoned his kindness with the living and with the dead." Naomi said to her, "The man is close to us. He is one of our kindred redeemers." ²¹Ruth the Moabite said, "Also, he even said to me, 'Stick with my servants until they finish my entire harvest.'" ²²Naomi said to Ruth her daughter-in-law, "It is better my daughter that you go out with his female servants so they will not attack you in another field." ²³So she stuck with Boaz's female servants to glean until the barley harvest and wheat harvest were finished. Then she stayed with her mother-in-law.

Naomi's Instructions

3 ¹Naomi her mother-in-law said to her, "My daughter, shouldn't I seek a place of rest for you where it would go well for you? ²Now isn't Boaz our relative, whose female servants you were with? Look, he is winnowing near the threshing floor of the barley tonight. ³You should wash up, apply perfume, and put on your garments. Go down to the threshing floor. Do not make yourself known to the man until he finishes eating and drinking. ⁴When he lies down, you shall know the place where he lies. You shall enter, undress at his feet and lie down. He will tell you what you should do." ⁵She said to her, "All that you say to me I will do."

On the Threshing Floor

⁶So she went down to the threshing floor and did according to all that her mother-in-law had instructed. ⁷When Boaz ate and drank and his heart was merry, he entered to lie down at the edge of the pile [of barley]. Then, she entered secretly, undressed at his feet and lay down. ⁸In the middle of the night, the man was troubled and turned himself about and Look! A woman lying at his feet! ⁹He said, "Who are you?" She said, "I am Ruth, your handmaid. Spread your skirt over your handmaid because you are a kindred redeemer." ¹⁰He said, "Blessed are you to YHWH my daughter. You performed your latter kindness better than your earlier one. You did not go after the young men whether poor or rich. ¹¹And now my daughter, do not be afraid. All that you say I will do for you because the entire assembly of my people knows that you are a woman of worth. ¹²And now, it is certainly true that I am a kindred redeemer, but in fact there is a kindred redeemer closer than I. ¹³Lodge tonight. Then, in the morning, if he wishes to redeem you, that is fine, let him redeem. But if he does not want to redeem you, I will redeem you. As YHWH lives, lie down until the morning!" ¹⁴So she lay down at his feet until the morning. Then, she arose before a man could recognize another. For he thought, "May it not be known that the woman came to the threshing floor." ¹⁵He said, "Give me the garment that is on you and hold it." So she held it and he measured out six units of barley and set [the barley] on it. Then, he went into the city.

Ruth and Naomi's Conversation

¹⁶When she came to her mother-in-law, she said, "Whose are you my daughter?" She told her all that the man had done for her. ¹⁷She said, "These six units of barley he gave to me because he said to me, 'You should not go empty to your mother-in-law.'" ¹⁸She said, "Stay my daughter until you know how the matter plays out because the man will not rest unless the matter is finished today."

At the Gate

4 ¹Now Boaz went up to the gate and he sat there and, look, the kindred redeemer whom Boaz spoke of was passing by! He said, "Turn aside and sit here, So and So." So he turned aside and sat. ²He took ten men from among the elders of the town and said "Sit here" and they sat. ³He said to the kindred redeemer, "The portion of the field held by our kin Elimelech—Naomi, who returned from the territory of Moab, offers for sale. ⁴I thought I would uncover your ear by saying, 'Acquire [it] before the inhabitants and before the elders of my people.' If you want to redeem, redeem! But if you do not want to redeem, tell me so that I may know because there is no one except you to redeem and I am after you." Then, he said, "I want to redeem." ⁵Boaz said, "On the day you acquire the field from the hand of Naomi, also Ruth the Moabite, the wife of the dead man, you acquire her to establish the name of the dead man upon his inheritance."

⁶The kindred redeemer said, "I am not able to redeem for myself lest I ruin my own inheritance. You redeem my redemption for yourself because I am not able to redeem." ⁷(Now this was [the custom] formerly in Israel regarding redemption and substitution to establish any matter: a man would remove his sandal and give it to his friend. This served as the witness in Israel.) ⁸The kindred redeemer said to Boaz, "Acquire for yourself" and he removed his sandal. ⁹Boaz said to the elders and all the people, "You are witnesses today that I now acquire all that belonged to Elimelech and all that belonged to Kilyon and Mahlon from the hand of Naomi. ¹⁰Also, Ruth the Moabite, the wife of Mahlon, I now acquire for myself as a wife to establish the name of the dead man upon his inheritance so that the name of the dead man may not be cut off from among his kin or the assembly of his place. You are witnesses today." ¹¹All the people who were in the gate and the elders said, "(We are) witnesses. May YHWH make the woman who is entering your house like Rachel and Leah, who built, the two of them, the house of Israel, so that you act worthily in Ephrathah and proclaim a name in Bethlehem. ¹²May your house be like the house of Perez, whom Tamar bore for Judah, from the seed that YHWH gives to you from this female servant."

The Birth of Obed

¹³Then Boaz took Ruth and she became his wife. He entered her and YHWH gave her conception and she bore a son. ¹⁴The women said to Naomi, "Blessed be YHWH who has not removed a kindred redeemer for you today. May his name be proclaimed in Israel. ¹⁵He will become one who returns life for you and supports your old age because your daughter-in-law, who loves you, bore him, who herself is better for you than seven sons." ¹⁶Then, Naomi took the child and placed him in her bosom. She was a caregiver for him. ¹⁷The female inhabitants proclaimed his name saying, "For Naomi a son has been born!" They proclaimed his name [to be] Obed. He was the father of Jesse, the father of David.

The Generations of Perez

¹⁸These are the generations of Perez: Perez begot Hezron, ¹⁹and Hezron begot Ram, and Ram begot Amminadab, ²⁰and Amminadab begot Nahshon, and Nahshon begot Salmon, ²¹and Salmon begot Boaz, and Boaz begot Obed, ²²and Obed begot Jesse, and Jesse begot David.

NOTES AND COMMENTS

Residing in Moab (1:1–7a)

1 ¹In the days when the chieftains ruled, there was a famine in the land. So a man from Bethlehem of Judah went to reside as an alien in the territory of Moab—he and his wife and his two sons. ²The name of the man was Elimelech and the name of his wife was Naomi and the names of his two sons were Mahlon and Kilyon—Ephrathites from Bethlehem of Judah. They entered the territory of Moab and stayed there. ³Yet, Elimelech, the husband of Naomi, died and she was left, she and her two sons. ⁴They took for themselves Moabite wives—the name of the first was Orpah and the name of the second was Ruth—and then dwelled there for about ten years. ⁵The two of them, Mahlon and Kilyon, also died. The woman was left without her two children or her husband. ⁶She arose, she and her daughters-in-law, and she returned from the territory of Moab because she heard in the territory of Moab that YHWH had visited his people to give to them food. ⁷ªShe set out from the place where she had stayed. Her two daughters-in-law were under her authority.

Notes

1:1. *In the days when the chieftains ruled, there was a famine in the land.* Although the book of Esther also opens with "In the days of" (1:1; cf. Gen 14:1; Isa 7:1; Jer 1:3), Ruth 1:1 represents the only occurrence of this particular construction in the Hebrew Bible, in which a type of activity rather than a personal name follows "in the days." Although my translation aims for smooth English, a wooden translation of 1:1a would read: "It was [*wayhî*] in the days when the chieftains ruled. There was [*wayhî*] a famine in the land." As Robert D. Holmstedt suggested in a personal communication, the first *wayhî* functions as an initial discourse marker, as in the verses cited above. The second *wayhî* clause sets the scene and relates syntactically to the *wayyiqtol* clause that follows ("So a man from Bethlehem"). Some of the versions smooth out the syntax of this verse, for example, "In the days of the judges" (Syr.) or "When the judges ruled" (LXX[BL]). Yet, despite the unique syntax, the meaning of the first seven words is clear.

ruled. The word *šĕpōṭ* suggests "ruled" (cf. Deut 1:16) rather than "judged." Beginning with the first verse, the book contains several short spellings (e.g., 1:1, 9, 12, 20; 2:3, 20; 3:2, 8, 9, 12; 4:1, 3, 4, 6, 8, 14, 17; NOTE *Obed . . . David* on 4:17). The use of *plene* or full spellings occurs more frequently in later texts (e.g., Qumran literature). At points, 2QRuth[b] and the *qere* have a full spelling whereas the *ketib* has a short spelling (NOTE *at his feet* on 3:14; cf. 3:3). If the short spelling serves as evidence of SBH, 2QRuth[b] may reflect scribal updating of an older text. Nevertheless, the *ketib* also contains several full spellings (1:9–14, 19–21; 2:4–7, 15; 3:11; 4:14, 17), sometimes in the same verse as short spellings (1:9, 12; 4:14). Also, the *ketib* sometimes uses the full and short spellings for the same word (2:3, 5). If these full spellings reflect an updating of an older text, one may ask why the updating was not more consistent since many short spellings remain. The mixture of both full and short spelling suggests that this orthographic feature should not be used in attempts to date the book's composition.

the land. Here, "the land" most likely refers to the Cisjordan (Deut 4:21; 6:1; 12:1; 15:4; 19:14; Josh 18:4) in contrast to the "territory of Moab" across the Jordan (consult NOTE *territory of Moab* on 1:1). If "the land" referred to is the whole earth or had a wider international scope, one might expect "there was a famine in all the lands," as in Gen 41:54. While opinions differ on the likelihood of a famine limited to territory on one side of the Jordan but not the other (e.g., Block, 626; Gerleman, 14; Frevel, 46; Nielsen, 40–41), such scenarios, however unrealistic, were conceivable for biblical authors (e.g., Amos 4:7).

a man from Bethlehem of Judah went. The syntax also allows for the translation, "A man went from Bethlehem of Judah" (Bush 62–63; Campbell, 50; Joüon, 31; Rudolph, 37). Yet, despite the parallelism that such a translation would provide between traveling "from" Bethlehem "to" Moab (Korpel, 54, n. 3), other texts introduce a man with reference to his place of origin (Helmstedt, 56; Hubbard, 83, n. 2; Sasson, 14; Judg 17:1; 1 Sam 1:1; Job 1:1). In Ruth 1:2, the clause "Ephrathites from Bethlehem of Judah" supports my translation (cf. "The man from the town of Bethlehem of Judah went to reside as an alien"; Judg 17:8; cf. 17:7, 9; 19:1; 1 Sam 17:12). "Bethlehem of Judah" distinguishes this Bethlehem from the city of the same name in Zebulun (Josh 19:15). On the etymology of "Bethlehem" (*bêt leḥem*), consult "The Diction of the Hebrew in Ruth" in the Introduction and COMMENTS on 1:1–7a.

reside as an alien. Here, the term *lāgûr* refers to a settlement in a foreign land (for a detailed study of the term's possible legal nuances, consult Kidd). In Gen 12:10, Abram goes to Egypt to reside as an alien (*lāgûr*) because "there was a famine in the land" (the same phrase as in Ruth 1:1). Likewise, when "there was a famine in the land" (Gen 26:1), God instructs Isaac to reside as an alien (*gûr*) in Gerar rather than going down to Egypt (26:3; consult "Ruth and Ancient Israelite Literary Traditions" in the Introduction).

territory of Moab. My translation uses the word "territory" for two different Hebrew words. The first use of "territory" translates *śĕdê*, a singular construct form of the III-*y* root *śdy* ("field, land, territory"; 1:6a, 22). The second translates *śĕdēh*, a singular construct form of the III-*h* root *śdh* (1:6b; 2:6; 4:3). Both Hebrew words convey the same meaning, namely, a general reference to Moab since they are both singular forms rather than the plural "fields of Moab," which could imply a particular part of Moab. Indeed, 4QRuth[a] has a singular construct form of the III-*h* root *śdh* for the first word translated as "territory." Throughout Ruth, the Old Greek consistently translates both words with the Greek masculine singular form *agros* ("field"). Although Campbell discusses whether this reference designates a specific part of Moab (50–51), it refers simply to Moabite territory in distinction from the Israelite territory (cf. "territory of Moab" from the singular construct form of *śdh* in Gen 36:35; Num 21:20; 1 Chr 1:46; 8:8).

two sons. Unlike other versions, the Old Greek and Syr. do not have the word "two."

1:2. *Elimelech.* Ruth contains the only occurrences in the Hebrew Bible of this name, which means "my god is king" (1:3; 2:1, 3; 4:3, 9), although some scholars relate it to the names *i-li-milki* and *milki-ilu* in the Amarna Letters as well as *ili-milku* and *ilmlk* from Ugarit (consult Hubbard, 88, for references). A related name may occur in the Hazor 6 inscription (*'lm[lk?]*; Dobbs-Allsopp et al., 191). Some scholars read the etymology of the name against the backdrop of the concern over a lack of kingship at the end of Judges (Judg 17:6; 18:1; 19:1; 21:25; Moore, 2000, 310). Yet, Ruth and Judges do not have strong internal connections (consult "Canonical Placements" in the Introduction). While the Vulg., Syr., and Targum support MT[L], LXX[BL] read "Abimelech" ("my father is king"). If one took *abi* as reflecting a *y* genitive case ending from archaic Hebrew (so "father of"), LXX[BL] could reflect "father of the king" as a possible reference to the royal line that will descend from this character (Ruth 4:17, 22). LXX[BL] find little support, however, from the other versions. Most likely, the Old Greek reads "Abimelech" because it is a more common name than Elimelech (Gen 20–21; Gen 26:1–16; Judg 9; 2 Sam 11:21; Ps 34:1), just as elsewhere the Old Greek reads "Abimelech" for the Hebrew "Ahimelech" (1 Sam 21:2, 7, 9; 2 Sam 22:9, 11, 16).

Naomi. Although my translation follows the traditional English spelling for this name, the first vowel is a *qamets hatuf*, thus "Noʻomi" would reflect MT[L] more accurately. LXX[BL] and Theodoret, among other Old Greek witnesses, read "Noemin," although this spelling does not find support among the other versions. This name derives from the noun *nʻm* ("kindness"), which some scholars relate to Ugaritic epithets for Kirta and Aqhat and deities such as Anat, as well as feminine personal names such as *Nu-ú-ma-ya* and *Nu-ú-ma-ya-nu* (for the references, consult Campbell, 53; Hubbard, 88–89; Sasson, 17). The masculine personal name *Elnaʻam* meaning "God is kindness" appears in 1 Chr 11:46. Most likely, rather than a first common singular possessive suffix, the *y* at the end of *noʻomî* is an abbreviated form of a theophoric element (*yah*), as in the personal names *ʼûrî* ("light of Y[HWH]"; Exod 31:2) or *ʻabdî* ("servant of Y[HWH]"; Ezra 10:26), among others, although it is relatively rare in women's names. Thus, Naomi means "kindness of Y(HWH)" rather than "my kind one." The name is ironic since Naomi feels that YHWH has not treated her with kindness (NOTE *"Bitterness" [Mara] and Shaddai* on 1:20).

the names of his two sons were Mahlon and Kilyon. This clause has a singular subject ("name") but a compound predicate ("Mahlon and Kilyon"). Thus, a more wooden translation would be "the name of his two sons was Mahlon and Kilyon." On the basis of the introduction of Orpah and Ruth in 1:4, one might expect "two sons, the name of the first was Mahlon and the name of the second was Kilyon" (cf. Gen 10:25; 41:50–51; Exod 18:3–4; 1 Chr 1:19). In this case, the disagreement between the subject and predicate may introduce the brothers as a single unit (Holmstedt, 59; Linafelt, 1999, 5). As with several other personal names of brothers, "Mahlon" and "Kilyon" rhyme (cf. Gen 4:20–21; 22:21; 36:26; 46:21). This may further support the idea that they function as a pair. This is in keeping with the use of rhyme, assonance, and alliteration involving proper names throughout the book of Ruth (consult "The Diction of the Hebrew in Ruth" in the Introduction). The narrator does not develop these two brothers as distinct characters. Rather, as with Nabal ("fool") in 1 Samuel 25, their names describe the role that the brothers play in the narrative, assuming that the two names mean something involving sickness, death, or sterility (NOTE *Mahlon* on 1:2) and the annihilation of a lineage (NOTE *Kilyon* on 1:2). As the "name" of this pair suggests, sickness/sterility and annihilation threaten to bring Elimelech's lineage to a premature end.

Mahlon. Unlike the three other family members named in this verse, there are no known cognate names in other Semitic languages for the Hebrew name Mahlon. The name occurs only in Ruth (1:5; 4:9, 10) but may be related to other Hebrew names, such as the feminine names *maḥlâ* (Num 26:33; 27:1; 36:11; Josh 17:3; 1 Chr 7:18) and *māḥălat* (Gen 28:9; 2 Chr 11:18) or the masculine name *maḥli* (Exod 6:19; Num 3:20; 1 Chr 6:4 [Eng. 6:19], 14 [Eng. 29], 32 [Eng. 47]; 23:21, 23; 24:26, 28, 30; Ezra 8:18). Mahlon may mean "sick one" if it reflects the Hebrew word *maḥălâ* from *ḥlh* ("sick") with an *-ôn* suffix (*-ān*). Other suggestions based on *ḥlh/ḥly* include "sweet" (Joüon, 33; cf. the Aramaic *hālê*), "forgiveness" (Exod 32:11; 1 Kgs 13:6; 2 Kgs 13:4; Jer 26:19; 2 Chr 33:12; Dan 9:13; for rabbinic interpretations reflecting this meaning, consult Eskenazi and Frymer-Kensky, lxi, 6), and "ornament" (Prov 25:12; Song 7:2). Some scholars have also suggested that the name derives from *ḥûl,* meaning "dance" (Ps 30:12), or *ḥll,* meaning "pierce" (consult Hubbard, 89, n. 29, for references). Although usually in the context of war, *ḥll* may also refer to a dead person (Gen 34:27; 1 Sam 31:8; 1 Kgs 11:15; note Boaz's references to Mahlon as "the dead one" [*hammēt*] in Ruth 4:5, 10 [cf. 1:8; 2:20]). It would be easiest to explain the name as deriving from *mḥl* with an *-ôn* suffix, although this root is not attested elsewhere in Biblical Hebrew except in the personal names listed above. Nonetheless, some scholars cite the Arabic word *maḥala* ("sterile"; Joüon, 33; Sasson, 18) or the word *māhil* ("cunning"; Rudolph, 38). Although the etymology of the name Mahlon remains uncertain, it seems to be related to sickness, death, or sterility and thus creates a pun (consult "The Diction of the Hebrew in Ruth" in the Introduction). After providing his name, the narrator reports only that, like his brother, Mahlon had a ten-year marriage that was apparently childless and then he died (vv. 4–5). Boaz draws specific attention to the potential end of his lineage when he emphasizes the need to preserve Mahlon's lineage explicitly (4:10). Yet Boaz may also create a pun when he mentions preserving Mahlon's name upon "his inheritance" (*naḥălātô*) in 4:10 (Garsiel, 252; Porten, 1978, 46; Sasson, 19; cf. 4:5).

Kilyon. According to some scholars, this name may be related to the Ugaritic name *ki-li-ya-nu* (Campbell, 53; Hubbard, 89). While some derive the name from the Hebrew word *kĕlî* ("small vessel") with an *-ôn* suffix (Joüon, 33), it more likely derives from the Hebrew *klh* ("annihilation, completion") with an *-ôn* suffix. A similar form, *killāyôn* ("destruction"), occurs in Isa 10:22 (cf. Deut 28:65). LXX[B] supports the argument that Kilyon derives from *klh*. Various forms of *klh* are often used for the destruction of a people or lineage (Exod 32:10, 12; 33:3, 5; Lev 26:44; Num 16:21; 17:10; 25:11; 1 Sam 15:18).

Ephrathites from Bethlehem of Judah. Just as "Bethlehem of Judah" distinguishes this Bethlehem from the Bethlehem in Zebulun (Josh 19:15), this reference to Ephrathites should not be confused with members of the tribe of Ephraim or inhabitants of the geographic location Ephraim (Judg 12:5; 1 Sam 1:1; 1 Kgs 11:26 [LXX[B]]) or associated with the town of Zeredah in Transjordanian Israel (1 Kgs 11:26 [MT^L]; 2 Chr 4:17; Zarethan in 1 Kgs 7:46). The term "Ephrathite" (*'eprātîm*) in Ruth may refer to a small Judean clan (Ps 132:6) associated with Bethlehem. In 4:11, Ephrathah parallels Bethlehem (cf. Gen 35:19; 48:7). In the genealogy of Perez in 1 Chronicles (cf. Ruth 4:18–22), a woman named Ephrathah was either the great-grandmother (1 Chr 2:51) or the grandmother (4:4) of Bethlehem, the eponymous ancestor of the town. While the references to Ephrathah and Bethlehem as eponymous ancestors are unique to Chronicles and probably midrashic, they reflect an association between Ephrathah and Bethlehem. As in Ruth 1:1–2, 1 Sam 17:12 refers to Jesse, the father of David (Ruth 4:17, 22), as an Ephrathite "from Bethlehem of Judah." Micah 5:1 (Eng. 5:2) refers to "Bethlehem-Ephrathah" (*bêt-leḥem 'eprātâ*) as among the smallest or least significant "family units of Judah" (*'alpê yĕhûdâ*). In some contexts, the word *'elep* ("family unit") may be used to describe a social unit similar to the *mišpāḥâ* (Judg 6:25; McNutt, 88), which could suggest that Ephrathah was the name of Elimelech's clan (NOTE *clan* on 2:1).

stayed there. The verb *wayyihyû* suggests a less frequent meaning, "to remain," in this context (Exod 34:28; 2 Sam 4:3; 13:38; 1 Chr 12:40). 4QRuth^a reads *wyšbw* ("they dwelled"), although this reading may be influenced by 1:4 (*BHQ,* 51*). The Old Greek and Targum support MT^L but with the more common meaning of *hyh:* "they became." Thus, "they became royal adjutants" (Targum). The Syr. and Vulg. reflect the less common meaning, as does the verb *hāyĕtâ* in 1:7 in MT^L.

1:3. *she was left, she and her two sons.* The feminine singular passive form of the verb "to leave" (cf. 1:5) refers to Naomi, but it does not have an independently stated subject (contrast "the man" as an independently stated subject of the verb in v. 1; NOTE *she arose, she and her daughters-in-law, and she returned from the territory of Moab because she heard* on 1:6). The compound "she and her two sons" is not the subject of the singular verb. Rather, it specifies who was left after Elimelech died (Holmstedt, 62).

1:4. *They took . . . wives.* Bush and Joüon cite the use of a verb deriving from *nś'* rather than a verb deriving from *lqḥ* in regard to "taking" a wife as evidence that Ruth reflects LBH since the use of *nś'* in this idiom occurs more frequently in texts that pattern with LBH (e.g., Ezra 9:2, 12; 10:44; Neh 13:25; 2 Chr 11:21; 13:21; 24:3). Texts that pattern with SBH prefer the verb *lqḥ* in this idiom (e.g., Gen 4:19; 6:2; 11:29; Judg 14:2; 1 Sam 25:40; 2 Sam 12:9; 1 Kgs 3:1; 4:15). The idiom with *nś'* also occurs in Ben Sira 7:23 and the Mishna, which does not use *lqḥ* in this idiom (Holmstedt, 33; Young, Rezetko, and Ehrensvärd, 1:265). Yet, Campbell and Myers cite the use of *nś'* in this sense in a possibly earlier text (Judg 21:23). This allows for the possibility that Judg 21:23 and Ruth 1:4 are older texts that reflect an early adoption of an idiom that became commonplace in later texts (Kim). Also, Holmstedt cites the use of a verb deriving from *lqḥ* in regard to Boaz "taking" Ruth as a wife in 4:13. Ruth contains idioms for marriage that pattern with both SBH and LBH.

Orpah. The etymology of this name is uncertain. It occurs only twice in the Hebrew Bible (Ruth 1:4, 14), although some scholars suggest it may parallel the Ugaritic name for Ba'al's daughter Tal(a)ya, which possibly means "dewy" (Campbell, 55–56; "clouds," Ugaritic *'rpt,* Hebrew *'ărāpel*). Some propose etymologies based on possible Arabic cognates (Hubbard, 94, n. 14 for references), while others suggest that it is an otherwise unknown Moabite name (Joüon, 34). Some rabbinic traditions connect the name to the Hebrew word *'ōrep,* meaning "back (of the neck)" and suggest that the name refers to various actions for which Orpah is censured. For example, she does not accompany Naomi to Bethlehem (1:14–15). *Ruth Zuta* 1:4 connects her name with verb forms of *'rp*, meaning "to break one's neck" (Exod 13:13; 34:20; Deut 21:6). According to *Ruth Rab.* 2:9, the name refers to how Orpah "turned her back on Naomi" (Exod 23:27; 2 Sam 22:41; Jer 2:27; 32:33; 48:39 for this idiom, although unlike Ruth 1:14–15, the idiom does not use the verb *šûb*). According to *b. Sotah* 42b, 2 Sam 21:18 provides a different spelling of the name in the phrase "the offspring of *hārāpâ*" (more likely, the word means "the giants" collectively). In this interpretation, Orpah was also called *hārāpâ* because she had multiple sexual partners who ground her like "the grain" (*hāripôt*; 2 Sam 17:19; Prov 27:22). Thus, her name implies that she was sexually promiscuous. This interpretation suggests that her neck should be broken because of her unspecified actions. Nevertheless, the narrator in Ruth does not explicitly censure Orpah. In fact, Naomi endorses Orpah's choice to return to Moab (1:15).

Ruth. Throughout the book, the Syr. reads *rĕʿût*, meaning "friend, companion" (Hebrew *rĕʿût*, "female companion"; Exod 11:2; Esth 1:19) Yet, the other versions do not support this reading. There is no reason to assume the loss of an *'ayin* in this personal name. For similar reasons, the name does not derive from *r'h* ("to see"). Following Albright's translation (*ANET* 320–21), Campbell cites the word *ryt* in the Mesha Inscription line 12, "[I] slew all the people of the town as satiation (intoxication) [*ryt*] for Chemosh and Moab." Although it would be nice to have a Moabite etymology for Ruth's name, considering her ethnicity, the reading and meaning of *ryt* in the Mesha Inscription are disputed. The word could be read *hyt* rather than *ryt* (for differing opinions, consult Lemaire; Shade). Thus, the evidence from the Mesha Inscription is not necessarily helpful etymologically. Following Bruppacher, a number of commentators argue that the personal name derives from the same root as the Hebrew verb *rwh/rwy* ("saturate, sate") and as a noun would mean "refreshment" (for a detailed explanation, consult Rendsburg, 1999a). Although the noun form of this root does not occur in the Bible, it seems more probable than the root *rtt*, of which no form is attested in the Bible. Moreover, in Jer 31:14, a Hebrew verb deriving from *rwh* parallels a verb deriving from *śbʿ* ("to be satisfied, full"). If the name Ruth derives from this root, there could be a pun in the phrase "she [Ruth] was satisfied [*śbʿ*]" (2:14; cf. 2:18).

and then dwelled there for about ten years. My translation understands the *wayyiqtol* form of *yšb* as resuming the narration of the sequence of events after providing the names of the wives. Thus, the clause refers to the length of time that the brothers dwelled in Moab after their marriages (Campbell, 58; Hubbard, 91, n. 2) and does not refer to the length of time that elapsed since the family first left Bethlehem (contra Joüon, 34; Würthwein, 9–10). For further discussion of this phrase, consult "Divine Activity and Acts of *ḥesed* in Ruth" in the Introduction.

1:5. *without her two children and her husband.* Whereas v. 1 refers to Kilyon and Mahlon as *bānâw* ("his sons") and v. 3 refers to them as *bĕnêhā* ("her sons"), v. 5 refers to them as *yĕlādêhā* ("her children") although they are married adults at the time of their deaths. Frequently, this term refers to a newborn or small child, who is often dying or in distress (e.g., Exod 2:6–10; 21:22; 2 Sam 12:15, 18–19, 21–22; 1 Kgs 14:12; 17:21–23; 2 Kgs 4:1). Its use in v. 5 may provide poignancy to Naomi's loss that the more generic term "sons" would not (Bush, 66; NOTE *the child* on 4:16). Moreover, the reading in MT[L], supported by 4QRuth[a], the Vulg., and the Targum, reverses the order of Naomi's family members that is found in vv. 1–3. This reversal may also emphasize the extent of Naomi's loss rather than the chronology of events. The Syr. and Old Greek read "her husband and two sons" possibly to reflect the chronological order of the deaths (*BHQ*, 51*). The Syr. also reverses the order of the characters in the phrase "with the dead ones and with me" to "with me and my two sons who are dead" in 1:8b (Campbell, 60).

1:6. *She arose, she and her daughters-in-law, and she returned from the territory of Moab because she heard.* The three verbs ("to arise," "to return," and "to hear") are all feminine singular forms despite the plural form "daughters-in-law." The subject of these verbs is not "she and her daughters-in-law" but the singular "she" in reference to Naomi, who was the subject of the previous verse ("the woman was left"; Bush, 85; Campbell, 63; Holmstedt, 68). The syntax is similar to that at the end of v. 3 ("she was left, she and her two sons"). Several versions smooth out the syntax of this verse. For example, LXX[BL] read the second and third verbs as feminine plurals ("they returned" and "they heard"), and the Syr. reads the third verb as a feminine plural. Possibly because of haplography triggered by the *b* in *watāšāb* ("she returned") and *mô'āb* ("Moab"), a minority of Old Greek manuscripts omit the phrase "the territory of Moab" in v. 6a. Campbell notes that only Naomi can "return" to Judah because Orpah and Ruth were not among the party that originally left Bethlehem (Campbell, 63; cf. Hubbard, 129). Ruth and Orpah, however, ask to "return" to Naomi's people and her ancestors in v. 10, and Ruth "returns" to Bethlehem in v. 22.

daughters-in-law. The Old Greek, Syr., and Vulg. read "her two daughters-in-law." This reading may be influenced by the occurrences of the phrase "her two daughters-in-law" in 1:7, 8. The Targum supports MT[L].

because. The word "because" (*kî*) introduces a verb complement clause. This use of *kî* patterns with SBH (Bush, 23; Holmstedt, 26). Elsewhere in Ruth, *kî* introduces noun or verb complement clauses (1:18; 2:22; 3:11, 14; 4:9) whereas *'ăšer* is never used in this manner. Texts that pattern after SBH rarely use *'ăšer* to introduce complement clauses, but this use is much more frequent in texts that pattern after LBH. Whether this distribution indicates an earlier date for Ruth's composition, however, remains uncertain because such a conclusion would reflect an argument from silence on the basis of the absence of a syntactic feature rather than on the presence of certain syntactic features.

1:7a. *under her authority.* Various forms of the preposition *'im* occur fifteen times in Ruth. In two places, the form or context of the preposition suggests the translation "from" or "from among" (2:12; 4:10). In most cases, however, the form or context suggests the translation "with" (1:8b [three times]; 2:4, 8, 21, 22). Yet, scholars have recognized that *'im* has more technical nuances. Although Jacob Milgrom does not cite any examples from Ruth, he argues convincingly that one may translate *'im* as "under the authority of" in a variety of texts elsewhere in the Hebrew Bible (e.g., Gen 23:4; 29:14, 25, 30; 31:38; Deut 15:12, 16, 18; Judg 17:10; 1 Sam 2:21; 2 Sam 19:34; 1 Kgs 11:22) (2001, 2205–6). Milgrom translates *'im* with this technical sense in Lev 25:6, 23, 35–36, 39–41, 47, 50, 53. Both Ruth and Lev 25:23–55 frequently use the words "redeem" or "redeemer(s)" with a similar technical sense (e.g., consult the various forms of *g'l* for land redemption in Lev 25:25–26, 30, 33; Ruth 4:1, 3, 4 [five times], 6 [four times], 8, 14; "redemption" in Lev 25:24, 26, 29 [two times], 31, 32; Ruth 4:6, 7). Also, both texts discuss redemption performed by a close (*qrb*) relative (Lev 25:25;

Ruth 2:20; 3:12; cf. Lev 25:49) That both texts use similar technical language in regard to an impoverished relative increases the likelihood that they also use *'im* with a similar technical sense (Schipper, 2013, 665). The preposition may have this technical sense when used to describe asymmetrical relationships among household members in 1:7, 11, 22; 2:6; 2:19 (two times) (consult "Household Organization" in the Introduction).

Comments

The first verse of Ruth sets the narrative in a time when chieftains exercised localized legal authority in Israel. This does not necessarily serve as an allusion to the book of Judges since Ruth's description of the days when chieftains ruled resembles how some Deuteronomic traditions optimistically imagine this time period (consult "Canonical Placements" in the Introduction). Ruth, however, does not necessarily share the optimism of these Deuteronomic traditions regarding the utility of household and clan structures to provide for household dependents (consult "Household Organization" in the Introduction; cf. Butting, 45). In the opening verses, the narrator describes significant shifts in the relationships and statuses within a particular household that challenge the integrity of this social structure. The remainder of this chapter is dominated by dialogue whose addressees are, or presumably include, fellow household or clan members. Yet, the only speech that evokes a positive response from its addressee is Naomi's speech that persuades Orpah to leave her household and return to Moab.

After identifying the household members by name and by their relationships to each other and possibly the name of their clan (Ephrathites), the narrator notes the death of the household's senior member (vv. 2–3). Although their father is dead, Mahlon and Kilyon do not leave their birth household when they marry Orpah and Ruth. Rather, in keeping with the patrilocal nature of the household, their wives join the men's household and multiple generations live together as an extended family (*wayyēšbû*; 1:4). Although the narrator does not clarify which man marries which woman (consult "Selective Representation and Narrative Ambiguity" in the Introduction), Orpah and Ruth would be under the authority of the senior members of the household: their husbands and mother-in-law according to this model (Mic 7:6). Even after Mahlon's and Kilyon's deaths, Naomi's relationship to her daughters-in-law is structured according to a household model. As the surviving senior member of the household, Naomi retains authority over her daughters-in-law until they leave her household (NOTE *under her authority* on 1:7a). The word translated as "under her authority" (*'immāh*) in 1:7a implies that her daughters-in-law are still members of her household as they begin their journey to Bethlehem. It also plays off of "his people" (*'ammô*) in v. 6, which refers to members of a household or clan in its other occurrences in Ruth (1:10, 15, 16 [two times]; 2:11; consult "Household Organization" in the Introduction).

Moreover, in v. 6, Naomi still operates as one might expect a member of a clan to behave in this situation (consult "Household Organization" in the Introduction). She returns to her clan in Bethlehem, most likely to secure food. Although it is unclear whether Naomi's birth household is in Bethlehem, her return would not be unusual according to a social model structured around the household (cf. especially Lev 22:13; Gen 38:11). Even with the deaths of her husband and sons, she is not without a potential male provider and thus not an *'almānâ*, which is the term used for a woman bereft of male support within the household system (consult "Household and Clan Statuses of Ruth's Characters" in the Introduction). Although the narrator does not reveal this fact until 2:1, Naomi has relatives in Bethlehem who could potentially provide for her (consult NOTE *one of our kindred redeemers* on 2:20; Siquans, 445). In 1:8–15, Naomi will try to persuade her daughters-in-law to follow her example and return to or join households in their own native land. The opening verses of Ruth provide a context for the first conversation in the book by situating the main characters and their relationships within the household structure.

In keeping with the style of narration throughout the book, the opening verses create a play on the name Bethlehem and the word *leḥem* (consult "The Diction of the Hebrew in Ruth" in the Introduction). The famine serves as a catalyst for the journeys to and from Moab. It drives Elimelech and Naomi from the house of food (*bêt leḥem*) to Moab (1:1). Yet, in v. 6, Naomi hears that YHWH provided "food" (*leḥem*) for YHWH's people. Thus, she sets off to return to the house of food (cf. 1:19). The book ends only after the surviving members of her household acquire abundant food (2:17–18) and build up an abundant household (4:11–22; Garsiel, 250–53) although, throughout Ruth, the significance of a secure household may represent different priorities depending on whether the conversations involve women or men (cf. 1:8; 3:1; 4:11–12, 14–15).

Ruth Rab. 1:4 suggests that the famine was divinely orchestrated. It cites Amos 8:11 to describe what a "famine in the land" (Ruth 1:1) would involve. In Amos, YHWH declares, "I will send a famine in the land, not a famine of food and not thirst for water, but of hearing the words of YHWH." *Ruth Rab.* 1:4–5 also describes Elimelech's decision to leave Bethlehem as an abandonment of his responsibilities to his community (cf. *b. B. Bat.* 91a; among contemporary scholars, consult Berman, 27–29). When the introductory formula "there was a famine in the land" used in Ruth 1:1 occurs elsewhere in the Hebrew Bible, however, it does not imply divine disfavor (compare its other uses in Gen 12:10; 26:1; Gerleman, 13). Moreover, neither Abram nor Isaac is condemned for his temporary, if prolonged (26:8; cf. "stayed there," Ruth 1:2b), settlement as a resident alien (*gûr*) in Egyptian and Philistine territory, respectively. In fact, God specifically instructs Isaac to reside as a resident alien in Philistine territory because of the famine (Gen 26:3). Likewise, a Shunammite woman and her household follow Elisha's instructions and reside in Philistine territory without any divine censure (1 Kgs 8:1–2). Also, 1 Sam 17:12 describes David's father Jesse, the grandson of Boaz and Ruth (Ruth 4:17, 22), as an "Ephrathite from Bethlehem of Judah" (cf. Ruth 1:2). There is no censure of David's parents when they "dwell" (*wayyēšbû;* cf. Ruth 1:4) in Moab during a time of crisis (1 Sam 22:3–4; cf. Ruth 1:6).

The narrator does not indicate the cause or causes of the famine, but only its consequences: Elimelech and his household travel to Moab (consult "Actions, Events, and Consequences" in the Introduction). Likewise, while one could speculate that Elimelech hoped to acquire food from the Moabites (Deut 2:28–29; cf. Num 21:11–20; contrast Deut 23:4–5 [Eng. 23:3–4]), the narrator does not provide his motives. Nor does the narrator provide Mahlon's and Kilyon's motives for their marriages (contrast Gen 37:4–11). Moreover, although some scholars speculate that Mahlon's and Kilyon's deaths were divine punishments for marrying Moabite women (consult "Exogamy and Ethnicity" in the Introduction), YHWH does not punish or show disfavor toward anyone in the book of Ruth (contrast Gen 38:6–10). In fact, YHWH does not express any opinions or emotions in Ruth. Interpreting the famine or deaths as divine punishment develops YHWH's character beyond what the textual evidence supports. In Ruth, YHWH's characterization is limited to one single, but important, role in the book: the giving of human and agricultural fertility and fecundity in the Cisjordan (consult "Divine Activity and Acts of *ḥesed* in Ruth" in the Introduction).

Regarding YHWH's influence on human fertility, the deity's role in the Cisjordan provides a point of contrast with the events set in the Transjordan. What distinguishes Bethlehem from Moab is that YHWH allegedly intervenes in Bethlehem in the wake of disaster (1:6; cf. 2:20). While the narrator does not specify whether the famine extended to Moab and whether Elimelech and Naomi's family sojourned there in search of food (Note *the land* on 1:1), the lack of human fertility in Moab contrasts with the divinely enabled fertility in Bethlehem (4:13; Dube, 2001, 191–92; LaCocque, 42). Naomi's "children" die in Moab (1:5), but she acquires a "child" in Bethlehem (Note *the child* on 4:16).

This contrast does not imply that Moab is portrayed as cursed or punished in Ruth. After all, the opening verses may imply that Moab enjoyed agricultural fertility while Bethlehem experienced famine. It is more accurate to say that, in regard to human fertility, Moab is simply nonblessed whereas Bethlehem is blessed by the end of the book. This reflects the notion that YHWH will uniquely bless the Israelites, in distinction from all other peoples or regions, when they settle in the Cisjordan. While several biblical texts reflect variations of this ideology (cf. Exod 23:25–26; Lev 26:4–5, 9–10), it receives its fullest articulation in certain Deuteronomic texts (Deut 7:6; 14:2; 26:18–19), specifically in regard to Israel's agricultural and human fertility while in the Cisjordan (7:13–15; 11:11–15; 28:1–12; cf. Ruth 2:20; 4:13). In fact, the only reference to *ḥesed* in Deuteronomy outside of the Decalogue suggests that YHWH's *ḥesed* is manifested in the Cisjordan specifically through the extraordinary divine blessing that removes the harsh realities of everyday life that the community would normally experience, including sickness and a lack of fertility (Deut 7:12–15; cf. Exod 23:25–26; Ruth 2:20; 4:13; Baden, 14–17).

As with the famine, the narrator does not explain the reasons behind the deaths in Moab but notes only their consequences for Naomi. After Elimelech's death, she "was left" with her two sons (v. 3), and then, after they die, she "was left" without them (v. 5; on this chiastic structure, consult Bush, 60; Linafelt, 1999, 5). The narrative space devoted to her interpretation of these deaths (1:13, 20–21) further emphasizes their effect on her. In 1:1–7a, the narrator provides reasons only for Naomi's actions (cf. 1:18). She "returned" (*šûb*) from Moab "because she heard in the territory of Moab that YHWH had visited his people to give to them food" (1:6; consult "Actions, Events, and Consequences" in the Introduction). The dialogue in 1:8–17 will develop the characters' interiority further as they discuss whether to "return" (*šûb*) to Moab or Bethlehem (1:7, 8, 10, 11, 12, 15, 16). Yet, in the opening verses, the narrator explains only Naomi's thought process.

Following the deaths in Naomi's household, the narrator refers to Naomi as simply "the woman" (*hā'iššâ*; v. 5). For Trible, the use of "the woman" helps to show how Naomi is "stripped of all identity" through the deaths of her family (167). For Dubin, the reference to her merely as "the woman" signals that divine "kindness" is absent in v. 5 (132; cf. Note *Naomi* on 1:2). The description of Naomi as "the woman" in v. 5 also creates a contrast between her experience and that of "a man" in v. 1. "A man" travels to Moab with "his wife and his two sons" (v. 1), but "the woman" is left in Moab "without her two children or her husband" (v. 5).

In Ruth, blessings occur throughout the narrative once the characters leave Moab. Everything from a casual greeting (2:4) to an act of *ḥesed* invokes a blessing (3:10; consult COMMENTS on 1:7b–19a). Nonetheless, the book does not begin by presenting life in the Cisjordan during the time of the chieftains as particularly blessed. At best, the opening verses contain only a rumor of the type of blessings described throughout Deuteronomy. The narrator acknowledges this rumor but does not confirm its veracity (v. 6b). Instead, the narrator reports only the famine and the deaths as confirmed facts (vv. 1b, 3–5). Although there is a rumor that YHWH blessed Naomi's clan with food (1:6), her daughters-in-law would have no evidence that her clan is divinely blessed on the basis of their experience of a lack of human fertility since joining her household. In 1:7b–19a, Orpah and Ruth will have to decide whether to return to their birth households; to join another, presumably Moabite, household through marriage; or to remain members of Naomi's clan under her authority.

On the Road (1:7b–19a)

1 ⁷ᵇThey traveled along the road in order to return to the land of Judah. ⁸Naomi said to her two daughters-in-law, "Go! Return, each one to her mother's household. May YHWH deal with you kindly just as you have dealt with those who are dead and with me. ⁹May YHWH give to you . . . [Oh, forget it!] Find rest, each one in the household of her husband!" She kissed them and they lifted their voices and wept. ¹⁰They said to her, "We will certainly return with you to your people." ¹¹Naomi replied, "Return my daughters! Why should you travel under my authority? Are there still sons in my womb that could become husbands for you? ¹²Return my daughters! Go! For I am too old to belong to a man. For even if I thought, 'There is hope for me,' even if I were to belong to a man tonight and even if I bore sons, ¹³would you wait for them until they grew? Would you restrain yourselves for them by not being with a man? No, my daughters! For my bitterness is much greater than yours because the hand of YHWH has gone forth against me." ¹⁴They lifted their voices and wept again. Orpah kissed her mother-in-law, but Ruth clung to her. ¹⁵She said, "Look! Your sister-in-law has returned to her people and to her ancestors. Return after your sister-in-law." ¹⁶But Ruth said,

> "Do not pressure me to abandon you
> To return from after you
> For to [the place] where you may travel, I will travel
> And in [the place] where you may lodge, I will lodge
> Your people, my people
> Your ancestors, my ancestors
> ¹⁷In [the place] where you may die, I will die
> And there I will be buried.

Thus, may YHWH do to me and thus may he add if death should separate me from you!" ¹⁸When she saw that she was resolved to travel with her, she ceased to speak to her. ¹⁹ᵃThe two of them traveled until they entered Bethlehem.

Notes

1:7b. *They traveled along the road in order to return to the land of Judah.* Probably due to haplography produced by the final *h* in *wattēlaknâ* ("they traveled") and *yĕhûdâ* ("Judah"), some Targum manuscripts omit this clause. Yet, this reading is not supported by the other versions.

1:8. *two daughters-in-law.* The Syr., LXX^B, and most LXX^L manuscripts lack the word "two" before "daughters-in-law." The Targum and multiple Old Greek manuscripts support MT^L (consult NOTE *daughters-in-law* on 1:6).

her mother's household. LXX^A and multiple Old Greek manuscripts read "father's house." Most likely, this reading replaces "mother's household," a term that occurs less frequently (Gen 24:28; Song 3:4; 8:2; cf. "her house" in Exod 3:22; 1 Kgs 17:15; 2 Kgs 8:1–6; Prov 14:1; 31:21, 27; Jdt 8:5; "house of his mother's father," Judg 9:1) with one that occurs more frequently: "father's house" (Gen 24:38; 28:21; 38:11; Josh 2:12; Judg 9:18; 1 Sam 22:15; 2 Sam 14:9; Isa 7:17; Ps 45:11; 2 Chr 21:13, etc.). LXX^B and the Targum support MT^L. Although widowed women without children return to the "house of the father" (*bêt 'āb*) in other texts (Gen 38:11; Lev 22:13), the "house of the father" is not simply a physical location, but refers to a socially and economically integrated unit representing the basic element or foundational building block for the organization of Israelite and other ancient Near Eastern societies (consult "Household Organization" in the Introduction). Some scholars suggest that women played a part in the arrangement of marriages within this social structure (Gen 24:53; 27:46; Num 36:6; Tob 7:14–17; Campbell, 65–65; Hertzberg, 262; Meyers, 1993, 112–13; for a more cautious approach to this issue, consult Bush, 75). One should also note that the use of the less common reference to the mother's rather than the father's house creates a pun with v. 7a. MT^L vocalizes "her mother" in "her mother's household" as *'immāh* and vocalizes "under her authority" in "her two daughters-in-law were under her authority" as *'immāh*. The pun draws attention to the idea that Naomi is releasing her daughters-in-law from under her authority as their mother-in-law to return to the authority of their mothers in their birth households (Schipper, 2013; "The Diction of the Hebrew in Ruth" in the Introduction).

May YHWH deal. Rather than the modal *ya'aśeh* (*ketib*), the *qere* has a jussive *ya'aś* ("May YHWH deal"; cf. Vulg. and Old Greek). Yet the *ketib* could also be translated as a jussive (Korpel, 55, n. 16; Gen 41:34; Ruth 1:17; 1 Sam 3:18; 14:44; 20:13; 25:22; 1 Kgs 2:23). Strawn (2004) has a detailed discussion of the *ketib/qere*. The language of v. 8b reflects a formulaic blessing similar to the longer blessing in 2 Sam 2:5–6 (NOTE *May YHWH give to you . . . [Oh, forget it!]* on 1:9 and COMMENTS).

with you . . . you have dealt with. Although in both cases, "you" refers to the two daughters-in-law, both words have masculine plural suffixes (cf. Gen 31:9; Exod 1:21). In Ruth, there are eight examples in which a masculine plural independent pronoun (1:22), a pronominal suffix (1:8, 9, 11, 13, 19; 4:11), and a verbal suffix (1:8) have a feminine antecedent referring to two women. There are also two examples in 1:13 in which a feminine pronominal suffix refers to presumably two men. Instead of a mismatch in gender, some scholars have identified the masculine plurals as examples of supposedly archaic feminine dual forms (Bush, 24; Campbell, 24–25; Myers, 20; more recently,

Rendsburg, 2001). One could compare these pronominal and verbal suffixes to dual endings on pronominal or verbal forms in Ugaritic (Tropper). Yet, comparative linguistic evidence for the independent pronoun *hēmmâ* ("they," 1:22) as a dual form remains unclear (Davis, 110–11). Moreover, depending on whether one dates Priestly literature as postmonarchic, the distribution of masculine forms with two feminine antecedents may not be represented in early texts significantly more than in later texts (Exod 28:9, 11, 14, 26, 27; 30:4; 39:7, 18, 20). Also, accounting for the mismatch in gender by appealing to an archaic feminine dual does not explain the use of feminine plurals to refer to two men in Ruth 1:13 (Davis, 499).

A mismatch in gender, or "gender neutralization," in feminine plurals involving more than two parties is much more common than a supposed dual (JM §149b; Holmstedt, 24). Including the occurrences in Ruth, the pronominal suffixes *-hm* and *-km* with a feminine antecedent involving two parties occur thirty-eight and six times, respectively, in Biblical Hebrew, whereas they occur at least ninety-seven and twelve times, respectively, when the feminine antecedent involves more than two parties (Rendsburg, 2001, 30–31). Also, it is not always clear whether the examples involving only two parties as the feminine antecedent present these antecedents as a pair/dual (e.g., two eyes, two ears, etc.) or as a case of a plural that just happens to involve only two parties. In Judg 19:24, the two women are not necessarily a pair since they are otherwise unassociated with each other. Unlike the two cities personified as a pair of women in Ezek 23:45, 46, 47, they are simply two otherwise unconnected women from different households who tragically happen to be in the same location (cf. the plurals involving two items in Judg 16:3; Hos 2 14 [Eng. 2:12]; Zech 5:8–9). Even if such dual forms existed in archaic Hebrew, it does not necessarily mean that the examples of gender discord in Ruth must reflect these archaic forms and not simply "gender-neutralized" forms (Bar-Asher). Seven of the examples of gender discord come from Naomi's speech in Ruth 1 (vv. 8 [two times]; 9, 11, 13 [three times]). As with other supposedly archaic forms in Ruth, Naomi's use of a masculine rather than a feminine form could reflect archaized forms that distinguish Naomi's speech pattern from the narrator's pattern, which uses the typical feminine plural form *lāhen* ("[to] them") in reference to Orpah and Ruth in the same verse. This difference may simply reflect the variation often used for repeated words or phrases in biblical narrative (Rendsburg, 1995, 180). It could also help to distinguish the way that Naomi spoke back in the days when the chieftains ruled from the narrator's more "contemporary" speech pattern. Timothy H. Lim notes that most examples of gender discord "appear in the mouth of the aged, Naomi [*zāqantî* in 1:12] and the elders [*hazzĕqēnîm* who use the masculine form *šĕttêhem*, meaning 'two of them,' in reference to Rachel and Leah in 4:11]" (111). For Lim, these linguistic features distinguish the speech pattern of the elderly, although he does not account for the gender discord in the narrator's speech (1:19, 22). In short, scholars have raised enough reasonable doubt to caution against using these forms as solid evidence of the date of Ruth's written composition or to reconstruct Ruth's oral origins, if they ever existed, in a particular time period.

kindly. For a detailed discussion of the word translated as "kindly," consult "Divine Activity and Acts of *ḥesed* in Ruth" in the Introduction.

those who are dead. The article *h* in the words *hammētîm* ("those who are dead") and *haššābâ* ("who returned") in 1:22; 2:6; 4:3 introduces a relative clause, for example, "a viper on the path that bites [*hannōšēk*] a horse's heels" (Gen 49:17) or "a highway that goes up [*hāʿōlâ*] from Bethel" (Judg 21:19b). Ruth 1:22; 2:6; 4:3 introduce a relative clause by prefixing the article *h* to a finite verb as in 1 Kgs 11:9b, "the god of Israel, who appeared [*hanniręʾâ*] to him twice." On these and other examples, consult Holmstedt, 28–29, 74, 100; and NOTE *who returned from the territory of Moab* on 1:22.

1:9. *May YHWH give to you . . . [Oh, forget it!]* The jussive verb ("to give") does not have an object in either MT[L] or 4QRuth[a]. The other versions provide various objects for the verb to smooth out the syntax, for example, "mercy" (LXX[L]), "a full reward" (Targum), or *ḥsdʾ* (Syr.). Along these lines, Campbell suggests "recompense" from the Hebrew word *śākār* (cf. 2:12) as the object of the jussive. Others suggest that "find rest/security" is the object of the jussive, for example, "May God allow each one of you to find security" (Sasson, 22–24; also consult Bush, 76; Hubbard, 98, n. 11; Joüon, 36). Holmstedt proposes that the syntax of this clause is interrupted. As is common in everyday speech, the clause starts one way, pauses, and ends another way. He translates the interrupted clause as, "May YHWH give you . . . Find rest, each one in the house of her next husband!" (66, 75). In support of this proposal, one could also note the interrupted syntax in Moses' appeal to YHWH in Exod 32:32, which is also a tense, emotional, moment. My translation adds "Oh, forget it!" in brackets to emphasize a possible rhetorical reason for the interruption of the formulaic blessing that began in v. 8b. The beginning of v. 9 continues the blessing with "May YHWH give to you" but stops mid-sentence (cf. NOTE *this . . . her sitting . . . the house . . . a little* on 2:7). Naomi abruptly drops the pretense of piety in favor of the nonpious, practical advice that will characterize her speech for the rest of the chapter (for a more detailed discussion, consult Schipper, 2012).

Find rest, each one in the household of her husband. The noun translated as "rest" (*měnûḥâ*) is related to the noun translated as "place of rest" in 3:1 (*mānôḥa*). In both cases, the word relates the household of a husband to a place of material security (cf. "Household Organization" in the Introduction). In keeping with her instructions in v. 8, Naomi seems to instruct her daughters-in-law to return to Moab and find rest in the household of another, presumably Moabite, husband. Yet, the households of their respective deceased husbands are in Bethlehem. Thus, Orpah and Ruth could (mis)understand Naomi as changing her mind abruptly and instructing them to return with her to Bethlehem and remain as "wives of dead men" under the protection of the clan into which they married (NOTE *the wife of the dead man* on 4:5) rather than returning to their birth households. While Naomi's position becomes clear in vv. 11–13, her daughters-in-law's initial response could be interpreted as emphatic agreement with rather than resistance to Naomi's instructions (NOTE *We will certainly return* on 1:10).

give to you . . . kissed them. The words translated as "to you" and "them" are further examples of gender-neutralized pronouns (NOTE *with you . . . you have dealt with* on 1:8).

their voices. MT[L], supported by the Targum, Syr., and most Old Greek witnesses, reflects the expected feminine plural form *qôlān*. 4QRuth[a] reads *qwlm*. In MT[L], the same form (*qôlān*) occurs in 1:14, but that verse is not preserved in 4QRuth[a]. For 1:9, Campbell reads "their voice" with 4QRuth[a] and argues that the *m* ending reflects an early feminine dual ending. Thus, according to Campbell, "their voices" refers to only two voices, those of Orpah and Ruth (66). Although not cited by Campbell, the Vulg.

indicates that only the two women wept. Yet, most versions support MT^L. Moreover, the evidence of early feminine dual forms in Ruth is uncertain. It is also noteworthy that when characters kiss (*nšq*) and weep (*bkh*) elsewhere in the Hebrew Bible, the party doing the kissing always weeps (Gen 29:11; 45:15; 50:1). In some cases, this party weeps along with the party being kissed (Gen 33:4; 1 Sam 20:41). This suggests that "their voices" does not have a dual antecedent. 4QRuth^a may result from either a copying error or gender-neutralized pronouns (NOTE *with you . . . you have dealt with* on Ruth 1:8).

1:10. *We will certainly return.* Whereas *kî* functions in vv. 12, 13, 16b, and 20 to introduce clauses that provide evidence to support the speaker's claim and is translated as "for," in this verse, *kî* functions as an exclamation. It is unnecessary to emend the text to the more common term *lōʾ kî* to produce an adversative, as some scholars do (e.g., Rudolph, 40; Gen 18:15; 19:2; Josh 24:21; 1 Sam 8:19; 12:12; 2 Sam 24:24; 1 Kgs 2:30; 3:22; Isa 30:16; Jer 42:14). On its own, *kî* may function as an adversative (Gen 31:16; Bush, 77). The use of the *yiqtol* form *nāšûb* ("we will return") rather than the cohortative form *nāšûbâ* ("let us return") reinforces Orpah and Ruth's determination expressed by *kî* (Holmstedt, 77). Yet, since *kî* can serve as either a negative or a positive exclamation (e.g., "surely"; Gen 31:16 [in the NASB]; cf. Amos 4:2; 2 Sam 12:5; WO §40.2.2b; NOTE *it is certainly true that* on 3:12), Orpah and Ruth could understand Naomi as changing her mind midway through v. 9 and instructing them not to return to Moab but to return to Bethlehem with her and remain in her household (consult NOTE *Find rest, each one in the household of her husband* on 1:9), with which they emphatically agree: "We will certainly return with you to your people!" (*lĕʿammēk* meaning members of Naomi's clan; consult "Household Organization" in the Introduction). The fact that they kiss each other and weep does not clarify their use of *kî* since elsewhere relatives kiss and weep at reunions (Gen 29:11; 33:4; 45:15; 50:1) as well as departures. This would also explain why Orpah and Ruth say that they intend to return with Naomi *after* they kiss and weep. The translation "certainly" retains the ambiguity of this exclamation since it does not clarify whether they are agreeing or disagreeing with Naomi even though it expresses their determination to travel with her to Bethlehem (consult "Selective Representation and Narrative Ambiguity" in the Introduction). Nonetheless, Naomi clarifies her instructions in vv. 11–13.

to your people. The Syr. reads "to your land and to your people," but the other versions do not support this reading.

1:11. *Naomi replied.* The word translated as "replied" is a *wayyiqtol* form. Some scholars take the frequent use of *wayyiqtol* and *qatal* modals in main clauses as a possible indicator of SBH. Ruth uses these converted forms frequently (1:11, 12; 2:7, 9, 14, 16; 3:3, 4, 9, 13, 18; 4:5, 7). There are a few occurrences of *qatal* nonmodels in main clauses (1:14, 22 and 4:1, 18–22) which occur more frequently in Qumran and Mishnaic literature. This leads many scholars to argue that the less frequent use of converted forms is an indication of later Hebrew. Yet, Mark S. Smith documents a complex distribution of both converted and unconverted forms in Qumran literature (1991). The continued use of converted forms in Qumran literature suggests that their use is not a clear indicator of SBH. At the same time, the use of both converted and unconverted forms in main clauses in Ruth does not necessarily mean that Ruth patterns after later

Hebrew. The use of unconverted forms could reflect the type of semantic manipulation for literary effect that may occur in texts that pattern after both SBH and LBH. In 1:14, 22, and 4:1, the narrator uses *qatal* nonmodels in main clauses to shift to new subjects or agents: from Orpah to Ruth (1:14b), from Naomi to Naomi and Ruth (1:22b), and from Naomi to Boaz (4:1; cf. Holmstedt, 10, 12–13, 86–87, 101, 180–81). Moreover, the use of a *qatal* nonmodel (*hôlîd*) throughout 4:18–22 reflects a standard practice for genealogies in texts that pattern after both SBH and LBH (e.g., Gen 11:27; 25:19; Num 26:29; Neh 12:10–11; 1 Chr 9:34–44).

Return my daughters! Why should you travel under my authority? Reading with LXX[A], which includes the imperative "go" after "daughters," Myers translates v. 11a as, "Return, my daughters, [go]; Why will you go with me?" (54). Yet, this reading is not supported by the other versions. Most likely, the imperative form of *hlk* that follows the phrase "Return, my daughters!" in the following verse (1:12; cf. 1:8; Myers, 61, n. 4) influenced the insertion of the imperative form of *hlk* in v. 11 of LXX[A]. MT[L] uses a modal of *hlk* in this verse, thus, "why *should* you travel under my authority?" For the translation "under my authority," consult NOTE *under her authority* on 1:7a. In 1:11, Naomi associates authority over her daughters-in-law with a responsibility for their future marriages (3:1–2; NOTE *clung to her* on 1:14; COMMENTS on 1:7b–19a).

for you. The word translated as "for you" is another example of a gender-neutralized pronoun (NOTE *with you . . . you have dealt with* on 1:8).

1:12. *Go!* MT[L], supported by the Targum and Vulg., reads *lēknā*, which is a shortened spelling of the feminine imperative of *hlk*. MT[L] has the fuller spelling of this feminine imperative in 1:8 (*lēknâ*). Multiple Old Greek witnesses read this shorter spelling as the Hebrew word *lākēn* ("therefore, thus"). The Syr. and some Old Greek witnesses lack this word completely.

For even if I thought . . . even if . . . even if. The conditional nature of these statements is unmarked in MT[L] but represented in the translation with the word "if." The repeated use of *gam* introduces increasingly unlikely scenarios. Naomi emphasizes that even under the unlikeliest of circumstances, she could probably not produce another husband for either Orpah or Ruth in a timely fashion (cf. v. 13).

to belong to a man . . . I were to belong to a man tonight. A more wooden translation of "belong to a man" might read "to be to a man." This expression is often used as an idiom for marriage (cf. the translations of Lev 22:12; Num 30:7; Deut 24:2; Jer 3:1 in major English versions such as the KJV or NRSV; consult Lev 21:3; Ezek 44:25). Such texts reflect the assumption that a woman would be under the authority of her husband according to the household model discussed previously ("Household Organization" in the Introduction; NOTE *under her authority* on 1:7a). Yet, as Sasson notes (24–25), the expression may also refer to sexual intercourse, as in Hos 3:3, which the NRSV translates as "you shall not have intercourse with a man." Along these lines, the Targum translates the term as a reference to sexual intercourse. The second occurrence of the term in this verse refers to an action that may occur that night and result in pregnancy. Thus, the context of the verse suggests that Naomi refers to reproductive sexual activity rather than simply marriage.

tonight. MT[L], the Vulg., and the Targum read "tonight." Old Latin reads "today." The Syr. and LXX[BAL] lack this word. Other Old Greek witnesses read "profaned," with a possible sexual overtone based on the Hebrew root *hll*. Yet, this reading probably results from a confusion of the Hebrew letters *h* and *ḥ* when reading the first letter in *hallayĕlâ* ("tonight").

I bore sons. 4QRuth^b may read "two sons," although the word "two" must be reconstructed because the scroll is damaged (DJD XVI, 194). The versions do not support the reading in 4QRuth^b.

1:13. *for them.* The word *hălāhēn* ("for them") occurs twice in this verse. This form does not occur elsewhere in the Hebrew Bible. It seems to combine an interrogative *h* with the preposition *l* and a third-person feminine plural suffix. As the antecedent of this word is Naomi's male "sons" mentioned in the previous verse, one might expect a third-person masculine plural suffix. Yet, this probably does not reflect a confusion of a *-m* for a *-n* suffix because 4QRuth^b also reads *hlhn* rather than *hlhm*. According to Zevit, this word provides evidence of LBH because it shows "a loss of distinction between final *mem* and *nun* as in Rabbinic Hebrew under the influence of Aramaic" (592; for examples from Qumran literature, consult Qimron, 27, §200.142). The spelling of *lāhēn* in MT^L is the same as the Aramaic words for "therefore" and "except, but" (*lāhēn*; Dan 2:6, 9, 11, 30; 3:28; 4:24; 6:6, 8, 13 [Eng. 6:5, 7, 12, respectively]), but the other versions (Old Greek, Syr., Targum, Old Latin, Vulg.) support the reading "for them." The most likely explanation of the feminine rather than masculine suffix is that the word has a gender-neutralized suffix (NOTE *with you . . . you have dealt with* on Ruth 1:8).

wait . . . restrain. The verb "to wait" is a *piel* inflection of the root *śbr*, which occurs in only nine other biblical verses (*piel:* Isa 38:18; Pss 104:27; 119:116, 166; 145:15; 146:5; Esth 9:1; *qal:* Neh 2:13, 15). Some scholars argue that this verb, along with the verb "to restrain" from the root *'gn*, reflects a word borrowed from Aramaic and therefore indicates that Ruth was composed during the Second Temple period. Even if these verbs reflect Aramaic borrowing, it remains uncertain when they were incorporated into Hebrew on the basis of these few occurrences. Regarding *śbr*, since other more frequently occurring Hebrew words for "wait," such as *yḥl* or *qwh*, were available (for examples, consult Bush, 29), this verb could have been used in 1:13 because it was not yet incorporated into Hebrew. Before the period of Aramaic linguistic dominance, this verb could reflect "casual speech that introduced the occasional chic 'foreign' element as an innovation" (Zevit, 575). If so, one could interpret Naomi's use of foreign words as evidence of characterization rather than for the date of composition. Naomi, who just spent at least ten years in a foreign country, sounds like a non-Israelite while encouraging her Moabite daughters-in-law to return to Moab. Even if it is Aramaic rather than Moabite, her speech still sounds foreign. Moreover, the root *'gn* is a hapax legomenon; thus, it remains uncertain when it was incorporated into Hebrew or whether it reflects Aramaic borrowing (Sasson, 244).

my bitterness is much greater than yours. The Hebrew syntax allows for multiple translations, including, "my bitterness is too much for you (to handle)" and "great bitterness is mine because of you." The Old Greek reads, "I am made bitter on behalf of you," whereas the Syr. includes two options when it reads "I am very bitter on your account, and it is more bitter for me than for you." The major commentaries reflect these various options (for a review of opinions, consult Sasson, 27). One's translation of this clause depends partly on how one understands Naomi's attitude toward her daughters-in-law. Naomi's feelings in this regard are open to interpretation (Fewell and Gunn, 1990, 73; Linafelt, 1999, 14; consult "Characterization" in the Introduction). Since the syntax does not endorse one translation over another, the issue is an interpretative one rather than a grammatical one. As in this verse, verb forms from *mrr* ("to be bitter") can describe someone whose child has died (2 Kgs 4:27; Zech 12:10; Ruth 1:20; also possibly Job 27:2). This would be contextually appropriate.

hand of YHWH. The expression "hand of [a given deity]" occurs at several points in Akkadian diagnostic texts in connection with various illnesses (Roberts; Schipper, 2006, 81; cf. "hand of YHWH is against *X*" in Exod 9:3; 1 Sam 5:6, 9). This may be an appropriate expression for Naomi to use, considering that her husband and sons have all died and the imagery of illnesses that Mahlon's name invokes (NOTE *Mahlon* on 1:2).

1:14. *they lifted their voices.* The word translated as "they lifted" is spelled differently than it is in 1:9 because quiescent *alephs* may be omitted in verb conjugations of III-*aleph* roots. Yet, this spelling is grammatically acceptable and does not necessarily reflect a scribal error. Although the quiescent *aleph* occurs more frequently in later texts (e.g., Qumran literature), it also occurs in earlier ones (e.g., Jer 9:17; *lqrt* rather than *lqr't* in line 4 of the Siloam Inscription; Myers, 9). Likewise, object suffixes attached directly to the verb instead of the use of the object marker *'t* with the suffix are not clear indications of LBH. Habakkuk and certain sections of 1 Kings use suffixes attached to the verb despite the general consensus that these are early texts (Young, Rezetko, and Ehrensvärd, 1:261–62). Thus, although Ruth has only suffixes attached to the verbs (1:21; 2:4, 13, 15; 3:6, 13 [two times]; 4:15 [two times], 16), the distribution of this linguistic feature makes its relevance for the book's composition date uncertain (Holmstedt, 27; contra Bush, 25). For the word translated as "their voices," consult NOTE *their voices* on 1:9.

kissed her mother-in-law. The Syr. follows this clause with "and she returned and went" (cf. Vulg., Old Latin, and Targum). Old Greek witnesses follow this clause with "and returned to her people," most likely influenced by Naomi's statement to Ruth in v. 15 ("your sister has returned to her people"). In different ways, these versions make explicit what MT[L] implies, namely, that Orpah's kiss is a farewell gesture (*BHQ*, 52*). Naomi's statement in v. 15 makes this obvious. 4QRuth[b] seems to support MT[L] (DJD XVI, 194), although only the first two letters in the word following "mother-in-law" are extant. Moreover, it is unclear whether the second of the two letters is the *r* in *wrwt* ("but Ruth," so MT[L]) or the *t* in *wtšb* ("and [Orpah] returned," so Old Greek).

clung to her. Although most witnesses support MT[L], the Old Greek reads *ēlolouthēsen* ("followed after her"). This reading may result from confusion with a similar sounding form of the Greek word *kollaō* ("to adhere"; 2:8, 21, 23; Campbell, 72). In MT[L], the object of the verb has a *b-* prefix (*dābaqâ bāh;* cf. 2:23), unlike the objects of this verb in 2:8, 21. In 2 Sam 20:2, the verb with an object with a *b-* prefix describes how the people of Judah stuck with David while the people of Israel left to follow Sheba (cf. the similar contrast in Deut 4:3–4). Ruth's narrator may use this verb to describe the contrast between Orpah's and Ruth's respective decisions whether to remain with Naomi.

Although the verb often describes loyalty to God (Deut 10:20; 11:22; 30:20; Josh 22:5; 2 Kgs 18:6), it is also used for a marriage between two people (e.g., Gen 34:3; 1 Kgs 11:2). In these examples, forms of *dbq* occur with forms of *'hb* ("to love"), which is the verb the townswomen use in 4:15 to describe how Ruth relates to Naomi, although '*hb* has a variety of nonerotic or nonmarital nuances that could support other interpretations, such as loyalty. The verb *dābaq* may describe an individual relationship that is closer than a previous kinship relationship (Gen 2:24; cf. Prov 18:24). Moreover, in the other texts that describe a personal relationship between people with the verb *dābaq* and an object with a *b-* prefix, the context involves the attempted incorporation of a person into an Israelite household through marriage (Gen 2:24; 34:3; Josh 23:12; Callaham, 2012, 179–84). In these cases, household members who have authority over the unmarried party negotiate their marriages (Gen 34:9). Regarding Gen 2:24, it reads, "A man abandons his father and his mother and clings [*ya'ăzāb-'îš 'et-'ābîw wĕ'et-'immô wĕdābaq*] to his wife and they become one flesh." Similarly, Boaz recalls "all that you [Ruth] did for your mother-in-law after your husband died, namely, how you abandoned your father and your mother" (*wata'azbî 'ābîk wĕ'immēk*; Ruth 2:11b). Ruth's relationship with Naomi is described as abandoning one's birth family and clinging to a new party in the same terms that Gen 2:24 uses to describe a marriage between a woman and a man. As Gen 2:24 involves a male-female union, some scholars suggest that Ruth's act of "clinging" has sexual or erotic connotations (e.g., Exum, 138, 145–46; West, 191). Yet, Gen 2:24 discusses the formation of a kinship relationship without emphasizing the sexual aspect of marriage. In the previous verse, Adam refers to Eve as "bone of my bone and flesh of my flesh" (2:23). Other texts use "bone and flesh" as an idiom for kinship relationships without a sexual or erotic connotation (Gen 29:14; Judg 9:2; 2 Sam 5:1; 19:13–14 [Eng. 19:12–13]). In other words, Gen 2:24 refers to the creation of a new kinship and household relationship when the man and woman "become one flesh." Likewise, Ruth's clinging to Naomi may indicate a desire for a continued kinship relationship or household affiliation despite Naomi's objections that she cannot provide a husband for her daughters-in-law (Ruth 1:11–13; 3:1–2; NOTE *Return my daughters! Why should you travel under my authority?* on 1:11).

Nevertheless, to argue that the verb *dābaq* does not have a sexual or erotic implication in this verse does not discredit a queer reading of Ruth and Naomi's relationship unless one holds extremely reductive and mistaken ideas about queer identities. As with heterosexual desire, culturally conditioned expressions of queer desire include but are not limited to or solely defined by physical acts. Often, when we use labels for various sexual expressions, even in a derogatory sense, we are referring to more than simply physical activity. The possibility of a queer interpretation is not solely dependent on how one analyzes the verb *dābaq*. In fact, some of the most frequently cited queer interpretations of Ruth never cite 1:14 (e.g., Alpert; Duncan). Similarly, although Mona West refers to 1:14 and Gen 2:24 as descriptions of a "physical relationship" (191), her reading focuses on several other aspects of queer relationships, including the creation of families through kinship bonds that are not always recognized within dominant culture and may require legal manipulation comparable to aspects of Ruth 4. Koosed develops this idea further with more specific contemporary parallels (103–13; consult "Sexual Desire in Ruth" in the Introduction).

1:15. *She said.* Multiple Old Greek witnesses specify Naomi as the speaker in this verse and Ruth as the one to whom Naomi is speaking. The Vulg. also specifies Naomi as the speaker. The Targum supports MT^L.

your sister-in-law. Noun and verb forms of the Hebrew root *ybm* occur in only two other passages in the Bible (Gen 38:8; Deut 25:7, 9). Sasson cites a text from Tell

Al-Rimah that mentions "the house of her brother-in-law (*bītya-ba-mi-ša*)" in a context that does not involve marriage to one's brother-in-law as in Genesis 38 or Deuteronomy 25 (29). The relationship between this word and levirate marriage terminology or practices remains unclear (contra Campbell, 73).

to her people and to her ancestors. 4QRuth[b] reads *l['] m[h] wl'[lhyh]* whereas MT[L] reads *'el-'ammāh wĕ'el-'ĕlōhêhā*. Nonetheless, as with the handful of orthographic differences between MT[L], 4QRuth[a], and 4QRuth[b] (consult DJD XVI, 188), this difference does not affect the translation. Often, *'ĕlōhêhā* is translated as either "her god" or "her gods." If one reads the word as singular, it may refer to a Moabite deity such as Chemosh (Num 21:29; Judg 11:24; 1 Kgs 11:17, 33; 2 Kgs 23:13; Jer 48:46; Mesha Inscription, lines 3, 5, 8, 12, 13, 14, 17, 18, 19, 32, 33). The versions offer a variety of readings, including "her gods" (Old Greek, Vulg.) and "house of her family" (Syr.). Yet, the context suggests translating *'ĕlōhêhā* as "her ancestors" (possibly supported by the Syr.). Regardless of whether ancestors were deified in ancient Israel, other texts use *'ĕlōhîm* when referring to ancestors (Gen 31:30; Judg 17:5; 18:24; 1 Sam 28:13; Isa 8:19–20; possibly Exod 21:6; 32:4; Num 25:2 [cf. Ps 106:28]; 2 Sam 14:16; Lewis 602–3; van der Toorn, 1990, 203–22). In Ruth 1:16b–17a, Ruth declares "Your people, my people / Your *'ĕlōhîm*, my *'ĕlōhîm* / In [the place] where you may die, I will die / And there I will be buried." In these verses, the context of kinship, death, and burial with one's relatives suggests that *'ĕlōhîm* refers to ancestors rather than gods. Ruth intends to join Naomi's ancestors upon her death and be buried in the same place as Naomi and her ancestors (NOTE *or the assembly of his place* on 4:10 and COMMENTS on 4:1–12). Her oath that even death will not separate her from Naomi further reflects this idea. Along these lines, Naomi praises her daughters-in-law for dealing with her and "those who are dead" (*hammētîm;* NOTE *those who are dead* on 1:8; cf. 2:20) with kindness (*ḥesed;* in a personal communication, Susan Ackerman suggested that, in this context, *ḥesed* may have a more specific connotation, such as "according to what is required by kinship obligation"). For a parallel use of *hammētîm* and *'ĕlōhîm* as references to ancestors, consult Isa 8:19. In 1:15, Naomi notes that Orpah's return to her ancestral home of Moab involves returning to her people and her ancestors. In 2:12, however, "YHWH *'ĕlōhê yiśrā'ēl*" refers to "YHWH, god of Israel."

Return after your sister-in-law. The Syr. and LXX[BAL] read "return you also after your sister." The Targum supports MT[L] but includes "to your people and to your gods" at the end of the verse. These versions seem to add emphasis to Naomi's command that Ruth should do as Orpah did.

1:16–17. *Do not pressure me to abandon you . . . And there I will be buried.* On the basis of the heightened use of parallelism and rhyme in vv. 16b–17 and 20–21, Linafelt identifies these verses as poetry or "formally marked lines of verse" (2010, 123; for a detailed and convincing treatment of lineation as a constitutive feature of poetry, consult Couey; Dobbs-Allsopp, especially 186–95). Regarding the line "And there I will be buried" in the final couplet of the poem, Linafelt notes that it "introduces more variety into the parallel structuring of the lines, such final variation being a not uncommon way of marking closure in biblical poems" (125). For Linafelt, vv. 16b–17 and 20–21 represent the only occurrences of "formal lines of poetry" in the book (124). My translation indicates the shift from prose to poetry by offsetting these verses (cf. vv. 20–21). For a detailed discussion of poetic characteristics of vv. 16b–17, consult Linafelt, 2010,

123–25. On the possible significance of this shift into poetry, consult "Speech" in the Introduction.

1:16. *pressure.* The word translated as "pressure" is a *qal yiqtol* from *pgʿ* ("to meet, encounter") followed by the preposition *b*. This construction has a range of meanings, including "encounter" and "meet" but also "attack" or "kill" (Note *attack* on 2:22). Other texts that use this construction with the sense of "pressure" include Jer 7:16; 27:18 (cf. Jer 36:25 in the *hiphil*).

abandon. The word translated as "abandon" comes from *ʿzb* (cf. 2:11, 16, 20). In 2:11, Boaz uses this root when describing how Ruth "abandoned" her birth household and maintained her household affiliation with Naomi. Similarly, Gen 2:24 uses this root to describe how a man leaves his birth household upon marriage (Note *clung to her* on 1:14). Here, Ruth is telling Naomi not to pressure her to revoke Ruth's affiliation with the household that she joined through marriage by returning to her birth household or joining the household of another husband (consult "Household Organization" in the Introduction).

Your people, my people / Your ancestors, my ancestors. In Hebrew, this couplet is only four words: "Your-people, my-people, Your-ancestors, my-ancestors." Although it does not have any verbs, many interpreters understand it as "Your people will be my people, Your god(s) will be my god(s)" (Exod 6:9; Lev 26:12; 7:23; 11:4; 30:22; 31:33; 32:38; Ezek 36:28; 37:27, although these clauses include verbs). The Targum and several rabbinic texts understand these statements as indicating Ruth's conversion (for a detailed discussion of the Targum, consult Brady; for a discussion of rabbinic traditions, consult Eskenazi and Frymer-Kensky, 19; for a review of contemporary scholarly opinions, consult Mark S. Smith, 2007, 243–47). Nevertheless, unlike the references to traveling, lodging, dying, and being buried, which have yet to occur, the nominal clauses in this couplet do not indicate on the basis of the syntax alone whether Ruth means that Naomi's people and ancestors will become Ruth's people and ancestors or will remain Ruth's people and ancestors (Holmstedt, 90; Note *a foreign woman* on 2:10). My wooden translation does not supply a verb in order to convey the ambiguity of Ruth's statement. For further discussion, consult Comments on 1:7b–19a.

Your ancestors, my ancestors. As in v. 15, the Hebrew word *ʾĕlōhîm* may be plural or singular. The versions favor the singular (e.g., Old Greek, Vulg.). Yet, context suggests translating the forms of *ʾĕlōhîm* in both verses as "ancestors," which refers to multiple deceased parties rather than one particular ancestor or deity (Note *to her people and to her ancestors* on 1:15).

1:17. *And there I will be buried.* Unlike the other versions, LXX^L does not include this clause. Although this clause may not reflect the parallel structure of the previous lines, it serves as a means of poetic closure (Note *Do not pressure me to abandon you . . . And there I will be buried* on 1:16–17).

Thus, may YHWH do to me and thus may he add. As discussed in the corresponding Comments, Ruth concludes her dialogue in v. 17b with a common oath formula (cf. 1 Sam 3:17; 14:44; 20:23; 25:22; 2 Sam 3:9, 35; 19:14 [Eng. 19:14]; 1 Kgs 2:23; 19:2; 20:10; 2 Kgs 6:31). The oath should not be considered part of the poem as it does not exhibit the heightened parallelism or rhyme structures of the previous lines (Linafelt, 2010, 124; contra the lineation in the NRSV as well as Bush, 70; Campbell, 62; on

vv. 16b–17 as poetry, consult NOTE *Do not pressure me to abandon you . . . And there I will be buried* on 1:16–17).

if death should. Whereas *kî* functions in vv. 12, 13, 16b, and 20 to introduce clauses that provide evidence to support the speaker's claim and is translated as "for," here it functions as a conditional. For a detailed review of the use of *kî* in biblical oaths, consult Conklin, who argues that *kî* functions as a complementizer ("that") rather than an asseveritive or a conditional particle (46–59). Yet, as Jeremy M. Hutton notes, the Akkadian particle *kî* does function as a conditional in some oath formulas (for references, consult *CAD* K: 318, *kî* 2' b'). Given the contact between Israelite and Assyrian cultures, one should account for possible Akkadian influence on the use of *kî* in biblical oaths (Hutton, 2012, 130). As this influence was well established long before my proposed date for Ruth's composition, the use of *kî* as a conditional particle is viable. The verb translated as "separate" is a *yiqtol* modal with "death" as its subject.

me from you. This represents the only use of the construction *bên-X . . . bên-Y* (1:17) in Ruth. According to Bush, SBH prefers the construction *bên-X . . . bên-Y,* whereas LBH prefers *bên-X . . . l-Y* (e.g., Neh 3:32; Mal 3:18; Jonah 4:11; Bush, 24). Yet, the former construction occurs in several texts that pattern after LBH (e.g., Zech 11:14; Mal 2:14; 1 Chr 21:16; 2 Chr 4:17; 13:2; Young, Rezetko, and Ehrensvärd, 1:123–24), and the latter occurs in those that pattern after SBH (e.g., 1 Kgs 3:9). Thus, Ruth's single use of *bên-X . . . bên-Y* (1:17) without any uses of *bên-X . . . l-Y* should not factor into decisions about the book's date of composition (cf. Kim, 122–28).

1:18. *to her.* Some versions make the last phrase in this verse more specific. Old Greek reads "to her still." The Syr. reads "to [persuade] her to go back." The Targum supports MT^L.

1:19a. *The two of them traveled until they entered.* The words "traveled" and "entered" have the expected feminine suffixes. Yet, the word translated as "two of them" is another example of a gender-neutralized suffix (NOTE *With you . . . you have dealt with* on 1:8). Multiple medieval Hebrew manuscripts seem to have "corrected" the grammar by replacing the masculine suffix with a feminine suffix (*BHS* critical apparatus). Although grammatically correct, the final *h* in the two occurrences of the infinitive *bō'ānâ* in this verse ("entered"; cf. *kěbō'ānâ* in v. 19b) is not grammatically necessary. The use of the less common feminine suffix *-nâ*, however, provides assonance with the verb "traveled" (*wattēlaknāh*), which is in keeping with the use of rhyme and alliteration throughout the book (consult "The Diction of the Hebrew in Ruth" in the Introduction).

Comments

The scene in 1:7b–19a does not take place in either Moab or the Cisjordan, but "on the road" between these two regions (v. 7). Most likely, this road would run through the Israelite occupied territory between the Wadi Arnon and Mount Hermon (Num 21:22; Deut 2:27; cf. Josh 12:1–5). Thus, one might imagine the conversation between Ruth and her daughters-in-law as happening somewhere in the Israelite Transjordan. Several biblical texts represent the Israelite Transjordan as ethnically and politically part of Israel but enough of a geographic "other" that it was not associated with YHWH's presence and its inhabitants were considered ambiguously Israelite. As Jeremy M. Hutton notes, Transjordan Israel is in "a liminal position . . . physically and metaphorically at the edge of Israelite existence" (2009, 6; cf. Havrelock; Jobling, 1986, 116–17). Just as the barley harvest (1:22) provides an appropriate backdrop for the scenes in Ruth 2, a Transjordanian backdrop fits well with a scene in which Orpah and Ruth, who are "foreign-kinswomen" within Naomi's clan (consult "Household and Clan Statuses of Ruth's Characters" in the Introduction), will decide with which household or clan they will ultimately identify.

In v. 8, a character speaks for the first time in the book. Naomi urges each daughter-in-law to return to the household of her mother (*'immāh*) with the hope that YHWH will do *ḥesed* for them. While one's birth household is often referred to as the "house of the father" (*bêt 'āb*; consult "Household Organization" in the Introduction), the reference to the mother's house allows for a pun. Naomi is releasing both women from under her authority (*'immāh*; v.7a) and encouraging them to leave her household and join another household in Moab (NOTE *her mother's house* on 1:8).

The dialogue that will dominate the rest of the book begins with a blessing formula. Blessings occur throughout the book of Ruth in a wide variety of situations (2:4, 19, 20; 3:10; 4:14). In 2:4, a blessing serves as a greeting (NOTE *May YHWH bless you* on 2:4). Elsewhere, acts of *ḥesed* become catalysts for blessings (1:8; 2:19; 3:10; 4:14; consult "Divine Activity and Acts of *ḥesed* in Ruth" in the Introduction). Often, characters speak in the formulaic language of blessing even when they do not use the specific word "bless" (NOTE *May YHWH compensate your deed* on 2:12). In 1:8–9, Naomi begins to bless her daughters-in-law but aborts the blessing before its completion (NOTE *May YHWH give to you . . . [Oh, forget it!]* on 1:9). In 4:11–12, the community declares a blessing on Ruth and Boaz's union. The Syr. labels their speech as a blessing, which presumably makes explicit what is assumed in the other versions (NOTE *All the people who were in the gate and the elders said, "(We are) witnesses"* on 4:11).

In contrast to dated scholarship which associates blessings with magic that assumes the inherent power of words, Rüdiger Schmitt provides a working definition of blessings as "ritual acts of speech that mediated or anticipated God's favor or disfavor and were performed by a person endowed with authority, even when the authority was merely situational. This authority in familial contexts would usually have resided in the *pater familias* [and in some cases] widows could act in the role of *pater familias*" (410, 411 [italics in original]; cf. Meyers, 2013, 187–93).

Upon her return to Bethlehem, Naomi would qualify as the surviving senior member of her household. Along these lines, the women of Bethlehem announce Obed's birth with a formula that applies to the paterfamilias in almost every other occurrence in the Bible (NOTE *For Naomi a son has been born!* on 4:17). Although it is unclear whether her husband is still alive, the Shunammite woman also acts as the paterfamilias in 2 Kgs 8:1–6 (cf. 4:8–37).

Senior members of an extended family could also bless other family members upon their departure from the household. In Gen 24:60, Rebekah's brothers and probably her mother (v. 55) bless her as she leaves to marry Isaac and join his household (cf. Tob 7:13). Laban kisses and blesses his married daughters and their children when they leave his household with Jacob to return to Canaan (Gen 32:1 [Eng. 31:55]; Schmitt, 411). After settling his dispute with Jacob, he releases them from under his authority (31:26–31). Similarly, Naomi kisses her daughters-in-law after beginning to bless them, releasing them from under her authority as the senior member of her household (Ruth 1:8–9, 14; Thompson and Thompson, 96). One could contrast Naomi's blessing in 1:8–9 with the Bethlehemites' blessings in the book's final chapter. The blessing in 4:11–12 anticipates divine favor toward Ruth and Boaz's union in regard to the couple's fertility (cf. 4:14; 1 Sam 1:17; "Divine Activity and Acts of *ḥesed* in Ruth" in the Introduction; Schmitt, 411). The various uses of blessings throughout Ruth reflect the various circumstances and statuses of the members of the household and clan as those circumstances and statuses evolve.

Naomi's blessing refers to acts of kindness toward both the living and dead members of her household (*ḥesed;* cf. "Divine Activity and Acts of *ḥesed* in Ruth" in the Introduction). An Israelite household or clan consisted of multiple generations, including the living and the dead. Naomi's reference acknowledges the unspecified kindness her daughters-in-law have shown toward her household. Nonetheless, the reference to YHWH in relation to her daughters-in-law subtly reinforces their status as foreign-kinswomen. The blessing formula that Naomi uses in vv. 8–9 differs from the references to divine *ḥesed* in the ancestral promises to Israel (Exod 20:6; 34:7; Num 14:18–19; Deut 5:10; 7:9). Instead, her blessing resembles the formula that David uses when he blesses the inhabitants of Transjordanian Jabesh-gilead after they did *ḥesed* with a deceased Saul: "Blessed are you to YHWH because you did this kindness to your lord Saul and you buried him. Now may YHWH deal kindly and truthfully with you" (2 Sam 2:5–6a). As with David's blessing of these "ambiguous Israelites" inhabiting the Transjordan, Naomi appeals to the *ḥesed* that her daughters-in-law have done. She blesses them as a Judahite might bless a Transjordanian resident on the basis of merit rather than ancestral promises (cf. the use of *ḥesed* in 3:10; Ps 62:13 [Eng. 62:12]).

Naomi's blessing may suggest that she hopes YHWH will treat her daughters-in-law better than YHWH has treated her (cf. 1:20–21; Strawn, 2004; Trible, 170). Yet, she does not complete the blessing formula but trails off mid-sentence and then begins a new train of thought (NOTE *May YHWH give to you . . . [Oh, forget it!]* on 1:9). It is unclear how convinced she is that YHWH will bless her Moabite daughters-in-law or show concern for their future security. One may interpret Naomi's aborted blessing as Naomi abruptly dropping the pretense of pious language in favor of practical advice. The pragmatic rhetoric that she uses in the rest of her conversation with her daughter(s)-in-law (vv. 9aB, 11–13, 15) suggests a dramatic shift in tone midway through 1:9a (Schipper, 2012). Reading 1:9aβ as a new train of thought independent of the blessing, Naomi's speech shifts toward matters of practical advice that no longer involve YHWH. None of her rhetorical questions in 1:11–13 suggests that YHWH will assist her daughters-in-law in finding rest in the household of a new husband.

Scholars debate whether Naomi's rhetorical questions refer to levirate marriage (Gen 38:1–11; Deut 25:1–10; cf. Matt 22:23–33). Some argue that Naomi does not refer to levirate marriage because the specifics of her situation differ from those addressed by levirate marriage customs, including, but not limited to, the fact that her future sons would not be related to Mahlon and Kilyon paternally (for discussions, consult Eskenazi and Frymer-Kensky, xxxvi; Weisberg, 31–34). Also, Naomi's stated concern in v. 9 is not with the continuation of her deceased husband's lineage but with the security of her daughters-in-law (cf. 3:1; Berlin, 1983, 105; Bush, 97; Hubbard, 109–10). These objections, however, do not mean that she does not refer to this custom but only that she dismisses it as irrelevant to this particular situation. For example, both Naomi and Judah discuss with their widowed daughter(s)-in-law whether they should remain unmarried until a younger brother reaches marital age (cf. *'ad-yigdal* ["until he grew"] in Gen 38:11 with *'ad 'ăšer yigdălû* ["until they grew"] in Ruth 1:13). Yet, while Judah endorses the idea that his daughter-in-law should wait for the son to grow up, Naomi rejects it. If Naomi refers to some version of levirate marriage, it is only to offer it as an unrealistic solution to the issue of finding rest or security for her daughters-in-law (1:9; 3:1). As Trible observes, the female characters in Ruth discuss children in the context of material security, whereas the male characters associate children with the continuation of patrilineal descent (192). Throughout the book, marriage and children represent the continuation of a male's "name" only when men are involved in the conversation (4:1–12). Marriage and children are associated with security in conversations between women (1:8–9; 3:1; cf. 4:14–15, in which the townswomen suggest that Obed is a source of security for an elderly Naomi)

As Naomi's authority over her daughters-in-law operates within a household structure in which she is a more senior member, she imagines a highly improbable scenario that would stabilize her relationship to them as their mother-in-law. Marriage arrangements often involved the household member(s) who had authority over an unmarried household member, whether it was a mother, a father, or a brother of a daughter; a father-in-law of a daughter-in-law whose husband had died; or a man or woman with a male or female servant (cf. Gen 16:3; 21:21; 24:2–4, 32–58; 27:46–28:4; 29:28; 30:4, 9; 34:10–11; 38:6–11; Exod 2:16–21; 34:16; Deut 7:3; 22:15–16; Josh 15:16–17; Judg 14:3, 10; 1 Sam 18:27; Jer 29:6; Neh 13:25; 1 Chr 2:34–35; on familial involvement in marriage arrangements of unmarried household members in the ancient Near East, consult Marsman, 43–106). In Ruth 3:1–2, Naomi implies that she has some responsibility to find a husband for Ruth, who still remains under her authority at that point in the book. Naomi's seniority notwithstanding, she implies in 1:12 that her daughters-in-law were under no obligation to marry her future sons. Orpah and Ruth had the choice whether or not to "restrain" themselves. Similarly, in 3:10, Boaz implies that Ruth could have chosen to "go after" a younger man if she so desired (cf. Num 36:6). Ultimately, Naomi's arguments persuade Orpah, who returns to her people and her ancestors (NOTE *to her people and to her ancestors* on 1:15).

Naomi expresses Orpah's return to her native land of Moab as a return to her people and ancestors. It remains uncertain whether this idea accurately reflects historical practices in Moab, but the association between one's land and both the living and dead members of one's clan may imply that land was considered the clan's inalienable inheritance throughout its generations (consult "Household Organization" in the Introduction). The connection between the clan's inherited land and its deceased members will become more explicit in Ruth 4.

In contrast to Orpah, Ruth expresses her resolve to settle in Bethlehem by affirming her connection with Naomi and her clan (on the poetic quality of her speech, consult "Speech" in the Introduction; Linafelt, 2010). Her speech has little to do with religious conversion although some scholars read it in that sense (for a review of scholarship, consult Glover; Saxegaard, 130–34; Mark S. Smith, 2007, 243–47). In the Targum, Ruth becomes an exemplar for all converts (Brady). In v. 16, however, she appeals to her current relationship to both the living and dead members of Naomi's clan. One could interpret "your people, my people, your ancestors, my ancestors" as meaning "your people will remain my people, your ancestors will remain my ancestors," rather than "your people will become my people, your ancestors will become my ancestors" (NOTE *Your people, my people,/Your ancestors, my ancestors* on 1:16; for discussions of this issue in rabbinic literature, consult Bernard S. Jackson, 20, nn. 4, 5). As her speech reacts to Orpah's decision to leave Naomi's household, I would interpret her statement as indicating her commitment to maintain rather than change her household status relative to Naomi. There is no change or conversion. Ruth continues to express her commitment to Naomi's household when she states that she will be buried where Naomi dies (1:17a), presumably in the family tomb, since her reference to her burial comes immediately after her reference to the ancestors (cf. Gen 49:29–32). In her death and burial, Ruth will join Naomi and other deceased ancestors of the clan. Even death will not separate them, as her oath sworn by YHWH indicates (1:17b). Also, Ruth pledges to lodge with Naomi, and, later in the story, Boaz, a member of Naomi's clan, will encourage Ruth to "lodge" with him (3:13).

As in 1:6, the narrator provides the reason for Naomi's silence in 1:18. She does not continue the conversation because Ruth's poetic speech convinced her of Ruth's resolve. Yet, the narrator does not indicate how Naomi felt about what she interpreted as Ruth's resolve. One could read her silence as indicating a range of emotions regarding Ruth (for a review of scholars' opinions, consult Saxegaard, 84–85). As with the deaths of Naomi's husband and sons, the narrator focuses on the effect of Ruth's speech on Naomi. With the conversation over, the narrator notes the completion of their journey to Bethlehem (1:19a) with language similar to that used to narrate the beginning of their journey (1:7b).

The nature of Ruth's relationship with Naomi has received significant scholarly attention. Often, 1:16–17 have been used in marriage and commitment ceremonies as an expression of love, although the context of Ruth's speech to Naomi has little to do with such unions, especially heterosexual ones. Some scholars compare Ruth's words to those of a Judean king who promises to go to war with an Israelite king against a third party when he states "like your people, like my people" (1 Kgs 22:4; 2 Kgs 3:7; 2 Chr 18:3; Frymer-Kensky, 241). Noting this similarity, Mark S. Smith reads Ruth's speech as "an explicit expression of shared resources" (2007, 250). If one follows this interpretation, however, one should note the asymmetrical power dynamic in the Israelite and Judean kings' relationship. In the contexts of these stories, the Judean king who pledges his resources to the Israelite king may offer them because he is at a political disadvantage relative to his more powerful counterpart. Thus, a similar statement in Ruth 1:16 does not necessarily mean that the two parties are relating to each other as peers. Along these lines, some have compared Ruth's pledge to the pledge of a Hebrew slave to remain forever under the authority (*'im*) of the senior member of the household (Exod 21:5; Deut 15:16; cf. Brenner, 1999b; Dube, 2001; Sasson, 123–25). While the similarities are not precise, they should caution one against an overly romantic understanding of Ruth's relationship with Naomi.

Arriving in Bethlehem
(1:19b–22a)

1   ¹⁹ᵇWhen they entered Bethlehem the whole town was abuzz over them. The [women of the town] said, "Isn't this Naomi?!" ²⁰But she said to them,

"Do not call me 'Kindness of YHWH' [Naomi]
Call me 'Bitterness' [Mara]
For Shaddai has made me very bitter.
²¹I left full,
YHWH made me return empty.
Why should you call me 'Kindness of YHWH' [Naomi]?
YHWH has testified against me,
Shaddai has brought disaster upon me."

²²ᵃSo Naomi returned. Now Ruth the Moabite, her daughter-in-law, was under her authority, the one who returned from the territory of Moab.

Notes

1:19b. *When they entered Bethlehem.* LXX^BL do not have this clause. These readings probably result from haplography triggered by the first occurrence of "Bethlehem" in the verse immediately preceding the omitted clause (Campbell, 75). The Vulg. (which reads "city"), Syr., and Targum support MT^L. I translate *wayhî* with the word "when" in this clause. Although some scholars claim that Ruth reflects SBH because it uses *wayhî* or *wĕhāyâ* to introduce a clause or follows these words with a preposition followed by an infinite construction (1:19; cf. 3:4, 8, 13; Bush, 23), distribution calls this claim into question. Although less frequent, both of these constructions occur in texts that pattern after LBH (e.g., Esth 2:8; 3:4; 5:2; Dan 8:2, 15; Neh 1:4; 13:3; 2 Chr 12:1; 22:8; 25:14, 16; 26:5; Holmstedt, 25–26; for a detailed discussion, consult Kim, 107–16).

abuzz. The spelling of the word *wattēhōm* ("abuzz") in MT^L could indicate a *qal* from *hwm* or a *niphal* from *hmm* or *hwm*. The roots are possible biforms. All of the possible Hebrew roots include the meaning "abuzz." As Bush notes, the question is whether the "buzz" expresses agitation and consternation (Isa 22:2) or delighted excitement (1 Sam 4:5; 1 Kgs 1:45; cf. Syr.) over Naomi and Ruth's arrival (Bush, 91; cf. Linafelt, 1999, 18–19). The versions interpret the word in various ways, including "resound" (Old Greek; possibly from the Hebrew *hmh,* cf. Joüon, 43), "rejoice" (Syr.), and the rapid spread of the report (*fama,* Vulg.).

over them. MT[L] has a plural suffix for the word translated as "over them" in reference to both Naomi and Ruth. LXX[B] has a singular genitive object, and LXX[AM] have a singular dative object. All of these Greek versions understand the "buzz" in the town to be over Naomi's return rather than the presence of both Naomi and Ruth. The Targum and Vulg. support MT[L]. Although the women of the town ask only about Naomi, the nearest antecedent of the object is plural: "they entered Bethlehem."

[women of the town] said. Although the subject is unmarked in Hebrew, the verb translated as "said" is a feminine plural form. Thus, the implied subject is the women of the town. In 4:14, "the women" marks the subject of the same feminine plural verb as in 1:19. Consult COMMENTS on both verses.

1:20–21. *Do not call me "Kindness of YHWH" [Naomi] . . . Shaddai has brought disaster upon me.* As with vv. 16b–17, Linafelt identifies vv. 20–21 as poetry or "formally marked lines of verse" on the basis of their heightened use of parallelism. In this poem, the lines are structured in a triplet, couplet, triplet pattern (2010, 123, 126; NOTE *Do not pressure me to abandon you . . . And there I will be buried* on 1:16–17).

20. *"Bitterness" [Mara].* When it takes a feminine ending, the Hebrew adjective *mar* (from *mrr,* "to be bitter") usually has a *h* as a mater lectionis (2 Sam 2:26; Ezēk 27:30; Prov 5:4; Job 21:25). Thus, multiple medieval manuscripts read *mrh* rather than *mr'* (*BHS* critical apparatus). Yet, in this case, the *aleph* serves as the mater lectionis (Num 11:20; Isa 19:17; Ps 127:2; Lam 3:12; *GKC* §80h). In v. 20b, Naomi uses a verb form of the root *mrr* ("to be bitter") to describe her treatment by Shaddai (NOTE *Shaddai* on 1:20). Verb forms from *mrr* can describe someone whose child has died (NOTE *my bitterness is much more than yours* on 1:13 for references). Thus, Naomi may be claiming that Shaddai made her bereft of children. As she explains further in v. 21, she no longer accepts the name Naomi, meaning "kindness of YHWH" (NOTE *Naomi* on 1:2), because, according to her, it no longer describes how God has treated her. Instead of treating her kindly, God has made her bereft. Thus, "bitterness" is a more suitable name for her.

Shaddai. Although the precise etymology of Shaddai remains uncertain, scholars have made a number of proposals. The name may refer to a mountain deity based on the Akkadian word *šadû* "mountain" or to a demon or demons (cf. Akkadian *šedu*). It may be related to the Hebrew words *šaday* ("my breasts," Song 1:13; 8:10; cf. Ugaritic *td* or Aramaic *tĕdayyā'*) or *śādeh* ("field"). For reviews of scholarship, consult Hubbard, 124–25; *TDOT,* 14: 429–22. For Ruth 1:20–21, some of the versions associate the name with divine power, for example, *omnipotens* (Vulg.) and "sufficient one" (Old Greek; cf. the rabbinic entomology "who [*šĕ*] is sufficient [*dâ*]"). These translations reflect the sense of Shaddai in Ezek 1:24; 10:5; Ps 68:15 (Eng. 68:14) and the traditional English translation of Shaddai as "Almighty" (cf. Greek *pantokratōr* used to translate Shaddai elsewhere in the Hebrew Bible). Some biblical texts create puns on Shaddai, as with *šōd,* "devastation" (Isa 13:6; Joel 1:15), or the promise that Shaddai will provide "blessings of the breasts [*šadayim*] and the womb" (Gen 49:25; cf. the associations of Shaddai with fertility in Gen 17:1–2; 28:3; 35:11; 48:3–4). Likewise, Naomi may use Shaddai to invoke fertility imagery regardless of Shaddai's historical etymology (consult "The Diction of the Hebrew in Ruth" in the Introduction). Rather than blessing her with fertility, however, Naomi claims that Shaddai made her bitter (or bereft; NOTE *my bitterness is much more than yours* on 1:13) and YHWH emptied her. Job, whose children also died, uses a nearly identical expression in Job 27:2: "Shaddai has made my life bitter" (cf. 27:13b–14). Not only had Naomi's sons died, but, in Ruth 1:11, she doubted that she still had sons in her womb (although she uses a different word for "womb" than in Gen 49:25). In regard to matters of offspring, Shaddai had made her bitter rather than blessed.

In Ruth, the name Shaddai occurs only in Naomi's speech (1:20, 21). Campbell, who dates the book to the early monarchic period, identifies "Shaddai" as an archaic name that was revived only in the exilic period (76–77). On the basis of its distribution alone, however, it remains difficult to determine whether the occurrences of Shaddai reflect the book's archaic origins or archaizing in a later text. Also, considering the use of Shaddai in Balaam's oracles (Num 24:4, 16; cf. *šdyn* in Deir 'Allā 1:6; Moore, 1993), the ancestral narratives (cf. Exod 6:3), and most often in Job (a text from the post-monarchic period that contains thirty-one of the forty-eight occurrences of Shaddai in the Hebrew Bible), the name seems to have been associated with divine activity in the Transjordan (for discussions of linguistic features in Job that reflect its Transjordanian setting, consult Greenstein; Rendsburg, 1995, 179–81). This association would fit with Naomi's description in vv. 20–21 of her experience while in Transjordanian Moab. Rather than using the name because it reflects a particular time period, Naomi may use it simply because it fits the context of her dialogue.

1:21. *I left.* This verse opens with the independent personal pronoun *'ănî* ("I"). Scholars have cited the use of the pronoun *'ānōkî* ("I") rather than the shorter form *'ănî* elsewhere in Ruth as evidence for the book's date of composition. Some argue that texts that pattern after LBH rarely use the pronoun *'ānōkî* (Dan 10:11; Neh 1:6; 1 Chr 17:1) but prefer the shorter form *'ănî*, which Qumran literature uses almost exclusively (Qimron). Texts that pattern after SBH alternate between *'ānōkî* and *'ănî* (Bush, 22; Holmstedt, 33; Polzin, 126). Yet, Ruth uses *'ānōkî* seven times (2:10, 13; 3:9, 12, 13; 4:4 [two times]) and *'ănî* two times (1:21; 4:4). This mixture is not a clear indicator of SBH in the book. Moreover, many languages use different pronouns depending on the circumstances or the relative social statuses of the conversation partners (e.g., the German pronouns "du" and "sie"). E. J. Revell argues that biblical characters use *'ānōkî* and *'ănî* in this way, with *'ănî* used by "status-marked speakers" or those expressing personal concerns and *'ānōkî* used as an expression of deference or politeness (201–2). A thorough assessment of whether this theory accounts for the use of these pronouns throughout the Hebrew Bible is beyond the scope of this commentary; nevertheless, in the book of Ruth, Naomi uses *'ănî* when expressing emotion or urgency (1:21), and Boaz uses *'ănî* when asserting his social status in 4:4a. Yet, as the negotiations develop, both Boaz and the unnamed kindred redeemer use *'ānōkî* in a context requiring mutual deference or politeness (4:4b). Also, Ruth uses *'ānōkî* when claiming a lower social status as a foreign woman and calling herself Boaz's maidservant or handmaid (2:10, 13; 3:9), and Boaz uses *'ānōkî* when claiming that another person has the right to redemption before him because he is "closer than I [*'ānōkî*]" (3:12b). If Revell is correct that the two forms reflect a character's status or circumstances, one should not use these first-person pronouns as linguistic evidence for the date of the book's composition.

Why should you call me "Kindness of YHWH"? LXX[ABL] begin this clause with "and." The Vulg. reads "therefore" (*igitur*). The Old Latin omits this clause, possibly as a result of haplography triggered by the word "YHWH," which immediately precedes and follows this clause. On Naomi meaning "kindness of YHWH," consult NOTE *Naomi* on 1:2.

YHWH has testified against me. MT[L] spells the verb in "testified against me" (*ʿānâ bî*) as a *qal* (from *ʿānāh;* Exod 20:16; 1 Sam 12:3; 2 Sam 1:16; Isa 3:9; Hos 5:5; Job 15:6). The Targum supports MT[L] with "my sin has been testified against me" (Isa 59:12; Jer 14:7). The Old Greek, Vulg., and Syr. translate the verb as "humbled," reflecting a *piel* (*ʿinnāh*). A number of commentators note, however, that the *piel* of *ʿnh* is never followed by the preposition *b* elsewhere in the Hebrew Bible. Talmon cites the use of *ʿnh* followed by the preposition *l* as a legal idiom meaning "to testify on behalf of" in the Yavneh-Yam inscription and suggests that it has the opposite meaning of the biblical *ʿānâ b-*, even though *ʿnh* followed by the preposition *b* does not occur in the Yavneh-Yam inscription (36). Some scholars understand the use of *ʿnh* as intentionally multivalent in this verse (e.g., Moore, 1997, 237–38; Sasson, 36). Considering the use of rhyme and alliteration throughout the book, the word translated as "testified against me" (*ʿānâ bî*) may have been used simply because it rhymes with the name Naomi (cf. Hubbard, 122, n. 14; Sasson, 36; Witzenrath, 20).

Shaddai has brought disaster upon me. LXX[A] and some LXX[L] manuscripts omit this line. The Syr. reads "with his hands" instead of Shaddai. The Vulg. and Targum support MT[L]. One finds a similar construction in Gen 43:6.

1:22a. *under her authority.* The Vulg. and LXX[BL] do not have the word translated as "under her authority." The Targum supports MT[L]. The Syr. includes "who wanted to return with her out of purity of heart" (Campbell, 62). For the translation "under her authority," consult NOTES *under her authority* on 1:7a, and *who returned under the authority of Naomi* on 2:6.

the one who returned from the territory of Moab. On the basis of the accent mark, MT[L] reads *haššābâ* as a perfect rather than a participle. Thus, "(she) returned." In this case, the article *h* introduces a relative clause (Holmstedt, 28, 100; cf. *haššābâ* in 2:6; 4:3). On this use of the article, consult NOTE *those who are dead* on 1:8. The Syr. translates "return" in the sense of both "to return" and "to convert" (NOTE *who returned with Naomi* on 2:6). On the reference to Moab, consult NOTE *territory of Moab* on 1:1. The Vulg. reads "land of pilgrimage [*peregrinationus*]" for "territory of Moab" (also 1:7 [Vulg.]), but this reading is not supported by the other versions. This clause further distinguishes Ruth from Orpah. Orpah is the daughter-in-law who returned to her ancestral home in Moab and is therefore no longer under Naomi's authority. Ruth, however, is the daughter-in-law who remained with Naomi (1:16–17), under her authority (2:6).

Comments

In 1:19b, the plural verb indicates that both Naomi and Ruth arrive in Bethlehem. Nevertheless, as many commentators note, Ruth does not speak and is not acknowledged upon her arrival. Instead, the female residents of Bethlehem focus their curiosity on Naomi. They ask the first of four questions that the characters will ask about the identity and status of either Naomi or Ruth (2:5; 3:9, 16). Their question about her identity allows Naomi to reject her name in favor of the name Mara, meaning "bitterness," which probably refers to her bereavement (NOTES *my bitterness is much more than yours* on 1:13, and *"Bitterness" [Mara]* on 1:20). As with Ruth in 1:16–17, Naomi speaks in poetry in 1:20–21. This may add a sense of emotional depth to her speech (consult "Speech" in the Introduction).

If Ruth's poetic speech conveys her deep commitment to Naomi's household, Naomi's speech conveys a deep level of poverty (although we discover later that she may have land at her disposal). Despite the fact that Ruth remains with her, Naomi declares that she is "empty" (cf. 3:17). Her emptiness may refer to a lack of a male who can assume responsibility for the household's well-being (NOTE *one who restores life* on 4:15). Instead of blessing her with fertility, Shaddai has been a source of bereavement (on possible puns, consult NOTE *Shaddai* on 1:20). From Naomi's perspective, the deity has not only failed to bless her during her Transjordanian residence, but has acted against her. Scholars often note the legal language similar to what one finds in Job or Jeremiah (*Ruth Rab.* 2:10; Campbell, 83; Lapsley, 94–99; Ostriker, 348; NOTE *YHWH has testified against me* on 1:21). Yet the judicial process will not provide relief for Naomi regardless of her innocence (Nielsen, 52).

Unfortunately, the clan structure does not necessarily ensure relief for Naomi either (consult Butting, 45). The whole town was abuzz over her arrival, and now they know that she does not have a male provider in her immediate family. In a sense, she is declaring her need for a kindred redeemer by emphasizing her emptiness upon her arrival in Bethlehem (cf. NOTE *one of our kindred redeemers* on 2:20). A few verses later, the narrator reveals that Naomi has male kin living in Bethlehem (2:1, 3). Thus, she has potential redeemers within her clan. Just as Ruth's poetic speech had declared her status among Naomi's clan (1:16–17), Naomi's poetic speech declares her status among this clan. Nevertheless, just as Ruth's poetic speech evokes no response from her kinswoman Naomi (1:18), Naomi's speech is met with silence from any kin present. The narrator does not indicate that any eligible redeemer comes forward despite the buzz that filled Bethlehem (1:19; 2:11). The clan structure does not necessarily guarantee that the ideals for the support of certain household dependents depicted in some Pentateuchal texts (e.g., Lev 25:25–55) will be realized. While still operating within the household structure, Naomi and Ruth may have to resort to other methods to evoke action from either YHWH or kin who are in a position to help (Hackett, 2014). While the situations are very different, there is precedent for a woman whose husband has died to try to find relief through other means when the conventional mechanisms of the clan fail her (cf. 2 Sam 14:5–7).

In 1:22a, the narrator reiterates Naomi's status within the current configuration of her household by restating that Ruth is under Naomi's authority (1:22a; cf. 1:7a). The narrator refers to Ruth as Naomi's daughter-in-law and further specifies that she, as opposed to Orpah, is "the one who returned from the territory of Moab." The fact that Naomi has authority over Ruth also explains why Ruth asks her permission to glean two verses later (2:2).

Ruth and Naomi's Conversation (1:22b–2:2)

1 ²²ᵇThey entered Bethlehem at the beginning of the barley harvest.
2 ¹Now Naomi had a relative of her husband, a mighty man of worth from the clan of Elimelech. His name was Boaz. ²Ruth the Moabite said to Naomi, "Let me go to the field so I may glean the ears of grain after anyone in whose eyes I may find favor." She said to her, "Go, my daughter."

Notes

1:22b. *They entered Bethlehem.* Although the antecedents of the clause are both feminine subjects (Naomi and Ruth), the pronoun "they" is masculine (*hēnnâ*). Nonetheless, the word *hēnnâ* is a pronoun rather than a demonstrative adjective (contra Campbell, 78). This is an example of a gender-neutralized pronoun (NOTE *With you . . . you have done* on 1:8).

2:1. *relative.* MT^L *ketib* reads *myōdāʿ*, which may reflect the *pual* participle of *ydʿ* (*mĕyuddāʿ*; cf. 2 Kgs 10:11; Pss 31:12; 55:14; 88:9, 19 [Eng. 31:11; 55:13; 88:8, 18]; Job 19:14). If MT^L *ketib* represents the common confusion of a *w* for a *y* (for examples, consult Tov, 246–47), it may assume the absolute form of the noun (*mōdāʿ*), which occurs elsewhere only in Prov 7:4 in parallel with "sisters" (the Old Greek uses the same word to translate this Hebrew word in both Ruth 2:1 and Prov 7:4). Moreover, many Kennicott manuscripts have the consonants *mwdʿ* (Campbell, 88). MT^L *qere* reads a construct form from the same root (*môdaʿ*). A feminine version of the *qere* occurs in Ruth 3:2, but this word is morphologically problematic and does not help to specify the meaning of the word in 2:1 (NOTE *relative* on 3:2). Nonetheless, the various Hebrew spellings, as well as the other versions, suggest some type of relative or intimate acquaintance. (According to the genealogy in 1 Chr 2:9–12, Boaz and the descendants of the Ephrathites' eponymous ancestress [2:19, 50], which would presumably include Elimelech, can both trace their ancestry back to Herzon, the son of Perez [cf. Ruth 4:18].) Although the specific nature of the relationship remains uncertain, references to Boaz elsewhere in Ruth suggest that he is a relative. Naomi identifies him as "close (kindred)" (2:20; cf. 3:12; 2 Sam 19:43 [Eng. 19:42]; Neh 13:4). Also, in Ruth 2:20; 3:9, 12, 13, he is referred to as a *gōʾăl* ("kindred redeemer"), which is kinship terminology elsewhere in the book (NOTE *one of our kindred redeemers* on 2:20). Campbell makes an extensive but strained argument for translating this word as "covenant-brother" on the basis of an unconvincing parallel with 2 Kgs 10:11 and an unconvincing theological analysis (88–90; cf. the critiques of Campbell in Bush, 100; Sasson, 39). Campbell's translation has not been generally accepted in subsequent scholarship. The English word "relative" identifies Boaz as a kinsman without specifying the exact nature of his relationship to Elimelech.

mighty man of worth. My translation takes *gibbôr* ("mighty") as an adjective, in construct with the noun *ḥayil* ("worth"), that modifies the noun *ʾîš* ("man"), although *gibbôr* could also be read as a noun. A more wooden translation would be, "a man, a mighty one of worth." The noun *ḥayil* ("worth") has a wide semantic range when used with *gibbôr*, including a wealthy landholder (1 Sam 9:1; 2 Kgs 15:20; 24:14; cf. Deut 8:17, 18); a powerful, influential, or competent person (1 Kgs 11:28; 1 Chr 9:13; 26:6, 31); a mighty warrior (2 Chr 13:3; 17:13–14, 16–17; 25:6; 32:21); and a person with honor or high character (1 Sam 16:18; cf. 1 Kgs 1:42, 52; NOTE *woman of worth* on Ruth 3:11), among others. With the exception of a mighty warrior, all of these meanings could describe Boaz at various points in the story. While the English word "worth" is not very specific, it could cover a range of meanings of *ḥayil*. Campbell, who translates *ḥayil* as "substance," writes, "The translation 'man of substance' has just the right ambiguity to cover the term in Hebrew!" (90). His point applies equally as well to my translation of *ḥayil* as "worth."

clan. The word *mišpāḥâ* ("clan") has a broad semantic range. In some cases, it may be better translated as "lineage" in the sense of descendants (Lemche, 245–90), although this sense does not apply to its use in 2:1, 3. Gottwald prefers the more cumbersome "protective association of families," arguing that a "clan" is exogamous whereas a "protective association of families" may be endogamous (301–5). This objection, however, would not apply to Ruth's use of the term since the members of Elimelech's clan practiced exogamy (1:4; 4:13; consult "Exogamy and Ethnicity" in the Introduction). A *mišpāḥâ* also refers to the maximal projection of the *bêt ʾāb* ("house of the father"; NOTE *her mother's household* on 1:8) through an association of socially and economically integrated extended families (consult "Household Organization" in the Introduction). It may be a unit larger than a single household but smaller than an entire tribe (Num 1:2; Josh 7:14), although it occasionally refers to an entire tribe (Judg 18:19) or all of Israel (Jer 8:3; Amos 3:1; Mic 2:3). According to Num 27:11 and Lev 25:48–49, a *mišpāḥâ* may include uncles and cousins (NOTE *The man is close to us* on 2:20). In Num 33:54, land is apportioned according to Israel's *mišpāḥôt* rather than by the so-called tribes. In this text, the clan represents the social unit by which land was allotted and held as "its inheritance" (*naḥălātô*; Num 26 52–56; Ruth 4:5, 10), which seems to be the context in which Ruth's narrator uses the term *mišpāḥâ*. As members of the same clan, Boaz and Elimelech each held a portion of their clan's field (*ḥelqat haśśādeh*; cf. Ruth 2:3; 4:3, respectively). However the exact structure or parameters of the *mišpāḥâ* was configured, a member of one's *mišpāḥâ* was expected to perform the role of the kindred redeemer under certain circumstances, including, but not limited to, land redemption (NOTES

The man is close to us and *one of our kindred redeemers* on 2:20). Boaz operates largely within the context of his clan. These technical nuances of *mišpāḥâ* notwithstanding, the term rhymes with *šipḥâ* ("maidservant"), which would seem in keeping with the use of rhyme and alliteration throughout the book (consult "The Diction of the Hebrew in Ruth" in the Introduction). In 2:8, Ruth refers to herself as Boaz's *šipḥâ* without knowing that she is a member of his *mišpāḥâ* (NOTE *maidservant* on 2:8).

Boaz. Despite numerous proposals (consult Campbell, 90–91; Hubbard, 124–35; Sasson, 40–42, for references), the etymology of this name remains uncertain. The name occurs only in the book of Ruth and the genealogy in Chronicles (2 Chr 2:11–12; cf. Matt 1:5; Luke 3:32). Although the northern pillar in Solomon's temple is called "Boaz" (1 Kgs 7:21; 2 Chr 3:17), proposals that connect the Boaz in Ruth with the Davidic dynasty via this pillar remain unconvincing. Some scholars relate the name to the Ugaritic expression *b'l 'z* ("Baal is strong") or an abbreviated form of the Hebrew *bēn 'ōz* ("son of strength"). Yet, it is hard to account for the absence of the *l* or the *n* in these proposals. LXX^B, some LXX^L manuscripts, Theodoret, and the Old Latin read "Boos," which may reflect the Hebrew *bô 'ōz* ("in him is strength") or *bĕ'ōz* ("in the strength of"). Yet, "Boos" may represent an interpretive gloss by these versions, possibly influenced by the following description of him as a "man of worth." Along these lines, some LXX^L manuscripts read "in strength" after "Boaz" in 2:4 and after "Boaz said" in 2:8. Its historical etymology notwithstanding, the name Boaz creates a play on words like other personal names in Ruth (NOTES *Naomi, Mahlon, Kilyon,* and *Ruth* on 1:2, 4, respectively). The consonants in the name *b'z* are an anagram for the Hebrew root *'zb* ("to abandon"). In 2:19b–20a, both *b'z* and *'zb* occur in the context of the disclosure of Boaz's identity. After Ruth mentions him by name, Naomi replies, "Blessed is he who has not abandoned [*'zb*] his kindness" (Garsiel, 252; cf. *'zb* in 1:16; 2:11, 16).

2:2. *Let me go to the field so I may glean.* The verbs translated as "go" and "glean" are both cohortatives (*'ēlĕkāh . . . wa'ălaqqătāh;* reading with MT^A and MT^Y; MT^L and Tiberian manuscripts misspell *wa'ălaqqătāh* as *wa'ălaqăttāh*). Scholars differ as to whether the cohortative form of the verbs signals a question (so Sasson, 38, 43), a declaration (so Campbell, 91–92; Hubbard, 136, n. 1; Sakenfeld, 1999, 39), or a request (so Bush, 102; Holmstedt, 106). Sasson provides little evidence that it is a question. Moreover, cohortatives do not serve as declarations of one's intention unless one addresses oneself (cf. Exod 3:3; Isa 5:1; Bush, 102). Here, the cohortatives function as a polite request, as is common when addressing someone of a higher social status (cf. Deut 3:25; Exod 4:18; 2 Sam 15:7; Bush, 102). The fact that Naomi grants permission ("Go my daughter"; cf. Judg 11:38) suggests that these cohortatives function as a request.

ears of grain. The word translated as "ears of grain" (*šibbŏlîm*) refers to grain that has not been cut off of the stalk, that is, grain that has yet to be harvested (cf. Gen 41:5–7, 22–24; Isa 17:5; Job 24:24). It is difficult to explain the function of the preposition *b* in *baššibbŏlîm* (reading with MT^A and MT^Y; MT^L and Tiberian manuscripts misspell *baššibbŏlîm* as *bašibbŏlîm*). It could function spatially, for example, "among the ears of grain" (so Sasson, 38; cf. the use of the dative in the Old Greek). Yet elsewhere, *šibbŏlîm* is the object of the gathering rather than the location of the gathering (cf. Isa 17:5; Holmstedt, 107). The preposition could function as a partitive, for example, "some of the ears of grain" (Hubbard, 136, n. 3; cf. "Let me not eat some of their delicacies [*bĕman'ammêhem*]" Ps 141:4b; cf. WO 11.2.5f). Yet, the partitive use of the preposition *b* is uncertain, since one could also explain its use in Ps 141:4 as a nonaccusative complement, as with the *l* in *lāhem* in the prepositional phrase in Ruth 1:9: "she kissed them" (Holmstedt, 5, 107). Thus, "gather the ears of grain" remains grammatically possible and conveys the sense of the clause.

after anyone in whose eyes I may find favor. This clause uses a standard biblical idiom, "to find favor in the eyes of" (e.g., Gen 6:8; 39:4; Exod 33:12, 17; 1 Sam 16:22; 2 Sam 15:25; 16:4; 1 Kgs 11:19; Esth 5:8, etc.), which Ruth repeats in her conversation with Boaz (cf. Ruth 2:10, 13). The use of this idiom may indicate that Ruth intends to glean because of the generosity of others rather than because of any legal precedent recorded in the laws for gleaning in various Pentateuch sources (cf. Lev 19:9–10; 23:22; Deut 24:19; Comments on 1:22b–2:2; and Notes *let me glean [ears of grain] and gather [them] into bundles behind the harvesters* on 2:7, and *a foreign woman* on 2:10). Such generosity, however, may not result from altruism. Jon L. Berquist argues that when the idiom refers to women finding favor in men's eyes, it may imply sexual attraction (28, n. 11; Deut 24:1; cf. the slightly different idiom in Esth 2:15, 17). The words translated as "after anyone" (*'aḥar 'ăšer*) could be translated more woodenly as "after that," as in "after that I may find favor in his eyes." One could interpret these two words in this temporal sense on the basis of Ezek 40:1, which reads, "in the fourteenth year after [*'aḥar 'ăšer*] the city was struck down" (cf. Josh 9:16; 23:1; 24:20). Along these lines, Sasson proposes that Ruth asks whether she should "glean among the ears of grain in the hope of pleasing him" (Sasson's translation, 38). Taking the pronoun "him" as a reference to Boaz, Sasson argues that Ruth targets Boaz's field so that her action will result in Boaz favoring her. Yet, there is no textual evidence that Ruth knows of Boaz's existence at this point in the story. In fact, Naomi does not explain to Ruth who Boaz is until 2:20, and Naomi does not seem to know in whose field Ruth worked when she asks Ruth, "Where did you glean today?" (2:19). Among the versions, the Syr. would not endorse Sasson's proposal as it interprets the party that Ruth will glean after as the harvesters.

She said to her. LXX^L specifies the speaker as Naomi (cf. Note *she said* on 1:15), although this reading does not find much support among the other versions.

Comments

In 1:1–2, the narrator states that there was a famine in the land and lists the members of Naomi's household who left Bethlehem and "entered the territory of Moab." In 1:22b, the narrator states that the remaining members of the household left Moab and "entered Bethlehem at the beginning of the barley harvest" (cf. 1:19). As in 1:1, the land's agricultural state serves as a catalyst for the characters' actions in the subsequent verses. Also, the narrator once again explains Naomi's relationships to surviving members of her clan through their marriages. In Moab, she had a husband, two sons, and eventually two daughters-in-law (1:2–4). In Bethlehem, Naomi has a daughter-in-law (1:22a) from her son's marriage and a relative named Boaz from her marriage to Elimelech (Note *Boaz* on 2:1). The exact nature of Boaz's relationship to Elimelech, however, is unspecified (Note *relative* on 2:1), and closer relatives will emerge as the story continues (3:12). The vague term "relative" does not clarify what, if any, kinship obligations Boaz has to Naomi. This leaves open the question of who, if anyone, among her clan is going to provide for her. Later, we learn that Boaz is a close relative and one of her potential kindred redeemers (2:20), but not the closest one (3:12; 4:1–8).

The description of Boaz as a "mighty man of worth" is equally ambiguous (cf. NOTE *mighty man of worth* on 2:1). Scholars differ on whether Boaz is depicted in a positive light (e.g., contrast Shlomo Dov Goitein, 1988, with Fewell and Gunn, 1988). In part, the issue depends on whether one interprets the term "worth" as a reference to his integrity (1 Sam 16:18) or his wealth (Deut 8:17–18). If the former, the narrator indicates that Boaz will act properly. If the latter, one may ask why he does not act as a kindred redeemer for Naomi upon her arrival if he has the means to do so since the narrator introduces him in the wake of Naomi's declaration in Ruth 1:20–21. In 2:11, Boaz claims to have complete knowledge of Naomi and Ruth's situation, possibly because the town was "abuzz" regarding their return (1:19b). If Boaz is speaking the truth, then he would have known of Naomi's lack of a provider long before he acts on her behalf after the harvests are complete (2:23; cf. Trible, 179).

Although it is unclear whether any member of the clan acts on Naomi's behalf upon learning of her situation, Ruth's actions conform to what one would expect given her household status relative to Naomi. Ruth's request to glean does not necessarily reveal her feelings toward Naomi. The narrator does not indicate whether it reflects her concern for Naomi's well-being or simply the fact that she is under Naomi's authority. Likewise, Naomi's approval of her request does not reveal her feelings toward Ruth. Naomi's reference to Ruth as "my daughter" may be a term of affection, but it is also an appropriate term for an unmarried woman within the household (consult "Household and Clan Statuses of Ruth's Characters" in the Introduction). Thus, the use of this term throughout the book is not necessarily an indication of warm feelings toward Ruth on the part of Naomi or later Boaz (1:11–13; 2:8, 22; 3:1, 10–11, 16, 18).

Pentateuchal legislation that assumes a clan structure includes provisions for aliens to glean (Lev 19:9–10; 23:22; Deut 24:19). Nevertheless, although Ruth would qualify as a "foreign kinswoman" when she resides in Bethlehem (consult "Household and Clan Statuses of Ruth's Characters" in the Introduction), she never self-identifies as an alien (cf. Ruth 2:10), and her request to glean is not necessarily made on the basis of such legislation (NOTES *after anyone in whose eyes I may find favor* on 2:2, *let me glean [ears of grain] and gather [them] into bundles behind the harvesters* on 2:7, and *a foreign woman* on 2:10). According to her statement, Ruth assumes that her successful gleaning depends on the favor of others rather than on the faithful application of legally mandated provisions for aliens. Even if Ruth is aware of the Pentateuchal gleaning laws, and that is not certain, there is no reason to assume that she would have faith that the residents of Bethlehem would follow these laws in a fair or just manner, especially considering that a kindred redeemer has yet to step forward in accordance with Pentateuchal law. Whether in ancient Israel or the contemporary United States, it is often only the socially privileged who assume that the law will protect them. As the story continues, Ruth may have to resort to other methods for support.

In the Field Held by Boaz (2:3–17)

2 ³When she went and came and gleaned in the field behind the harvesters, she chanced upon the portion of the field held by Boaz who was from the clan of Elimelech. ⁴Look! Boaz came from Bethlehem. He said to the harvesters, "YHWH be with you" and they said to him, "May YHWH bless you." ⁵Boaz said to his male servant who was set over the harvesters, "To whom does this female servant [belong]?" ⁶The male servant who was set over the harvesters answered and said, "She is a Moabite female servant, who returned under the authority of Naomi from the territory of Moab. ⁷She said, 'Let me glean [ears of grain] please and gather [them] into bundles behind the harvesters.' She came and stood from then, the morning until now, this . . . her sitting . . . the house . . . a little." ⁸Boaz said to Ruth, "Haven't you heard my daughter? Do not go to glean in another field. In fact, you should not leave this one so that you may stick with my female servants. ⁹Your eyes should be on the field that they harvest and you may go after them. Haven't I instructed the male servants not to assault you? So, if you become thirsty, you may go to the vessels and drink from whatever [water] the male servants may draw." ¹⁰Then she fell on her face and bowed down to the ground. She said to him, "Why have I found favor in your eyes that you have paid attention to me although I am a foreign woman?" ¹¹Boaz answered and said to her, "It has been completely reported to me—all that you did for your mother-in-law after your husband died, namely, how you abandoned your father and your mother and the land of your birth and traveled to a people that you did not know previously. ¹²May YHWH compensate your deed. May your wage be complete from YHWH, the god of Israel, whom you came to seek refuge under his skirts." ¹³She said, "I must have found favor in the eyes of my lord because you comfort me and because you speak to the heart of your maidservant, even though I am not like one of your maidservants." ¹⁴Boaz said to her at the time of the meal, "Come here and eat some of the food and dip your morsel in the vinegar." So she sat alongside the harvesters. He heaped together for her parched grain and she ate and was satisfied and left over [some of the parched grain]. ¹⁵Then she arose to glean. Boaz instructed his servants, "Even among the bundles, she may glean. Do not humiliate her! ¹⁶In fact, you should even pull out for her some of the heaps and abandon [them] so that she may glean [them]. Do not rebuke her!" ¹⁷So she gleaned in the field until evening and she beat out what she had gleaned. Now it was about an ephah of barley.

Notes

2:3. *When she went.* LXX^L specifies the subject of the verb as Ruth (NOTE *she said to her* on 2:2), although this reading does not find much support among the other versions.

and [she] came. Possibly because of haplography triggered by the letters *wt* at the beginning of *wtbw'* ("and she came") and *wtlqt* ("and she gleaned"), respectively, LXX^BL, the Vulg., and the Syr. do not have the word translated as "and [she] came." The Targum supports MT^L.

she chanced upon. One could translate this clause more woodenly as "her chance chanced upon" (cf. Eccl 2:14 translated woodenly as "one chance chanced all of them"). A number of scholars interpret this "chance" encounter as evidence of YHWH working behind the scenes of otherwise mundane events (e.g., Bush, 106; Campbell, 112; Hals, 8; Hubbard, 141; Nielsen, 55; Sakenfeld, 1999, 40, 80; Trible, 176, 178). Yet, the noun *miqrehā* ("her chance") occurs in only two other places in biblical prose (1 Sam 6:9; 20:26). In 1 Sam 6:9, the Philistines return the ark of YHWH to the Israelites after a plague broke out in their land. The priests and diviners advise the Philistines to watch the direction that the oxen pull a cart that contains the ark when they send it back to the Israelites. The direction that the oxen travel will determine whether the plague on the Philistines was the result of YHWH's actions or just "chance." This passage suggests that events that result from "chance" are not inspired by YHWH. Jennifer L. Koosed asks, "Why should the word carry a meaning that is the antithesis of its plain meaning only in the book of Ruth?" (79). Some scholars cite the use of verb forms of the root *qrh* ("to chance") in Gen 24:12 and 27:20 as examples of places where "chance" is granted by God (e.g., Eskenazi and Frymer-Kensky, 30–31). In both of these examples, however, God is the explicit subject of the *hiphil* verb form of *qrh* (Ruth 2:3 has a *qal* verb). In contrast, the subject of the verb ("chanced") in Ruth 2:3 is the noun *miqrehā* ("her chance"), rather than the noun God or name YHWH. Thus, these citations from Genesis are irrelevant because the stated subjects of the respective verbs are different from those in Ruth 2:3, and these subjects, God and chance, are contrasted in 1 Sam 6:9. The use of *miqrehā* in this verse does not justify attributing the encounter to divine manipulation (cf. Sasson, 45; Holmstedt, 110; Linafelt, 1999, 27–28; "Divine Activity and Acts of *ḥesed* in Ruth" in the Introduction). The word could just as easily be a byproduct of Ruth's narrative style since *miqrehā* creates alliteration and rhyme with *mākĕrâ* in 4:3, a verse that contains the only other occurrence in the book of the infrequent term "the portion of the field" (*ḥelqat haśśādeh;* consult "The Diction of the Hebrew in Ruth" in the Introduction).

from the clan of Elimelech. My translation interprets the antecedent of this clause as a reference to Boaz's identity. The syntax also allows "the portion of the field" to serve as the antecedent, as in "the portion of the field held by Boaz, that was from the clan of Elimelech." This reading emphasizes the fact that Boaz held the usufruct to a field that the clan apportioned to him from land that they held as an inheritance (*naḥălâ;* consult "Household Organization" in the Introduction).

2:4. *Look!* This use of *wĕhinnēh* has generated much discussion among scholars. For Adele Berlin, it introduces a new figure into a scene after the scene has already started (Num 25:6; Judg 4:22; 1 Sam 11:5; 1 Kgs 13:1, 24–25). She argues that it does not mark Ruth's perception of the content of the *hinnēh* clause as Ruth would not be able to identify Boaz at this point in the story (1983, 94–95; Berlin translates the word as "at that point"). Robert Kawashima argues that this use of *wĕhinnēh* represents the perception of the harvesters since, unlike Ruth, they would know Boaz's name and possibly that he was arriving from Bethlehem. Kawashima compares it to *wĕhinnēh* in 1 Sam 11:5 where it introduces Saul's arrival (*bw'*) from the field, which Kawashima argues reflects the perception of "the people" (120–22). For Kawashima, this use of *wĕhinnēh* serves as an example of "represented consciousness," a concept related to free indirect discourse in which a narrator refracts a scene from a character's viewpoint without explicitly marking it as the character's viewpoint (consult Sternberg, 52–53; for objections, consult Miller, 88–89). These interpretations may not be mutually exclusive since a *hinnēh* clause in third-person narration could introduce a new figure into an ongoing scene by refracting this introduction through a character's viewpoint. On another possible literary technique used to represent a servant's consciousness, consult NOTE *this . . . her sitting . . . the house . . . a little* on 2:7 and COMMENTS.

Boaz came. The word translated as "came" could be analyzed as either a perfect ("Boaz came") or a participle ("Boaz was coming"). One finds both options reflected in the versions. As Hubbard notes, "LXX (aorist, *ēlthen*) implies a perfect, the Vulg. (imperfect, *veniebat*) a participle" (143, n. 9). The Targum (Vaticanus Urbinas 1 manuscript) spells it as a perfect (*'ătā'*). Scholars differ on how much time elapses between Ruth's arrival and Boaz's arrival, but this question is irrelevant in regard to the progression of the narrative itself. Boaz's arrival simply represents the next event necessary to move the story forward (consult "Selective Representation and Narrative Ambiguity" in the Introduction).

May YHWH bless you. The language of this verse reflects a formulaic blessing used as a greeting (cf. 2 Kgs 4:29; 10:15). One finds similar blessing formulas used as greetings in Hebrew inscriptions. For example, Arad 16.2–3 and 21.3–4 read *brktk lyhwh* ("I bless you by YHWH," Dobbs-Allsopp et al., 32, 44).

2:5. *To whom does this female servant [belong]?* The word translated as "to whom" (*lĕmî*) can function as a genitive (e.g., Gen 38:25; Exod 32:24; 2 Sam 3:12). The Syr. reads, "What is the good of this young woman?" (Campbell, 93). The Old Latin and a minority of Old Greek manuscripts read, "Who is this young woman?" (Campbell, 93). Reading with MT^L, the question may assume that Ruth is a servant in an unidentified household. The Targum reads, "Of which people ['*ûmmā'*] is this female servant?" In Gen 32:18 (Eng. 32:17), Jacob tells his servant, "If [Esau] asks you, 'To whom [*lĕmî*] do you belong?' . . . Say, 'To your servant Jacob.'" Likewise, in 1 Sam 30:13, David asks an unidentified man, "To whom [*lĕmî*] do you belong and where are you from?" The man responds, "I am an Egyptian, a servant of an Amalekite." Along these lines, the response of Boaz's male servant to this question identifies Ruth's ethnicity (Moabite) and her household status as under the authority of Naomi, but not her name or other personal details (cf. Trible, 261; NOTE *who returned under the authority of Naomi* on

2:6). One could also interpret the question about to whom Ruth belongs as an inquiry about her marital status.

2:6. *The male servant who was set over the harvesters.* The Syr. does not have "who was set over the harvesters." The Vulg. reads "who answered" (*qui respondit*). The Targum and some Old Greek manuscripts support MT^L, although "who was set over the harvesters" does not occur in multiple Old Greek manuscripts.

She is a Moabite female servant. The Targum and Old Latin support MT^L, whereas the Old Greek, supported by the Syr., reads, "the Moabite."

who returned under the authority of Naomi. As indicated by the word's accent mark, MT^L reads *haššābâ* as a perfect rather than a participle. Thus, "(she) returned." Yet, in this case, the article *h* introduces a relative clause (Note *who returned from the territory of Moab* on 1:22). The Targum and Syr. translate the word in the sense of both "to return" and "to convert" (cf. 1:22 [Syr.]; *Ruth Rab.* 4:3; Jerusalem Talmud Yebamot 8:3). For the translation "under her authority," consult Note *under her authority* on 1:7a. Ruth is first granted permission to glean by Naomi (2:2), and she stays with Naomi after the barley and wheat harvests (Note *Then she stayed* on 2:23b). The use of *ʿim* by Boaz's male servant communicates that Ruth not only accompanied Naomi upon her return from Moab, but that Naomi has authority over her.

from the territory of Moab. On the reference to Moab, consult Note *territory of Moab* on 1:1.

2:7. *She said.* My translation interprets the dialogue in 2:7a as a continuation of the male servant's speech. It is possible, however, that the narrator is reporting what Ruth spoke to Boaz directly. This would explain why Boaz responds to her instead of his male servant in 2:8. Yet, this would mean that 2:7b represents the narrator's speech, which seems unlikely because the reference to Ruth standing "until now" would not make sense if spoken by the narrator, who sets the story a minimum of three generations before its narration (4:7, 17). Boaz's response to Ruth rather than his male servant could simply indicate that he either interrupted or ignored his male servant's rambling (Note *this . . . her sitting . . . the house . . . a little* on 2:7).

Let me glean [ears of grain] please and gather [them] into bundles behind the harvesters. The Syr. and Vulg. do not have "and gather [them] into bundles." The other major versions support MT^L. It is difficult to determine whether the readings in the Syr. and Vulg. result from haplography produced by the final *aleph* in *nāʾ* ("please") and the initial *aleph* in *ʾāḥărê* ("behind"). Although this verse does not include the object of the verbs "glean" and "gather," one can assume that it is "ears of grain" on the basis of 2:2 (Note *ears of grain* on 2:2). Moreover, aside from 2:2, the object of the verb "to glean" is implied but not stated elsewhere in Ruth (2:3, 7–8, 15–19, 23; cf. Isa 17:5; Yavneh-Yam inscription, lines 4–5; Bush, 117). Similarly, in 2:9, the implied object of the verb "to draw" is "water," but the word "water" is not included (cf. Gen 24:11; contrast Gen 24:13). One can assume that the verb "gather" shares the same implied object as the verb "glean" because the latter verb is a *wĕqatalti* form that follows a cohortative and thus expresses the consequence of the request, that is, "let me glean . . . and so gather" (cf. Judg 19:13; WO 32.2.2b). As "ears of grain" is the implied object, the preposition *b* in *bāʿŏmārîm* ("into bundles") probably indicates the result of the verb "gather" and not its object (contrast the use of *b* in *baššibbŏlîm* in 2:2). Thus, there is no need to repoint the Hebrew to read *bāʾămirîm*, meaning "stalks of grain" (singular, *ʾāmîr*), so it can serve as an object as in "let me glean the stalks of grain" (contra Joüon, 49–50; for reviews of this and other proposals for repointing or emendation, cf. Bush, 117; Hubbard, 148–49). According to the male servant's report, Ruth presumably requested to glean ears of grain as they were cut off the stalks. Since Ruth asks to do her gleaning and gathering "behind the harvesters," Eskenazi and Frymer-Kensky argue that "Ruth is asking for a place immediately behind the reapers so that she can get the first pickings, rather than trailing behind other gleaners. For this she needs permission" (33). If this interpretation is correct, Ruth's request would go above and beyond any provisions provided by the laws for gleaning in Pentateuchal legislation (cf. Lev 19:9–10; 23:22; Deut 24:19). These laws may not necessarily serve as the basis for her request.

from then, the morning until now. Some Old Greek manuscripts read "until evening" (cf. 2:17), reflecting the Hebrew word *'ereb* rather than *'attâ* ("now"). Yet, most other versions, including multiple Old Greek manuscripts, support MT^L. The Hebrew construction *wĕ'ad-'attâ* ("until now") is not unusual, although other occurrences do not use it with the word translated as "morning" (cf. "from our/my youth until now" in Gen 46:34; Ezek 4:14; and "from the day . . . until now" in Exod 9:18; 2 Kgs 4:6). Moreover, the mention of evening in v. 17 implies that this conversation took place before the evening (Campbell, 95).

this . . . her sitting . . . the house . . . a little. The last four words of v. 7 represent the most difficult syntax and grammar in the book. In fact, Campbell does not even offer a translation of the last half of this verse. After reviewing proposed readings that others offer, he warns, "Let the reader of the Bible, note well, however, that a hundred conjectures about a badly disrupted text are all more likely to be wrong than any one of them absolutely right!" (96). Most of the scholarly discussion focuses on the word translated as "her sitting" (*šibtāh*). On the basis of the spelling in MT^L, one could analyze this word either as an infinitive from *yšb* ("to sit, dwell") with a feminine singular suffix or as a segholate noun from *šbt* ("to cease, rest") with a feminine singular suffix. While the Targum supports MT^L with a form of the Aramaic root *ytb* ("to sit, dwell"), the Vulg. takes the Hebrew *zeh* as a negative and reflects a *qal* perfect feminine singular verb from *šwb*, thus, "she has not returned home." The Old Greek also takes the Hebrew *zeh* ("this") as a negative and reads "she has not rested" (cf. Old Latin without the negative). Along these lines, many scholars repoint the word as *šābĕtāh*, a *qal* perfect feminine singular from *šbt* ("she rested"; cf. Rudolph, 46–47).

Other influential proposals include those of Daniel Lys and Avi Hurvitz. Lys provides an extensive review of proposed readings and argues that *zeh* refers to the field in v. 3 and *šibtāh* derives from *yšb*. Reading against the accents in MT^L, he divides the last four Hebrew words as two parallels lines, which allows for the translation, "This (field) would be her residence/the house means little to her." (For other reviews of proposed readings, consult Hubbard, 147–52; Moore, 1993, 238–42. With modifications, both scholars follow Lys, although Hubbard provides past tense verbs, and Moore interprets *šibtāh* as a wordplay invoking the roots *yšb*, *šwb*, and *šbt*.) Hurvitz's proposal explains MT^L as it is without the need for a different lineation or an emendation. Taking *šibtāh* from *yšb*, he interprets the syntax as an attempt to convey the hesitant and inarticulate speech of a nervous servant addressing his superior (1983, 122–23; cf. 1 Sam 9:12–13; Mesad Hashavyahu inscription, lines 2–3; Carasik; Rendsburg, 1999b, 3–4). As is common in everyday speech, the clause starts one way, pauses, and ends another way, as if the servant begins to explain Ruth's presence but ends up trailing off (for further discussion, consult COMMENTS on 2:3–17). Elsewhere in Ruth, unusual syntax depicts a character's speech in a similar manner (NOTE *May YHWH give to you . . . [Oh, forget it!]* on 1:9). The concern over whether Ruth is allowed into the "house" in this verse may be interpreted as anticipating whether she will be accepted into Boaz's household (cf. 4:11).

2:8. *Haven't you heard?* The Syr. uses this clause to begin a proverb. It reads, "Haven't you heard what the proverb says, 'Do not glean in a field that is not yours.'" Old Greek supports MT^L. Possibly influenced by the Hebrew's use of "field" in references to the territory of Moab elsewhere in the book (cf. NOTE *territory of Moab* on 1:1), the Targum supports MT^L but interprets Boaz's command not to leave as meaning not to go to "another people" (*lĕ'ummā' 'āḥārîtî*).

in fact . . . so that. The adverbs *gam* ("in fact") and *kōh* ("so that") introduce the respective clauses "you should not leave this one" and "you may stick with" as emphatically building on and specifying the intention of the first clause in the verse (Holmstedt, 118–19). Not only should Ruth avoid gleaning in other fields, but, more specifically, she should stay in Boaz's field.

leave. The spelling in MT^L of the verb translated as "leave" (*ta'ăbûrî*) is unusual because one would expect *ta'ăbĕrî*. The spelling would be unusual even if it were analyzed as a pausal form, which is typically not indicated by a *wāw* (but cf. Exod 18:26; Prov 14:3; *GKC* §47g). Nonetheless, the meaning of the verb is clear regardless of the unusual spelling. The other versions did not have difficulty understanding the meaning of the verb. Scholars have cited the full or plene spelling with the *wāw* as evidence for the date of the book (NOTE *ruled* on 1:1).

stick with. As with Bush's translation ("stick close to," 107), my translation uses an idiom for staying close to or partnering with another party to translate *tidbāqîn 'im* (also 2:21, 23), although I have translated the third-person feminine singular form of *dbq* where the object of the verb has a *b*-prefix (*dābaqâ bāh*) as "clung" (1:14). The word *tidbāqîn* is spelled with a paragogic, or "word-extending," *nûn* (on the paragogic *nûn*, consult *GKC* §47o; WO 31.7.1). Some scholars (e.g., Myers, 17–20; Campbell, 25; Hubbard, 156) claim that the paragogic *nûn* is a genuine archaic feature (cf. 2:8, 9 [two times], 21; 3:4, 18). Yet, it occurs in many biblical texts that reflect a wide variety of dates. Its wide distribution throughout the Hebrew Bible should caution one against using this feature to date Ruth's composition as either early or later (Sasson, 245; Holmstedt, 23). Moreover, in Ruth, this possibly archaized linguistic feature occurs in speech by only Boaz and Naomi (2:8, 9 [two times]; 3:4, 18) or Ruth's (mis)quotation of Boaz's words (2:21). Thus, Humbert argues that it helps to characterize their speech patterns as sounding elderly (92), although Naomi is not necessarily depicted as more than fifteen to twenty years older than Ruth if, in keeping with cultural customs in ancient Israel, one imagines Naomi as relatively young when she was married (Exum, 146–50). Lim notes that extant Moabite texts use a final *nûn* on masculine nouns and adjectives. Thus, when Boaz uses the paragogic *nûn* in reference to his female servants (2:9), Ruth the Moabite may think he is referring to male servants since she uses a masculine ending in reference to the servants when she (mis)quotes Boaz's words to Naomi (Lim,

108). For Lim, this confusion on Ruth's part helps to characterize her as a foreigner. In short, one could analyze the paragogic *nûn* as evidence of characterization rather than a date of composition.

2:9. *Your eyes should be on the field.* One could translate MT^L woodenly, supported by the Old Greek, as "your eyes on the field." The Targum includes a jussive verb, which makes explicit what is implied in MT^L.

harvest . . . draw. MT^L spells both of these verbs with a paragogic *nûn* (consult NOTE *stick with* on 2:8).

go after them. Whereas the pronoun "they" in the clause "that they harvest" reflects a masculine plural form that could refer to both the male and female servants inclusively, the word translated as "after them" has a feminine plural suffix. Thus, it specifically refers to the female servants that Boaz instructed Ruth to "stick with" in v. 8. MT^L misspells the verb translated as "go" with a *hîreq* under the *tāw* instead of a *šěwă'*. MT^A spells it correctly.

Haven't I instructed. Rather than an interrogative, LXX^{BL} introduce this clause with *idou* ("Look!" or "Behold") as in "Look! I have instructed." MT^L reads *hălô'* (Haven't . . . ?). Other Old Greek manuscripts support MT^L and translate *hălô'* in 2:8 and *hălô'* in 3:1 as interrogatives.

So, if you become thirsty. The *wāw* in *wěṣāmit* ("so, if you become thirsty") is an apodosis *wāw* in that it serves to introduce a consequential clause in a *wěqatalti* construction (cf. Gen 44:4; 1 Kgs 20:36; JM §166b). My translation includes the word "so" to indicate that Ruth's ability to drink water is dependent on Boaz's instruction to his male servants not to abuse her. As in 1:14, the verb form *wěṣāmit* from *ṣm'* is not spelled with the *aleph* because quiescent *alephs* may be omitted in verb conjugations of III-*aleph* roots.

vessels. The Old Latin, Vulg., and Syr. do not have "vessels." The Old Greek and Targum support MT^L.

from whatever [water] the male servants may draw. My translation adds "water" in brackets to indicate the implied but unstated object of the verb "draw" (NOTE *let me glean [ears of grain] please and gather [them] into bundles* on 2:7). The Targum and Syr. include the object "water" explicitly.

2:10. *although I am.* The *wāw* in *wě'ānōkî* introduces a nominal clause that follows a verbal clause. In this construction the nominal clause may present a fact that seems to contradict the expectations of the previous verbal clause (cf. Gen 18:27; 48:14). In such cases, one may translate the *wāw* as "although" (*GKC* §141e). MT^L misspells the pronoun as *wě''ānōkî*. MT^A spells it correctly. On the use of *'ānōkî*, consult NOTE *I left* on 1:21.

a foreign woman. Ruth self-identifies as a "foreign woman" (*nākriyyâ*) rather than a "resident alien" (NOTE *reside as an alien* on 1:1). The latter identification would align her with one of the parties addressed by the laws for gleaning in various Pentateuchal sources, such as the poor, alien, widowed, or orphaned (Lev 19:9–10; 23:22; Deut 24:19). Some scholars argue that Ruth assumes that such laws apply to her on the basis of her request in 2:2. Yet, unlike resident aliens, none of the legal texts in the Pentateuch extends special privileges to male or female foreigners. Her identification as a foreign woman rather than a resident alien may have several implications. Many scholars note the wordplay, assonance, and rhyme in her words *lĕhakkîrēnî wĕ'ānōkî nākriyyâ* ("you have paid attention [from *nkr*] to me although I am a foreign woman"). The wordplay and assonance would not work as well if she did not refer to herself as a foreigner. Also, while the term occurs once in Ruth, elsewhere it can describe a woman of a different, non-Israelite ethnicity (1 Kgs 11:1, 8; Ezra 10:2, 10–11, 14, 17–18, 44; Neh 13:26–27). This use would fit with the male servant's identification of Ruth as a "Moabite" (cf. 1 Kgs 11:1; Neh 13:26). Yet, in Proverbs, the term refers to a woman who is under the authority of another man, be it a husband or father (Prov 2:16; 5:20; 6:24; 7:5; 23:27). In this case, the woman is not necessarily a non-Israelite but could simply be the wife of another man (thus, the NRSV's translation of *nākriyyâ* as "adulteress" in the above references from Proverbs). This sense of the term would also fit if Ruth interprets Boaz's question "To whom does this female servant belong?" in 2:5 as an inquiry into her marital status or into her current household affiliation. Rather than identifying as a Moabite, which she herself never does anywhere else in the book, Ruth may be identifying herself as another man's wife or as part of another household or clan. (At this point in the story, there is very little evidence that she would know of Boaz's relation to Elimelech [cf. 2:20]). If Ruth is identifying herself as a member of Elimelech's household by marriage (NOTE *Your people, my people / Your ancestors, my ancestors* on 1:16), she may not necessarily identify as a resident alien or assume that any legal provisions for the resident alien, if she is even aware of them, apply to her. This may explain why Boaz mentions that he knows about her deceased husband when he replies to her in 2:11. At the same time, Boaz's reference to the fact that Ruth left the land of her birth and traveled to a people she "did not know previously" may suggest that he identifies her as an ethnic foreigner. Ultimately, the use of *nākriyyâ* conveys the multiple nuances and complications of her status within the Bethlehem community that terms such as "resident alien" or even "Moabite" would not capture.

2:11. *all that you did for your mother-in-law.* This clause uses the preposition *'et* ("for") with a verb form from *'śr* ("did"). In 1:8 and 2:19, the preposition *'im* ("with") occurs with a verb form from *'śr* ("did"). As Campbell notes, various Old Greek witnesses indicate "confusion in rendering an ambiguous situation in the Hebrew, some manuscripts using the dative, some *meta* with genitive, 'along with,' and one *meta* with the accusative, 'after, next after'" (86 [italics in original]). Nevertheless, as with the verb forms of *'śr* in 1:8; 2:11, 19, the book of Ruth varies the use of prepositions with other verbs (e.g., the preposition *b* [1:14; 2:23] and the preposition *'im* [2:8, 21] with verb forms from *dbq* ["to cling, stick with"]). The use of the preposition *'et* in this verse may reflect variation for stylistic reasons rather than a textual difficulty (Holmstedt, 48–49, 127; Rendsburg, 2013).

namely, how you abandoned. The *wāw* in *watta'azbî* has "explanatory value" (JM §118j; Joüon, 55), as in Judg 11:30; 1 Sam 8:8; 1 Kgs 18:13; 21:4. Along these lines, the Old Greek translates the Hebrew *wāw* as *pōs* ("how").

your father. MT^L misspells "your father" as *"ābîk*. MT^A spells it correctly as *'ābîk*.

previously. The idiom *tĕmôl šilšôm* ("previously") could be translated woodenly as "yesterday and three days ago." The word *šilšôm* ("three days") functions as an adverb that probably derives from "a composite form from **šāliš* third, and from **yōm/yām* day; the same as Akk. *šalšūmi*" (*HALOT* 2:1545 [italics in original]). Yet, rather than a reference to a particular number of days, this idiom usually simply refers to a previous event or situation (Gen 31:2, 5; Exod 5:7, 8; 21:29, 36; Deut 4:42; 19:4, 6; Josh 3:4; 4:18; 20:5; 1 Sam 21:6 [Eng. 21:5]; 2 Sam 3:17; 2 Kgs 13:5; 1 Chr 11:2).

2:12. *May YHWH compensate your deed.* The language of this verse reflects a formulaic blessing similar to the longer blessing in 2 Sam 3:39b (NOTE *May YHWH do* on 1:8 and COMMENTS). A very similar blessing occurs in a Hebrew inscription. Arad 21.4 reads *yšlm yhwh l'dn[y]* ("May YHWH compensate my lord"; Dobbs-Allsopp et al., 44). The LXX^L (*soi*), Vulg. (*tibi*), and Targum (*lîk*) read "compensate to you." MT^L reads "compensate your deed." Other Old Greek manuscripts support MT^L. The Syr. and Targum translate this blessing rather freely.

from YHWH. The word "from" translates the compound preposition *mē'im*, which reflects the prepositions "from with" (*min 'im*). The Targum renders this compound preposition as "from before" (*min qādam*). The Old Greek reads "from" (*para* as a genitive). When used with YHWH, the compound preposition *mē'im* often means "from" in the sense of something being provided by YHWH (1 Kgs 2:33; Isa 7:11; 8:18; 28:29; Ps 121:2).

2:13. *I must have found favor . . . speak to the heart of your maidservant.* Variations of the same idiom occur in 2:2, 10. The Old Greek reads the verb as an optative aorist active form ("May I"). One could translate the *yiqtol* form *'emṣā'* as an indicative or a modal. Ziba uses a nearly identical expression after David grants him all of Mephibosheth's land (2 Sam 16:4). Since in both situations Ruth and Ziba use this expression after Boaz and David have already shown favor toward them, respectively, these two texts reflect "epistemic modality," in which "speakers express their judgments about the factual status of a proposition" (Callaham, 2010, 22). Although the use of *kî* ("because") introduces the following two clauses as providing the evidence to support Ruth's judgment (cf. 1:12, 13, 16b, 20), Ruth makes her judgment through a deduction based on Boaz's words just as Ziba makes his judgment through a deduction based on David's words. Unlike Ruth, Ziba does not state the evidence for his deduction.

maidservant. Ruth refers to herself as *šipḥātēk* ("your maidservant" serves as an approximate translation). Joüon and Sasson argue that the term may refer to a woman of low social status (Joüon, 57) who may be expected to perform menial labor such as fieldwork (Sasson, 53–54; cf. vv 15–16). Later, in a more intimate setting, Ruth refers to herself as a "handmaid" (*'āmāh;* NOTE *handmaid* on 3:9). Yet, even though only *'āmāh* is used in conjugal contexts outside of Genesis, it is unclear whether Ruth uses these two terms in technically distinct fashions because they are used interchangeably in contexts similar to that in 2 13 (e.g., 1 Sam 25:27–28; cf. Bridge). Together with the use of the pronoun *'ānōkî* ("I"), the term *šipḥātēk* may simply reflect a polite form of address since "your maidservant" occurs elsewhere in biblical prose when a woman makes a request of a man in a position of authority under the circumstances (1 Sam 1:18; 25:27; 28:21, 22; 2 Sam 14:7, 12, 14, 17, 19). Moreover, Ruth's use of *šipḥāh* creates assonance and rhyme with the narrator's use of *mišpāḥâ* ("clan") in vv. 1, 3 (NOTE *clan* on 2:1; "The Diction of the Hebrew in Ruth" in the Introduction; Campbell, 101). Although Ruth claims that she is not Boaz's *šipḥâ*, she will later discover that she is part of his *mišpāḥâ* (2:20).

I am not like one of your maidservants. While the Vulg. and Targum support MT^L, the Old Greek, Syr., and Old Latin do not reflect the negative particle. In these versions, Ruth states her intention to become one of Boaz's maidservants or her current status as one of his maidservants. One may account for the reading in the Old Greek, Syr., and Old Latin if the negative particle (*lōʾ*) were read as an asseverative (*lû*): "Surely, I am like" (Campbell, 101; on the asseverative *lamed*, consult WO 11.2.10i). This proposal, however, has not gained widespread acceptance among other scholars (cf. Bush, 125; Rudolph, 47; Sasson, 54), and MT^L makes sense as it is.

2:14. *to her.* One expects a *mappiq* in the *h* of the first *lāh* ("to her") in the verse, as in *loh* following *wayyiṣĕbbaṭ* ("heaped together") later in the verse as well as in 2:2, 11, 16, 18–20; 3:1, 16; 4:13. Yet, one finds *lāh* without a *mappiq* in Num 32:42 and Zech 5:11 (Campbell, 87).

at the time of the meal. My translation interprets this clause as part of the narrator's discourse rather than as the beginning of the direct discourse attributed to Boaz. The LXX^L, Targum, Vulg., and Syr. support this interpretation of the syntax in MT^L. Other Old Greek witnesses, however, read the clause as the beginning of Boaz's dialogue: "Boaz said to her, 'Now it is time to eat'" (cf. Old Latin). My reading agrees with most of the versions, but the accents and syntax of MT^L also allow for the latter interpretation (cf. Holmstedt, 132–33).

Come. MT^L spells this word as *gōšî*, which is difficult to explain because, although the word seems to be an imperative from *ngš* ("to approach, draw near"), it is spelled as if it comes from *gwš*, as with the imperative form of *bwʾ* (Joüon, 58). Yet, the imperative form of *ngš* is spelled in a similar manner (*gōšû*) in Josh 3:9; 1 Sam 14:38; 2 Chr 29:31 (Myers, 18), which differs from the expected form *gĕšû* (cf. Gen 45:4; 1 Kgs 18:30). Nonetheless, despite the unexpected spelling, the other versions did not have difficulty translating this word as if it derives from *ngš*.

the food. LXX^L reads "my bread" and the Old Latin reads "your bread." Other Old Greek witnesses, the Targum, Vulg., and Syr. support MT^L.

vinegar. The Syr. reads "milk." My translation follows the traditional English translation in the KJV. Yet, this is an approximate translation for some type of liquid associated with some unpleasant beverage (Ps 68:22) or with alcohol, thus the NRSV translation "sour wine" (cf. Judg 6:3). The Old Greek uses the same word in reference to a liquid that aggravates a wound (Prov 25:20).

heaped together. The verb translated as "heaped together" (*wayyiṣbbaṭ*) is a hapax legomenon whose precise meaning remains uncertain, although 2QRuth^a supports MT^L. The verb creates alliteration with the noun *haṣṣĕbātîm* ("the heaps") in 2:16, which is also a hapax legomenon (consult "The Diction of the Hebrew in Ruth" in the Introduction). The Targum translates it with a verb meaning "to stretch out, extend" (*yšṭ*; cf. 4:7, 8 Targum; cf. Syr., Old Latin). The Old Greek reads "to heap up" (cf. 2:16). This Greek neologism possibly takes the word from the Hebrew *ṣbr* ("to heap up" used in reference to a great quantity of food or grain in Gen 41:35, 49) or, assuming an interchange of the letters *ṭ* and *t*, represents an otherwise unattested verb form of the noun *ṣebet* ("bundle, heap"; a hapax legomenon in 2:16). Along these lines, Sasson argues that the Hebrew roots *ṣbṭ* in v. 14 and *ṣbt* in v. 16 are alternative spellings of the root attested in Akkadian *ṣabātu* ("to seize"; 55–56). The Vulg. reads "she heaped up barley for herself." Campbell relates the Hebrew word to the Ugaritic noun *mṣbṭm*, possibly meaning "tongs" (102).

For a review of other scholarly proposals, including evidence from later Aramaic and Arabic words, consult Hubbard, 174. Although the specifics of Boaz's action remain vague, my tentative translation of the verb communicates the point that he provided Ruth with food.

and left over [some of the parched grain]. The Old Latin does not have the verb "and left over" (*wattōtar*), whereas according to the Vulg., Ruth "took away" the leftover portion. Talia Sutskover argues for a play on words between the root of *wattōtar* (*ytr*) and the consonants in the personal name Ruth (*rwt*) so that "a connection is indirectly created between Ruth and the idea of being satisfied" (294; cf. the anagram *bʿz* [Boaz] and *ʿzb* ["abandon"] in 2:20). Yet, this connection is more likely made through a play on the etymology of the name Ruth as "refreshment" and the previous verb "she [Ruth] was satisfied" (*wattiśbaʿ*; cf. 2:18; NOTE *Ruth* on 1:4).

2:15. *servants.* The word translated as "servants" is a masculine form that I translate elsewhere as "male servant(s)." Yet, as with the plural pronoun "they" in "they harvest" (2:9), the word could refer to both the male and the female servants inclusively (NOTE *go after them* on 2:9).

Even among the bundles she may glean. Do not humiliate her! The particle *gam* ("even") emphasizes the special access to the bundled grain that Boaz grants Ruth (cf. the use of *gam* in 2:16 ["in fact"]; NOTE *in fact . . . so that* on 2:8). The Vulg. reads "even if she wants to reap with you, do not prevent her," but this reading is not supported by other versions. As Campbell notes, the Vulg. may clarify an interpretation assumed by MT^L (103; contra Joüon, 60). Although the specifics of Boaz's instructions remain unclear, they go above and beyond both what Ruth had requested according to the male servant in 2:7 and any provisions provided by the laws for gleaning in various Pentateuchal sources. This becomes clear as his instructions continue in v. 16 (consult COMMENTS and NOTES *after anyone in whose eyes I may find favor* on 2:2, *let me glean [ears of grain] please and gather [them] into bundles behind the harvesters* on 2:7, and *a foreign woman* on 2:10).

2:16. *In fact, you should even pull out.* The particle followed by the infinite construct and a *yiqtol* from *šll* (*wĕgam šōl tāšōllû*, "even pull out"; [*wgm šl*] *tšl*[*w*], 2QRuth^a) is difficult to translate because elsewhere the root usually means "to plunder," whereas in this verse alone, the context suggests "to pull out." The Targum translates this construction with forms of the Aramaic root *ntr* ("to shed, fall off, make drop"). The Syr. omits v. 16, possibly triggered by Boaz's repeated use of the particle *gam* ("even" in 2:15; "in fact" in 2:16) or, as some scholars suggest, the assumption of the instruction's repetition (Campbell, 103; Hubbard, 171, n. 6). LXX^B woodenly translates both the infinite construct followed by the *yiqtol* and then repeats this construction with a second verb after translating the particle *gam,* resulting in the reading "Lifting up, lift up for her; and indeed throwing out, throw out to her" (translation of LXX^B by Hubbard, 171, n. 6). LXX^L reads "you shall heap up." Some scholars cite an Arabic cognate used for drawing a sword (Bush, 126; Campbell, 104).

some of the heaps. The verb "pull out" does not have an object in MT^L. Whereas many commentators assume an implied object such as "ears of grain" (NOTE *let me glean [ears of grain] please and gather [them] into bundles behind the harvesters* on 2:7), it is easier to explain the clause as it is by reading the *min* as a partitive ("some of";

Joüon, 61; cf. Vulg.). This means that Boaz instructs the servants to leave entire heaps of grain rather than merely some of the ears of grain from the heaps. Bush objects that this interpretation "surely stretches kindness to the point of incredibility" (127), but this objection misses the point that Boaz's actions toward Ruth in this passage are depicted in hyperbolic terms. (What motivates his actions, however, can be debated, as discussed in the COMMENTS on 2:3–17.) Moreover, since the syntax makes sense as it is, there is no need to supply an object for the verb and then explain the practice by appeals to later but supposedly analogous so-called Arab practices, as some scholars do (Humbert, 206–7; followed by Bush, 126–27; Hubbard, 177, among others). The word translated as "the heaps" (*haṣṣĕbātîm*) is a hapax legomenon whose precise meaning remains uncertain. It must be reconstructed in 2QRuth^a. Assuming an interchange of the letters *ṭ* and *t*, the noun may be related to the verb form of *ṣbṭ* (2:14), which possibly means "to heap together" (although that verb is also a hapax legomenon). The Old Greek uses verb and noun forms of the same neologism respectively to translate the two words in 2:14, 16, which suggests something related to heaps (NOTE *heaped together* on 2:14). Regardless of its precise meaning, the noun creates alliteration with the verb *wayyiṣbbaṭ* in 2:14, which is in keeping with Ruth's narrative style (consult "The Diction of the Hebrew in Ruth" in the Introduction).

and abandon [them]. LXX^B reads "and she shall eat." Some LXX^L manuscripts conflate this reading to produce "and leave it and she shall eat it" (Campbell, 87).

2:17. *she beat out.* Forms of the root *ḥbṭ* ("to beat out") occur exclusively in contexts of agricultural production (Deut 24:20; Judg 6:11; Isa 27:12 [metaphorically]; 28:27). Here, it refers to the threshing of grain.

about an ephah. An ephah is a unit of measurement. Old Greek witnesses transliterate this word in a variety of ways. Unlike other versions, including the Vulg., the Old Latin does not account for this word. On the basis of various methods of calculation, scholars have estimated that an ephah would be the equivalent of nearly six gallons, or nearly thirty pounds by U.S. measurement. Others have estimated it as high as just over thirty-six liters, or nearly fifty pounds. For a review of opinions, consult Campbell, 104; Hubbard, 179. Regarding attempts to arrive at an absolute measurement, Campbell cautions rightly, "the base of calculation is not certain . . . we do not know what variations developed throughout the biblical period" (104). Nonetheless, a relative measurement conveys the point that Ruth gleaned an abundance of grain that day. As Sasson notes, the ration for a male worker at Mari was rarely more than two pounds per day, and in 1 Sam 17:17, David delivers one ephah of parched grain and ten loaves for his three brothers to share. If these comparisons are relevant, Ruth had enough grain to sustain herself and Naomi for quite some time (Sasson, 57). Although the precise unit of measurement remains uncertain, the term "ephah" (*'êpāh*) creates alliteration with the word "where" (*'êpoh*) in 2:19 (Campbell, 105; "The Diction of the Hebrew in Ruth" in the Introduction). Following Talmon's discussion of the use of the preposition *k* in the Yavneh-Yam inscription, Bush argues that *kĕ'êpāh* indicates "exactly an ephah" rather than "about an ephah" (NOTE *according to all that her mother-in-law had instructed* on 3:6). He writes, "the point of the passage is to stress the extremely large amount of grain that Ruth threshed from her gleanings" (133). Yet, even if one uses a conservative estimate for how much an ephah was, this point would be obvious regardless of whether Ruth threshed nearly an ephah or exactly an ephah. There is no reason to argue for an obscure use of the preposition *k* when a much more common use (*k* as "about, roughly"), which occurs elsewhere in Ruth (cf. 1:4), conveys the same point.

Comments

By chance, Ruth gleans in Boaz's field. Although generally all events were thought to be controlled by divine forces in the ancient Near East, the text does not provide evidence that this chance event indicates specifically YHWH's providence. Rather, the word "chance" creates alliteration with 4:3, which is in keeping with the use of alliteration throughout Ruth (NOTE *she chanced upon* on 2:3; "Divine Activity and Acts of *ḥesed* in Ruth" in the Introduction). Although the narrator does not specify how Boaz is related to Elimelech, that both men already hold a portion of the clan's field (2:3; 4:3) suggests that Boaz would not be obligated to serve as a levirate for Elimelech's widow even if he were Elimelech's brother. The situation described in Genesis 38 or Deut 25:5–10 assumes that the brothers are still living together and that the inherited field of their father's household has not yet been divided among them, presumably because their father is still alive when one of his sons dies (Westbrook, 118–41). In fact, Gen 38:4–10 make it clear that Judah is still alive when his sons die. If, however, Boaz and Elimelech already hold a portion of the inherited field and are not living together on the same portion, the levirate marriage custom as described in those texts would not apply to Boaz. He would not have been obligated to serve as a levirate even if he were Elimelech's brother because the estate already would have been divided between them. Furthermore, although Elimelech's land was not divided among his sons after his death because they were living together in Moab rather than on the inherited field in Bethlehem, Boaz would not be obligated to serve as a levirate to Elimelech's sons since Boaz is not Elimelech's son (4:21; 1 Chr 2:11) and he was not living together with them on Elimelech's portion of the field. Although Boaz's expected kinship obligations may include land redemption, serving as a levirate would be voluntary rather than mandatory. In a sense, although other differences exist, the voluntary nature of marrying the wife of a dead kinsman in Ruth (4:5–6) is in keeping with the Deuteronomic version (Deut 25:7–8; cf. Weisberg, 27).

In v. 4, Boaz arrives from Bethlehem, which would be walking distance from the field if one assumes common physical layouts for Israelite villages (3:15; Borowski, 14; Meyers, 2013, 107). Upon his arrival, he greets the harvesters with a blessing (NOTE *May YHWH bless you* on 2:4) and he inquires about Ruth. The narrator does not indicate why he notices her, although speculation has ranged from divine to sexual motivation (consult "Sexual Desire in Ruth" in the Introduction). His question identifies her is a member of an unidentified household. Rather than assuming that she is a woman bereft of support under the patriarchal household system (an *'almānâ*; consult "Household and Clan Statuses of Ruth's Characters" in the Introduction), his question assumes that she is under the authority of more senior members within her household (NOTE *to whom does this female servant [belong]?* on 2:5).

Boaz's servant identifies Ruth as a Moabite and as member of Naomi's household. The servant's use of the preposition *'im* communicates that Ruth not only accompanied Naomi upon her return from Moab, but that Naomi has authority over her (cf. 1:22).

Unlike the narrator in 1:22, however, the servant does not identify Ruth as Naomi's daughter-in-law but leaves the precise nature of her relationship to Naomi undefined. For all the servant knows, as a Moabite under Naomi's authority, Ruth could simply be a foreign maidservant or handmaiden within Naomi's household (2:13; 3:9; cf. Lev 25:44). Nevertheless, Boaz is aware of Ruth's status within Naomi's household (2:11).

Regarding 2:7, there is no previous record of the request that the servant claims Ruth made. This may result from the narrator's selective representation (consult "Selective Representation and Narrative Ambiguity" in the Introduction), or it could suggest that the servant is lying and that Ruth never spoke to him (for similar cases, consult 2:8, 11; 3:17). He could be lying to explain why Ruth is not just gleaning, but gleaning directly behind the harvesters, which would go above and beyond any of the Pentateuchal gleaning laws (NOTE *let me glean [ears of grain] and gather [them] into bundles behind the harvesters* on 2:7). If Ruth acted without authorization, it might reflect poorly on the servant's management of the harvest of Boaz's field. While this interpretation is not prohibited or mandated by the text, it could nonetheless account for the difficult syntax of v. 7b as his response deteriorates into a string of nonsensical jabbering until he simply drops his story altogether, possibly because Ruth could contest his version of the events. She may be within earshot since Boaz addresses her directly in v. 8 rather than responding to his servant's babbling (cf. Naomi's difficult syntax when she aborts her blessing in 1:9).

In 2:8, Boaz refers to Ruth as "my daughter," which would be an appropriate term for an unmarried female member of a household (consult "Household and Clan Statuses of Ruth's Characters" in the Introduction). This may indicate that he knows something about her current status, as he claims in 2:11. He instructs her to stay in his field with his female servants. He also claims to have told his male servants not to assault her, which acknowledges that Ruth is not only economically vulnerable, but also vulnerable in terms of her physical safety (NOTE *attack* on 2:22). Yet, there is no record of any instructions to his servants regarding her until 2:15. This may result once again from the narrator's selective representation, or it could indicate that Boaz is telling Ruth what he thinks she wants to hear even if it is not quite true.

Ruth's response shows an awareness of the difference in status between her and Boaz. The narrator describes her as falling on her face and bowing to the ground (2:10). Although this gesture is not limited to such gendered situations, descriptions of it occur elsewhere in biblical prose when a woman makes a request of a man in a position of authority over her (1 Sam 25:23, 41; 2 Sam 14:4; 1 Kgs 1:16, 31; 2 Kgs 4:37). In her verbal response to Boaz, Ruth uses a common biblical idiom employed in similar circumstances (NOTE *after anyone in whose eyes I may find favor* on 2:2). Moreover, in 2:13, Ruth refers to herself as "your maidservant" (*šipḥāh*). Elsewhere, women sometimes refer to themselves as maidservants when making a request of a man in a position of authority relative to their relationship (NOTE *maidservant* on 2:13).

Ruth's verbal response emphasizes further that her ability to glean depends on Boaz's favor rather than on any legal obligation. She concludes that she "must have found favor in the eyes of my lord" (2:13). In 2 Sam 16:4, Ziba uses almost an identical phrase in reaction to David's decision to grant him all that belonged to Mephibosheth. David's ruling is not based on legal precedent but on his royal prerogative considering his position within the structure of the royal household. In both cases, Ruth and Ziba perform obeisance (cf. Ruth 2:10) and use very similar language to acknowledge that Boaz and David show them favor unrelated to any legal obligation. Furthermore, Ruth self-identifies as a foreign woman (as well as a maidservant) rather than as an alien resident or one of the other parties with gleaning privileges under various Pentateuchal legislation. She consistently assumes that Boaz's instructions result from his favor rather than from his legal obligation (2:10, 13; cf. 2:2). In fact, in 2:13, she distinguishes herself from the rest of Boaz's maidservants, who would presumably be dependents within Boaz's household and thus fall under his authority and guardianship according to the clan structure (e.g., Gen 24:35; 29:24, 29).

It remains unclear whether Ruth's response to Boaz assumes legal overtones. For example, one does not need to assume that her use of "foreign woman" or "maidservant" reflects technical legal terminology, since both terms create alliteration and rhyme within their present context (NOTES *a foreign woman* on 2:10, and *maidservant* on 2:13). Even if Ruth knew of the relevant Pentateuchal laws, there is no reason to assume that she believes she would find protection under these laws, considering her status as a minority in Bethlehem and the fact that none of Naomi's relatives had come forward to serve as a kindred redeemer at this point in the story. In fact, in v. 11, Boaz states that he has received a full report about everything Ruth has done for Naomi. This implies that he knows that his relative Naomi does not have a provider but he has yet to act as a redeemer for her (COMMENTS on 1:7b–22a, 1:22b–2:2). Later, he explains that Naomi has a closer relative (3:12), although Naomi assumes that Boaz is one of potentially several relatives eligible to serve as a redeemer (2:20b).

Moreover, in 2:12, Boaz uses a blessing formula that involves the language of wage payment (*maśkōret*). Elsewhere, this language is used in reference to the earnings of a relative residing as an alien and working under the authority of a wealthier, more senior member of the clan (e.g., Jacob's work for Laban; Gen 29:15; 31:7, 41). Yet, Boaz does not use the term with reference to how he will support Ruth. Instead, he uses it to describe how YHWH may provide for her. This divine payment may be a reference to future children (cf. Jer 31:16–17; Ps 127:3; Novick, 713), but at this point, Boaz does not indicate that he intends to be the one who will have children with her. His emphasis on all that Ruth has done for Naomi creates a striking contrast with his own lack of action on her behalf to this point in the story. While Boaz claims that Ruth is seeking refuge under YHWH's skirts, Ruth will use the image of skirts when requesting that Boaz serve as a kindred redeemer (Ruth 3:9). At this point, it remains unclear whether Boaz's favor toward Ruth would extend beyond the harvest seasons since it is not done to fulfill a legal obligation. Boaz's provisions of food and safe working conditions for Ruth during the harvest notwithstanding (2:15–16), her request in the next chapter may imply that Boaz has yet to fulfill his role as a kindred redeemer before her direct request in 3:9.

This does not mean that Boaz is not ostensibly generous toward Ruth. He provides food and drink for her until she is satisfied (v. 14) and gives instructions to his male servants to abandon some of the barley, which ensures that her gleaning will be successful (v. 16). One could read the inclusion of these details as emphasizing Boaz's kindness. Their inclusion, however, creates wordplays with the names of both Ruth and Boaz (NOTES *Ruth* on 1:4, and *Boaz* on 2:1). Also, alliteration occurs when the narrator details the results of Ruth's gleaning (NOTE *about an ephah* on 2:17; "The Diction of the Hebrew in Ruth" in the Introduction). In other words, one could interpret the inclusion of details of Boaz's provisions for Ruth and the large amount of grain that she gleans as a result as evidence either of his generosity or of a literary style that revels in alliteration and wordplay unrelated to any implicit comment on Boaz's character one way or the other. As these interpretive options are not mutually exclusive, it is up to readers' discretion as to how they use this textual evidence for understanding Boaz and Ruth's relationship. Nonetheless, if Boaz shows generosity toward Ruth independent of any legal mandate, questions regarding how or whether he will serve as a kindred redeemer will continue as the story unfolds.

Ruth and Naomi's Conversation (2:18–23)

2 ¹⁸She carried [the grain] and entered the city. Her mother-in-law saw what she had gleaned. She brought out [the grain] and gave to her what she had left over because of her fullness. ¹⁹Her mother-in-law said to her, "Where did you glean today and where did you work? May the one who paid attention to you be blessed." She told her mother-in-law under whose authority she worked. She said, "The name of the man under whose authority I worked today is Boaz." ²⁰Naomi said to her daughter-in-law, "Blessed is he to YHWH, who has not abandoned his kindness with the living and with the dead." Naomi said to her, "The man is close to us. He is one of our kindred redeemers." ²¹Ruth the Moabite said, "Also, he even said to me, 'Stick with my servants until they finish my entire harvest.'" ²²Naomi said to Ruth her daughter-in-law, "It is better my daughter that you go out with his female servants so they will not attack you in another field." ²³So she stuck with Boaz's female servants to glean until the barley harvest and wheat harvest were finished. Then she stayed with her mother-in-law.

Notes

2:18. *carried [the grain].* The implied object of the verb is grain, probably the threshed barley mentioned in 2:17 rather than the parched grain mentioned in v. 14. Verb forms from *nś'* ("to carry, lift up") occur elsewhere with various implied objects (2 Sam 23:16; 2 Kgs 5:23–24; 7:8; 9:25, 26; Ezek 10:7), including parched grain (1 Sam 17:20).

Her mother-in-law saw. MT^L, supported by the Old Greek and Targum, spell the verb as a *qal wayyiqtol* form from *r'h* (*wattēre'*, "she [her mother-in-law] saw"). Two Kennicott manuscripts (18 and 109; cf. *BHQ*, 53–54*), supported by the Vulg. and Syr., read the verb as a *hiphil* and include an object marker before "her mother-in-law" (*wattarĕ' 'et;* thus "she [Ruth] showed her mother-in-law"). Although the verb needs to be reconstructed in 2QRuth^a, the object marker in 2QRuth^a occurs before *'ăšer* ("what"), which would seem to support MT^L.

She brought out [the grain] and gave. The Syr. does not have the verb "to bring out" but simply reads "she gave." The other versions do not support the Syr.

left over. LXX^L specifies the object as "left over to eat." The other versions do not support this reading.

because of her fullness. One could analyze the word translated as "her fullness" in MT^L as an infinitive construct with the preposition *min* having an ablative sense in which it marks the cause or means of a situation (WO §11.2.11d). Thus, Ruth had food left over "because of her fullness" (2 Sam 3:37; Ezek 28:18 for this use of the preposition *min*). One could also analyze the word as the noun *śōba'* ("fullness") with the preposition having a temporal sense (WO §11.2.11c). Thus, Ruth had food left over "after her fullness" (Hos 6:2; Ps 78:20 for this use of the preposition *min*). The context suggests the former option (Holmstedt, 138–39). 2QRuth^a, supported by the Vulg., reads *bśb'h*, whereas MT^L, supported by the Old Greek and Targum, has *min* as the preposition. One Kennicott manuscript does not have the word (DJD III, 72). If the preposition *min* in MT^L has an ablative sense, the word could convey the same meaning as *bśb'h* in 2QRuth^a.

2:19. *Where did you glean today and where did you work?* I have used the English word "where" to translate two different relatively rare Hebrew words (*'ēpoh* and *'ānâ*). The use of *'ēpoh* creates alliteration with the word "ephah" (*'ēpāh*) in 2:17 (Campbell, 105). With Campbell and several others, I translate the forms of *'śh* ("to do, make") as "work" in this verse. LXX^L reads "Where have you done your work?," which specifies the object of the verb (NOTE *left over* on 2:18). One Old Greek manuscript reads, "Where did you work today?" Most versions support MT^L.

May the one who paid attention to you be blessed. Although it is rare (1 Kgs 10:9 = 2 Chr 9:8; Prov 5:18; "may it not be blessed," Jer 20:14), this blessing formula is not unusual (so Bush 133–34; contra Campbell, 105–6). As Campbell discusses, LXX^L and Theodoret continue this blessing with "because he satisfies the hungry soul as he has done with which he has done." The clause "because he satisfies the hungry soul" comes from Ps 107:9. One Old Greek witness has "because he satisfies the hungry" but not "as he has done with which he has done." For further discussion, consult Campbell, 106.

under whose authority she worked. The Old Greek and Syr. read "where she worked." The Targum and Vulg. support MT^L. Although the word translated as "under whose authority" (*'immô*) needs to be reconstructed, 2QRuth^a could also support MT^L (DJD III, 73). For the translation of the preposition *'im* as "under the authority of," consult NOTE *under her authority* on 1:7a. This preposition is used in this technical sense with various forms of the verb "to serve" (*'bd*; cf. Lev 25:40; Deut 15:12). In Gen 29:14, 25, 30; 31:38, Jacob does not serve (*'bd*) "with" or alongside of his uncle Laban. Rather, he serves "under the authority" of Laban (Milgrom, 2001, 2205). While working in the field, Ruth sticks "with" (*'im*) Boaz's servants rather than with Boaz himself (cf. 2:8, 21). Although Boaz grants Ruth permission to work in his field (2:8–9), the text does not indicate that he worked in the field that day alongside her. As with Jacob and Laban, Ruth does not work with Boaz. Rather, she works under his authority (Schipper, 2013, 665–66). To be sure, Ruth's relationship to Boaz differs from Jacob's relationship to Laban. Laban's authority over Jacob results from the fact that Jacob entered a household in which Laban is the senior member (consult "Household Organization" in the

Introduction). Ruth, however, does not necessarily acknowledge Boaz's authority over her because he is a senior member in the household that she entered, but because he controls the portion of the field in which she worked. In this sense, the nature of Boaz's authority over Ruth in 2:19 is not necessarily household authority (as in 1:7a, 11, 22; 2:6) but the authority of a holder of a field over a laborer in the field.

The name of the man under whose authority I worked today is Boaz. Boaz's name occurs at the beginning of Ruth's dialogue in the Syr. (Campbell, 88). My translation reflects the word order in MT^L, which is supported by the Targum and Old Greek.

2:20. *Blessed is he to YHWH.* The dative use of the preposition *l* in *lyhwh* ("to YHWH") indicates the goal of the action, as in "May he be pronounced blessed to YHWH," rather than the source of the blessing (WO §11.2.10d; Note *blessed are you to YHWH* on 3:10). Rather than "to YHWH," the Old Latin, Syr., and one de Rossi manuscript read "YHWH," as in "blessed is YHWH." This reading could clarify the antecedent of the following clause (Note *who has not abandoned his kindness with the living and with the dead* on 2:20). Yet, 2QRuth^a, the Targum, Vulg., and Old Greek support MT^L, and the formula "blessed . . . to YHWH" is not unusual (Judg 17:2; 1 Sam 15:13; 23:21; 2 Sam 2:5; Ps 115:5; *GKC* §121f). Similar blessing formulas occur in Hebrew inscriptions. For example, Kuntillet 'Ajrûd 9 reads *brk hʾ lyhwh* ("blessed be he to YHWH"; Dobbs-Allsopp et al., 283–84; cf. Arad 40.3; Dobbs-Allsopp et al., 70–71), Kuntillet 'Ajrûd 19A.5–6 reads *brktk lyhwh tmn* ("blessed are you to YHWH of Teman"; Dobbs-Allsopp et al., 293–94), Khirbet el-Qôm 3.2 reads *brk ʿryhw lyhwh* ("blessed is [Personal Name] to YHWH"; Dobbs-Allsopp et al., 407), and Arad 16.2–3 and 21.3–4 read *brktk lyhwh* ("I bless you to YHWH"; Dobbs-Allsopp et al., 32, 44).

who has not abandoned his kindness with the living and with the dead. Often, scholars discuss two issues in relation to this clause. The first is whether "his kindness" is the subject or object of the verb "abandoned." I read it as the object with an implied masculine singular subject. Yet, one could also translate the clause as "because his kindness has not abandoned the living and the dead." The Hebrew syntax allows for either possibility. Both translations convey similar meanings. The second and more difficult issue is whether the subject of the clause refers to Boaz or YHWH. To whose kindness does Naomi refer? Naomi may be blessing Boaz because of his kindness. Some scholars cite 2 Sam 2:5 as a parallel blessing in which David provides the reason that the people of Jabesh-gilead should be blessed by YHWH (e.g., Bush 135–36; Glueck, 41–42). Along these lines, Naomi provides the reason that YHWH should deal kindly with her daughters-in-law when she begins to bless them in 1:8. Yet, rather than providing the reason for Boaz's blessing, the clause could provide the reason to ascribe praise to YHWH. Some scholars (e.g., Gerleman, 28; Sakenfeld, 1978, 105; Zenger, 61) cite similar language in Gen 24:27 where YHWH is blessed "because he has not withheld his kindness [*ʾăšer lōʾ-ʿāzar ḥasdô*] and truth from my lord [Abraham]." The women of Bethlehem use a similar formula in Ruth 4:14. Along these lines, Naomi may be ascribing praise to YHWH because, upon seeing the abundant grain that Ruth gleaned (2:18), she has confirmation of the rumor that she heard back in Moab that YHWH had provided food for the people (1:6b). Thus, the context could support interpreting the clause as the reason either for a blessing of Boaz or for the praise of YHWH (for a different opinion, consult Bush, 135–36). Although not conclusive, the syntax favors interpreting YHWH as the implied subject of the clause. YHWH is the nearest antecedent, and in most cases, the nearest grammatically acceptable antecedent serves as the referent of a relative clause (Holmstedt, 141–42). This does not necessarily mean that one should question the sincerity of Naomi's earlier concerns about whether YHWH's kindness would extend to her daughters-in-law or to herself in 1:8–9, 20–21, respectively. Rather, it simply means that she may not have been convinced of or previously committed to the idea that YHWH will treat her daughters-in-law kindly or that YHWH will show concern for their future security through marriage (1:8–9), considering the fate of her family in Moab (vv. 20–21). For further discussion, consult COMMENTS on 2:18–23.

his kindness. For a detailed discussion of this word, consult "Divine Activity and Acts of *ḥesed* in Ruth" in the Introduction.

The man is close to us. The term "close to us" (*qārôb lānû*) identifies Boaz as a close relative (NOTES *relative* and *clan* on 2:1). According to Lev 21:2, a person who is "close to one" (*haqqārōb 'ēlâw*) could include one's parents, children, or siblings. Elsewhere, in the absence of any children, siblings, or paternal uncles, the term is used more generally for a remaining relative from the same clan (*haqqārōb 'ēlâw mimmišpaḥĕtô;* Num 27:11; cf. Lev 25:25, 49; Ruth 2:1, 3).

one of our kindred redeemers. The word translated as "one of our kindred redeemers" (*miggō'ălēnû*) is singular in form ("one of our kindred redeemer"). Yet, the partitive use of the preposition *min* ("one of") seems to require a plural sense. Thus, one might expect *miggō'ălēnû* with a *y* between the *l* and the *n* serving as a mater lectionis to clarify the ambiguous consonantal spelling. This reading occurs in some Kennicott manuscripts. The Old Greek and Syr. read a plural form. Yet, 2QRuth[a] supports the consonantal spelling in MT[L] if one follows the reconstruction in DJD III, 73. One may best explain the Hebrew consonantal spelling as a shortened spelling (Gerleman, 24; *GKC* §91k).

The form of *g'l* ("to redeem") is a *qal* active participle. Elsewhere in Ruth, the *qal* active participle of *g'l* refers to Boaz, another unnamed member of the clan, or Obed (3:9, 12; 4:1, 3, 6, 14). A kindred redeemer is simply a close relative who redeems through "the restoration of the status quo" (Milgrom, 2001, 2189). Depending on how the status quo has been disrupted, this restoration may require the relative to perform various activities including, but presumably not limited to, buying back an inherited field of an indebted relative (Lev 25:25–28; cf. Prov 23:10–11), buying a relative out of slavery (Lev 25:47–55), receiving reparation due the deceased (Num 5:8), serving as an avenger of blood (Num 35:12, 19, 21, 24, 25, 27; Deut 19:6, 12; Josh 20:3, 5, 9; 2 Sam 14:11; cf. 1 Kgs 16:11), or providing for relatives of advanced age in unspecified ways (Ruth 4:14). In Ruth, the Syr. consistently glosses the *qal* active participle of *g'l* as "the one who asks for the inheritance" (*tb' yrtwt;* cf. Moore, 2000, 344). Certain cases require a divine being to serve as the redeemer (Gen 48:16; Pss 19:15 [Eng. 19:14]; 78:35; 103:4; Isa 41:14; 43:14; 44:6, 24; 47:4; 48:17; 49:7, 26; 59:20; 54:4, 8; 60:16; 63:16; Jer 50:34). In its depiction of YHWH as a redeemer, Isa 54:4–5 reflects a custom in which the redeemer restores the status quo by marrying a woman outside the protection of a household (*'almānâ*), thus providing security for her. Although Ruth is not an *'almānâ,* Naomi's statement in Ruth 3:1–4 seems to associate Boaz with a place of rest for Ruth through marriage (cf. 1:9), Naomi may refer to Boaz as a kindred redeemer with a sense similar to that in Isa 54:4–5, although this does not necessarily mean that Ruth's narrator alludes to Isaiah. Moreover, Boaz describes his marriage to

Ruth after her husband had died as an act of redemption (3:13). As with other types of redemption, Boaz's marriage to Ruth helps to restore the status quo, presumably through material security.

2:21. *the Moabite.* The Old Greek, Old Latin, Vulg., and Syr. do not have "the Moabite." 2QRuth[a] and the Targum support MT[L], although only a stroke of the final *h* in *hmw'byh* ("the Moabite") is extant in 2QRuth[a]. The Old Greek reads "Ruth said to her mother-in-law." This reading, supported by the Old Latin, specifies Ruth's conversation partner (NOTE *she said* on 1:15; NOTE *she said to her* on 2:2).

Also, he even said to me. The combination of the words translated as "Also . . . even" (*gam kî*) occurs seven other times in MT[L] (Josh 22:7 [with a *wāw*]; Ps 23:4; Prov 22:6; Isa 1:15; Lam 3:8; Hos 8:10; 9:16), but only here does a *paseq* separate the words, which indicates that they should not be read together (Holmstedt, 143, who translates the words as "It is also that"). My translation renders *gam* as "also" and takes *kî* as emphatic (Isa 27:29–30; Ps 3:8; WO §39.3.4e) and smooths the English as "Also, he even said." 2QRuth[a] reads *ly* ("to me") whereas MT[L] reads *'ēlâ* ("to me"). This difference does not affect the translation.

Stick with. The word translated as "stick" is spelled with a paragogic *nûn* (NOTE *stick with* on 2:8).

my servants. Although the word translated as "servants" is a masculine form, it could refer to both the male and female servants inclusively (NOTE *servants* on 2:15). Multiple Old Greek manuscripts read "young women" (cf. Old Latin), but most Old Greek manuscripts, the Syr., and 2QRuth[a] support MT[L] (for a review of scholarship on this issue, consult Lim). My translation is gender inclusive because Boaz actually recommends that Ruth stick with the female servants in 2:8 (COMMENTS on 2:18–23).

my entire harvest. The Syr. and Vulg. do not have "my entire harvest." The Old Greek, Targum, and 2QRuth[a] support MT[L], although only *kl hq* in *kl hqṣyr* ("entire harvest") is extant in 2QRuth[a].

2:22. *It is better.* My translation takes *ṭôb* ("good") as a comparative (thus, "it is better"; cf. 1 Sam 27:1; 2 Sam 18:3), although the syntax allows for the translation "Good, my daughter, certainly [*kî*] go out" (Sasson, 62; consult NOTES *We will certainly return* on 1:10, and *it is certainly true that* on 3:13). The former option is supported by the Vulg. (which also uses *melius* in 1 Sam 27:1; 2 Sam 18:3), whereas the latter option is supported by the Targum and Old Greek. My translation interprets Naomi's words as specifying that Ruth should stick with the female servants, as Boaz instructs her in 2:8, rather than the male servants (NOTES *stick with* and *my servants* on 2:21). Alternatively, one could take *ṭôb* as a superlative ("it is best") and interpret Naomi's words as advising Ruth that staying in Boaz's field is her best available option (cf. Bush, 130, 139; Holmstedt, 144–45).

his female servants. 2QRuth[a] reads *n'rwtw*, whereas MT[L], supported by the Old Greek, Vulg., Targum, and Syr., reads *na'ărôtâw*. Most likely, the reading in 2QRuth[a] results from a scribal error.

attack. The word translated as "attack" is a *qal yiqtol* from *pg'* ("to meet, encounter") followed by the preposition *b*. This word has a range of meanings, including "encounter" and "meet" (Gen 28:11; 32:2) but also "attack" or "kill" (Judg 18:25; 1 Sam

22:18; 2 Sam 1:5; 1 Kgs 2:25, 34, 46). Ruth uses a similar construction (*qal yiqtol* followed by the preposition *b*) in 1:16 when she tells Naomi, "Do not pressure me" (NOTE *pressure* on 1:16). Yet, the context of Naomi's use of this word seems to suggest something stronger than "pressure," something more like "attack" (cf. Judg 15:12), possibly including a sexual assault. The location of another open field does not lessen the threat of rape or murder (contra Hubbard, 192; Sasson, 62). It is not clear that Naomi imagines that others will be nearby in this other unidentified field (cf. Deut 22:25–27). More importantly, whether in ancient Israel or the contemporary United States, public safety is a social privilege that is hardly universally enjoyed or assumed by all parties, especially women and ethnic or racial minorities.

in another field. The Syr. reads "in the field of someone you do not know" (Campbell, 88). The other versions, however, do not support this reading.

2:23. *to glean*. 2QRuth^a has *llwṭ*, whereas MT^L, supported by the Old Greek, Syr., and Targum, has *lĕlaqqēṭ*. Most likely, 2QRuth^a reflects a scribal error because there seems to be a trace of a *q* in the space above the word between the second *l* and the *w* (cf. DJD III, 73). This may suggest a recognition and correction of the error.

barley harvest and wheat harvest. The "entire harvest" that Ruth mentions in 2:21 seems to include both the barley and wheat harvests. Although these harvests are distinct, these crops are associated with each other elsewhere in the Hebrew Bible (Exod 9:31–32; Deut 8:8; 2 Sam 17:28; Jer 41:8; Ezek 45:13; Joel 1:11; Job 31:40; 2 Chr 2:10, 15; 27:5). Some texts indicate that the harvest seasons would last about two months (Gezer Calendar, *ANET*, 320; but *Ruth Rab*. 5 claims that the beginning of the barley harvest until the end of the wheat harvest lasted three months; Milgrom, 2001, 1991; cf. Lev 23:15–16; Deut 16:9). According to Deut 16:11, the festival at the conclusion of the harvest should include, among others, the handmaids (NOTE *I am your handmaid* on 3:9) and resident aliens, widows, and orphans living among the Israelites (Deut 16:14) among its participants. While an association between the harvest's conclusion and a time for the inclusion of these parties would make an appropriate backdrop for the events of Ruth 3 and 4, the literary relationship between Ruth and Deuteronomy 16 is uncertain. Against such a connection, one could note that although Ruth 4 may engage other traditions that are also reflected in Deuteronomy, the book of Ruth never discusses any specific festivals despite its later liturgical association with Shavuot.

were finished. The word translated as "were finished" (*kĕlôt*) is a *qal* infinitive form from *klh* ("to complete, finish"). The Old Greek seems to read a *piel* infinitive form (*kallôt*) from the same root but may mean basically the same thing. LXX^L reads "they completed." The Vulg. expands this clause to have Ruth continuing to glean until all the barley and wheat was stored in barns. The Vulg. begins the next verse (3:1) with the last clause in 2:23 (NOTE *Then she stayed* on 2:23).

Then she stayed. Two de Rossi manuscripts read the verb as a *wayyiqtol* form from *šwb* (*wattāšāb;* "she returned"). This reading is supported by the Vulg., which takes this clause as the opening of chapter 3 rather than as the end of chapter 2. The word is not attested in Old Latin, and 2QRuth^a is in need of reconstruction. The Old Greek, Syr., and Targum support MT^L. My translation takes the *wayyiqtol* form as indicating a temporal sequence in which Ruth stayed with Naomi after the harvests were finished (Bush, 140), although this clause could indicate that Ruth stayed with Naomi during the harvests. Whereas Ruth 1 began with Naomi and her sons "staying" in Moab (consult 1:4), by the end of chapter 2, Naomi's Moabite daughter-in-law is "staying" with her in Bethlehem.

Comments

Ruth 1 ends by noting that Naomi and Ruth arrived in Bethlehem at the beginning of the barley harvest (1:22b). Ruth 2 takes the audience through the ends of both the barley and the wheat harvests (2:23). In v. 18, Ruth returns to the city with her threshed barley. The narrator makes a point that Naomi saw the yield from her daughter-in-law's gleaning and that a satisfied Ruth gives Naomi what is left over from her gleaning (2:17). In 1:6, Naomi left Moab because she heard a report that YHWH had provided his people with food, although the narrator does not confirm the veracity of the rumor at that point. When Ruth arrives with an abundance of food, it may put to rest any of Naomi's doubts about the rumor (2:20).

Just as Ruth and Naomi were greeted with questions when they first entered Bethlehem (1:19), Ruth is greeted with questions when she once again enters the city (2:18). These questions continue the inquiry surrounding her character and those associated with her (1:19; 2:5; 3:9, 16). Naomi asks her where she worked and invokes a blessing upon Ruth's yet-to-be-identified benefactor. Once again, a blessing results from an act on behalf of others in need (1:8; 3:10; 4:14; cf. "Divine Activity and Acts of *ḥesed* in Ruth" in the Introduction). Naomi's questions use vocabulary similar to the vocabulary used in the previous verses. As already discussed (COMMENTS on 2:3–17), these repetitions continue to create alliteration. Before Naomi learns the benefactor's identity, she refers to him as "the one who paid attention to you," which is a participle from the root *nkr*. Ruth used an infinitive form of the same root when she asks why Boaz has "paid attention" to her (2:10).

Ruth replies that she worked under the authority (*'im*) of Boaz (NOTE *under whose authority she worked* on 2:19). The narrator states that Ruth answered Naomi's questions regarding her benefactor (v. 19bα) and then includes Ruth's direct discourse to Naomi (v. 19bβ). In other words, the audience learns not only that Ruth answered her mother-in-law's questions, but also what she told her. One can contrast this narrative technique with the one used in 3:16, where Naomi again inquires about Ruth's activities but the narrator states only that Ruth answered Naomi without specifying what she told her (consult "Selective Representation and Narrative Ambiguity" in the Introduction). As I will discuss shortly, Ruth's answer may imply that Boaz is acting as a kindred redeemer by taking Ruth under his authority since kindred redeemers took impoverished relatives under their authority (the particle *'im* has this technical sense in the legislation regarding kindred redeemers in Lev 25:6, 23, 35–36, 39–41, 47, 50, 53; NOTE *under her authority* on 1:7a).

In Ruth 2:20, Naomi blesses Boaz by name. One could connect Naomi's reference to divine kindness (*ḥesed*) in this blessing with the reference to divine kindness in her aborted blessing of her daughters-in-law in 1:8, although some scholars suggest that Naomi attributes this kindness to Boaz rather than to YHWH (NOTE *who has not abandoned his kindness with the living and with the dead* on 2:20). In regard to 1:8–9, Trible and others have suggested that Ruth and Orpah's kindness toward Naomi and her dead relatives serves as a model or at least a reason for YHWH to show kindness to her daughters-in-law (consult "Divine Activity and Acts of *ḥesed* in Ruth" in the Introduction for references). If so, one could interpret Naomi's reference to YHWH's kindness in 2:20 as her claim that she finally has evidence that YHWH has shown the kindness that Naomi had called for in 1:8 but that she did not believe was extended to her in Moab (1:20–21).

Naomi's blessing contains the verb "abandon" (cf. 1:16; 2:11, 16), which creates a play on Boaz's name (NOTE *Boaz* on 2:1). Ruth had abandoned her Moabite household (2:11) but refused to abandon Naomi (1:16). As with Ruth's kindness to Naomi and her deceased relatives, Naomi's blessing suggests that YHWH's kindness has not abandoned Naomi's household, which includes its living members and the household ancestors who had died (COMMENTS on 1:7b–19a). Naomi continues to use language associated with the household in 2:20. She includes Ruth as part of her household when she describes Boaz as one who is close to both of them and one of their kindred redeemers.

Up to this point, it is unclear whether any of Naomi's potential kindred redeemers is willing to fulfill this role since the narrator does not indicate whether anyone came forward when Naomi declared that she was bereft of a male provider (1:21). In fact, in 4:6, a potential kindred redeemer will explicitly express his reluctance to provide redemption for her and Ruth. In 2:19, Naomi learns that Boaz took notice of Ruth and had her work under his authority. This fits with legislation regarding the responsibilities of kindred redeemers. When Naomi explains to Ruth the nature of Boaz's relationship to them, Naomi may be interpreting Boaz's favor as an indication that he is willing to serve as a kindred redeemer. A kindred redeemer could potentially perform a variety of functions on behalf of other household or clan members in need. Broadly understood, a kindred redeemer was a close relative who performed whatever functions were necessary to restore the status quo (NOTE *one of our kindred redeemers* on 2:20). For Naomi and Ruth, the status quo had been profoundly disrupted. They were bereft of husbands and sons (1:3–5), and the field held by Elimelech was in need of redemption (4:3). Thus, their situation required a potential kindred redeemer to perform multiple duties before the status quo was restored.

In 2:21, Ruth responds to Naomi by paraphrasing what Boaz said to her in vv. 8–9 (cf. 3:17). There is a potential misunderstanding on Naomi's part because Ruth conjugates the Hebrew word for "servants" with a masculine form, whereas Boaz had used a feminine form in v. 8 (NOTE *my servants* on 2:21). In response, Naomi advises Ruth to stick with the female servants rather than the male servants to avoid being attacked. Naomi's final response has led some scholars to question whether Naomi has Ruth's best interests in mind. If Naomi was aware of this potential danger, it is unclear why she did not warn Ruth of it when Ruth first requested permission to glean in 2:2. The fact that Naomi gives these instructions only after she sees that Ruth can provide her with food could reflect ulterior motives on her part rather than a more altruistic concern for Ruth's well-being (Fewell and Gunn, 1990, 76; COMMENTS on 3:1–5). These questions remain unanswered because, in keeping with the style of narration throughout the book, the narrator does not usually explain the motivations behind the characters' words or actions (consult "Actions, Events, and Consequences" in the Introduction).

Ruth's paraphrase of Boaz's words also raises questions about whether Boaz will do all that is necessary to fully restore the status quo for Naomi and Ruth. In vv. 8–9, he did not indicate how long Ruth should stick with his female servants. Yet, Ruth specifies that he said she should stick with them "until they finish my entire harvest" (v. 21). Ruth may assume that Boaz's favor will extend only through the barley and wheat harvests when she can glean in the field that he holds. Moreover, although he knows that she is an impoverished kinswoman, the provisions that he offers differ for what Leviticus 25 requires a kindred redeemer to do for impoverished kin. For example, according to Lev 25:35, an impoverished relative who is under the authority of a kindred redeemer (cf. Ruth 2:19) should live with the kindred redeemer. Yet, once the harvests are finished, Ruth lives with Naomi rather than Boaz (NOTE *Then she stayed* on 2:23). In 3:1, Naomi's expression of concern over Ruth's future security may assume that Boaz will not serve as a kindred redeemer once the harvest seasons are finished unless more drastic measures are taken (Eskenazi and Frymer-Kensky, 47).

Naomi's Instructions (3:1–5)

3 ¹Naomi her mother-in-law said to her, "My daughter, shouldn't I seek a place of rest for you where it would go well for you? ²Now isn't Boaz our relative, whose female servants you were with? Look, he is winnowing near the threshing floor of the barley tonight. ³You should wash up, apply perfume, and put on your garments. Go down to the threshing floor. Do not make yourself known to the man until he finishes eating and drinking. ⁴When he lies down, you shall know the place where he lies. You shall enter, undress at his feet and lie down. He will tell you what you should do." ⁵She said to her, "All that you say to me I will do."

Notes

3:1. *to her.* LXX^L specifies "to her" as "to Ruth." The other versions do not support this reading. The Vulg. reads the last clause in 2:23 as the beginning of 3:1 (NOTE *Then she stayed* on 2:23).

shouldn't I seek a place of rest. As with Boaz in 2:8–9, Naomi asks a rhetorical question (cf. 3:2). Yet, unlike Boaz, she uses a *yiqtol* modal form rather than a *qatal* form. Thus, her question begins "shouldn't I" rather than "haven't I" (cf. 2:8–9). The noun translated as "place of rest" (*mānôḥa*) is related to the noun translated as "rest" in 1:9 (*měnûḥâ*). In both cases, the word portrays the household of a husband as a place of material security.

where it would go well for you? This clause carries an implicit comparison to Ruth's present circumstances, in which she does not have an ideal place of rest (Holmstedt, 148; Sasson, 63–64). In Deut 6:3, a masculine form of "that it may go well for you" expresses a hope for multiple generations of descendants in the Cisjordan (Deut 4:40; Jer 42:6; Myers even claims that the expression is "apparently a Deuteronomic phrase," 25). In these other texts, this expression is not associated with the continuation of a dead relative's lineage. Naomi may use the idiom with a connotation similar to that in

Deut 6:3, thus expressing hope that Ruth has multiple generations of descendants in a new household (cf. 1:9; Trible 192–93).

3:2. *our relative.* The word translated as "our relative" (*mōdaʿtānû*) seems to be related to the word translated as "relative" in 2:1 (NOTE *relative* on 2:1), although one would expect *mōdaʿtēnû* rather than *mōdaʿtānû*. The Syr. uses a word from *khkm*, which is a different word for "relative" than it uses in 2:1. This Syr. root has the sense of "to know sexually" (Moore, 2000, 347). This interpretation may imply that Naomi views Boaz as a potential sexual partner for Ruth.

winnowing near the threshing floor of the barley. My translation is a fairly wooden rendering of MT[L]. The preposition *ʾet* indicates proximity (Judg 4:11; 1 Kgs 9:26; WO §11.2.4). It does not mark the object of the participle "winnowing." The word translated as "threshing floor" is in construct with "the barley," and thus "the barley" is not the object of the participle (cf. the wooden translation in the Old Greek). As the object is implied although unspecified, one should not make too much of the fact that barley is mentioned but not wheat since both the barley and wheat harvests are finished (2:23). Despite Campbell's argument on the basis of Gen 26:12; Judg 7:13; 1 Kgs 23:8 (117–18), arguments for repointing *haśśĕʿōrîm* ("the barley") as *haśśĕʿārîm* ("the gates") are not supported by the versions (cf. Old Greek, Vulg., Targum).

tonight. The Old Greek, Syr., Old Latin, and Vulg. read "this night" for the MT's *hallāyĕlāh* ("tonight"), although the meaning is the same.

3:3. *You should wash up, apply perfume, and put on your garments.* LXX[B] begins this verse with "But you." MT[L] *ketib* reads the first two verbs as *qal waqqatal* modals with Ruth's own body as the implied object that is washed and perfumed. Although these forms do not suggest a reflexive translation ("wash yourself," "perfume yourself"), the implication may be the same. The third verb is also a *qal waqqatal* modal but with an explicit object ("your garments"). LXX[L] manuscripts read "and rub yourself with myrrh" either after the verb translated as "apply perfume" or in place of the verb (Campbell, 120). The other versions do not support this reading.

your garments. The Targum reads "finery" (cf. Vulg.; *Ruth Rab.* 5:12; *b. Shab.* 113b). 2QRuth[a] reads "garments" as a plural noun ([*śml*]*tyk*; cf. MT[L] *qere*, Syr., Vulg., Targum), whereas MT[L] *ketib* and the Old Greek have a singular form ("garment, clothing"). MT[L] *ketib* may use the singular form as a collective or a shortened spelling because the *y* between the *t* and the *k* could serve as a mater lectionis in 2QRuth[a].

Go down. The Old Greek reads "go up" (cf. 4:1) but reads "go down" for a *wayyiqtol* form of the same root in 3:6. The other versions do not support the Old Greek. MT[L] *qere* corrects the *ketib* to conform to the three previous *qatal* modal forms in the verse. Some scholars argue that the *-tî* suffix on this second feminine singular verb in the *ketib* reflects a remnant of archaic Hebrew, as the verb's morphology fits proto-Semitic reconstructions for second feminine singular forms (for a review of scholarship, cf. Irwin, 332, n. 2). In 4:5, however, the *qere* corrects the *-tî* suffix on *qānîtî* in the *ketib* to a masculine rather than a feminine second-person singular suffix. This suggests that the *-tî* suffix should not be read as a feminine singular in 3:3, 4 (Irwin, 332, n. 3; Irwin argues that the first-person singular form reflects a scribal emendation). Also, it is difficult to determine whether these verbs represent genuine archaic forms or archaized Hebrew (as in possibly Jer 2:33; Ezek 16:18; 31:21, and so on; cf. the list in Myers, 11). Many other second feminine singular forms in Ruth do not reflect reconstructed proto-Semitic morphology. If one assigns an archaic date to Ruth on the basis of only two verbs in 3:3, 4 (NOTE *and lie down* on 3:4), then the majority must have been updated by later scribes at some point. Yet, it seems unlikely that these two verbs went unchanged but the rest were updated (Holmstedt, 24, 152–53). Moreover, since Naomi is the speaker, one could explain these verbs as distinguishing her speech pattern as unusual or old-fashioned rather than as reflecting genuine archaic forms (cf. NOTE *Shaddai* on 1:20).

Do not make yourself known. The verb translated as "make yourself known" comes from *yd'*. Forms from this root, which is often used as a euphemism for sexual intercourse, occur several times in this chapter (3:3, 4, 11, 14, 18; NOTE *undress at his feet and lie down* on 3:4 and the corresponding COMMENTS). Naomi's instructions may reflect a double entendre. She could be telling Ruth not to make Boaz aware of her presence or not to make herself sexually available to him immediately (NOTE *our relative* on 3:2; Moore, 2000, 348–49).

eating and drinking. LXX^B and several LXX^L manuscripts read "drinking and eating" (consult NOTE *without her two children or her husband* on 1:5).

3:4. *undress at his feet and lie down.* Although the noun translated as "his feet" (*margĕlōtâw*) derives from *rgl* ("foot"), it is unclear exactly which body part Naomi is referring to. In addition to Boaz's feet, *margĕlōtâw* could refer to his legs, as in Dan 10:6 where it parallels "arms." It could also serve as a euphemism for the genitals (cf. *raglâw* in 1 Sam 24:4 [Eng. 24:3]). Bush suggests that a rare form of the word for feet is used to avoid any sexual implication that would have been clear if a more common spelling of the word for feet were used (153; cf. Eskenazi and Frymer-Kensky, 53). Yet, as Julie Pfau notes, there is no reason why one spelling of a word for feet can be euphemistic but not another spelling (4–5). The Targum and 2QRuth^a, the latter of which reads *wglyt mr[gltyw* . . .], support MT^L but do not clarify this issue. As Campbell notes, other versions offer different renderings of this clause, for example, "reveal the (place) at his feet" (Old Greek), "remove the coverlet which hides the place at his feet" (Vulg.), and "cover yourself at his feet" (Old Latin) (Campbell's translations, 121). The Syr. does not account for the verb "uncover." Instead of the object of the verb (i.e., what Ruth uncovers), most of these versions interpret "his feet" as the location where the uncovering happens, that is, at his feet. This reflects the use of the locative *mem* (cf. *margĕlōtâw* in 3:8, *margĕlôtâw* in 3:14 [*qere*], or various forms of the noun *mĕra'ăšôt*, "at the place of the head," in Gen 28:11, 18; 1 Sam 26:7, 11, 12, 16; 1 Kgs 19:6). The object of the verb "uncover" (*wĕgillît*) is unstated or implied (cf. "the place" as the gapped object of the previous verb "enter" in the previous clause). Elsewhere, other *piel* verb forms of the root *glh* ("to uncover") frequently refer to the uncovering of one's body (Lev 18:6–19; 20:11, 17–21; Deut 23:1 [Eng. 22:30]; 27:20; Ezek 16:37; 22:10; 23:10, 18; Nah 3:5; cf. Hos 2:12; as *niphal* forms, 2 Sam 6:20; Exod 20:26; Isa 47:3; Jer 13:22; Ezek 16:36; 23:29). In the majority of these references, the body that is uncovered is a female body (Nielsen, 69–70). Thus, Naomi is probably instructing Ruth to undress and lie down at Boaz's feet, as Ruth does in the following verses (3:7, 8, 14). Nevertheless, exactly what type of activity Naomi implies and Ruth carries out remains unclear because in some of the references above, uncovering the body is used with the various forms of the root *škb* ("to lie down") as a euphemism for sexual activity (cf. Lev 20:11, 18, 20; Deut 27:20; cf. Ezek 23:8–10 and possibly Ruth 3:7, 13). The fact that these activities may or may not happen in close proximity to Boaz's genitals only adds to their ambiguity. Moreover, other verbs that Naomi uses in this verse ("know" and "enter") derive from roots that are often used as euphemisms for sexual intercourse (*ydʿ* and *bwʾ*, respectively; e.g., Gen 4:1, 17, 25; 30:16; 38:8–9; Judg 19:22; 1 Sam 1:19; 2 Sam 17:25; 1 Kgs 1:4; Ps 51:2 [Eng. 51:1]; cf. Linafelt, 1999, 52). For further discussion, consult COMMENTS on 3:6–15.

and lie down. As in the previous verse (NOTE *go down* on 3:3), the *qere* corrects the *ketib* to conform to the three previous *qatal* modal forms in the verse.

you should do. MT[L] and 2QRuth[a] spell the verb translated as "you should do" with a paragogic *nûn* (cf. NOTE *stick with* on 2:8).

3:5. *She said to her.* The Old Greek specifies the speaker in this verse as Ruth. The Targum and Vulg. support MT[L]. The clause must be reconstructed in 2QRuth[a].

you say. The use of a *yiqtol* verb form (cf. 3:11) suggests an ongoing commitment by Ruth to follow Naomi's instructions. If she were simply agreeing to follow Naomi's plan as stated in 3:4, one would expect the use of a *qatal* verb form, for example, "Everything that you said." The Old Greek and Vulg. reflect the latter option.

to me. Possibly triggered by the *aleph* at the beginning of *ʾēlâ* ("to me") and *ʾēʿĕśeh* ("I will do"), MT[L] *ketib* has only the vowel points (*ē a*) without the corresponding consonants (*ʾly*) above them. The consonants are attested in MT[L] *qere* and multiple MT manuscripts. Multiple Old Greek manuscripts, Old Latin, the Targum, and the Syr. also support the *qere*. 2QRuth[a] must be reconstructed (DJD III, 74). The Vulg. and other Old Greek manuscripts do not have "to me." According to the Masorah parva, the *ketib* represents one of ten occasions where the vowels of a word are written without the corresponding consonants in MT[L] (cf. Judg 20:13; Ruth 3:17; 2 Sam 8:3; 16:23; 18:20; 2 Kgs 19:31, 37; Jer 31:38 50:29). Elvira Martín-Contreras argues that Ezra 9:11 represents an eleventh occasion.

Comments

Toward the end of chapter 2, Naomi recognized Boaz as a potential kindred redeemer. As the third chapter begins, she explores other ways in which Boaz might continue to restore the status quo for her and Ruth. Naomi asks a rhetorical question about whether she should seek a place of rest for Ruth. Earlier, she instructed her daughters-in-law to "find rest, each one in the house of her husband" while encouraging them to leave her and return to Moab (1:9). At that point, she was attempting to end her household affiliation with Ruth and Orpah (but consult NOTES *Find rest, each one in the household of her husband* on 1:9, and *We will certainly return* on 1:10). In 3:1, however, Naomi associates a place of rest for Ruth with the household of a close relative within her own Judahite clan instead of either Ruth's birth household or the household of a future husband in Moab. Naomi once again identifies Boaz as a relative (cf. "close to us" in 2:20), although she uses a different word than in 2:20. The word for "relative" in 3:2 derives from the root *ydʿ* and may imply a sexual relationship in this context (NOTE *Do not make yourself known* on 3:3; COMMENTS on 3:6–15).

As in 1:9, Naomi's reference to rest for Ruth implies Ruth's integration into a stable household. In this case, Naomi probably does not mean that Ruth should return to her birth household in Moab since Ruth had already abandoned it to align herself with Naomi's household (1:16–17; 2:11). Naomi seems to be functioning as the remaining senior member in her household (cf. "Household Organization" in the Introduction).

In this capacity, it would not be unusual for her to be involved in the marriage arrangements of a household member under her authority (consult COMMENTS on 1:7b–19a for references). Elsewhere, the idiom "it would go well for you" expresses hope for multiple generations of descendants, which could apply to Ruth's present circumstances (NOTE *it would go well for you* on 3:1). As already noted, marriage and children are associated with a continuation of a male's lineage and inheritance during conversations involving men (4:1–12), whereas they are associated with security in conversations between women (1:8–9; 4:14–15).

A second marriage with a member of Naomi's clan could help to restore the status quo for Ruth and thus could qualify as an act of kindred redemption. In the book of Isaiah, God is referred to as Zion's "kindred redeemer" in a metaphor that depicts God as Zion's husband (54:5). The prophet imagines exiled Zion, who is barren and bereaved, as restored through this marriage (NOTE *one of our kindred redeemers* on 2:20). Despite the obvious contextual differences between Ruth and Zion in two texts that may be otherwise unrelated, both texts may depict marriage as an acceptable form of kindred redemption if it is necessary to restore the status quo (cf. Bush, 168–69; Hubbard, 212). If Naomi thought Boaz showed a willingness to act as a kindred redeemer when he allowed Ruth to glean in the portion of the field that he held, Naomi may figure that he would continue to serve in this capacity not only through the provision of food, but through marriage as well. As already noted, Naomi and Ruth's restoration would require the kindred redeemer to perform multiple tasks, considering how profoundly the lives of these women had been disrupted (COMMENTS on 2:18–23). As Boaz suggests in the final chapter, the kindred redeemer should not only buy the land held by Elimelech, but also marry Ruth (4:5, 10). This is not because of a legal mandate but because the situation requires it.

The narrator still does not clarify whether Boaz will in fact provide redemption beyond the favor that he showed to Ruth during the harvests. It remains unclear whether his knowledge of the women's circumstances (2:11) is motivation enough for him to act. The fact that Naomi feels the need to propose that Ruth meet him at night at the threshing floor hardly suggests that she assumes he will continue to act as a kindred redeemer once the harvest is over. When Ruth returns from the threshing floor, Naomi insists that Boaz "will not rest unless the matter is finished" (3:18). Yet, Naomi does not display the same level of confidence in Boaz's persistence before Ruth's visit to the threshing floor. Although Naomi and Boaz never appear in a scene together anywhere in the book, Naomi seems to possess detailed knowledge of how Boaz will act in 3:2–4 (cf. 4:3). Yet, it is not until after his nocturnal encounter with Ruth that Naomi mentions that he will work without rest until he resolves the matter. The women are clearly in need of a kindred redeemer, but they may need to provide Boaz with a motivation beyond obligations assumed within the structure of the clan (Hackett, 2014). The utility of the clan structure to provide rest for Ruth remains an open question.

It is also unclear whether Naomi's concern for Ruth's security reflects an altruistic attitude toward her daughter-in-law. As already noted, Naomi's reference to Ruth as "my daughter" may be a term of affection, but it could also simply reflect an appropriate term for an unmarried woman within the household who is under Naomi's authority (consult "Household and Clan Statuses of Ruth's Characters" in the Introduction). Moreover, in 2:23, the narrator states that Ruth stayed with Naomi after the harvests, although the Hebrew syntax is somewhat ambiguous (NOTE *Then she stayed* on 2:23). The narrator does not clarify whether Ruth continues to provide food for her mother-in-law during the harvests if one interprets 2:23 as indicating that Ruth does not stay with Naomi again until after the harvests. If Ruth did not continue to provide food for Naomi, one could interpret Naomi's instructions in 2:23 and 3:1–4 as expressing concern for Ruth's interests over her own well-being. As in 1:8–14, Naomi may be encouraging Ruth to abandon her to ensure Ruth's own security. Yet, as in chapter 1, one could also interpret Naomi's instructions as reflecting a desire to rid herself of Ruth, the wife of her deceased son. If Ruth gleaned in the field to provide food for Naomi during the harvests, it is striking that Naomi addresses the subject of Ruth's security, which presumably involves joining another household, only after the harvests are finished.

Unlike in 1:6, 18, the narrator does not provide the reason for Naomi's instructions in 3:1–4. One could read her instructions as indicating a range of opinions regarding Ruth. In 2:2, Naomi allows Ruth to glean in an unknown field without warning her of the potential danger of which Naomi is well aware (2:23). In 3:2–4, she once again allows Ruth to enter a potentially dangerous situation by arranging an encounter between a well-groomed Ruth and a possibly inebriated man despite the concern she expresses over Ruth's security. Yet, as with Naomi's instructions in 2:22–23, the narrator focuses on the effect of the instructions on Ruth's subsequent actions: in both cases, Ruth follows the instructions of the senior member of her household (3:5). In keeping with the book's style of narration (consult "Actions, Events, and Consequences" in the Introduction), the narrator does not indicate the motives behind the characters' speech, but only the consequences of their speech. Ruth's actions conform to what one would expect given her status relative to Naomi. Thus, Ruth's statement of obedience in v. 5 does not necessarily reveal her feelings toward Naomi. As in 2:2, the narrator does not indicate whether Ruth's obedience reflects her respect and affection for Naomi or simply the fact that she is under Naomi's authority within the structure of the household (consult NOTE *under her authority* on 1:7a, and "Household Organization" in the Introduction).

On the Threshing Floor (3:6–15)

3 ⁶So she went down to the threshing floor and did according to all that her mother-in-law had instructed. ⁷When Boaz ate and drank and his heart was merry, he entered to lie down at the edge of the pile [of barley]. Then, she entered secretly, undressed at his feet and lay down. ⁸In the middle of the night, the man was troubled and turned himself about and Look! A woman lying at his feet! ⁹He said, "Who are you?" She said, "I am Ruth, your handmaid. Spread your skirt over your handmaid because you are a kindred redeemer." ¹⁰He said, "Blessed are you to YHWH my daughter. You performed your latter kindness better than your earlier one. You did not go after the young men whether poor or rich. ¹¹And now my daughter, do not be afraid. All that you say I will do for you because the entire assembly of my people knows that you are a woman of worth. ¹²And now, it is certainly true that I am a kindred redeemer, but in fact there is a kindred redeemer closer than I. ¹³Lodge tonight. Then, in the morning, if he wishes to redeem you, that is fine, let him redeem. But if he does not want to redeem you, I will redeem you. As YHWH lives, lie down until the morning!" ¹⁴So she lay down at his feet until the morning. Then, she arose before a man could recognize another. For he thought, "May it not be known that the woman came to the threshing floor." ¹⁵He said, "Give me the garment that is on you and hold it." So she held it and he measured out six units of barley and set [the barley] on it. Then, he went into the city.

Notes

3:6. *according to all that her mother-in-law had instructed.* This clause (*kĕkōl ʾăšer ṣiwwattāh ḥămôtāh*) reflects a common idiom for following commands or directions thoroughly (cf. *kĕkōl ʾăšer ṣiwwāh/ṣiwwāhû*; Gen 6:22; 7:5; Exod 39:32, 42; 40:16; Num 1:54; 2:34; 8:20; 9:5; 2 Kgs 11:9; 16:16; Jer 35:18; 36:8; 2 Chr 23:8). Possibly because of haplography triggered by the two *k*s in *kĕkōl* ("according to all"), a few medieval Hebrew manuscripts (*BHS* critical apparatus), supported by the Vulg. and Syr., read *kōl* ("all"). Yet the Old Greek and Targum support MT[L]. 2QRuth[a] must be reconstructed (DJD III, 74). The word translated as "instructed" (*ṣiwwattāh*) has a *dagesh* in the *t* because of the assimilation of the *h* from the feminine suffix, referring to "her mother-in-law," into the *t*. The *h* at the end of the word does not have a *mappiq* because that *h* is a mater lectionis (1 Sam 1:6; Isa 34:17; Jer 49:24; GKC §59g; Holmstedt, 158), rather than the feminine suffix.

3:7. *and drank*. Probably because of haplography triggered by *wy* in *wayyēšet* ("and drank") and *wayyîṭab* ("was merry"), LXX^BL do not have "and drank." 2QRuth^a, the Old Latin, Vulg., Syr., and Targum support MT^L.

his heart was merry. As Sasson correctly notes, it is "impossible to ascertain Boaz's condition at the end of the meal" (73). The problem is that various forms of the idiom "one's heart was merry" (*ṭjb/yāṭab lēb*) may refer to inebriation (1 Sam 25:36; 2 Sam 13:28; Esth 1:10, although in these cases wine or drunkenness is mentioned explicitly), but the idiom may also refer to one being in generally good spirits (Judg 18:20; cf. Eccl 7:3), often at the end of a feast (1 Kgs 8:66 = 2 Chr 7:10) or a good meal (Judg 19:6, 22; 1 Kgs 21:7; Eccl 9:7; cf. Prov 9:7). Whether alcohol-induced or not, the idiom signals that Boaz was content and satisfied after his meal.

secretly. In MT^L and 2QRuth^a, this word derives from *lwṭ* ("secrecy, mystery"; cf. Old Greek ["secretly," *kruphē*] and Targum ["in secret," *bĕrāz*]). It conveys the sense of something done in private (1 Sam 18:22) or without another party's knowledge (Judg 4:21; 1 Sam 24:5; contra Joüon [71], who incorrectly takes the word from the adverb *'aṭ* ["gently"] and the preposition *l*, cf. 2 Sam 18:5; Isa 8:6).

undressed at his feet and lay down. On this clause, consult NOTE *undress at his feet and lie down* on 3:4.

3:8. *was troubled and turned himself about*. The meaning of these verbs remains uncertain. The verb translated as "was troubled" (*wayyēḥĕrad*) often results from fear (e.g., Exod 19:16, 18; 1 Sam 28:5) but may also result from confusion over one's circumstances. This can be seen when Isaac is troubled when Esau identifies himself after Isaac asks him, "Who are you?" (*mî 'attāh*; Gen 27:32–33). The situation is similar when Boaz, who may not be able to see Ruth since it is the middle of the night, is troubled and, upon awaking, asks her, "Who are you?" (*mî 'att*), and she identifies herself as Ruth (Ruth 3:9). The verb translated as "turned himself about" (*wayyillāpēt*), which derives from *lpt*, is a *niphal* form that suggests a reflexive sense. This root, which occurs in only two other places in the Hebrew Bible (Judg 16:29; Job 6:18), seems to suggest turning, groping, or twisting about (for a detailed discussion of this verb's meaning, consult Sasson, 78–80). Thus, the image expressed by these verbs is of a fitful sleep in which Boaz is tossing and turning about. The reason for his fitful sleep, however, remains a matter of speculation. For a review of various theories, consult Beattie, 229; Bush, 162–63.

and Look! MT^L and 2QRuth^a, supported by the Old Greek, have the particle *wĕhinnēh* ("look!"), whereas the Targum, Vulg., and Syr. have a verb form meaning "he [Boaz] saw." Yet, the verb forms are most likely an interpretation of the particle (Campbell, 115). The use of a *hinnēh* clause may convey a sense of surprise on Boaz's part. While it does not introduce a new character into an ongoing scene, as in 2:4 or 4:1, it conveys Boaz's awareness of Ruth's presence after the scene has already started (NOTE *look!* on 2:4).

3:9. *He said*. LXX^L, generally supported by the Vulg. and Syr., reads "he said to her." Yet other Old Greek manuscripts and the Targum support MT^L.

Who are you? MT^L misspells the feminine pronoun translated as "you" by omitting the *šĕwā'* under the *tāw*. MT^A spells it correctly.

I am Ruth, your handmaid. Scholars have cited the use of the pronoun *'ānōkî* ("I") rather than the shorter form *'ănî* as evidence for the date of the book or the theory that *'ānōkî* reflects a polite form of speech for addressing one's superior (consult NOTE *although I am* on 2:10). Although Ruth refers to herself as *šipḥātēk* ("your maidservant") when speaking to Boaz in 2:13, in this verse she refers to herself as *'ămātek* ("your handmaid" serves as an approximate translation). The switch to *'ămātek* may reflect the conjugal context of this scene. Uses of *'āmāh* have a conjugal sense more frequently than *šipḥâ*, including references to a so-called slave-wife (Gen 30:3; cf. Exod 21:7–10), although *šipḥâ* may refer to a slave-wife as well (Gen 16:2–3; 30:4, 9; 33:1–6). If *'āmāh* has a conjugal sense, however, it remains unclear whether it describes a free-wife or a slave-wife in this case on the basis of biblical and inscriptional evidence. For example, the Silwan 1 inscription refers to the senior member of the household's *'mht*, who is buried with him, and an Elamite tomb inscription mentions a king's *'amātu*, whom he loves, but these texts do not clarify the woman's status within the household (consult Dobbs-Allsopp et al., 507–10; Bridge, 5–7). One cannot assume much about Ruth's status as a slave or free woman simply because she uses *'āmāh* rather than *šipḥâ* in this verse (contra Sasson, 53–54). For further discussion, consult NOTE *maidservant* on 2:13.

your skirt. The consonants of the word translated as "your skirt" (*knpk*) could be read as a shortened dual form ("his skirts," *kĕnāpâw* in 2:12) or a singular form. MT *ketib* Tiberian (*kĕnāpēk*) reflects the dual form with the fuller spelling *kĕnāpêk* in multiple manuscripts (*BHS* critical apparatus), whereas MT *ketib* Babylonian, supported by MT^L *qere*, Old Greek, and the Syr., reads a singular form. As many scholars note, the spreading of a man's skirt in the singular serves as an idiom for conjugal activity (Ezek 16:8, or negatively Deut 23:1 [Eng. 22:30]; 27:20, where "uncovering" a man's skirt refers to sleeping with his wife; for further parallels, consult Kruger), although Eskenazi and Frymer-Kensky interpret it as Ruth's more general request for protection (59). Nevertheless, Boaz seems to interpret Ruth's words as a reference to marriage in his reply in the following verse (Ruth 3:10). The context suggests that Ruth is using an idiom for marriage that elsewhere uses "skirt" in the singular.

kindred redeemer. On this term, consult NOTE *one of our kindred redeemers* on 2:20.

3:10. *Blessed are you to YHWH.* LXX^B has "the Lord God," and some LXX^L manuscripts read "the Lord your God." The Targum, Vulg., and Old Latin support MT^L. On the translation of *lyhwh* as "to YHWH" and examples of similar blessing formulas found in Hebrew inscriptions, consult NOTE *Blessed is he to YHWH* on 2:20.

kindness. For a detailed discussion of the word translated as "kindness," consult "Divine Activity and Acts of *ḥesed* in Ruth" in the Introduction.

the young men. Old Greek reads "young men" rather than "the young men."

poor or rich. The Syr. has "rich or poor," whereas other versions read "poor or rich." For other examples of reversals, consult NOTES *without her two children or her husband* on 1:5, and *eating and drinking* on 3:3.

3:11. *you say.* On the translation of this *yiqtol* form, consult NOTE *you say* on 3:5. A few medieval Hebrew manuscripts, supported by the Syr., Targum, Vulg., and some

Old Greek manuscripts, include *ēlâ* ("to me") after "you say." Yet, most Hebrew and Greek manuscripts do not include "to me." The inclusion of "to me" in certain versions may be influenced by the similar phrase in 3:5 (NOTE *to me* on 3:5).

the entire assembly of my people. The Syr. reads "our people," but the other versions do not support this. One could translate the phrase *šā'ar 'ammî* more woodenly as "the gate of my people" (cf. Mic 1:9). In this idiom, "gate" functions as a metonym for the political body responsible for the legal or political affairs of the town. According to Deut 16:18, the people must appoint judges and officials in all their gates (cf. 21:19). In Ruth 4:1, Boaz goes up to the "gate" in order to conduct legal transactions involving marriage and property, which are approved by "the people in the gate and the elders" (4:11; cf. Deut 22:15–16; 25:7). The versions seem to have recognized the idiomatic quality of *šā'ar 'ammî* because they gloss it in various ways, such as "tribe of my people" (Old Greek; cf. Old Latin; Syr.) or "all who sit at the gate of the great Sanhedrin" (Targum). As discussed further under "Canonical Placements" in the Introduction, this idiom provides further evidence that the book of Ruth is set in the time and place in which Deuteronomy assumes that its idealized model for life in the Cisjordan will be enacted.

woman of worth. Boaz's use of "woman of worth" (*'ēšet ḥayil*) to describe Ruth is similar to the narrator's use of "mighty man of worth" to describe Boaz in 2:1. Thus, some commentators have suggested that Boaz and Ruth are a good match for one another (e.g., Eskenazi and Frymer-Kensky, 63). Along these lines, Boaz's use of the pronoun *'ānōkî* in 3:12, 13 may indicate that he addresses Ruth as his social equal (NOTE *I am a kindred redeemer* on 3:12), although this rhetoric may disguise the power dynamic in their relationship. On the translation of *ḥayil* as "worth," consult NOTE *mighty man of worth* on 2:1. The phrase "woman of worth" occurs elsewhere only in Prov 12:4 and 31:10, where it is used to describe a wife who is considered desirable for a wide variety of reasons, be it her ability to teach kindness (*ḥesed*; Prov 31:26) or her skills in land management (31:16), which would also be contextually appropriate in the present circumstance (consult COMMENTS on Ruth 3:6–15).

3:12. *And now.* Possibly influenced by the use of *wĕ'attâ* ("and now") at the beginning of v. 11, multiple Old Greek witnesses do not account for *wĕ'attâ* at the beginning of v. 12. The Targum supports MT^L.

it is certainly true that. The Hebrew (*kî 'omnām kî 'm*) is awkward in part because the word *'m* has the consonants but is unpointed in the *ketib*. The *qere*, supported by multiple medieval Hebrew manuscripts, proposes that the word should be "written, not read." This is one of eight occurrences of this type of *qere* (2 Sam 13:33; 15:21; 2 Kgs 5:18; Jer 38:16; 39:12; 51:3; Ezek 48:16). The first *kî* in this verse functions as an exclamation ("certainly"; NOTE *We will certainly return* on 1:10). The second *kî*, however, introduces the following clause, "I am a kindred redeemer," and thus may be translated as "that" (cf. *'omnām kî* in Job 12:2). The Targum simply reads "that" (*'ărûm*). The unpointed consonants *'m* probably do not represent the word *'im* ("if"). Rather, the final form of the *m* notwithstanding, these consonants probably result from dittography triggered by the first *kî* and the consonants *'m*, which begin the word *'omnām*. The mistake was probably corrected before the word *'omnām* was spelled completely for a second time. The Old Greek, Vulg., and Syr. do not account for either the second *kî* or the consonants *'m*.

I am a kindred redeemer. Boaz uses the pronoun *'ānōkî* ("I") rather than the shorter form *'ănî*. Some scholars have argued that *'ānōkî* reflects a polite form of speech for addressing one's superior, whereas *'ănî* is often used when addressing one's social equal or inferior (Notes *although I am* on 2:10, and *maidservant* on 2:13). If this is correct, at least for the book of Ruth, the conversation's intimate context may explain why Boaz addresses Ruth as his social equal (Note *woman of worth* on 3:11; Holmstedt, 167). On the word translated as "kindred redeemer," consult Note *one of our kindred redeemers* on 2:20.

but in fact. The word translated as "but in fact" is *wĕgam*. On this use of *gam*, consult Note *in fact . . . so that* on 2:8 and the use of *gam* in 2:15, 16.

closer than I. Naomi uses a similar term to refer to Boaz as a close relative (Note *the man is close to us* on 2:20).

3:13. *Lodge.* Multiple Hebrew manuscripts enlarge the consonants *l* and *n* in *lînî* ("lodge"). A verb form from the same root occurs in 1:16 without enlarged consonants. In both cases, the location of the lodging is implied rather than explicit. Despite scholarly speculation (e.g., Joüon, 75), the reason for the enlarged letters remains unknown. The feminine imperatives in this verse translated as "lodge" and "lie down" (*šikĕbî*), respectively, do not have locative adjuncts (cf. the implied reference to "the place" in 1:17). Thus, Boaz could mean "lodge/lie down here on the threshing floor" or "lodge/lie down with me" (consult Note *lie down* on 3:13). The narrative remains ambiguous (consult "Selective Representation and Narrative Ambiguity" in the Introduction).

if he wishes to redeem you, that is fine, let him redeem. My translation takes *ṭôb* as a *qatal* verb (e.g., among others, Num 11:18; Esth 1:19; 1 Chr 13:2), with the act of redemption as its subject. As Boaz does not state this other relative's name, a midrash takes *ṭôb* as the proper name of this relative (*Ruth Rab.* 6:3) since the syntax allows one to translate this clause as "if Tov wants to redeem you, let him redeem." Yet, none of the versions, including the Targum, supports this translation. Moreover, this man is never referred to as "Tov" during his cameo in chapter 4 (Note *So and So* on 4:1). Possibly influenced by the clause later in this verse, some LXX[L] manuscripts have "I will redeem you." Other versions do not support this reading.

I will redeem you. As in 3:12, Boaz continues to use the pronoun *'ānōkî* ("I") rather than *'ănî* (Note *I am a kindred redeemer* on 3:12). Three of the four uses of the root *g'l* ("redeem") in this verse have a second-person feminine suffix ("you"), which marks Ruth as the object of the redemption. Since Ruth is already a member of Boaz's clan (cf. 2:20; 3:11), Boaz seems to frame a marriage to her as a type of kindred redemption since under these circumstances it would be one way to help to restore the status quo within his clan (4:6; Note *one of our kindred redeemers* on 2:20 and Comments on 3:1–5, 3:6–15, and "Household Organization" in the Introduction).

As YHWH lives. The Syr. does not include the oath formula "as YHWH lives." LXX[B] has "live, Lord, you are the Lord" (*zē kurios su ei kurios;* Campbell, 115). Other Old Greek manuscripts and the Targum support MT[L]. This oath formula needs to be reconstructed in 2QRuth[b] (DJD III, 74).

lie down. The feminine imperative translated as "lie down" (*šikĕbî*) does not have a locative adjunct. Thus, Boaz could mean "lie down here on the threshing floor" or "lie down with me" (Note *lodge* on 3:13). If the latter, Boaz could be instructing Ruth to have intercourse with him. When this particular imperative form occurs elsewhere in the Hebrew Bible, it includes the adjunct "with him" and "with me" (Gen 19:34; 2 Sam 13:11, respectively) and refers explicitly to sexual intercourse. Thus, if "with me" is the implied adjunct of the imperative, Boaz is probably referring to sexual intercourse. The fact that the narrator specifies that Ruth "lay down at his feet until the morning" in the next verse may support this interpretation, especially if "feet" is read as a euphemism for Boaz's genitals (NOTE *undress at his feet and lie down* on 3:4). The syntax does not endorse one of these interpretations over the other, but it is a distinct possibility that Boaz is referring to sexual intercourse.

3:14. *at his feet.* MT^L misspells the word translated as "at his feet" as *margĕlōtāô*. MT^A and MT^Y have *margĕlōtāw*, which reads the Hebrew consonantal spelling as a shortened spelling without a mater lectionis. The *qere* reads *margĕlōtâw* with a mater lectionis. 2QRuth^b, which reads *m[rg]ltyw*, supports the *qere*. The *m* in *margĕlōtâw* is a locative *m* in that it specifies the location where Ruth lay down. Yet, as in 3:4, 7, 8, it remains unclear exactly to which body part the "feet" refers (NOTE *undress at his feet and lie down* on 3:4).

before a man. The *ketib* misspells the word translated as "before" as *bĕṭerewm*. The *qere* offers a correct spelling with *bĕṭerem*. My translation does not use gender-inclusive language for *'îš* ("a man") in order to preserve the gendered nature of Boaz's concern that a man might recognize the woman (*hā'iššâ*) at the threshing floor.

recognize. This verb derives from the same root (*nkr*) as the *hiphil* infinitive in 2:10, which I translated as "paid attention to me" (*lĕhakkîrēnî;* cf. 2:19).

he thought. The verb translated as "he thought" is a *yiqtol* form from *'mr*, which often means "to say." When *yiqtol, wayyiqtol,* or *qatal* forms of *'mr* that introduce direct speech occur without specifying to whom the speaker is talking, the direct speech may reflect the character's inner thoughts (e.g., Gen 32:20; Judg 16:20; 1 Sam 18:11; 2 Kgs 20:19 = Isa 39:8). The Old Greek and Vulg. specify the speaker as Boaz. In the Targum, Boaz speaks to his servant (cf. *Ruth Rab.* 2:1). Another midrash presents the direct speech as a prayer to God by Boaz (*Ruth Rab.* 7:1). Multiple Old Greek manuscripts have Boaz speaking to Ruth, which is also implied in the Vulg. The Syr. reads "she said to him" as if Ruth, who is the subject of the first two verbs in the verse, speaks to Boaz. Thus, in the Syr., Ruth rather than Boaz speaks the last line of the verse. LXX^L specifies the subject of the verb "arose" as Ruth.

the woman. 2QRuth^b, supported by the Vulg. and Syr., does not have "the woman" but simply reads *ky b'h hgrn* ("that she came to the threshing floor"). Possibly, this reading results from haplography triggered by the multiple occurrences of the letter *h* at the beginning or end of the words in the clause *bō'â hā'iššâ haggōren* ("the woman came to the threshing floor"). The Old Greek and Targum support MT^L, although the Old Greek reads "a woman" rather than "the woman."

to the threshing floor. Old Latin reads "to me" and the Vulg. reads "here" (*hoc*) rather than "to the threshing floor." 2QRuth^b, the Targum, and Old Greek support MT^L.

3:15. *Give me.* LXX^{BL} do not have the imperative "give me" (*hābî*), which derives from *yhb*. The expected form of the imperative would be *hăbî* because of vowel reduction, but other imperative forms of *yhb* occur without the reduction of the first vowel (Gen 11:3, 4, 7; 29:21; Deut 1:13). In Gen 29:21, Jacob says to Laban, "Give me my wife," with the indirect object ("me") implied (*hābāh 'et-'ištî*). Likewise, in Gen 47:16, Joseph says to his brothers, "Give me your cattle," with the indirect object ("me") implied (*hābû miqnêkem*). Boaz uses an imperative form of *yhb* in a similar sense in this verse.

he measured out. 2QRuth^b reads *wymd šm šš š'ry[m]* ("he measured out there six units of barley"). The Syr. follows "he measured" with "he threw." The Old Greek, Vulg., and Targum support MT^L.

six units of barley. One could translate *šēš-šĕʿōrîm* more woodenly as "six of barley" (cf. *šēš-haśśĕʿōrîm* in v. 17). Yet, MT^L, supported by the Old Greek and 2QRuth^b, implies six unspecified measurements, as the Vulg. and Syr. suggest with the translation "six measures" and the Targum suggests with the translation "six seahs of barley."

set [the barley] on it. The unstated or gapped object of the verb "set" is the units of barley from the previous clause (cf. the gapped or unstated objects in 2:7, 9, 14; 3:4). The suffix in the word translated "on it" (*ʿālêkā*) is a feminine form, which refers to the garment (*hammiṭpaḥat*), a feminine noun, rather than to Ruth. Boaz sets the barley on her garment rather than on her.

he went into the city. Multiple Kennicott and de Rossi manuscripts, multiple Old Greek manuscripts, the Vulg., and the Syr. read a feminine subject for the verb, implying Ruth as the subject. Some LXX^L manuscripts specify "Ruth" as the subject of the verb. Other Old Greek manuscripts support MT^L. The Targum and some LXX^L manuscripts specify "Boaz" as the subject of the verb.

Comments

In 3:5, Ruth had said that she would do all that her mother-in-law told her to do. In vv. 6–7, the narrator first states that she did indeed do as instructed. Then, the narrator describes her following these instructions with vocabulary similar to Naomi's in vv. 3–4. Yet, aside from telling Ruth that Boaz will provide further instructions, Naomi did not explain what Ruth should do when Boaz inevitably becomes aware of her presence. Thus, the situation requires Ruth to improvise once Boaz discovers her (Wojcik, 149). Although the situations are very different, one could compare Ruth's actions to the way the woman from Tekoa improvises beyond Joab's instructions when she claims to be a widow seeking relief from David because the conventional mechanisms of the clan had failed her (2 Sam 14:1–20).

Ruth encounters a content Boaz who, just as Naomi had said, has lain down following a meal. The narrator does not explain how Naomi knew of his plans, considering that she and Boaz have no direct contact anywhere in the book (although Naomi may anticipate such behavior if sleeping on the threshing floor reflected a common practice during harvest time possibly analogous to the shelter in the field referenced in Isa 1:8; cf. Hopkins; Meyers, 2013, 107). Nor does the narrator clarify whether Boaz is inebriated during his nocturnal encounter with Ruth, which Naomi does not inform Ruth may be possible (COMMENTS on 1:22b–2:2; NOTE *his heart was merry* on 3:7). This lack of clarity regarding Boaz's state fits with the ambiguity surrounding much of what happens that night on the threshing floor. After Ruth follows Naomi's instructions as far as they go, Boaz awakes "in the middle of the night" (cf. Judg 16:3) and is surprised to find an undressed woman at his feet (cf. NOTE *and Look!* on 3:8). Ruth's location and state of undress could suggest intimate physical contact (cf. NOTE *undress at his feet and lie down* on 3:4).

A surprised Boaz asks Ruth to identify herself. His question continues the questions that surround her character (cf. 2:5, 19; 3:16). Ruth replies that she is his handmaid, which may position her as a dependent within Boaz's clan and describe her status relative to his status. Boaz uses terminology that reflects his senior status relative to her when he refers to Ruth as "my daughter," a term for a subordinate unmarried female member of a clan. Although Naomi had told Ruth that Boaz will tell her what to do (3:4), Ruth is the first one to give instructions when she tells Boaz to spread his skirt over her because he is a kindred redeemer (3:9). Ruth's response not only reveals to Boaz who she is in relation to him, but also reminds him who he is in relation to her (Landy, 301). Throughout their conversation, both characters use terminology that structures their relationship within their Judahite clan framework.

Boaz ultimately agrees to do all that Ruth says (3:11), just as Ruth had previously agreed to do all that Naomi had said (3:5). In 2:12, Boaz had referred to YHWH's skirt as an image of refuge for Ruth. Now she uses the image of a skirt with a similar sense of refuge, possibly found in a secure marriage (NOTE *your skirt* on 3:9). Yet, unlike Boaz, she does not connect this image with YHWH. For her, the refuge should come through Boaz serving as a kindred redeemer. As already discussed (COMMENTS on 3:1–5), marriage could qualify as an act of redemption. There is no clear reference to land redemption until Ruth 4. Thus, a marriage with a member of Elimelech's clan would be a contextually appropriate form of redemption because the death of Ruth's husband was one of the events that disrupted the status quo for Ruth and the clan (cf. 4:10).

Although Boaz claims that Ruth has performed an act of kindness (*ḥesed*) that surpasses her earlier one, he does not specify to which earlier act he is referring. In keeping with other acts of kindness throughout the book, Ruth's kindness serves as the catalyst for a blessing (consult "Divine Activity and Acts of *ḥesed* in Ruth" in the Introduction). After blessing Ruth, Boaz claims "the entire assembly of my people knows that you are a woman of worth" (3:11). The description seems positive even if it is imprecise (cf. NOTE *woman of worth* on 3:11). One could also interpret Boaz's description of Ruth as countering her earlier statement when she described herself to Boaz as a "foreign woman" (*nākriyyâ;* 2:10). The term *nākriyyâ* could refer not only to an ethnic foreigner but to a woman who is not suitable for marriage because she is married to another man (NOTE *a foreign woman* on 2:10). To invoke imagery found in Proverbs (cf. Camp, 129; Koosed, 92), Boaz does not describe Ruth as a woman to be avoided because she is a *nākriyyâ* (Prov 2:16; 5:20; 6:24; 7:5; 23:27), but as a woman to be desired because, in his opinion, she is a woman of worth (*'ēšet ḥayil;* 12:4; 31:10).

Similar to Prov 31:31, Boaz claims that a *'ēšet ḥayil* is acknowledged by the assembly of his people (Ruth 3:11). Throughout the book of Ruth, one's "people" (*'am*) refers to living members of one's clan (except in 1:6; consult "Household Organization" in the Introduction). In other words, Boaz explains that he is willing to serve as a kindred redeemer because the clan has recognized that Ruth is a woman of worth. This explanation, however, may raise questions once again about why members of the clan have not done more to restore the status quo for Ruth, especially if they know of her circumstances and her good standing within their community. In fact, Boaz goes on to mention that there is another member of the clan who is a closer relative than he is (3:12). This disclosure highlights the lack of aid offered by potential kindred redeemers other than Boaz up to this point. One should not assume that the book presents an optimistic view of how well household dependents are provided for within the structure of the clan.

Boaz's willingness to act on Ruth's behalf in contrast to his peers does not necessarily confirm or deny his virtue. When Boaz blesses Ruth because she did not go after a younger man, he seems to acknowledge that she has some autonomy in her choice of a husband and that she was not obligated to marry Boaz (cf. 1:13; Num 36:6). Naomi had told Ruth that Boaz is one of potentially several relatives who would qualify as kindred redeemers (2:20). Similarly, in 3:9, Ruth had referred to Boaz as "a kindred redeemer" rather than "the [only] kindred redeemer." There is no reason why Ruth would have to marry her closest surviving kinsman. Eskenazi and Frymer-Kensky question whether Boaz construes Ruth's request for Boaz to spread his skirt over her as a marriage proposal in part because Boaz "seem[s] remarkably sanguine about the prospect of Ruth's marrying another man" (64). Even though Boaz interprets Ruth's proposal as an act of kindness worthy of a blessing, he does not raise any objections to the possibility of her marrying someone else, unlike Orpah and Ruth, who object explicitly to the possibility of marrying into a Moabite household (1:10, 16–17). One could interpret Boaz as expressing concern for Ruth's potential happiness over his own interests by informing her of other marital possibilities (although the narrator never indicates that the unnamed kinsman is younger than Boaz).

If one interprets Boaz's motives less generously, he may bring up the unnamed kinsman in the hope that Ruth would pursue another man instead of himself even though she is not legally obligated to do so. In fact, in 3:13, the word translated as "fine" (*tôb*) could also be read as a superlative meaning "that is best." If so, Boaz may imply his preference that another member of the clan serve as Ruth's redeemer (consult "Sexual Desire in Ruth" in the Introduction). As emphasized throughout this commentary, the narrator does not clarify the motivations for most of the characters' actions in the book (consult "Actions, Events, and Consequences" in the Introduction). Whether one understands Boaz's sanguine attitude about Ruth marrying another man as reflecting his self-sacrifice on her behalf or his hope that someone else will serve as her redeemer depends in part on how one chooses to interpret his character. One could be equally cautious about whether Boaz's instructions in v. 13 should be interpreted as an endorsement of his integrity. As discussed further below, some scholars cite Boaz's use of the word "lodge" rather than the possibly sexually charged term "lie down" when instructing Ruth to spend the night on the threshing floor as evidence of his pure intentions (v. 13a). Yet, this argument seems strained since he instructs her to "lie down" later in the same verse (v. 13b).

The narrator provides rare access into a character's thought process by supplying Boaz's internal monologue. Here, he shows concern that Ruth's presence on the threshing floor remain undiscovered (3:14; cf. 1:6, 18; "Actions, Events, and Consequences" in the Introduction). Although this monologue explains the motivation behind Boaz's instructions, it does not explain why he instructs Ruth to spend the night on the threshing floor (Fentress-Williams, 99). As Ruth does in 1:18, Boaz uses an oath formula that seems to help persuade her to stay until morning (consult "Genre[s] in Ruth" in the Introduction). According to v. 8, this conversation occurs in "the middle of the night" when it is presumably dark. If Boaz simply wanted Ruth's presence to go undetected, it is unclear why she could not leave the threshing floor in the middle of the night under the cover of darkness. Why risk waiting "until the morning," as Boaz says, even if it is still too dark for others to recognize her? More specifically, Boaz does not want her simply to lodge with him but to "lie down" with him (NOTE *lie down* on 3:13). As discussed below, this is a very sexually charged instruction, considering that it persuades an undressed Ruth to lie not only on the threshing floor, but, as the narrator specifies in 3:14, at Boaz's feet, which could be a euphemism for his genitals (NOTE *undress at his feet and lie down* on 3:4).

After spending the night with Boaz, Ruth arises "before a man could recognize another" (3:14). The word translated as "recognize" comes from the same root (*nkr*) as words translated as "paid attention" in 2:10, 19. Questions have surrounded Ruth and those associated with her since she arrived in Bethlehem and will continue in her next conversation with Naomi (3:16). Even Boaz seems aware of the questions surrounding her. His concern is not simply with the possible discovery of any woman with him on the threshing floor, but specifically with "the woman" (*hā'iššâ*), which presumably singles out Ruth (cf. the use of *hā'iššâ* to specify Naomi in 1:5). When Ruth was gleaning in the field, it was beneficial that Boaz noticed her. Naomi even blesses Boaz for noticing her. Now, however, Ruth arises in the morning presumably to leave the threshing floor and return to Bethlehem (cf. 2:4) before she is noticed.

As in 2:17–18, Ruth will return to Naomi with barley. In 3:15, Boaz puts six measures of barley on Ruth's garment before they part ways. Naomi's initial instructions to Ruth in 3:3–4 involved what to do with her clothing. The conversation on the threshing floor begins and ends with instructions also involving clothing. In v. 9, Ruth had told Boaz to spread his skirt over her. Before Boaz leaves, he tells Ruth to give him her garment, which he fills with barley. He does not, however, explain why he is giving her this barley. Although Ruth will discuss his intentions behind this gesture upon her return to her mother-in-law, what the gesture suggests about how Boaz understands his relationship with Ruth remains difficult to determine (consult COMMENTS on 3:16–18). In this sense, it is in keeping with much of the interaction between Ruth and Boaz during their nocturnal encounter.

Eskenazi and Frymer-Kensky are representative of many scholars when they write, "the reader is left in the dark as to what exactly transpires [at the threshing floor]" (48). Danna Fewell and David Gunn note the sexual overtones already present in Boaz and Ruth's initial encounter, especially in his instructions to his male servants (2:9, 15, 16) (84). Terms that can have sexual overtones occur frequently and repeatedly throughout Ruth 3, including the verbs "to know" (five times; vv. 3, 4, 11, 14, 18), "to lie down" (eight times; vv. 4 [three times], 7 [two times], 8, 13, 14), "to enter" (seven times; vv. 4, 7 [two times], 14, 15, 16, 17), and "to undress" (two times; vv. 3, 7), as well as euphemistic nouns such as "feet" (four times; vv. 4, 7, 8, 14; NOTE *undress at his feet and lie down* on 3:4) and the reference to the spreading of Boaz's skirt over Ruth (NOTE *your skirt* on 3:9). Also, some scholars identify sexual overtones in the phrase "to go after" in 3:10 because similar phrases may describe how one goes after a seductive woman (Prov 7:22; cf. Hos 2:7 [Eng. 2:5]; Hubbard 214; Linafelt, 1999, 57). Although each of these terms has a broad semantic range and is not used exclusively in a sexual sense in this chapter (e.g., "to know" in vv. 11, 14, 18; "to enter" in vv. 16, 17), the density of the terminology, which is comparable to that in other texts in which intercourse occurs overtly, is very suggestive (cf. Gen 19:32–35; 2 Sam 11–12, 13; Eskenazi and Frymer-Kensky, 53). Moreover, the narrator uses the verb "to enter" as an explicit sexual reference in Ruth 4:13.

In addition to vocabulary that could serve as sexual innuendo, scholars have noted several points of comparison between Gen 19:30–38 and Ruth 3 (consult "Moabites as Descendants of Lot" in the Introduction). The fact that Ruth undresses and lies down close to Boaz, possibly even at his genitals, is extremely suggestive, even if the narrator does not clarify exactly what happened on the night in question (consult "Selective Representation and Narrative Ambiguity" in the Introduction). Among the versions, Targumic expansions to v. 8 draw attention to the sexually charged nature of the encounter even as they deny that intercourse occurred, in part because Boaz's genitals "were made soft," according to the Targum. Similarly, a midrash portrays Boaz as resisting the evil inclination and swearing not to touch Ruth (*Ruth Rab.* 6:4; cf. 7:1).

This does not mean that all of the language used to describe this encounter possesses sexual overtones. Some scholars argue that the verb "lodge" lacks a sexual connotation when Boaz tells Ruth to "lodge tonight" (3:13; cf. 1:16; although its uses in sexually charged scenes in the Song of Songs might suggest otherwise [Song 1:13; 7:12; Pfau, 12, n. 26]). Some cite this verb as evidence that Boaz and Ruth did not engage in any sexual activity (e.g., Block, 695; Bush, 138; Campbell, 175). Noting much of the sexually suggestive language cited above, however, Julie Pfau argues convincingly that the presence of a verb that (possibly) lacks sexual overtones does not somehow negate the cumulative evidence for the strong possibility of sexual activity on the basis of several other terms and images in this passage (12). Moreover, she notes that denials of such activity tend to be rooted ultimately in scholars' assumptions about the characters' integrity rather than decisive textual evidence (12). For example, Bush writes, "Finally, one can only comment that such an action is so inconsistent with the character of Ruth as portrayed in the story as to be utterly implausible" (153). And Campbell writes, "It is not prudery which compels the conclusion that there was no sexual intercourse at the threshing floor; it is the utter irrelevance of such a speculation" (138). Yet, as argued repeatedly throughout this commentary, the narrator rarely clarifies the characters' desires. Their desires, motives, and possible virtue remain largely opaque and could be interpreted in a variety of ways (e.g., consult the discussion of Boaz or Naomi under COMMENTS on 1:22b–2:2 or 2:18–23; "Characterization" in the introduction).

Ultimately, the narrator does not clarify what happened during Ruth and Boaz's nocturnal encounter. The narration of this encounter is ambiguous not simply because of what is not described, but because of *how* it is described. The ambiguity is not only introduced by the gaps in information in the narration but by the multiple interpretative possibilities introduced by the innuendo-laced narration (consult "Selective Representation and Narrative Ambiguity" in the Introduction). Questions remain regarding whether Ruth and Boaz consummated their relationship and, if so, the implications that it would have for Ruth's household affiliation. In fact, Naomi confronts Ruth with these questions when Ruth returns from the threshing floor in 3:16–18.

Ruth and Naomi's Conversation (3:16–18)

3 ¹⁶When she came to her mother-in-law, she said, "Whose are you my daughter?" She told her all that the man had done for her. ¹⁷She said, "These six units of barley he gave to me because he said to me, 'You should not go empty to your mother-in-law.'" ¹⁸She said, "Stay my daughter until you know how the matter plays out because the man will not rest unless the matter is finished today."

Notes

3:16. *she came.* Old Greek specifies the subject of this verb as "Ruth" (NOTE *when she went* on 2:3).

Whose are you my daughter? 2QRuth[b] (*mh*) and the Vulg. (*quid*) read "what"; the Targum and Syr. (*mn*) read "who"; and multiple Old Greek manuscripts support MT[L] (*mî*) (for Old Greek variants, consult Quast, 183). As in 3:9, Ruth answers the question in the Syr. with "I am Ruth." LXX[B] reads "my daughter" but does not include Naomi's question. Naomi does not ask the question because she is uncertain of Ruth's identity, as some scholars suggest (e.g., Köhlmoos, 67). Unlike in Boaz's otherwise identical question in 3:9 to which Ruth responds by identifying herself by name, Naomi refers to Ruth as "my daughter," as she had done previously (2:2, 22; 3:1; Block, 699), and Ruth does not respond by identifying herself (contrast Gen 27:18–19). A number of scholars follow Rudolph's analysis of *mî* as an "accusative of condition" (Rudolph, 57) and cite Amos 7:2, 5 and the Ugaritic cognate *my* as parallels (e.g., Gray, 419). Read with this sense, Naomi is inquiring about Ruth's well-being, that is, "How are you?" My translation reads *mî* in a genitival sense (cf. *mî* in Gen 24:23, 47; Num 22:9; 1 Sam 12:3; 17:55, 56, 58; Jer 44:28; *GKC* §137b). Read with this sense, Naomi asks a question similar to that which Boaz asked regarding Ruth in 2:5, "To whom [*lĕmî*] does this female servant [belong]?" (cf. Gen 24:23, 47; 32:18 [Eng. 32:17]; 1 Sam 30:13). After the events of the previous night with their conjugal subtext, Naomi is inquiring about Ruth's current household affiliation (NOTE *to whom does this female servant [belong]?* on 2:5). As Sasson notes, "Naomi could simply be asking whether Ruth should still be considered as the widow of Mahlon or whether she has become the wife of Boaz" (100; cf. *Ruth Rab.* 7:4). This question would be in keeping with Naomi's stated concern in 3:1 that Ruth find rest in a new household (NOTES *find rest, each one in the house of her husband* on 1:9, *shouldn't I seek a place of rest* on 3:1, and *where it would go well for you* on 3:1).

3:17. *She said.* Old Greek reads "she said to her." The other versions do not support the Old Greek.

These six units of barley. On the meaning of this term, *šēš-haśśĕʿōrîm hāʾelleh,* consult NOTE *six units of barley* on 3:15, although in 3:17 it occurs with the article and the demonstrative pronoun ("these").

to me. The word translated as "to me" (*ʾēlâ*) is attested in MT^L *qere* and multiple Kennicott and de Rossi manuscripts. The Old Greek, Targum, and Syr. also support this reading (NOTE *to me* on 3:5). Possibly triggered by the *aleph* and *lemed* at the beginning of *ʾēlâ* and *ʾal-tābôʾî* ("you should not"), respectively, MT^L *ketib* has only the vowel points (*ē a*) without the corresponding consonants (*ʾly*) above them. Similarly, the Vulg. does not have "to me."

empty. The adverb translated as "empty" (*rîqām*) is related to the adverb "empty" (*rêqām*) in 1:21 (NOTE *one who restores life* on 4:15).

3:18. *She said.* The Vulg. specifies Naomi as the subject of this verb. The other versions do not support the Vulg.

Stay. The feminine imperative translated as "stay" (*šĕbî*) derives from *yšb* ("to sit, stay, dwell"), but this form may imply an instruction to wait until a certain event has occurred (cf. Gen 38:11; 1 Sam 1:23). Whereas Naomi and her sons "stayed" (*wayyēšbû*) in Moab at the beginning of the first chapter (1:4), the second chapter ended with the indication that Naomi's Moabite daughter-in-law "stayed" (*wattēšeb*) with her in Bethlehem after the harvests were "finished" (*kĕlôt;* 2:23). Now chapter 3 ends with Naomi instructing Ruth to stay (*šĕbî*) with her until the matter, which will further solidify her place in a Judahite household, is "finished" (*killâ*). For further discussion, consult COMMENTS.

know. MT^L spells this verb with a paragogic *nûn* (NOTE *stick with* on 2:8).

how the matter plays out. One could translate this idiom more woodenly as "how a matter will fall." Although English requires an article before the noun "matter" to smoothly translate *dābār* ("word, matter, thing") in this clause, MT^L does not include the article. It reads *dābār* rather than the expected *haddābār,* which occurs later in this same verse. For other examples, such as 2 Sam 19:36 (Eng. 19:35), of forms that lack the expected definite article, consult JM §137p. The Syr. does not have this clause at all. LXX^B provides a wooden translation without the expected article, but LXX^L witnesses include the article and use various inflections of the verb "to be" rather than equivalents of the *yiqtol* verb, translated idiomatically as "plays out," in MT^L. The verb in MT^L derives from *npl* ("to fall"). Verbs from this root are used with forms of the noun *dābār* to convey the fulfillment, or lack thereof, of a judgment or promise. In these contexts, *npl* often carries a negative connotation and is translated as "to fail," as in "Not a word failed [*lōʾ nāpal dābār*] from all the good words that YHWH spoke" (Josh 21:45; cf. 23:14; 1 Kgs 8:56; 2 Kgs 10:10; Esth 6:10). Yet, in Ruth 3:18, it conveys a sense of fulfillment of a judgment or promise, as in Isa 9:7 (Eng. 9:8), "YHWH sent a word [*dābār*] against Jacob and it fell [*wĕnāpal*] on Israel." In this sense, Naomi advises

Ruth to stay until she knows how this matter is fulfilled or resolved. In the Targum, Naomi advises Ruth to wait for the decree to come from the divine council in heaven. Some commentators suggest that this verse hints at divine providence controlling the outcome of this matter (e.g., Campbell, 129; Trible, 187; cf. Hals, 13–15). For further discussion, consult "Divine Activity and Acts of *ḥesed* in Ruth" in the Introduction.

today. Unlike the other versions, the Vulg. and two Old Greek manuscripts do not have "today" (Campbell, 116).

Comments

As in 2:18, Ruth is once again greeted with questions upon her return to Naomi (3:16; cf. 2:5; 3:9). In 2:5, Boaz had inquired about Ruth's household affiliation; now, Naomi asks a similar question. In 3:1, she had expressed concern for Ruth's security, which could be found presumably through a second marriage (1:8–9, 11–13). Ostensibly, this concern provided the pretext for Naomi's instructions that Ruth go to the threshing floor. Thus, one could expect Naomi to ask whether Ruth has joined Boaz's household upon her return. Given the possibility that Ruth and Boaz consummated their relationship on the threshing floor, Naomi inquires whether Ruth is under Boaz's authority as his wife (NOTE *Whose are you my daughter?* on 3:16). Naomi's question continues to scrutinize not only Ruth's exact status within her clan, but also whether Boaz is willing to serve as a kindred redeemer. In Ruth 2, his actions on behalf of Ruth were credited to the favor that he showed toward her during the harvests rather than being an explicit commitment to serve as a kindred redeemer. It is only during the nocturnal encounter arranged by Naomi that he actually agrees to serve as a kindred redeemer.

In 3:16b, the narrator states that Ruth told Naomi "all that the man had done for her." Thus, Naomi learns exactly what happened during the night in question. Yet, unlike in 2:19, the narrator states that Ruth provided Naomi with a full report but does not reveal what Ruth told her. Ultimately, Naomi learns more about Ruth's household status than the audience does in v. 16. This narrative technique ensures that the audience still does not know exactly what happened on the threshing floor. Ruth's status in relation to either the household of her first marriage or the household of Boaz remains an open question.

In 3:17, Ruth claims that Boaz gave her six units of barley and said that she should not go empty when she returns to Naomi. Although it is true that Boaz gave her this amount of barley in 3:15, there is no indication that he told her the reason for giving her these provisions (for possibilities, consult *b. Sanh.* 93a; Wojcik, 150). This silence could simply result from the narrator's selective representation, or it could indicate that the characters may have the capacity to lie (cf. 4:3; "Characterization" and "Selective Representation and Narrative Ambiguity" in the Introduction). One could also understand Ruth's supposed quotation of Boaz as her interpretation of what his gesture means since the characters' speech and actions do not necessarily provide unambiguous access to their intentions. This would fit with other points in the story where a character must infer another character's intentions behind her or his speech or actions (e.g., 1:18; 2:13; "Selective Representation and Narrative Ambiguity" in the Introduction).

Ruth's explanation of Boaz's gesture, however, does not necessarily clarify the meaning(s) that she attributes to it. For example, in 1:21, Naomi announced that she was bereft of a male provider when she declared that YHWH made her return from Moab "empty" (*rêqām*). Yet, the narrator did not indicate that any of her relatives came forward to serve as a kindred redeemer at that time. Now Ruth, who was presumably with Naomi when she made this declaration, claims that Boaz said she should not go to her mother-in-law "empty" (*rîqām*). Ruth could infer that his provision of barley is an indication that he will serve as a kindred redeemer. Just as Ruth's reference to Boaz's skirt (3:9) used an image that Boaz had previously connected with YHWH (2:12), her reference to a lack of emptiness uses an image that Naomi had previously connected with YHWH.

Yet, Ruth could also infer that Boaz's gesture signals that he is releasing her from under his authority as a dependent who has worked in the field that he holds. The infrequent word "empty" (*rîqām*) occurs in some texts that address the release of a member of a clan who has worked under the authority (*ʿim*) of a wealthier member of the clan. Although the circumstances in each of these texts differ significantly from one another, the dependent member of the clan in each text is expected not to depart empty when she or he is sent out from under the authority of another member of the clan (e.g., Gen 31:42). In fact, Deut 15:13–14 specifies that a male or female Hebrew slave should not be sent out from under one's authority empty but should be provided for from not only the flock and winepress but also the threshing floor (*gōren;* cf. Ruth 3:2, 3, 6, 14). Ruth's Moabite ethnicity notwithstanding, her explanation for why Boaz gave her provisions from the threshing floor may assume that he no longer considers her to be under his guardianship. If so, her explanation does not confirm whether he will serve as a kindred redeemer after that night.

The conversation in 3:16–18 is the last time that either Ruth or Naomi will speak in a book dominated by dialogue. Naomi instructs her "daughter," a term that can apply to an unmarried member of one's household, to stay, presumably with her, until the matter is finished. Within the patrilocal structure of the household model, a woman usually went to live with her husband's household upon marriage (consult "Household Organization" in the Introduction). Thus, to whom Ruth is married, if to anyone, remains unclear at this point. In fact, whether Ruth was previously married to Mahlon or to Kilyon is only clarified in 4:10. As Naomi implies, whatever happened on the threshing floor, the matter is not yet finished. What is the status of Ruth's relationship to Boaz? How will Boaz, whom Ruth and Naomi never refer to by name in this conversation, resolve this matter? Who, if anyone, will serve as a kindred redeemer for Ruth and Naomi? Considering how profoundly the status quo has been disrupted, how far would a kindred redeemer be willing to go for it to be restored? In a sense, Naomi's instructions set up the climax to the story in the final chapter.

At the Gate (4:1–12)

4 ¹Now Boaz went up to the gate and he sat there and, look, the kindred redeemer whom Boaz spoke of was passing by! He said, "Turn aside and sit here, So and So." So he turned aside and sat. ²He took ten men from among the elders of the town and said "Sit here" and they sat. ³He said to the kindred redeemer, "The portion of the field held by our kin Elimelech—Naomi, who returned from the territory of Moab, offers for sale. ⁴I thought I would uncover your ear by saying, 'Acquire [it] before the inhabitants and before the elders of my people.' If you want to redeem, redeem! But if you do not want to redeem, tell me so that I may know because there is no one except you to redeem and I am after you." Then, he said, "I want to redeem." ⁵Boaz said, "On the day you acquire the field from the hand of Naomi, also Ruth the Moabite, the wife of the dead man, you acquire her to establish the name of the dead man upon his inheritance." ⁶The kindred redeemer said, "I am not able to redeem for myself lest I ruin my own inheritance. You redeem my redemption for yourself because I am not able to redeem." ⁷(Now this was [the custom] formerly in Israel regarding redemption and substitution to establish any matter: a man would remove his sandal and give it to his friend. This served as the witness in Israel.) ⁸The kindred redeemer said to Boaz, "Acquire for yourself" and he removed his sandal. ⁹Boaz said to the elders and all the people, "You are witnesses today that I now acquire all that belonged to Elimelech and all that belonged to Kilyon and Mahlon from the hand of Naomi. ¹⁰Also, Ruth the Moabite, the wife of Mahlon, I now acquire for myself as a wife to establish the name of the dead man upon his inheritance so that the name of the dead man may not be cut off from among his kin or the assembly of his place. You are witnesses today." ¹¹All the people who were in the gate and the elders said, "(We are) witnesses. May YHWH make the woman who is entering your house like Rachel and Leah, who built, the two of them, the house of Israel, so that you act worthily in Ephrathah and proclaim a name in Bethlehem. ¹²May your house be like the house of Perez, whom Tamar bore for Judah, from the seed that YHWH gives to you from this female servant."

Notes

4:1. *the gate.* The Syro-Hexapla reads "of the city" after "the gate." Although the clause is marked with an asterisk in the Syro-Hexapla to indicate that this reading is attested in Hebrew, the asterisk may not necessarily come from Origen but probably reflects the influence of the Syr., in which Boaz sat "at the gate of the city," as compared with MT^L, in which Boaz "sat there" (Campbell, 139). Multiple Old Greek manuscripts, the Targum, and the Vulg. support MT^L, although the Targum reads "sat there with the elders" (cf. 4:2).

and, look, the kindred redeemer whom Boaz spoke of was passing by! As in 2:4, this use of *wĕhinnēh* ("and look") introduces a new character into a scene after the scene has already started by presenting this introduction through a character's viewpoint (Note *look!* on 2:4). A more wooden translation of this clause would read, "and look the kindred redeemer was passing by that Boaz spoke of." Although this construction is rare, one finds other texts in which a participle ("was passing by") intervenes between a relative clause ("whom Boaz spoke of") and its antecedent ("kindred redeemer"). For example, a wooden translation of Gen 24:15 reads, "and look Rebekah was coming out, who was born to Bethuel" (Holmstedt, 182). I have adjusted the word order for a smoother English translation.

kindred redeemer. On this term, consult Notes *one of our kindred redeemers* on 2:20, *I am a kindred redeemer* and *closer than I* on 3:12, and *I will redeem you* on 3:13.

So and So. The nouns translated as "So and So" (*pĕlōnî 'almōnî*) do not represent the kindred redeemer's proper name. The etymology of this idiom remains uncertain. The versions provide little clarity in this regard, with "secret one" (LXX^BL), "such a one" (multiple Old Greek manuscripts; cf. Matt 26:18), and the gloss "calling him by his name" (Vulg.). For a detailed survey of the versions as well as scholarly opinions regarding the etymologies of the idiom, consult Campbell, 141–43, and Hubbard 233–34, although Campbell's proposal that the etymology relates to secrecy or hiddenness does not find support in the only other uses of this idiom in the Hebrew Bible. In 1 Sam 21:3 and 2 Kgs 6:8, the idiom is used in reference to a geographic location that remains unspecified because the speaker is summarizing another party's statements rather than recounting those statements verbatim (cf. Dan 8:13). Thus, "So and So" conveys the sense of this idiom in 4:1 as in the English sentence, "She said that she would meet me at such and such a place." Along these lines, the use of this idiom draws attention to the fact that the narrator in Ruth summarizes the characters' dialogue without claiming to provide a verbatim record of actual dialogue (Berlin, 1983, 99–101). The use of this idiom may also subtly draw attention to the narrator's presence in anticipation of the narrator's more overt presence in 4:7, when the narrator provides direct commentary on the characters' actions (Note *now this was [the custom] formerly in Israel* on 4:7). A midrash suggests that the man's name is not provided because he refused to establish the name of the dead man upon his inheritance. According to *Ruth Rab.* 7:7, the man did not know that the legislation prohibiting Moabites and Ammonites from joining the assembly of YHWH applied to men but not to women. Deuteronomy 23:4–7 (Eng. 3–6) uses masculine forms of the words for Moabite and Ammonite (cf. Neh 13:1–2). Nonetheless, as illustrated in the example discussed above, the use of the idiom "So and So" does not have a negative connotation elsewhere in the Hebrew Bible. Likewise, one should not read a negative or dismissive evaluation of the character into Boaz's use of the idiom (contra Bush, 197; Hubbard, 234–35; Zenger, 81), even if the NRSV's translation of the idiom as "friend" may be too generous (Linafelt, 1999, 5, 65). For the purposes of the narrative, the use of this idiom helps maintain the focus on this character's role as a potential kindred redeemer similar to the way the rhyming names of Naomi's sons maintain the focus on their roles (NOTE *the names of his two sons were Mahlon and Kilyon* on 1:2; "Characterization" in the Introduction). As discussed in the Introduction ("The Diction of the Hebrew in Ruth"), rhyme occurs throughout the book.

4:2. *He took.* The Old Greek and Vulg. specify Boaz as the subject of the verb, possibly to clarify that the subject is not the kindred redeemer. The Targum supports MT^L.

4:3. *field . . . territory.* On the translation of these nouns, which reflect the absolute and construct forms of the III-*h* root *śdh*, respectively, consult NOTES *territory of Moab* on 1:1, and *territory* on 1:6.

Naomi . . . offers for sale. LXX^B has "was given to Naomi" rather than "Naomi . . . offers for sale." The other versions support MT^L, although the Syr. has "to me" after "sale." Since the verb *mākĕrâ* ("offers for sale") is a *qatal* form, one could translate it as "Naomi sold" (Westbrook, 65–66). Naomi's situation would conform to the situations described in Leviticus 25 in which a close relative redeems one's land after it has been sold to an outside party (e.g., Lev 25:25, 27). Yet, a relative may also redeem land preemptively (Jer 32:7–8). The unnamed kindred redeemer uses the same language in Ruth 4:8 as Jeremiah 32 uses to describe a preemptive land redemption (NOTE *acquire for yourself* on 4:8). The *qatal* verb that Boaz uses here probably functions as a performative, in which a state is created or an action is performed through its declaration (Gen 23:10–11, 13; 2 Sam 24:22–23; Jer 40:4; WO §30.5.1d; cf. NOTE *I now acquire* on 4:9). In this case, Naomi's offer to sell the property is actualized through Boaz's statement that she is offering it for sale. For a detailed review of scholarship on this verb, consult Sasson, 108–15. The technical nuances of *mākĕrâ* notwithstanding, one should note that the term rhymes with *miqrehā* ("her chance") used in 2:3 when Ruth "chanced upon the portion of the field [*ḥelqat haśśādeh*] held by Boaz" (NOTE *she chanced upon* on 2:3). The rhyme that *mākĕrâ* creates with 2:3 may help to explain its use in a way that is in keeping with the narrative style throughout the book (consult "The Diction of the Hebrew in Ruth" in the Introduction and COMMENTS on 4:1–12).

who returned from the territory of Moab. On the translation of this clause, consult NOTE *who returned from the territory of Moab* on 1:22.

4:4. *I thought I would uncover your ear.* On the translation "I thought," consult NOTE *he thought* on 3:14. Elsewhere, various forms of the idiom woodenly translated as "uncover your ear" (*'eglê 'ozĕnkā*) indicate the disclosure or revelation of information (1 Sam 9:15; 20:2, 12–13; 22:8, 17; 2 Sam 7:27; Job 33:16; 1 Chr 17:25). A wooden translation of this idiom preserves the assonance between Boaz's "uncovering" (*glh*) the kindred redeemer's ear and Ruth's "uncovering" (*glh*) herself at Boaz's feet (3:4, 7). Also, the word *'eglê* forms a consonantal anagram with the word *haggō'ēl* ("the kindred redeemer"; 4:1, 6, 8; "The Diction of the Hebrew in Ruth" in the Introduction).

If you want to redeem. LXX^L reads "if, therefore." This reading does not find support among the other versions. The Hebrew verb is a modal form, as are two other verbs from the same root later in the verse (cf. 3:13).

But if you do not want to redeem. MT^LA read the verb as a third-person rather than second-person form: "But if he will not redeem" (*wĕ'im-lō' yig'al*). Multiple Kennicott and de Rossi manuscripts, supported by the Old Greek and Syr., have a second-person form (*tig'al*). Nevertheless, how a *y* would be confused with a *t* in this case remains hard to explain (Rudolph, 59). Unlike most commentators, Sasson retains the third-person form, explaining this clause as an aside that Boaz directs toward the elders before resuming his address toward the kindred redeemer (118). Yet, nothing in the text endorses this interpretation, and Sasson does not cite comparable examples from other biblical texts. It is more likely that the readings in MT^LA are corrupt (consult the discussion in *BHQ,* 55*).

I may know. MT^L *qere* has *w'd'h*, whereas the *ketib* has *wĕ'ēda'*. Although the *qere* marks the verb explicitly as a jussive with the *h* suffix, one could translate both forms as a jussive (NOTE *may YHWH do* on 1:8).

I am after you . . . I want to redeem. Although Boaz uses the pronoun *'ănî* ("I") when describing his thought process at the beginning of the verse, in these two clauses, both Boaz and the kindred redeemer use the pronoun *'ānōkî* ("I"), which may reflect a more polite form of speech for addressing one's superior (NOTES *although I am* on 2:10, and *I am a kindred redeemer* on 3:12). If this is correct, both parties may be addressing each other with deference during these negotiations regardless of their social standing relative to one another (Holmstedt, 189).

4:5. *also Ruth.* In MT^L, the word translated as "also" is *ûme'et,* which, if one analyzes the word as the conjunction *wāw* and the preposition *min* ("from") joined to an untranslated object marker *'et,* occurs elsewhere when property or possessions are given to or taken from multiple parties (Num 35:8; cf. Lev 16:5; Zech 6:10). Although the verb in Ruth 4:5 is "acquire" rather than "take" or "give," as in these other texts, the context of acquiring property related to one's inheritance (cf. Num 35:8) from more than one individual could fit the present context. Moreover, Lev 25:14–15 uses both *miyyad* ("from the hand of") and *me'et* with forms of the root *qnh* ("to acquire") in the context of property acquisition. In this sense, the relative is acquiring the field from the hands of both Naomi *and* Ruth. Yet, in v. 10, Boaz states that he acquires from Naomi but does not mention Ruth alongside her. Also, if one takes both Naomi and Ruth as the objects of the first clause, the verb "acquire" would not have an explicit object in the latter clause. One could account for the object if one moved the *'atnāḥ* from under the word "Naomi" to under the word "Moabite." Thus, the object of the verb would be "the wife of the dead man" (Zevit, 596, n. 35; cf. Holmstedt, 190–92), which could refer to either Naomi or Ruth, although Ruth is the closest antecedent. Some scholars analyze the *m* in *ûme'et* as an enclitic *mem,* which may place emphasis on Ruth as the object of the following clause in the sense of "indeed [*m*], Ruth the Moabite, the wife of the dead man, you shall acquire her" (cf. Bush, 216–17; Campbell, 146). This allows *'et* to mark Ruth as the object of the following clause rather than as one of the parties from whom the field is acquired. This analysis, however, requires a unique use of the enclitic *mem* that is unattested elsewhere in Biblical Hebrew, since the enclitic *mem* usually appears at the end of a word in Biblical Hebrew (WO §9.8; but contrast Rendsburg, 1987). Other scholars emend *ûme'et rût* to read *gam 'et rût* ("also Ruth") or *wĕgam 'et rût* as in 4:10 ("and also Ruth the Moabite, the wife of Mahlon"; for various opinions, consult Hubbard 243, n. 8). These emendations assume that the *gîmel* was either deleted or mistaken for a *wāw* in MT^L, possibly because of a confusion between the two letters, as in the name *yg'l* (MT^L)/*yô'ēl* (LXX^L) in 2 Sam 23:36 (cf. 1 Chr 3:22). Overall, the other versions do not provide decisive support for reading with or against MT^L. The restoration of a *gîmel* finds support in the Vulg., which reads "Ruth also" (*Ruth quoque*; cf. Old Latin). The Old Greek reads "the field from the hand of Noemin [NOTE *Naomi* on 1:2] and from Ruth the Moabite, the wife of the dead man, you must also buy her." The Targum reads "from the hand of Naomi and from the hand of Ruth" and "you must acquire by levirate marriage [*lĕyabbāmâ*]." These readings seem to conflate the options in both the Vulg. and MT^L. Context, however, seems to support a reading of Ruth as the object of the second clause because, in v. 10, the "wife of Mahlon" (a dead man) modifies "Ruth the Moabite" in nearly the same context. Also, a similar construction occurs in 1:22 ("Ruth the Moabite, her daughter-in-law"). The reading "also Ruth" is supported by context (4:10) and is an option acknowledged in the multiple versions.

the wife of the dead man. The term "the wife of the dead man" (*'ēšet-hammēt*) occurs only here and in Deut 25:5. While the NRSV translates it as "widow," one should avoid confusing it with the term *'almānâ*, which describes a woman outside of the protection of the household or clan into which she married. In Deut 25:5, the term "the wife of the dead man" functions as a technical description of a woman who remains under the protection of her husband's household or clan after her husband's death rather than returning to her birth household as an *'almānâ* (cf. Gen 38:11; Lev 22:13; Sasson, 132). Deuteronomy 25 describes a scenario in which a wife and her husband had been living with his kin as an extended family whose inherited land (*naḥălâ*) had not been divided yet between the husband's brothers as an inheritance (Westbrook, 118–41). As part of an extended family, the wife would still be under the authority of its more senior members after her husband's death (cf. Gen 38; "Household Organization" in the Introduction). If Naomi and Ruth were dwelling together (2:23), and their household's portion of the inherited land held by Elimelech had not been divided between his sons, Ruth's legal status would be "the wife of the dead man" since she refused to return to her birth household as an *'almānâ* (1:16–17). Boaz acknowledges Ruth's legal status, which may assume her entitlement to security within the clan even if the specifics of her case differ from what Deut 25:5–10 or Genesis 38 describe.

you acquire her. While MT^L *ketib* reads *qānîtî* ("I [shall] acquire"; cf. Gen 47:23), my translation reads with the *qere* (*qnyth*) and analyzes the verb as a second-person masculine form with a feminine object, *qānîtāh* (NOTES *go down* on 3:3, and *and lie down* on 3:4). The Old Greek, Vulg., and Targum support the *qere*. Boaz repeatedly uses verb forms from *qnh* in reference to both the field and Ruth (4:4, 5, 9, 10). Elsewhere in the Hebrew Bible, *qnh* describes the purchase of property, animals, and/or people (e.g., Gen 25:10; 39:1; 47:23; Exod 21:2; Lev 22:11; 25:14; 2 Sam 24:21; Eccl 2:7). Often, scholars have explained this use of *qnh* as indicating the payment of a "bride-price," which may reflect Babylonian marriage laws (for a review of scholarship, consult Bush, 217–18; Sasson, 123). Yet, considering that this negotiation seems heavily influenced by the redemption laws reflected in Leviticus 25, Boaz may claim to acquire Ruth as one would acquire (*qnh*) a foreign handmaid (*'āmāh*) in Lev 25:44 (NOTE *handmaid* on 3:9), since no other biblical texts use *qnh* to describe a marriage outside of Ruth 4, although some Mishnaic and Talmudic texts do (for references, consult Weiss). Nevertheless, as Sasson notes, Gen 31:15 and Hos 3:2 also use commercial language to describe a marriage, although the verbs and context are different (*mkr* and *krh,* respectively; for further discussion, consult Lemos). Although the use of each of these verbs in the context of marriage is unique in the Hebrew Bible, collectively they demonstrate that the use of commercial language in such contexts is not unique.

to establish the name of the dead man upon his inheritance. Among other uses, *hiphil* infinitive forms of *qwm* meaning "to establish" (*lĕhāqîm* or *hāqîm*) can serve as an idiom for the continuation or restoration of one's reign or lineage (Deut 29:12; 1 Kgs 15:4; Isa 49:6). This represents the sense of *lĕhāqîm* in Ruth 4:5, 10. In Deut 25:7, *lĕhāqîm* together with the technical term *'ēšet-hammēt* (25:5; NOTE *the wife of the dead man* on 4:5) are used in the context of continuing the lineage of a dead relative through levirate marriage (for a detailed study of levirate marriage, consult Weisberg). Unlike Boaz, Deut 25:5–10 and Genesis 38 do not connect levirate marriage with land redemption or mention inheritance explicitly. Yet, as noted in the Introduction (consult "Ruth and Ancient Israelite Literary Traditions"), details mentioned in one legal text but not another do not mean that the texts contradict each other but simply that neither text represents a comprehensive account of the possible applications of that particular legal idea. Genesis 38, Deuteronomy 25, and Ruth 4 may represent different ways in which a marriage to the wife of a dead man could function to continue the deceased's lineage under various circumstances. Also, Boaz's reference to "his [Mahlon's] inheritance" (*naḥălātô*) creates a pun with the name of the dead man Mahlon (*maḥlôn*) that would not apply in these other cases (consult "The Diction of the Hebrew in Ruth" in the Introduction). This pun may subtly reframe the association of Mahlon with sickness or sterility in Moab to an association with a continued lineage and inheritance in Bethlehem (NOTE *Mahlon* on 1:2; Garsiel, 252; Porten, 1978, 46; Sasson, 19). The inheritance refers to inalienable land passed from one generation to the next, including the portion of the field where one is buried in the family tomb, as in the case of Joseph (Josh 24:32), who, like Mahlon, died in a foreign land (Gen 50:25; "Household Organization" in the Introduction). In 4:10, Boaz explains that the reason the dead man's name should be established upon his inheritance is so that it is not "cut off" through either the destruction of his lineage or the separation from his ancestors in death (NOTE *or the assembly of his place* 4:10 and COMMENTS on 4:1–12).

4:6. *to redeem for myself.* MT^L *ketib* has the longer or fuller spelling of the infinitive construct translated as "to redeem" (*ligĕʾôl-lî*), whereas the *qere* reflects the shorter spelling (*ligĕʾol-lî*). The vowel in question should be shortened because a *maqqep* connects the infinitive to *lî* ("for myself"). The *ketib* and *qere* convey the same meaning.

You redeem my redemption. Both the imperative translated as "redeem" and the noun translated as "my redemption" derive from *gʾl* (NOTE *one of our kindred redeemers* on 2:20). Although the kindred redeemer instructs Boaz to redeem his "redemption," this noun does not function as the object but as a cognate accusative (cf. "dreaded a dread" [*pāḥădû pāḥad*] in Ps 14:5 or various forms of "dreamed a dream" in Gen 37:5, 9; 40:5, 8; 41:11, 15; Dan 2:3; WO §10.2.1g). The object is implied as in Num 11:4, where the noun "craving" is a cognate accusative of the verb "to crave" in the clause "they craved a craving" (*hitʾaûû taʾăwâ*), but the implied object of the craving is "food." Whether the implied object is the field or Ruth in this clause or in the previous one is unclear, but Ruth is the nearest antecedent (v. 5b) and seems to be the reason for the closer kinsman's refusal to redeem in v. 6. If Ruth is the implied object of redemption, then the kinsman understands a marriage to Ruth as a possible form of kindred redemption (NOTE *one of our kindred redeemers* on 2:20; COMMENTS on 3:1–5 and 4:1–12).

4:7. *Now this was [the custom] formerly in Israel.* The Old Greek, supported by the Targum, Syr., and Vulg., has "this was the declaration formerly in Israel," as if the Hebrew reads *wĕzōʾt hammišpāṭ lĕpānîm bĕyiśrāʾēl* (cf. Jer 32:7–8; 39:7–8 [Old Greek]). Yet, since *hammišpāṭ* is a masculine form, one might expect the masculine demonstrative pronoun *wĕzeh* instead of the feminine form *wĕzōʾt* if *hammišpāṭ* were somehow deleted (Campbell, 147). Yet, *zōʾt* may be used in a neuter sense (Sasson, 141). Most likely, *hammišpāṭ* or a term with a similar meaning is implied in MT^L (cf. the gapped or unstated terms in 2:7, 9, 14; 3:4, 15), and the versions provide specificity to the terseness reflected in MT^L.

formerly. The word translated as "formerly" (*lĕpānîm*) can refer to the very recent past (Judg 3:2; Neh 13:5) as well as to the distant and even mythic past (1 Chr 9:20; Ps 102:26 [Eng. 102:25]). In a number of texts, it signals a contrast between a former and a current tradition, circumstance, or name of a place (Deut 2:10, 12, 20; Josh 14:15; 15:15; Judg 1:10, 11, 23; 1 Sam 9:9). In this sense, the narrator's commentary draws attention to the fact that this particular custom is no longer practiced (Levinson, 33–45; NOTE *So and So* on 4:1).

substitution. This word (*tĕmûrâ*) is rarely attested (elsewhere only in Lev 27:10, 33; Job 15:31; 20:18; 28:17), but its use here creates assonance with the proper name Tamar (*tāmār*) in 4:12. Terminology that carries technical legal nuances elsewhere in the Hebrew Bible does not necessarily clarify the nature of the legal transactions that this terminology describes in Ruth 4 but tends to create rhymes, puns, assonance, and alliteration (e.g., *mākĕrâ, haggōʾēl, naḥălātô*; consult COMMENTS on 4:1–12; "The Diction of the Hebrew in Ruth" in the Introduction).

would remove his sandal. My translation analyzes the verb *šālap* ("would remove") as a *qatal* modal that expresses a routine activity in the past (cf. 1 Sam 9:9; Bush, 236; Holmstedt, 196). The Old Greek and Targum have a copula before this verb. This is the only use of this verb with a sandal as its object in the Hebrew Bible (cf. v. 8). Other texts use verbs from *nšl* or *ḥlṣ* for the word translated as "remove" in the phrase "remove his/your sandal" (Exod 3:5; Deut 25:9, 10; Josh 5:15; Isa 20:2). Some Targumim use the Aramaic cognate *šlp* to translate the Hebrew verbs *ḥlṣ* (Lev 14:40, 43) and *nšl* (Deut 19:5), as in the Aramaic translation of the clause "remove your/his sandal" (Exod 3:5; Deut 25:9; Isa 20:2; cf. Bush, 28; Hurvitz, 1975; Zevit, 593). Considering that Hebrew had its own verbs that were used to express the removal of sandals, there was no need to borrow the phrase from Aramaic. Thus, the borrowing does not happen out of necessity, as in cases where Hebrew lacks a necessary word. Rather, it possibly happens out of the growing prestige of Aramaic (Holmstedt, 38). If so, the use of *šālap* in Ruth 4:7 could reflect an increased influence of Aramaic as a linguistically dominant language. Nevertheless, an attempt to determine whether Ruth's author's use of this term reflects an early adoption of the term would require additional research into the author's idiolect, which is well beyond the scope of the present commentary. Despite the involvement of a sandal, this custom does not necessarily reflect the version of the levirate marriage custom in Deut 25:9, in which a woman removes her brother-in-law's sandal, spits in his face, and verbally humiliates him. In Ruth 4:7, a man (*'îš*) performs a saliva-free custom in which he removes his own sandal and gives it to his friend with no required verbal proclamation. Also, the narrator in Ruth clearly states that this custom concerns redemption (4:6; cf. Lev 25:24–34; Jer 32:7, 8) and substitution (cf. Lev 27:10, 33) and never mentions a connection with marriage unless one assumes that marriage could serve as a form of redemption (COMMENTS on 3:1–5, 6–15). More important, the narrator specifies that this custom applies to "any matter" involving redemption and substitution, which would include, but would not be limited to, levirate marriage (Eskenazi and Frymer-Kensky, 79).

4:8. *Acquire for yourself.* The Old Greek specifies what Boaz is acquiring with its reading "acquire my redemption for yourself" (cf. NOTE *you redeem my redemption* on 4:6, although the Old Greek uses a different imperative in 4:6). The other versions do not support the Old Greek. In MT^L, the same clause *qěnê-lāk* ("acquire for yourself") occurs elsewhere only in Jer 32:7, 8, 25, where it always includes "field" as the object. Also, various forms of *qnh* ("to acquire") in Lev 25:14–15 and possibly Ruth 4:5 do not have an explicit object, although the implied object is property (cf. NOTE *also Ruth* on 4:5).

he removed his sandal. The Old Greek and Old Latin follow this clause with "and gave it [the sandal] to him," possibly to specify that the kindred redeemer's actions conformed completely with the narrator's description of this custom in 4:7. Some scholars, however, argue that the clause *wayyittēn lô* ("gave it to him") dropped out of MT^L because of haplography triggered by the *lô* in *na'ălô* ("his sandal") and *wayyittēn lô* (Rudolph, 60; cf. Joüon, 88). It remains unclear whether the masculine subject of the verb "remove" refers to the kindred redeemer or to Boaz and whether "his sandal" refers to the kindred redeemer's sandal or Boaz's sandal (cf. *b. B. Meṣ.* 47a). The fact that the kindred redeemer is the subject of the clause before the dialogue in this verse suggests that he remains the subject of the clause that follows the dialogue. Yet, the versions are divided on this issue and do little to clarify it. For a more detailed review of the versions, as well as scholarly opinions, consult Campbell, 149–50.

4:9. *I now acquire.* As with the *qatal* verb *mākěrâ* ("offers for sale") in 4:3, the *qatal* verb *qānîtî* ("I now acquire") in 4:9 and 10 is a *qatal* verb form that functions as a performative (NOTE *Naomi . . . offers for sale* on 4:3).

all that belonged to Elimelech. The Syr. does not have this clause, probably because of haplography triggered by the words *'et-kōl 'ăšer* and *wě'ēt-kōl 'ăšer*, which begin the respective clauses "all that belonged to Elimelech" and "all that belonged to Kilyon and Mahlon." The Syr. does not find support among the other versions.

all that belonged to Kilyon and Mahlon. The Old Latin does not have this clause, probably because of haplography triggered by the words *'et-kōl 'ăšer* and *wě'ēt-kōl 'ăšer*, which begin the respective clauses "all that belonged to Elimelech" and "all that belonged to Kilyon and Mahlon." The Old Latin does not find support among the other versions. Boaz says "Kilyon and Mahlon," in contrast to the narrator, who pairs the brothers in the reverse order, "Mahlon and Kilyon" (1:2, 5). A minority of Old Greek, Hebrew, and Syr. manuscripts reflect the order of names in Ruth 1 in this verse. Scholarly speculation regarding the reasons for the difference between 1:2, 5 and 4:9 has not produced definitive results other than to note that the reversal of two terms after their initial use is a stylistic feature found throughout the book (e.g., 1:3, 5; NOTE *without her two children or her husband* on 1:5; also 1:8/1:12; 1:9/1:14; 1:20–21a/1:21b; 4:9/4:11; Campbell, 14).

4:10. *Also, Ruth.* Earlier, I cited the phrase "also Ruth" (*wĕgam 'et rût*) in this verse in support of emending v. 5 in MT[L] (cf. NOTE *also Ruth* on 4:5). The Syr. seems to have taken the object marker *'et* as the second-person feminine pronoun *'att* ("you") and has Boaz address this clause directly to Ruth, that is, "You, Ruth." The other versions do not support the Syr.

I now acquire. On the translation of this *qatal* verb, consult NOTES *I now acquire* on 4:9, and *Naomi . . . offers for sale* on 4:3.

to establish the name of the dead man upon his inheritance. On this clause, consult NOTE *to establish the name of the dead man upon his inheritance* on 4:5.

so that the name of the dead man may not be cut off. My translation takes the *wāw* that introduces this clause as an "epexegetical *wāw*" that clarifies the information given in the previous clause (cf. 2 Sam 14:5; WO §39.2.4). Boaz explains to the assembly that the reason he is taking Ruth as his wife is to ensure that the name of the dead man is not cut off. For the use of the term "cut off," consult COMMENTS on 4:1–12.

or the assembly of his place. One could translate the phrase *ûmiššā'ar mĕqômô* more woodenly as "or the gate of his place." In this idiom, "gate" functions as a metonym for some type of assembly (NOTE *the entire assembly of my people* on 3:11). The versions seem to have recognized the idiomatic quality of *šā'ar mĕqômô* because they gloss it in various ways: "of the local tribe" (Old Latin), "people" (Vulg.), "tribe of his people" (LXX[B]; cf. 3:11), "tribe of the people" (LXX[A]), or simply "tribe" (LXX[L]; cf. Theodoret). LXX[MN] and the Targum translate *šā'ar* woodenly as "gate," although the Targum has "gate of the Sanhedrin" (4:11, and "the gate of the great Sanhedrin" in 3:11). The idiom *šā'ar mĕqômô* also occurs in Deut 21:19, where it parallels "the elders of his town," which is the assembly to whom Boaz appeals (Ruth 4:2). In the present context, the assembly could also refer to Mahlon's deceased kin or ancestors. While *mĕqômô* usually means "place" in a more generic sense (e.g., *hammāqôm* in 1:7; 3:4), it can also mean a "resting place" (Job 16:18). It refers to the destination of all the dead in Eccl 3:20 and parallels "grave" (*qeber*) in Ezek 39:11 (cf. *KAI* 9.A3; 14.4; 214.14; Lewis, 64, n. 61). In 1:17a, Ruth insists that she will be buried (*'eqqābēr*) where Naomi dies after Ruth claims Naomi's ancestors as her own (NOTE *to her people and to her ancestors* on 1:15). Both 1:17 and 4:10 reflect a concern over being separated or cut off from one's ancestors in death. In this sense, those "assembled" at Mahlon's burial place could refer to his deceased ancestors. The idiom may invoke both of these senses, similar to Boaz's reference to Mahlon's "inheritance" (NOTE *to establish the name of the dead man upon his inheritance* on 4:5)

4:11. *All the people who were in the gate and the elders said, "(We are) witnesses."* The Old Greek has "the people who were in the gate, '(We are) witnesses.' And the elders said . . . ," as if reading the Hebrew as *'ēdim wayyōmrû hazzĕqēnîm*. In 4:4 and 9, however, the elders and the people are not differentiated (cf. Campbell, 152; *BHQ* 56*). Also, the Vulg., Old Latin, and Targum support MT[L], although the Targum has "gate of the Sanhedrin and the elders" (cf. 3:11; 4:10). The Syr. reads, "The elders answered and the people in the gate said, 'We are witnesses,' and they blessed him and said to him . . ." This reversal of the order of "people" and "elders" may be to conform to the order in 4:4, 9 (NOTE *without her two children or her husband* on 1:5). The people and the elders answer with one word, "witnesses," which implies their agreement to serve as witnesses (cf. Josh 24:22). The Vulg., Syr., and Targum represent the pronoun "we" explicitly.

May YHWH make. Verbs from the root *ntn* are used throughout the book to describe YHWH's action, or potential action (1:6, 9; 4:12, 13). In these other verses, however, the verb occurs with a person or people as its indirect rather than direct object: "give [something] to [Orpah and Ruth]" (1:6), "give [something] to [Boaz]" (4:12), "gave [something] to [Ruth]" (4:13). In 4:11, however, YHWH does not give anything to "the woman," as she is the direct rather than the indirect object. In this construction, *ntn* can mean "make" rather than "give." For other examples of this meaning of *ntn* in reference to a direct object that is made "like" ("*ntn* . . . *k* . . .") something or someone else, consult Lev 26:19; 1 Kgs 16:3.

the woman. Other versions are more specific than MT^L. Most Old Greek witnesses read "your wife," and the Targum and Vulg. read "this woman."

the two of them. The word translated as "the two of them" is a further example of a gender-neutralized pronoun (NOTE *with you . . . you have done* on 1:8).

the house of Israel. Although not supported by other major versions, the Targum reads "our father" after "the house of Israel." This reading specifies the use of "Israel" as a reference to the patriarch Jacob rather than the nation (Sasson, 154). The context supports this interpretation, as it discusses the activity of Jacob's wives Rachel and Leah followed by those of his son's daughter-in-law Tamar. The genealogical material in 1 Chronicles 1–9 also refers to Jacob as Israel consistently (1 Chr 1:34; 2:1; 5:1, 3; 6:23; 7:29; "house of Israel" in Ruth 4:11 in contrast to "house of Jacob" in Gen 46:27).

so that you act worthily. The word translated "so that you act" is a singular masculine imperative in MT^L, which is supported by LXX^L and other Old Greek manuscripts. The Targum has a jussive, "may you prosper." LXX^B and some other Old Greek manuscripts translate the verb as a plural indicative, with Rachel and Leah as the subject: "they made power" (cf. Old Latin). When it follows a jussive, an imperative with a *wāw* copulative may express the consequence of the previous clause (*GKC* §110i). In other words, Boaz will be able to act worthily and proclaim a name because of YHWH's actions. As with the translation of the noun *ḥesed* as "kindly" in 1:9, the noun translated as "worthily" (*ḥayil*; cf. 2:1; 3:11) follows a verb form of *'śh* ("to do, create, act") and functions as an adverb. The same word occurs in 2:1 and 3:11, where it could cover a range of activities (for options, consult NOTES *mighty man of worth* on 2:1, and *woman of worth* on 3:11). Although the idiom *'ōśeh ḥayil* or *'ōśāh ḥayil* ("act worthily/valiantly") can describe success in warfare (Num 24:18; Ps 118:15, 16), that sense would not fit the context of the book of Ruth. As a modifier of the word "to do, act, create," it could also refer to the creation of wealth, possibly by ensuring that the field remains in the clan; to procreation (Labuschange); or to a flourishing in general. Considering that a variety of actions are needed to restore the status quo for Naomi and Ruth as well as for the clan in general, a blessing with a wide range of semantic possibilities would be appropriate. For reviews of other scholarly opinions of the meaning of this idiom, consult Bush, 240–42; Hubbard, 253, n. 12.

Ephrathah. This name parallels the name Bethlehem in the following clause. Genesis 35:19 and 48:7 specify that Ephrathah "is also called Bethlehem" (cf. "Ephrathah" in Ps 132:6; NOTE *Ephrathites from Bethlehem of Judah* on 1:2).

proclaim a name. Although forms of the idiom "to proclaim/call a name" usually occur in popular etymologies for geographic locations, for example, "the name of the place is called . . ." (*qārā'-šēm lammāqôm* in Gen 33:17; Josh 7:26; 2 Sam 5:20), the idiom can also refer to honoring or acknowledging a name, as in 4:14 when the women declare, "May his name be proclaimed in Israel" (*wĕyiqqārē' šĕmô bĕyiśrā'ēl;* cf. *qĕrā'-šēm* in Exod 33:19; Deut 32:3; cf. Jer 44:26). It remains unclear, however, whether the people and elders are telling Boaz to proclaim the dead man's name (cf. 4:10) or Boaz's own name, since one can proclaim one's own name as YHWH does in Exod 33:19. It may also refer to having a child, since forms of the idiom "proclaim a name" may refer to an announcement at birth. For example, the female inhabitants of the town proclaim the name of Boaz and Ruth's son as Obed (4:17b). To proclaim a name could cover a similar range of meanings as "act worthily." It even could possibly serve as an adoption formula (Gen 48:5–6, 16; consult Sarna, 325–26), although this is less likely because of grammatical differences. As several varieties of this idiom occur in Ruth 4 (vv. 11, 14, 17 [two times]) with a range of applications, it is worth repeating that a blessing with a wide range of semantic possibilities would be appropriate, considering that a variety of actions are needed to restore the status quo for Naomi and Ruth as well as the clan in general (NOTE *so that you act worthily* on 4:11).

4:12. *seed that YHWH.* Probably triggered by dittography of the letter *s* at the end of the first word of *spermatos ou* ("seed that") in the Old Greek, LXX^L and Theodoret read *spermatos sou* ("your"). Most other versions, including most Old Greek witnesses, do not support this reading.

Comments

The final chapter of Ruth opens with Boaz's arrival at the gate. The "gate" functions as a metonym for the political body responsible for the legal or political affairs of the town (NOTE *the entire assembly of my people* on 3:11). Boaz may be seeking to resolve the matter of who will serve as a kindred redeemer (3:13, 18), but, as I explain below, one should not assume that he wants to marry Ruth just because he goes to the gate.

While Boaz sits at the gate, the kindred redeemer that he had told Ruth about happens to pass by. Boaz refers to this unnamed person only as "So and So" (NOTE *So and So* on 4:2). The two of them sit with ten of the town elders, which rabbinic texts later associate with a quorum (*minyan;* b. Ketub. 7b; cf. b. Meg. 23b). Boaz announces that Naomi is offering for sale the portion of the field held by Elimelech. Similar to other terminology in Ruth 4 that can have technical legal implications elsewhere in the Bible (e.g., "inheritance" or "substitution," discussed below), the verb that Boaz uses to announce the sale may not clarify the legal situation that it describes (whether Naomi has sold or is selling the field), but it rhymes with the word "her chance" (2:3; NOTE *Naomi . . . offers for sale* on 4:3; "The Diction of the Hebrew in Ruth" in the Introduction). This sale has raised questions about whether women could inherit or hold property in ancient Israel (e.g., Bush, 203–4; Zevit, 582–92, and the references they cite). Yet, as Westbrook notes, Boaz's announcement is unrelated to such questions because

Boaz only claims that Naomi is acting as the agent who acquires or alienates the field, as in Prov 31:16. Ruth 4 address issues of female management of the household's inherited field rather than issues of female property ownership (Westbrook, 79–80, n. 4). The idea of a senior female within the household in this type of management role fits with ancient Israelite household organization (Meyers, 2013, 187–92).

Boaz's announcement is the first explicit reference to the land resources at Naomi's disposal. This disclosure, however, does not necessarily mean that Naomi was secure economically. According to some texts, land was held as an inheritance by the clan, with various members controlling the usufruct of various plots that were apportioned by the clan (consult "Household Organization" in the Introduction). Yet, having the usufruct did not guarantee that one would not become impoverished. In fact, the land redemption legislation in Lev 25:25 assumes that some members of the clan can become impoverished enough to require the sale of their land holdings. Boaz's announcement does not mean that Naomi is not impoverished since it seems to assume a similar scenario.

The narrator does not explain how Boaz knows of Naomi's intentions to sell a portion of the field. As noted earlier, Naomi and Boaz seem to have knowledge of each other's actions even though they never appear in the same scene anywhere in the book (cf. 3:2–4). Naomi had not expressed a desire to make this sale previously. Boaz's announcement could simply result from the narrator's selective representation (consult "Selective Representation and Narrative Ambiguity" in the Introduction). The fact that no one raises any objections to the redemption of this portion of the field may imply that Boaz represents Naomi's intentions accurately. Yet, as with Ruth's statement regarding Boaz's intentions in giving her barley (3:17b), it is also possible that Boaz's claim about the sale shows that he has the capacity to lie or be manipulative. This could be appropriate depending on how one interprets his interaction with the unnamed kindred redeemer in the following verses.

Boaz discusses land redemption as a voluntary matter. Other texts regarding land redemption seem to present land redemption by close relative as mandatory, but they do not specify any type of punishment if one does not carry out this responsibility (Lev 25:25; Jer 32:7–8). In Ruth 4:4a, a kinsman finally volunteers to serve as a kindred redeemer (COMMENTS on 1:19b–22a). Once a redeemer comes forward, however, the question becomes to what extent he is willing to go to restore the status quo once he has volunteered (COMMENTS on 2:18–23). The current situation requires not only land redemption, but also a restoration of a household, since Naomi's sons, including Ruth's husband, died without children in Moab. If a kindred redeemer is one who restores the status quo (NOTE *one of our kindred redeemers* on 2:20), multiple activities are necessary before the status quo is fully restored in this case. Boaz addresses this issue when he stipulates that on the day that the closer kinsman acquires the field, he also acquires Ruth to continue her deceased husband's lineage. Boaz presents this marriage to the wife of a dead man as required of the kindred redeemer, although elsewhere other versions of it are presented as voluntary (e.g., Deut 25:7–10; cf. Weisberg, 27; NOTE *to establish the name of the dead man upon his inheritance* on 4:5). Boaz's requirement may assume that if one is volunteering to serve as a kindred redeemer, one should do all that it takes to restore the status quo.

This understanding of the kindred redeemer's responsibilities is based on what the situation requires rather than on specific legal precedent, assuming that the biblical examples of how a kindred redeemer can restore the status quo are representative rather than exhaustive. As many scholars note, Boaz seems to conflate two distinct legal ideas, because no other biblical text addresses land redemption and levirate marriage together (e.g., Chavel; Baruch Levine; Berlin argues that inheritance and redemption laws may have already been conflated in Jer 32:6–8 [2010, 17–18]). While this is true, legislation addressing various forms of kindred redemption usually considers individual, although sometimes elaborated, ways of how the status quo may be disrupted and what to do in each case (e.g., Lev 25:23–55; Num 5:8). Since Ruth's situation involves a case of multiple disruptions to the status quo, the one who volunteers as a redeemer may have to take on multiple responsibilities. In this sense, what qualifies as an act of redemption is situational. Although a marriage to the wife of a dead man is not technically always a form of redemption in and of itself, it could function as a way to help restore the status quo under certain circumstances. Along these lines, in 4:6, when the kindred redeemer claims twice that he is "not able to redeem," he does not specify the object (cf. 4:4b; NOTE *you redeem my redemption* on 4:6). He could mean "I am unable to redeem the field" or "I am unable to redeem Ruth." If he means the latter, then he seems to understand a potential marriage to Ruth as a means of redemption. Either way, he objects out of concern that he would ruin his own inheritance, although exactly how this would occur remains unclear since the closer kinsman's current family situation and the inheritance rights of any sons potentially produced through a marriage to Ruth are unspecified in the book.

In 4:5, Boaz refers to Ruth with a technical term: the wife of the dead man (NOTE *the wife of the dead man* on 4:5). In Deut 25:5, the wife of a dead man seems to be entitled to security within the clan through the birth of a son (Siquans, 450). In v. 10, Boaz declares that he acquires what belonged not only to Elimelech, but also to both of his sons Kilyon and Mahlon. The inclusion of both sons probably reflects the fact that multiple generations were dwelling together as an extended family and that their inherited land had not been divided among the sons before they died in Moab (Chavel; NOTE *acquire for yourself* on 4:8; for a differing opinion, consult Westbrook, 65–66, 138–39). If Naomi and Ruth are the surviving members of this extended family, then Ruth is entitled to this type of security within the clan structure, which Boaz seems to acknowledge when he refers to her as the wife of a dead man and the wife of Mahlon.

Although Boaz seems to go to the gate to clarify which kinsman will redeem Ruth, his personal desires regarding the outcome remain opaque (consult "Characterization" in the Introduction). In 3:13, Boaz had stipulated that he would serve as a kindred redeemer for Ruth *if* the closer kinsman does not want to. This does not necessarily mean that Boaz would prefer to serve in this role. Whether one understands Boaz as desiring a marriage with Ruth or hoping that he can find someone else to marry her partially depends on how one chooses to interpret his character. As already noted (COMMENTS on 3:6–15), the fact that there is a closer relative to Ruth than Boaz should not affect who, if anyone, she marries. The closeness (*qārôb*) of a member of one's clan is noted in discussions of land inheritance (Num 27:11) and land redemption (Lev 25:25), but not of marriage. Moreover, Naomi showed awareness of multiple kindred redeemers (2:20) but did not express concern that one of them would have the right to marry Ruth before Boaz when she instructed Ruth to go to the threshing floor (3:3–4). Assuming that Boaz could afford it, there would be no legal reason why he would need to clear any plans to marry Ruth with a closer kinsman, even though Boaz acknowledges that a closer kinsman would have the legal right to land redemption before him (4:4). Moreover, if one reads v. 5b with the *ketib* ("I am acquiring Ruth the Moabite," but consult NOTE *you acquire* on 4:5), Boaz seems to presume an ability to marry Ruth regardless of whether a closer kinsman retains his right of land redemption (vv. 4b–5a). Since Boaz had promised to ensure Ruth's redemption (3:13), the easiest way to do so would not be to approach a closer kinsman, but to simply marry her if he actually wants to.

Moreover, Boaz does not necessarily refer to Ruth as "the Moabite" in 4:5b to discourage the kindred redeemer from acquiring her so he could marry her instead. That would not explain why Boaz refers to her ethnicity again after the other kinsman has relinquished his right of redemption (v. 10). Both of Boaz's references to her ethnicity occur alongside references to her status within the clan as "the wife of the dead man" and in the context of sexual relations intended for procreation (vv. 5, 10). A procreative relationship with a Moabite would reunite the lines of Abram, the grandfather of Israel, with his brother Haran, the grandfather of Moab. Thus references to Ruth's ethnicity would be contextually appropriate considering the emphasis on lineages in the following verses, including explicit comparisons to how female descendants of Abram's other brother Nahor built up the household of Israel (v. 11; consult "Moabites as Kin in Ruth" in the Introduction).

Also, if Boaz desired to marry Ruth, his strategy in v. 5b could backfire if the kindred redeemer were to agree to acquire Ruth (Linafelt, 1999, 68). If this were to happen, Hubbard states that "the story would end in hollow happiness: romance would surrender to regulation, love capitulate to legality—unless, of course, Boaz had some shrewd scheme in mind" (242–43). Yet Hubbard implies that romance or love motivates Boaz to marry Ruth, even though Boaz repeatedly says the marriage is to "establish the name of the dead man upon his inheritance" (vv. 5, 10). It is worth noting that other marriages to wives of dead men in the Hebrew Bible are not motivated by love (Gen 38; Deut 25:5–10). Boaz never expresses romantic or erotic desire for Ruth explicitly (consult "Sexual Desire in Ruth" in the Introduction). Yet, regardless of whatever outcome Boaz may have desired, his negotiations result in his serving as the kindred redeemer (consult "Actions, Events, and Consequences" in the Introduction).

In Ruth 4:7, the narrator's interjection explains a custom that Boaz and the kindred redeemer perform in the following verse. The narrator claims that this custom reflects a former practice, implying its antiquity (cf. 1 Chr 4:22b; NOTE *formerly* on Ruth 4:7). Its supposed antiquity explains the need to clarify its purpose as a witness for redemption and substitution. The precise nature of the substitution and its relation to the word "redemption," however, remain unclear. As with the words *pĕlōnî ʾalmōnî* ("So and So"), the two terms could function as a hendiadys (Brichto, 18; for a review of further proposals, consult Bush, 233–34). While the word "substitution" (*tĕmûrâ*) may not clarify the nature of the transaction, it creates assonance with the name Tamar (4:12; COMMENTS on the words "sale" and "inheritance" in this section). The sandal exchange creates further ambiguity because the narrator does not specify which party removed his sandal. Was the substitution performed properly? As with the narration of Ruth and Boaz's encounter at the threshing floor (3:6–15), a moment that has tremendous implications for their relationship is unclear because of how it is narrated. It is only Boaz's announcement in vv. 9–10 that confirms the success of the exchange. As he had promised Ruth in 3:13, he will redeem her if the closer kinsman is unwilling. While Boaz's announcement does not confirm what he desires, it does confirm that he will follow through on his commitment regardless of his motives. A member of the clan has finally come forward as a kindred redeemer. Ironically, we learn the identity of Ruth's first husband (Mahlon) only when Boaz confirms that he will become her second husband (4:10).

In 4:10, Boaz explains that the reason for the establishment of the dead man's name upon his inheritance is to ensure that his name "may not be cut off from among his kin or the assembly of his place." As with other vocabulary in Ruth (NOTE *under her authority* on 1:7a; "Ruth and Ancient Israelite Literary Traditions" in the Introduction), Boaz may use the verb "cut off" (from the root *krt*) with a technical sense similar to its use in Priestly literature (including Holiness legislation). In Priestly literature, *krt* can refer to the destruction of a person's lineage or a person's inability to join her or his ancestors in death. As Jacob Milgrom notes, these two uses are not mutually exclusive (for a detailed discussion with biblical references, consult Milgrom, 1991, 457–60). Boaz's use could imply both senses of the verb, as Mahlon's lineage faces extinction and he presumably was not buried in his ancestral tomb because he died in Moab (NOTES *to establish the name of the dead man upon his inheritance* on 4:5, and *or the assembly of his place* on 4:10). In 1:16–18, Ruth showed concern over her burial place to ensure that she is not separated from Naomi either in life or in death. Now Boaz may show concern over Mahlon's threatened lineage and his separation from his ancestors.

The Bethlehemites unanimously agree to serve as witnesses and employ a blessing formula that would be appropriate for a marriage (consult "Genre[s] in Ruth" in the Introduction). One could contrast this blessing over Ruth's entry into Boaz's household with Naomi's aborted blessing over her daughters-in-law's potential departure from her household in 1:8–9 (COMMENTS on 1:7b–19a). The Bethlehemites' blessing traces three successive generations of Judahites: Judah's father Israel (= Jacob), then Judah, then his son Perez. In this sense, it situates Boaz's household within a much larger line of descent, or what other texts refer to as the "house of the fathers" (*bêt 'ābôt*). The marriage blessing does not simply celebrate Ruth's entry into Boaz's nuclear or even extended family ("the house of his father"; *bêt 'āb*) but frames it as her incorporation into a larger Judahite lineage (4:17–22; "Household Organization" in the Introduction). As evidenced in the Judahite genealogies in 1 Chronicles (cf. Knoppers, 2001), the house of the fathers could include substantial ethnic diversity in its lineages.

The references to acting worthily and proclaiming a name could cover a range of activities (for a review of proposals, consult Bush, 240–43). As stressed in the NOTES, a blessing with a wide range of semantic possibilities would be appropriate, especially considering that a variety of actions are needed to restore the status quo under the present circumstances (NOTES *mighty man of worth* on 2:1, *woman of worth* on 3:11, and *so that you act worthily* and *proclaim a name* on 4:11). Whatever the range of meanings, the syntax of v. 11 ("so that") indicates that Boaz's ability to carry out these activities rests on YHWH making Ruth like Rachel and Leah. This comparison to the matriarchal sisters also fits in a context where conception is framed as a divine blessing rather than the assumed norm (4:13; "Divine Activity and Acts of *ḥesed* in Ruth" in the Introduction). For recent discussions of the interplay between human fertility and agricultural fecundity in the book of Ruth, consult Koosed, Timothy Stone, and Sutskover.

The Bethlehemites compare Ruth to Rachel and Leah in that Ruth, a descendant of Abram's brother Haran, may "build" Boaz's household just as the matriarchal sisters, descendants of Abram's brother Nahor, did (consult "Moabites as Descendants of Lot" in the Introduction). The Bethlehemites also compare Ruth to Tamar, who, like Ruth, would be considered the wife of a dead man within the clan structure (NOTE "the wife of the dead man" on 4:5). Whatever the historical etymology of the name Tamar may be (for a review of possibilities, consult Leuchter, 222–23), the name has assonance with the word "substitution" (*tĕmûrâ;* 4:7), which is in keeping with the narrative style throughout the book. It is unlikely that Ruth's author would have been aware of the name's historical etymology if the book were written during the early Persian period (consult "The Diction of the Hebrew in Ruth" in the Introduction).

The Birth of Obed (4:13–17)

4 ¹³Then Boaz took Ruth and she became his wife. He entered her and YHWH gave her conception and she bore a son. ¹⁴The women said to Naomi, "Blessed be YHWH who has not removed a kindred redeemer for you today. May his name be proclaimed in Israel. ¹⁵He will become one who returns life for you and supports your old age because your daughter-in-law, who loves you, bore him, who herself is better for you than seven sons." ¹⁶Then Naomi took the child and placed him in her bosom. She was a caregiver for him. ¹⁷The female inhabitants proclaimed his name saying, "For Naomi a son has been born!" They proclaimed his name [to be] Obed. He was the father of Jesse, the father of David.

Notes

4:13. *and she became his wife. He entered her.* LXX^B does not include "and she became his wife. He entered her," possibly because of haplography triggered by the *wāw* in "and she became" and in "and YHWH gave."

YHWH gave her conception. The word translated as "conception" (*hērāyôn*) occurs elsewhere only in Hos 9:11. The word derives from *hrh* ("to conceive") with an *-ôn* suffix (*-ān*). Zevit cites this construction as evidence of LBH. He writes, "n-t-n + *hērāyôn* . . . is regularly used by the Targum to translate 'and DN opened her womb' (cf. Gen 29,31; 30,22)" (593 [italics in original]). Regardless of its relevance for the date of the book, this word rhymes with the names of Naomi's sons. The *-ôn* suffix also occurs in the names Mahlon and Kilyon. Whereas Naomi's sons die in the book's opening, another son is born for her (v. 17) through this conception (*hērāyôn*). The rhymes continue as three of the names in the genealogy that ends the book in 4:18–22 have an *-ôn* suffix (Hezron, Nahshon, and Salmon). The rhyme with Naomi's sons may explain this use of the rare nominal form of the root *hrh* to express divinely granted conception instead of the much more frequent verb form of *hrh*, as in *wattahar* ("and she conceived"), which often expresses conception explicitly associated with divine causation (Gen 4:1; 21:2; 25:21; 29:32, 33; Judg 13:3; 1 Sam 1:20). This rhyme is in keeping with the narrative style throughout the book (consult "The Diction of the Hebrew in Ruth" in the Introduction).

she bore. LXX^L and the Syro-Hexapla read "she bore to him a son" (Campbell, 162), possibly influenced by *wattĕhî-lô lĕ'iššâ*, woodenly translated as "she was to him a wife" earlier in the same verse. The other versions do not support this reading.

4:14. *May his name be proclaimed in Israel.* As with the clause "who has not abandoned his kindness" in 2:20 (NOTE *who has not abandoned his kindness with the living and with the dead* on 2:20), the implied subject of this clause is unclear. It may refer to either YHWH or to the kindred redeemer, both of whom are mentioned in the previous clause. It is possible, but unlikely, that the implied subject in MT^L is "the dead one" (4:5, 10; so Joüon, 93) or Boaz, depending on the identity of the kindred redeemer in v. 14. In v. 15, the women identify the kindred redeemer as the son whom Ruth bore (v. 13). Thus, the kindred redeemer in v. 14 and the subject of this clause is probably not one of Naomi's dead relatives or Boaz. The subject could be YHWH since YHWH is the object of the women's blessing in this verse. Also, variations of the idiom "to proclaim a name" as in honoring or acknowledging that name refer to YHWH elsewhere (consult NOTE *proclaim a name* on 4:11). Yet, the kindred redeemer is the nearest antecedent, and in most cases, the nearest grammatically acceptable antecedent serves as the referent of a relative clause (Holmstedt, 141–42). While the context suggests either YHWH or the kindred redeemer as the implied subject of the clause, one could make a stronger, though not decisive, case for the kindred redeemer on the basis of the syntax. Also, the subject of the women's dialogue in the following verse (v. 15) is the son whom Ruth bore, and there is no apparent change of subject from v. 14 to v. 15 (Campbell, 163–64). This makes the kindred redeemer the more likely subject of this clause. The Old Greek, supported by the Old Latin, clarifies the ambiguity of the subject by reading "your name" as a second feminine singular (*sou*) as if referring to Naomi. The Syr. does not clarify the ambiguity because it reads "his name," although it has a second-person subject for the verb in the clause. The Vulg. mentions "your [Naomi's] family" (*familiae tuae*) in the previous clause and thus takes the name as a reference to Naomi's household. The Targum supports MT^L, although it reads "the righteous of Israel."

4:15. *one who returns life.* The word translated as "one who returns" (*lĕmēšîb*) is a *hiphil* participle from *šûb* ("to return"; cf. 1:6–8, 10–12, 15–16, 21–22; 2:6; 4:3). Elsewhere the idiom "to return life" refers to the lifting of one's spirits rather than bringing one back to life, for example, the *hiphil* participle form of *šûb* with *nepeš* in *mēšîbat nāpeš* (Ps 19:8 [Eng. 19:7]; cf. Prov 25:13). As many commentators note, this *hiphil* participle is similar to the *hiphil* from *šûb* in Ruth 1:21 when Naomi claimed that "YHWH made me return [*hēšîbanî*] empty." Whereas YHWH returned her to Bethlehem empty, without her husband or sons alive, a kindred redeemer will ensure that her life is returned (4:15) and not marked by emptiness (3:17; cf. 1:21). For a similar wordplay, consult NOTE *the child* on 4:16.

your old age. Although not supported by the other versions, the Syr. has "your city," which probably results from reading the Old Greek *polian* ("old age") as *polin* ("city"; cf. Campbell, 162).

your daughter-in-law. LXX^B does not have "your," although it occurs in the other versions, including other Old Greek witnesses.

loves you. MT^L reads *'ăhēbatek* ("[she] loves you") instead of the expected conjugation *'ăhēbātek,* which the majority of Hebrew manuscripts attest. This difference in spelling, however, does not change the meaning of the word. For further discussion, consult COMMENTS on 4:13–17.

who herself is better for you than seven sons. My translation analyzes this clause as an independent relative clause in which *'ăšer* ("who") serves as a subject in a verbless clause (WO §19.3c), with the independent feminine singular pronoun *hî'* ("herself") included for emphasis. Elsewhere, the numbers seven and ten are used idiomatically in hyperbolic comparisons in which one party is contrasted positively to other parties, for example, "Am I not better for you than ten sons?" (1 Sam 1:8; cf. Prov 26:16; Eccl 7:19). Seven sons may also represent an ideal number of sons (Job 1:2; 42:13; Eskenazi and Frymer-Kensky, 91).

4:16. *the child.* The word *hayyeled* ("the child") comes from the same root as *yĕlādêhā* ("her children") in 1:5, where the narrator reported that Naomi "was left without her two children." Whereas Naomi loses her children in 1:5, she acquires a child in 4:16 (Campbell, 56; Nielsen, 44; NOTES *without her two children or her husband* on 1:5, and *one who returns life* on 4:15).

placed him in her bosom. The Syr. does not have this clause, possibly because of haplography triggered by the word "and" and the first letter of the verb in both the Hebrew and Old Greek renderings of "and she placed" and "and she was," respectively. Unlike other Old Greek witnesses, LXX^3, supported by the Vulg., does not have the pronoun "him," although it is implied. The word translated as "in her bosom" (*bĕhêqāh*) could refer to one's lap or chest as well as one's breast and can be used with a masculine suffix to describe a male embrace (Deut 28:54; 2 Sam 12:3, 8; Isa 40:11). It probably does not suggest that Naomi breast-fed the infant (NOTE *caregiver* on 4:16).

caregiver. The word translated as "caregiver" (*lĕ'ōmenet*) is a feminine participle from *'mn,* as in 2 Sam 4:4, where it refers to the caregiver of a four-year-old Mephibosheth. Elsewhere, texts use masculine participle forms of the same root to refer to male caregivers or guardians (e.g., Num 11:12; 2 Kgs 10:1, 5; Esth 2:7; Isa 49:23; cf. the passive participle in Lam 4:5). This term does not suggest that Naomi breast-fed the infant or that she served as a wet nurse, since Biblical Hebrew may use the *hiphil* participle of *ynq* ("to suck"; Exod 2:7) for a woman who nurses, but never uses any form of *'mn* in that context (Bush, 259)—the parallel use in Isa 49:23 of words from these roots with a masculine subject for *'mn* and a feminine subject for *ynq* notwithstanding. Sasson's argument that Naomi's action reflects ancient Near Eastern motifs involving divine breast feeding is unconvincing because the vocabulary used to describe Naomi's action is not the vocabulary used for breast feeding (so Bush, 250; contra Sasson, 235–39).

4:17. *proclaimed his name . . . proclaimed his name.* Possibly influenced by the occurrence of *wattiqre'nâ šĕmô* ("proclaimed his name") later in the verse, the Syr. does not account for *wattiqre'nâ lô . . . šēm* ("proclaimed his name") in the first clause of the verse. The Targum and Old Greek support MT^L. The Vulg. translates the two occurrences of *wattiqre'nâ* with two different verbs: "congratulate" and "call," respectively. Although the Vulg. may capture the sense of the verse well, I have translated *wattiqre'nâ* woodenly in order to capture how this verse may relate to the women's blessing in 4:14 that the child's name will "be proclaimed in Israel" (NOTE *may his name be proclaimed in Israel* on 4:14) as well as the people and elders' blessing (NOTE *proclaim a name* on 4:11).

For Naomi a son has been born! The verb translated as "has been born" is a *qal* passive rather than a *pual*. The root *yld* in the *qal* indicates "to give birth," whereas in the *piel* it indicates "to deliver" (Gen 35:17; 38:28; Exod 1:15–21). Thus, the *pual* would indicate "to be delivered" rather than "to be born" (cf. JM §58a). The indirect object ("Naomi") has a *l-* prefix. Elsewhere, when a *qal* passive form of *yld* has an indirect object with a *l-* prefix, the indirect object always refers to the newborn's father (Gen 4:26; 10:21, 25; 35:26; 41:50; 46:22, 27; 1 Chr 1:19; Jer 20:15), except in 2 Sam 2:20 where it refers to *hārāpâ* ("the giants"; NOTE *Orpah* on 1:4) and in Isa 9:5 where it refers to a common plural ("a son is born for us"). In Gen 46:19–22, the list of "sons of Rachel who were born for Jacob" includes both their sons and grandsons as members of Jacob's household. Although in 4:15 the women acknowledge Ruth as Obed's birth mother, implying that he is not Naomi's direct biological descendant, they still refer to Ruth as Naomi's daughter-in-law even after Ruth marries Boaz and gives birth to Obed (consult "Household Organization" in the Introduction). Thus, this declaration probably indicates that Obed is a grandson of Naomi and is a member of her household.

They proclaimed his name [to be] Obed. A minority of Old Greek witnesses have a singular verb, presumably referring to Naomi as the one who names the child Obed, meaning "one who serves." The other versions, however, do not support this reading. Outside of Ruth and 1 Chr 2:12, at least four other individuals have the name Obed in the Hebrew Bible. One of David's warriors is named Obed (1 Chr 11:47), as is one of the gatekeepers in 1 Chr 26:7. Interestingly, as with Boaz in Ruth 2:1, both the Obed in 1 Chr 11:47 and the Obed in 26:7 are listed among the *gibbôrê haḥăyālîm/gibbôrê ḥayil* ("mighty [men] of worth," 1 Chr 11:26; 26:6; consult NOTES *mighty man of worth* on 2:1, *woman of worth* on 3:11). Obed is also the name of the grandfather or father of Azariah (1 Chr 2:37–38 and 2 Chr 23:1, respectively).

Obed . . . David. One also finds this genealogy in 4:22 and 1 Chr 2:12, 15. The full spelling of the name "David" (*dwyd*) with a *y* is quite consistent in LBH. Chronicles, Ezra, and Nehemiah always use the full spelling for this name (271 occurrences), whereas there are only a few occurrences of the full spelling in older texts, and some of them may be later redactions (e.g., 1 Kgs 11:4). Thus, some scholars cite the short spellings of this name (*dwd*) in Ruth 4:17, 22 as evidence of SBH. Nevertheless, this orthographic feature should not be used in attempts to date the book's composition. The use of the full spelling (*dwyd*) in works that could come from the eighth century (Amos 6:5; 9:11) may indicate an updating of older texts. If Ruth had used the full spelling of David in 4:17, 22, one cannot be sure that this possible LBH feature does not result from a similar case of updating. Moreover, the genealogical material in Ruth may come from another, and possibly older, source. If so, while other texts that pattern after LBH update the spelling of David (1 Chr 2:15), Ruth 4:17, 22 may preserve the short spelling from its older source material. If, on the other hand, the author of Ruth created this genealogy, the short spelling may reflect archaizing to make the genealogical records seem ancient (cf. the claim about the antiquity of the Judean genealogical records in 1 Chr 4:22). Such archaizing seems in keeping with the possible archaized speech elsewhere in the book (cf. Ruth 1:20, 21;

3:3, 4). At any rate, these different scenarios should caution one against using the spelling of David as strong evidence for Ruth's date.

Comments

In 4:13, Boaz takes Ruth as a wife and YHWH gives her conception. The phrase "he entered her" is a common euphemism for sexual intercourse (Gen 29:23; 30:4; 38:2; Judg 16:1; 2 Sam 12:24). The use of this euphemism creates a pun with the people and elders' description of Ruth as "the woman who is entering your household" (Ruth 4:11). The people and elders anticipate Ruth's entry into Boaz's house as a way to build it through procreation, and indeed, Boaz's entry into Ruth leads to procreation (on the unusual word used for "conception," consult NOTE *YHWH gave her conception* on 4:13; COMMENTS on 4:18–22).

A second blessing by the women accompanies Obed's birth (vv. 14–15). This blessing creates several wordplays that are in keeping with the narrative style throughout the book (consult "The Diction of the Hebrew in Ruth" in the Introduction). For example, the word translated as "your old age" (*śēbātēk*) is not the same as the more common term that Naomi uses to describe herself in 1:12: "old" (*zāqantî*). Yet, as with other rare or unusual forms in Ruth, the use of this term allows for assonance and alliteration. The participle translated as "one who returns" earlier in the verse is *lĕmēšîb*, and the very rare construction "not removed" in the previous verse is *lō' hišĕbbît*. (The only other occurrence of this construction in the Bible is *lō' tašĕbbît* in Lev 2:13.) The women's blessing also uses vocabulary similar to that used in Ruth 1 to describe the tragedies that so severely disrupted the status quo for Naomi and Ruth. The claim that YHWH has not removed (*hišĕbbît*) a kindred redeemer and that Obed will be the one who returns (*lĕmēšîb*) life creates alliteration and assonance with Naomi's claim that "YHWH made me return [*hĕšîbanî*] empty" when she announced that she was without a male provider in her household (1:21). Following the women's blessing, the narrator refers to Obed as "the child" (*hayyeled*), which comes from the same root as the word translated as "her children" (*yĕlādêhā*) in 1:5 when the narrator reported that a bereft Naomi "was left without her two children."

The giving of conception in v. 13 is the only act in the entire book that the narrator explicitly attributes to YHWH. It could be interpreted as an act of divine *ḥesed* ("kindness") since YHWH fulfills a need that could not be fulfilled otherwise. The couple's fertility can hardly be assumed as the norm. As with other acts of kindness through the book, this act results in a blessing on the one who performed it: in this case, YHWH (for detailed discussions, consult "Divine Activity and Acts of *ḥesed* in Ruth" in the Introduction; COMMENTS on 1:1–7a). One could contrast this final blessing with the book's first blessing in which Naomi began to invoke YHWH's kindness but aborted the blessing before its completion (1:8–9).

The focus of the women's blessing, however, quickly moves from YHWH to Obed (although the syntax is somewhat ambiguous; NOTE *may his name be proclaimed in Israel* on 4:14). Despite the men's prolonged negotiations over who will serve as a kindred redeemer in 4:1–12, the women identify neither Boaz nor the unnamed kinsman as Naomi's kindred redeemer. Instead, Obed will be the one who returns life for Naomi and supports her in her old age (v. 15). Naomi becomes Obed's caregiver in his infancy

(v. 16), and he, rather than Boaz, will become her supporter in her old age (LaCocque, 142; NOTE *caregiver* on 4:16). In contrast to the conversation between Boaz and the unidentified kinsman earlier in the chapter, the women's blessing once again associates the role of kindred and children with material security (cf. 1:8–9; 3:1). As already noted (COMMENTS on 1:1–7a), in the book of Ruth, children represent the continuation of a male's "name" only when men are involved in the conversation (4:1–12). Yet, in a book in which characters are consistently uttering blessings, the final one does not praise Ruth for building a household on the scale of Rachel and Leah (v. 11) or even Tamar, who bore two sons (v. 12; cf. Gen 38:28–30). Rather, the final blessing praises Ruth, who had only one son, for loving Naomi and being better for her than seven sons, which is the idealized size for a family in other texts (Job 1:2; 42:13; cf. 1 Sam 2:5; El's marriage blessing that Kirta's bride may bear eight sons [*ANET,* 146]).

In v. 11, the people and the elders had associated proclaiming a name with either the dead man (Elimelech or more likely Mahlon) or Boaz (NOTE *proclaim a name* on 4:11). In v. 14, the women use this idiom with slightly different nuances to associate it with Obed rather than his father or one of his deceased ancestors. Whereas Boaz's or the dead man's name was to be proclaimed in Bethlehem (v. 11), the women expand the scope of the proclamation and call for Obed's name to be "proclaimed in Israel" (v. 14). They also apply this semantically flexible idiom to the announcement of Obed's birth, which further removes the focus from Boaz. As already noted, the women announce Obed's birth with a formula that applies to the paterfamilias in almost every other occurrence in the Bible (NOTE *For Naomi a son has been born!* on 4:17; COMMENTS on 1:7b–19a). Yet, they proclaim that a son is born for Naomi, not Boaz. Despite the elders and people's description of Ruth's marriage to Boaz as her entry to Boaz's household (v. 11), Naomi seems to continue to function as the senior member of the household into which Obed is born. If the birth announcement's reference to Naomi seems to displace Ruth as a Moabite mother in favor of a Judean mother, as some have argued (e.g., Gerleman, 37–38; Amy-Jill Levine, 90), the announcement's formula would also seem to displace Boaz as the household's paterfamilias (Eskenazi and Frymer-Kensky, 92, n. 234). Although Boaz is listed in the final genealogy (v. 21), he is never mentioned in the narrative portion of the book after he sleeps with Ruth in v. 13.

In 1:1–7a, the narrative opened with significant shifts in the relationships and statuses within a particular household. In 4:13–17, the narrative portion of the book ends with further shifts among these relationships and statuses. Although the sandal ritual and the blessing at the gate may have anticipated Boaz serving as the kindred redeemer and the building of his household, the women declare Obed as the kindred redeemer and celebrate the building of Naomi's household. They refer to Ruth as her daughter-in-law, in which case Ruth would remain under her authority within the household structure. Within this context, when they claim that Ruth "loves" Naomi, the verb carries a wide range of meanings. One could interpret it as an expression of deep affection, as in 1 Sam 1:5–8 where Elkanah is said to "love" Hannah and he claims that he "is better for [her] than ten sons." One could also interpret it as an expression of loyalty, as when an impoverished Hebrew relative working under the authority of a household's senior member declares her or his "love" for that household because it is "going well" for her or him in that situation (Deut 15:16; cf. Exod 21:5; cf. Ruth 3:1). In this case, the reference to Ruth's love would not be an emotional expression but a legal one related to her material security (Brenner, 1999b, 159). In this sense, it could serve as an acknowledgment that Ruth is a permanent member of a Judahite household, which would be appropriate considering the questions about her household status throughout the book (consult COMMENTS on 1:7b–19a). As these interpretive options are not mutually exclusive, it is up to readers' discretion as to how they use this verb to understand the motives that shape Naomi and Ruth's relationship. In keeping with the book's style of narration (consult "Actions, Events, and Consequences" in the Introduction), the women do not explain the motives behind Ruth's love, but only its consequences: namely, that for better or worse, she bore Naomi's kindred redeemer.

One could contrast the three births of Obed, Jesse, and David with the three deaths of male household members in Moab (1:3–5), or, shifting from a focus on extended family to larger lineages (consult "Household Organization" in the Introduction), one could also note that the blessing in vv. 11–12 begins to trace three successive generations of households (Israel [= Jacob], Judah, and Perez) in anticipation of Boaz's household becoming like them. A second genealogy (v. 17c) also traces three generations (Obed, Jesse, and David), but, unlike vv. 11–12, Naomi rather than Boaz is positioned as the household's senior member. In a book dominated by dialogue, the women of Bethlehem literally have the last word. Following the women's lead, the narrator also uses the idiom "to proclaim a name" in v. 17 to describe the women's announcement of Obed rather than the proclamation of either Boaz or the dead man's name. In doing so, the narrator positions Naomi as the senior member of the household that becomes the lineage of David, who is mentioned for the first time in the book: "'For Naomi a son has been born!' They proclaimed his name [to be] Obed. He was the father of Jesse, the father of David" (v. 17; cf. Trible, 195).

The Generations of Perez (4:18–22)

4 ⁱ⁸These are the generations of Perez: Perez begot Hezron, ¹⁹and Hezron begot Ram, and Ram begot Amminadab, ²⁰and Amminadab begot Nahshon, and Nahshon begot Salmon, ²¹and Salmon begot Boaz, and Boaz begot Obed, ²²and Obed begot Jesse, and Jesse begot David.

Notes

4:18–22. *Perez . . . David.* The names in the genealogy in vv. 18–22 are closely related to the names in Perez's genealogy in 1 Chr 2:5, 9–12, 15. In fact, the only difference in the spelling of any of these names in either genealogy in MT^L is the name Salmon (NOTE *Salmon* on 4:20). The other versions, however, reflect significant spelling differences in several of the names.

4:18. *Hezron.* Most Old Greek manuscripts, the Vulg., and Old Latin have "Hezrom," ending in an *m* rather than *n*. This character's name is also spelled with an *m* in the genealogies in Matt 1:3 and Luke 3:33 (*Esrōm*). Yet, the spelling in MT^L, supported by the Targum, LXX^B, and Syr., ends in an *n*. This fits with the spelling of this same name in 1 Chr 2:9 in MT^L and conforms to the spelling of several other male names in the book of Ruth, such as Mahlon, Kilyon, Nahshon, and Salmon (NOTE *YHWH gave her conception* on 4:13).

4:19. *Ram.* MT^L, supported by the Targum, spells this name *rām* in both v. 19 and 1 Chr 2:9, 10 (cf. Job 32:2; 1 Chr 2:25, 27, which includes a grandson of Hezron also named Ram). Other versions of both Ruth 4:19 and 1 Chr 2:9, 10 usually begin the name with an *a* vowel, although they differ on the spelling of the rest of the name, for example, Arran in Ruth 4:19 (LXX^{BA}) and 1 Chr 2:10 (LXX^B) or Aram in Ruth 4:19 (Vulg., Syr., multiple Old Greek manuscripts; cf. Matt 1:3–4 and Arni in Luke 3:33). For a detailed discussion of the various spellings among the versions, consult Campbell, 171.

Amminadab. Outside of Ruth, at least three individuals have the name Amminadab ("my kin is generous") in the Hebrew Bible. A son of Kohath is named Amminadab (1 Chr 6:7 [Eng. 6:22]). A son of Uzziel is named Amminadab (1 Chr 15:10). The father of Aaron's wife Elisheba from the tribe of Judah is named Amminadab (Exod 6:23), who is probably the same individual as the father of Nahshon (Num 1:7; 2:3; 7:12, 17; 10:14; Ruth 4:20; 1 Chr 2:10). The Targum explicitly identifies the Amminadab in Ruth 4:19 as the father of Nahshon from the tribe of Judah.

4:20. *Nahshon.* The Old Greek and Vulg. spell this name as Naasson. The Targum reflects the MT^L spelling *naḥšôn*. The etymology of this name remains uncertain, although it may be related to the noun "snake" (*nāḥāš;* Gen 3:1; 49:17; Exod 4:3; Num 21:6), the verb "to practice divination" (*niḥēš;* Gen 44:5,15; Lev 19:25; Deut 18:10; 2 Kgs 21:6; although this verb occurs only in the *piel*), or the Akkadian word "luxury" (*nuḥšu;* cf. Propp, 280). Consistent with the present genealogy, the only Nahshon mentioned elsewhere in the Hebrew Bible is the son of Amminadab from the tribe of Judah (cf. Exod 6:23; Num 1:7; 2:3; 7:12, 17; 10:14; 1 Chr 2:10–11).

Salmon. In MT^L, this name is spelled *śalmāh* in v. 20 but *śalmôn* in v. 21. The Targum also reflects this difference. Multiple medieval Hebrew manuscripts have *śalmāh* in v. 21 (*BHS* critical apparatus), although this spelling may reflect an effort to conform v. 21 to v. 20. Most Old Greek witnesses have *Salmōn* in both verses, which reflects *śalmôn,* although LXX^B has *Salman* in both verses and Luke 3:32 has *Sala* as Boaz's father. Whereas Ruth 4:20 has an *h* as a mater lectionis (*śalmāh*), 1 Chr 2:11 has an *aleph* as a mater lectionis (*śalmā';* cf. 1 Chr 2:51, 54; *Salma* in the Vulg. translation of both vv. 21, 22).

4:21. *Boaz.* For a discussion of the name Boaz, consult NOTE *Boaz* on 2:1.

4:22. *Obed.* For a discussion of the name Obed, consult NOTE *they proclaimed his name [to be] Obed* on 4:17.

David. For a discussion of the name David, consult NOTE *Obed . . . David* on 4:17.

Comments

The final genealogy ends with the same three names as listed in v. 17c (Obed, Jesse, and David) but begins with Perez (cf. v. 12). The general consensus is that this final genealogy is a later addition (e.g., Campbell, Gray, Gerleman, Hertzberg, Joüon, Nielsen, Rudolph, Sasson, Würthwein, Zenger; for counterarguments, consult Hubbard, Bush, Fischer, 2001). To be sure, no extant witness of Ruth includes the entire book except for vv. 18–22. Nonetheless, the repetitions with v. 17c suggest that it is an addition. This genealogy shares material with the genealogies in Gen 46:12 and 1 Chr 2:5, 9–12, 15 and possibly reflects common source material. Scholarly attempts to clarify the literary relationship, if any, between these texts has not led to a consensus, although most agree that Ruth 4:18–22 postdates the narrative portions of the book (for a review of scholarship, consult Sasson, 178–87; for counterarguments, consult Nielsen 98–99, Saxegaard, 36–38).

As Campbell correctly notes (173), the list of only ten generations is selective because it creates the impression that there are only five generations from the exodus (Nahshon is Aaron's brother-in-law; NOTE *Nahshon* on 4:20) to the time of David, which would include the wilderness years, the settlement, and the entire period of the chieftains! This selectivity suggests that the genealogy is telescoped for some rhetorical purpose (consult Wilson, 133–34), although scholars differ on what that purpose may be. The genealogy includes five names that have not appeared in the book thus far (Hezron, Ram, Amminadab, Nahshon, and Salmon). Given the selective nature of the telescoped genealogy, a different five names could have just as easily been used to bring the list up to ten. Yet, three of these five names (Hezron, Nahshon, and Salmon) rhyme with the names of Naomi's sons who died in Moab (Mahlon and Kilyon), as well as with the rare word for Ruth's "conception" in v. 13, which allowed the lineage to continue through Obed (*hērāyôn*; NOTE *YHWH gave her conception* on 4:13). The fact that Amminadab is listed as Nahshon's father in other texts beyond Ruth and Chronicles (for references, consult NOTE *Amminadab* on 4:19) may explain his inclusion. This, however, would not account for the inclusion of Ram.

Assuming that the genealogy is telescoped, scholars differ over why it begins with Perez as opposed to a more prestigious ancestor, such as his father Judah. Following Nielsen, Saxegaard argues that the order was fixed before the composition of Ruth's narrative and thus was not altered (37). For Fischer, the application of a *toledot* formula ("these are the descendants of *X*") to Perez connects this genealogy with the genealogies in Genesis that use this formula (e.g., Gen 2:4; 5:1; 6:9; 10:1 [all Priestly]). Fischer notes that the last *toledot* formula in Genesis refers to the descendants of Jacob (37:2a), who is Judah's father and Perez's grandfather (Ruth 4:11–12; NOTE *House of Israel* on 4:11). The genealogy of Perez in vv. 18–22 then allows the book of Ruth to continue the narrative from Genesis 38 without a break (Fischer, 2007, 142).

Many scholars find significance in the number of generations listed in the telescoped genealogies. For some, the ten generations of descendants serve as a counterpart to the ten years of marriage in Moab without children (1:4–5; Linafelt, 1999, 80). Also, as many scholars argue, the tenth position is considered prestigious in ancient Near Eastern king lists and thus it was reserved for David (Sakenfeld, 1999, 85; Sasson, 183). Some note that ten generations demarcate an epoch, as in the period from Adam to Noah (Gen 5:3–32), then Shem to Abraham (Gen 11:10–26; consult *'Abot R. Nat.* 5:2–3), and then from Isaac until Boaz (Ruth 4:11–12, 18–22; 1 Chr 1:34; 2:1–11; consult Zvi). This idea also reserves an important slot for David as the tenth name listed in the genealogy of Perez (Zakovitch, 65). Sasson argues that the list may be divided evenly between five generations who experienced life in Egypt (Perez [cf. Gen 46:8–12] through Nahshon, Aaron's brother-in-law) and five generations between the exodus and Davidic monarchy (184). Considering the significance of the numbers seven (cf. "seven sons" in v. 15) and ten, Sasson also argues that the genealogy begins with Perez so that Boaz occupies the seventh position and David the tenth (182, 84). Yet, if the genealogy is telescoped, there is no reason why it could not start with another name while still holding the seventh and tenth slots for Boaz and David, respectively (Eskenazi and Frymer-Kensky, 103, n. 242). For Eskenazi and Frymer-Kensky, "a genealogy that begins with Perez makes a breach and a blessing (both of which his name represents) an important interpretative key to the book" (94).

Aside from explanations based on the genealogy's supposed date of composition relative to the narrative, connections to Genesis, the order of names, or a popular etymology of Perez's name, the genealogy creates a bridge between the generations listed in the blessing in vv. 11–12 and the generations listed in v. 17c. The blessing left off with the name Perez, thus leaving Perez's connection to Boaz unaccounted for. The final genealogy fills in this gap by starting with Perez and tracing the lineage through the generations mentioned in v. 17c. This connects Boaz to the Judahites and positions him within a larger patrilineal framework, which other biblical texts refer to as a "house of the fathers" (consult "Household Organization" in the Introduction).

The demarcation of an epoch as ten generations could also place Boaz in an important slot since the final genealogy continues from the three generations listed in vv. 11–12: Israel (= Jacob), Judah, and Perez (cf. 1 Chr 1:34; 2:1, 3). One could trace ten generations from the generation of Isaac and Lot to that of Boaz. Their age difference notwithstanding, Isaac and Lot were cousins and part of the same generation since Abram and Haran were brothers. If Ruth descended from Lot through his son Moab, then her marriage to Boaz involves a reunion of Abram and Haran's descendants after ten generations, or an epoch, of separation (consult "Moabites as Descendants of Lot" in the Introduction).

Index of Subjects

Abraham/Abram, 14, 25, 34, 39, 41, 42, 43, 48, 80, 87, 134, 175, 177, 187, 188. *See also* Haran (person); Jacob/Israel; Lot; Nahor

Alien(s), 14, 45, 47, 48, 49, 80, 87, 115, 122, 123, 130, 137. *See also* 'almānâ; Foreign(ers); Gleaning laws; Widows

Alliteration, 7, 8–9, 15, 81, 101, 109, 113, 117, 125, 127, 128, 130, 131, 133, 138, 168, 182. *See also* Anagrams; Assonance; Etymology: popular; Puns; Rhymes; Wordplay

Allusion, 11, 13, 14, 20, 86, 135. *See also* Authorial intention; Canonical interpretation/placement; Comparisons to biblical and other ancient texts; Intertextuality

'almānâ, 47, 86, 128, 135, 163, 166. *See also* Gleaning laws; Legal terminology; Technical terminology; Widows; Wife of the dead man

Ambiguity, 24–26, 86, 94, 100, 101, 103, 112, 115, 118, 123, 129, 135, 138, 143, 146, 151, 153, 157, 160, 173, 175, 179, 182. *See also* Characterization; Narrator; Selective representation

Anagrams, 8, 113, 126, 164. *See also* Alliteration; Assonance; Etymology: popular; Puns; Rhymes; Wordplay

Ancestors, 14, 25, 41, 42, 83, 85, 99, 100, 104, 105, 139, 167, 170, 176, 183, 187. *See also* Burial; Family tomb

Assonance, 7, 8–9, 15, 81, 101, 123, 124, 164, 168, 175, 177, 182. *See also* Alliteration; Anagrams; Etymology: popular; Puns; Rhymes; Wordplay

Author(ship), 7, 8, 11, 14, 15, 16, 18–20, 21, 22, 23, 28, 29, 49, 80, 168, 177, 181. *See also* Commentator; Date of Ruth's composition; Narrator

Authorial intention, 9, 13, 14, 19, 20. *See also* Allusion; Canonical interpretation/placement; Intertextuality

Barley, 102, 114, 119, 125, 130, 132, 137, 138, 140, 142, 153, 156, 159, 160, 161. *See also* Harvest(s); Wheat

Bethlehem/Bethlehemites, 6, 7, 9, 11, 14, 24, 28, 37, 39, 40, 42, 43, 44, 47, 48, 50, 51, 79, 80, 82, 83, 84, 85, 86, 87, 88, 93, 94, 102, 103, 104, 105, 106, 107, 109, 110, 111, 114, 115, 118, 123, 128, 130, 134, 138, 156, 159, 167, 172, 176, 177, 179, 183, 184. *See also* Ephrathah/Ephrathites; Judahites

189

Blessing(s), 5, 11, 12, 18, 27, 29, 30, 33, 35, 38, 46, 88, 89, 91, 93, 102, 103, 107, 108, 110, 113, 118, 124, 123, 129, 130, 133, 134, 138, 139, 149, 154, 155, 156, 170, 171, 172, 176, 179, 181, 182, 183, 184, 187, 188. *See also* Curse(d); Nonblessed

Burial, 37, 42, 43, 45, 99, 100, 103, 105, 149, 167, 170, 176. *See also* Ancestors; Family tomb

Canonical interpretation/placement, 10–13, 81, 86, 150. *See also* Allusion; Authorial intention; Intertextuality

Characterization, 9, 21, 24, 26–28, 88, 96, 97, 122, 157, 160, 164, 174. *See also* Ambiguity; Selective representation

Chieftains/judges, 5, 11, 12, 39, 44, 79, 86, 87, 89, 92, 150, 187

Cisjordan, 12, 31, 80, 88, 89, 101, 141, 150. *See also* Transjordan

Clan(s), 7, 29, 39, 43–49, 51, 83 86, 87, 89, 93, 94, 102, 103, 104, 105, 110, 112, 113, 114, 115, 117, 118, 123, 124, 128, 129, 130, 135, 139, 144, 145, 151, 153, 154, 155, 160, 161, 166, 171, 172, 173, 174, 175, 176, 177. *See also* Ephrathah/Ephrathites; Extended family; Household: house of the father

Clothing, 142, 153, 156. *See also* Skirts

Commentator, xii, 7, 13, 14, 20, 23, 28–29. *See also* Author(ship); Narrator

Comparisons to biblical and other ancient texts, 4, 5, 13–16, 34, 35, 37, 43, 48, 105, 118, 127, 153, 156, 157, 165, 175, 176, 177. *See also* Allusion; Intertextuality; Ugaritic comparisons

Conception, 8, 29, 30, 33, 34, 176, 178, 179, 182, 187. *See also* Fertility

Curse(d), 33, 34, 35, 38, 88. *See also* Blessing(s)

Date of Ruth's composition, 9, 20–22, 40, 44, 46, 80, 85, 92, 96, 97, 101, 108, 109, 121, 122, 181, 187. *See also* Author(ship)

David/Davidic dynasty, 5, 11, 19, 22, 30, 39, 40, 83, 87, 97, 103, 113, 118, 124, 127, 129, 130, 134, 153, 181, 182, 184, 186, 187. *See also* Ephrathah/Ephrathites; Jesse; Judahites; Obed

Disability, 34. *See also* Conception; Fertility; Infertility

Divine activity, 5, 22, 29–35, 36, 42, 88, 102, 103, 108, 117, 128, 139, 160, 176, 182. *See also* Conception; Fertility

Elders, 12, 35, 37, 42, 43, 46, 92, 150, 163, 165, 170, 171, 172, 181, 182, 183

Elephantine, 40

Elimelech, 14, 39, 40, 45, 46, 47, 48, 81, 82, 83, 87, 88, 111, 112, 114, 117, 123, 128, 139, 145, 154, 162, 166, 169, 172, 174, 183. *See also* Kilyon; Mahlon

Ephrathah/Ephrathites, 11, 39, 40, 42, 43, 46, 80, 82, 83, 86, 87, 111, 172. *See also* Bethlehem/Bethlehemites; Clan(s); Ethnicity; Judahites; Moabites

Ethnicity, 14, 16, 18, 19, 23, 29, 37, 38–44, 46, 49, 84, 87, 101, 112, 118, 123, 137, 154, 175, 176. *See also* Ephrathah/Ephrathites; Judahites; Moabites

Etymology, 7–8; historical, 7, 80, 81, 82, 84, 107–8, 113, 126, 163, 177, 186; popular, 7, 8, 172, 187. *See also* Alliteration; Anagrams; Assonance; Puns; Rhymes; Wordplay

Exogamy, 14, 16, 29, 38–44, 87, 112. *See also* Marriage

Extended family, 43, 45, 46, 47, 48, 86, 102, 112, 166, 174, 176, 184. *See also* Clan(s); Household: house of the father

Family tomb, 105, 167, 176. *See also* Ancestors; Burial; Inheritance/inherited field

Famine, 7, 14, 24, 25, 28, 31, 32, 41, 42, 79, 80, 87, 88, 89, 114

Feminist interpretation, 49–51. *See also* Gender; Patriarchy

Fertility, 29, 31, 33–35, 42, 88, 89, 103, 108, 110, 176, 182. *See also* Conception; Divine activity

Field(s), 6, 9, 14, 45, 46, 48, 49, 80, 81, 107, 112, 113, 114, 117, 118, 120, 121, 122, 128, 129, 133, 134, 135, 136, 137, 139, 140, 145, 146, 153, 156, 161, 164, 165, 166, 167, 169, 171, 172, 173, 174. *See also* Harvest(s); Inheritance/inherited field

Food/bread, 7, 12, 29, 30, 31, 41, 86, 87, 88, 89, 125, 126, 130, 133, 134, 138, 139, 145, 146, 167; networks, systems, and production, 50, 51

Foreign(ers), 7, 21, 38, 42, 43, 44, 48, 80, 96, 102, 103, 108, 115, 122–23, 129, 130, 154, 166, 167. *See also* Alien(s); Gleaning laws

Gate, 12, 37, 150, 163, 170, 172, 174, 183

Gender, 8, 16, 18, 19, 23, 29, 30, 49–51, 129, 136, 152. *See also* Feminist interpretation; Patriarchy

Genealogy/genealogies, 5, 21, 26, 39, 40, 46, 83, 95, 111, 113, 171, 176, 178, 181, 183, 184, 185–88. *See also* Household: house of the father; Lineages

Genre(s), 10, 16–18, 27, 42, 155, 176

Gleaning laws, 15, 114, 115, 120, 122, 126, 129, 130. See also *'almānâ*; Foreign(ers); Legal terminology; Widows

Handmaids, 43, 47, 50, 108, 124, 129, 137, 149, 154, 166. *See also* entries *under* Household

Haran (person), 41, 42, 175, 177, 188. *See also* Abraham/Abram; Lot; Nahor

Haran (place), 42, 48

Harvest(s), 9, 31, 50, 102, 115, 119, 129, 130, 136, 137, 138, 140, 142, 145, 146, 153, 159, 160. *See also* Barley; Field(s); Threshing floor; Wheat

ḥesed, 29, 31–33, 88, 89, 92, 99, 102, 103, 135, 138, 139, 149, 150, 154, 171, 176, 182. *See also* Divine activity

Heteronormativity, 34–38, 49, 98, 105. *See also* Queer interpretation

Household, 44–51, 91; authority/status within, 8, 14, 16, 21, 25, 29, 41, 42, 43, 45, 46–49, 50, 51, 85, 86, 87, 89, 91, 95, 98, 102, 103, 104, 105, 108, 109, 110, 113, 115, 118, 119, 123, 124, 125, 128, 129, 130, 133, 134, 138, 139, 140, 145, 146, 149, 154, 160, 161, 166, 175, 183; dependents of, 45, 46, 86, 110, 130, 154, 155, 161 (*see also* Alien[s]; *'almānâ*; Foreign[ers]; Widows; Wife of the dead man); house of the father, 8, 45, 46, 91, 102, 112, 176, 188 (*see also* Genealogy/genealogies; Lineages); mother's, 8, 13, 42, 91, 102 (*see also* Puns; Wordplay); protection within, 46, 93, 112, 115, 130, 135, 149, 166 (*see also* Legal protection/provisions; Security); senior member of, 45, 46, 47, 51, 86, 102, 103, 104, 105, 128, 130, 133, 134, 144, 146, 149, 154, 166, 173, 183, 184 (*see also* Paterfamilias)

Infertility, 33–35. *See also* Conception; Fertility

Inheritance/inherited field, 9, 15, 17, 37, 45, 46, 48, 82, 104, 112, 118, 128, 135, 145, 165, 166, 167, 170, 172, 173, 174, 175, 176. *See also* Family tomb; Field(s)

Intertextuality, 7, 12, 20, 30, 35. *See also* Allusion; Authorial intention; Comparisons to biblical and other ancient texts

Jacob/Israel, 13, 14, 27, 36, 37, 40, 42, 43, 48, 49, 102, 118, 130, 133, 152, 171, 175, 176, 181, 184, 187, 188. *See also* Abraham/Abram; Laban; Leah; Nahor; Rachel

Jesse, 39, 83, 87, 184, 186. *See also* David/Davidic dynasty; Ephrathah/Ephrathites; Obed

Judahites, 39–40, 42, 43, 44, 48, 49, 103, 144, 154, 176, 188. *See also* Genealogy/genealogies; Lineages

INDEX OF SUBJECTS 191

Kilyon, 8, 25, 38, 81, 82, 84, 86, 87, 103, 113, 161, 169, 174, 178, 185, 187. *See also* Elimelech; Mahlon

Kin/kinship, 10, 14, 33, 43, 44, 46, 48, 49, 87, 98, 99, 102, 103, 110, 112, 114, 115, 128, 130, 135, 140, 155, 166, 168, 170, 174, 175, 176, 183, 186. *See also* Genealogy/genealogies; Household; Lineages

Kindred redeemer, 8, 10, 14, 33, 43, 46, 87, 108, 110, 112, 115, 130, 131, 135, 138, 139, 140, 144, 145, 149, 151, 154, 155, 160, 161, 163, 164, 165, 167, 168, 169, 172, 173, 174, 175, 176, 179, 182, 183, 184. *See also* Land redemption; Levirate; Status quo

Kinship terminology, 43, 44, 47, 48, 112. *See also* Legal terminology; Technical terminology

Laban, 42, 48, 49, 102, 130, 133, 152. *See also* Jacob/Israel; Leah; Nahor; Rachel; Rebekah

Labor(ers)/work(ers), 12, 29, 49, 124, 127, 130, 133, 134, 139, 161, 183. *See also* Servants

Land redemption, 9, 14, 15, 85, 112, 128, 154, 164, 167, 173, 174, 175. *See also* Kindred redeemer; Legal terminology

Leah, 13, 14, 26, 33, 37, 42, 43, 92, 171, 176, 177, 183. *See also* Jacob/Israel; Laban; Nahor; Rachel; Rebekah; Sarai; Tamar

Legal idea(s), 14, 15, 16, 167, 174. *See also* Levirate

Legal protection/provisions, 115, 120, 123, 126, 130, 131, 140. *See also* Household: protection within

Legal terminology, 8, 14, 15, 130. *See also* Kinship terminology; Technical terminology

Levirate, 9, 15, 35, 50, 99, 103, 104, 128, 166, 167, 169, 174. *See also* Kinship terminology; Legal terminology; Technical terminology; Widows; Wife of the dead

Lineages, 9, 40, 41, 42, 50, 82, 103, 112, 141, 145, 167, 173, 175, 176, 184, 187, 188. *See also* Household: house of the father; Kin/kinship

Lot, 5, 39, 40–44, 48, 157, 177, 188. *See also* Abraham/Abram; Haran (person); Moab (person)

Lot's daughters, 41. *See also* Haran (person); Moab (person)

Mahlon, 8, 9, 25, 38, 39, 43, 45, 48, 81, 82, 84, 86, 87, 97, 103, 113, 159, 161, 165, 166, 167, 169, 170, 174, 176, 178, 183, 185, 187. *See also* Elimelech; Kilyon

Maidservants, 7, 25, 43, 47, 50, 108, 113, 124, 125, 129, 130, 149. *See also* Handmaids; Household; Servants

Marriage, 8, 9, 12, 15, 17, 18, 25, 29, 33, 34, 37, 38–44, 45, 46, 47, 48, 49, 50, 82, 83, 84, 86, 87, 89, 91, 93, 95, 97, 98, 99, 100, 102, 103, 104, 105, 114, 121, 123, 128, 135, 136, 145, 149, 150, 151, 154, 155, 160, 161, 166, 167, 168, 169, 172, 173, 174, 175, 176, 181, 183, 187, 188. *See also* Exogamy

Moab (person), 41, 175, 188. *See also* Haran (person); Lot; Lot's daughters

Moab (place), 6, 8, 9, 14, 25, 27, 28, 31, 32, 35, 39, 41, 43, 45, 48, 80–81, 84, 85, 86, 87, 88, 89, 93, 94, 96, 99, 101, 102, 104, 108, 109, 110, 114, 119, 121, 128, 134, 135, 138, 139, 144, 159, 161, 162, 164, 167, 173, 174, 176, 184, 187

Moabites, 14, 19, 38–43, 49, 50, 87, 89, 93, 163, 175, 177, 188

Nahor, 25, 42, 43, 48, 175, 177. *See also* Abram/Abraham; Haran (person); Leah; Lot; Rachel; Rebekah

Narrator, 5, 7, 8, 9, 14, 17, 23–28, 29, 30, 31, 32, 33, 34, 35, 36, 37, 39, 42, 43, 45, 46, 47, 48, 82, 84, 86, 87, 88, 89, 92, 95, 97, 105, 110, 112, 114, 115, 118, 119, 124, 125, 128, 129, 135, 138, 139, 145, 146, 150, 152, 153, 155, 156, 157, 160, 161, 163, 168, 169, 173,

175, 180, 182, 184. *See also* Ambiguity; Author(ship); Characterization; Selective representation
Nonblessed, 33, 35, 88. *See also* Blessing(s); Curse(d)

Obed, 30, 43, 50, 102, 104, 135, 172, 181, 182, 183, 184, 186, 187. *See also* David/Davidic dynasty; Jesse
Old Age/elderly, 92, 104, 121, 179, 182, 183
Orpah, 23, 25, 26, 27, 32, 33, 34, 43, 45, 47, 81, 83–84, 85, 86, 89, 92, 93, 94, 95, 97, 99, 102, 104, 105, 109, 110, 138, 144, 155, 171

Paterfamilias, 51, 102, 183. *See also* Household: senior member of
Patriarchy, 16, 29, 47, 49–51, 128, 171. *See also* Feminist interpretation; Gender; Household
Perez, 5, 13, 26, 40, 42, 83, 111, 176, 184, 185, 186, 187, 188. *See also* Household: house of the father; Lineages; Tamar
Poetry, in Ruth, 6, 16, 26, 27, 99, 100, 101, 104, 105, 107, 110
Polemics, in Ruth, 38, 39, 43
Poverty/impoverished, 29, 47, 48, 49, 86, 110, 138, 140, 173, 183. *See also* Land redemption; Wealth
Puns, 7, 8, 9, 15, 82, 84, 91, 102, 107, 110, 167, 168, 182. *See also* Alliteration; Anagrams; Assonance; Rhymes; Wordplay

Queer interpretation, 34, 36–38, 98. *See also* Heteronormativity; Sexual desire

Rachel, 13, 14, 26, 33, 34, 35, 36, 37, 42, 43, 92, 171, 176, 177, 181, 183. *See also* Abraham/Abram; Jacob/Israel; Laban; Leah; Nahor; Rebekah; Sarai; Tamar
Rebekah, 33, 34, 35, 42, 47, 48, 102, 163. *See also* Abraham/Abram; Laban; Leah; Nahor, Rachel; Sarai; Tamar
Rhymes, 7, 8–9, 15, 81, 99, 100, 101, 109, 113, 117, 123, 124, 130, 164, 168, 172,
178, 179, 187. *See also* Alliteration; Anagrams; Assonance; Puns; Wordplay

Sandal, 168, 169, 175, 183. *See also* Levirate; Substitution; Widows; Wife of the dead
Sarai, 14, 25, 34, 35. *See also* Leah; Rachel; Rebekah
Security, 87, 93, 103, 104, 135, 136, 140, 141, 145, 146, 154, 160, 166, 173, 174, 183, 184; physical safety, 129, 136–37, 139; public safety, 136–37, 139. *See also* Household: protection within
Selective representation, 24–26, 28, 86, 94, 118, 129, 138, 151, 157, 160, 173. *See also* Ambiguity; Characterization
Servants, 15, 42, 47, 118, 120, 121, 126, 127, 128, 129, 136, 139, 152; female, 45, 46, 50, 104, 118–19, 121, 122, 123, 126, 128, 129, 139, 140, 158, 162; male, 24, 27, 45, 50, 104, 118, 119, 120, 121, 122, 123, 126, 129, 130, 139, 156. *See also* Handmaids; Maidservants
Sexual desire, 29, 24, 35–38, 49, 98, 105, 114, 128, 142–44, 152, 155–57, 175. *See also* Heteronormativity; Queer interpretation
Shavuot/Feast of Weeks, 11, 137
Skirts, 10, 23, 30, 130, 149, 154, 155, 156, 161. *See also* Clothing
Status quo, 46, 135, 136, 139, 144, 145, 151, 154, 161, 171, 172, 173, 174, 176, 182. *See also* Kindred redeemer
Substitution, 8, 168, 169, 172, 175, 177. *See also* Land redemption; Sandal

Tamar, 8, 13, 26, 40, 41, 42, 168, 171, 175, 177, 183. *See also* Abraham/Abram; Laban; Leah; Nahor; Perez; Rachel
Technical terminology, 4, 7, 8, 11, 12, 14, 15, 16, 17, 85, 86, 113, 130, 133, 138, 164, 166, 167, 168, 172, 174, 176. *See also* Kinship terminology; Legal terminology

Threshing floor, 25, 41, 142, 145, 151, 152, 153, 155, 156, 157, 160, 161, 174, 175. *See also* Barley; Harvest(s); Wheat

Transjordan, 83, 88, 101, 102, 103, 108, 110. *See also* Cisjordan

Ugaritic comparisons, 7, 8, 33, 81, 82, 83, 92, 107, 113, 125, 158. *See also* Comparisons to biblical and other ancient texts

Wealth, 47, 48, 112, 115, 130, 161, 171. *See also* Poverty/impoverished

Wheat, 119, 137, 138, 140, 142. *See also* Barley; Harvest(s)

Widows, 45, 47, 51, 91, 102, 104, 122, 128, 137, 153, 159, 163, 166. See also *'almānâ;* Wife of the dead man

Wife of the dead man, 9, 12, 43, 48, 93, 165, 166, 167, 174, 175, 177. See also *'almānâ;* Kinship terminology; Legal terminology; Technical terminology; Widows

Wordplay, 7, 8, 10, 15, 86, 87, 113, 120, 123, 126, 130, 131, 139, 179, 182. *See also* Alliteration; Anagrams; Assonance; Puns; Rhymes

Index of Modern Authors

Ackerman, Susan, 51, 99
Aguilar, Grace, 49
Alpert, Rebecca, 36, 98
Alter, Robert, 26
Anderson, Francis I., 32
Aschkenasy, Nehama, 51
Auerbach, Erich, 24, 27
Avalos, Hector, 34

Baden, Joel S., 33, 34, 88
Bal, Mieke, 49
Bar-Asher, Elitzur Avraham, 92
Bar-Efrat, Shimon, 6
Barr, James, 8
Beattie, D. R. G., 4, 22, 30, 36, 148
Ben-Dor, S., 45
Berger, Yitzkah, 20, 42
Berlin, Adele, 9, 24, 26, 103, 118, 163, 174
Berman, Joshua, 87
Berquist, Jon L., 51, 114
Bertman, Stephen, 5
Bird, Phyllis, 50
Block, Daniel I., 5, 19, 80, 157, 158
Boer, Roland, 49
Borowski, Oded, 128
Brady, Christian M. M., 100, 104
Braulik, Georg, 41

Brenner, Athalya, 19, 23, 25, 49, 105, 184
Brichto, Herbert C., 175
Bridge, Edward J., 124, 149
Bronner, Leila Leah, 36
Bruppacher, Hans, 84
Bush, Fredric, 5, 16, 17, 20, 21, 30, 40, 80, 83, 84, 85, 88, 91, 93, 94, 96, 97, 100, 101, 103, 106, 107, 108, 112, 113, 117, 119, 120, 121, 125, 126, 127, 133, 134, 136, 137, 143, 145, 148, 157, 164, 165, 166, 168, 171, 172, 175, 176, 180, 186
Butting, Klara, 86, 110

Callahan, Scott N., 20, 98, 124
Camp, Claudia, 154
Campbell, Edward F., 5, 7, 11, 16, 19, 21, 22, 30, 80, 81, 82, 83, 84, 85, 91, 93, 97, 99, 100, 106, 108, 109, 110, 111, 112, 113, 117, 118, 120, 121, 123, 124, 125, 126, 127, 133, 134, 137, 142, 143, 148, 151, 157, 160, 163, 165, 168, 169, 170, 179, 180, 185, 186
Carasik, Michael, 120
Chavel, Simeon, 9, 174
Childs, Brevard S., 11, 30
Chu, Julie, 49
Clark, Gordon R., 31, 32

Collins, John J., 46
Conklin, Blane, 101
Couey, J. Blake, 99
Coxon, Peter W., 41

David, Martin, 20
Davies, Eryl W., 15
Davis, Andrew R., 26, 27, 49, 51, 92
Dobbs-Allsopp, F. W., 81, 99, 118, 124, 134, 149
Donaldson, Laura E., 37
Dube, Musa W., 25, 49, 88, 105
Dubin, Lois C., 5, 88
Duncan, Celena M., 35, 36, 37, 38

Ebach, Jürgen, 41
Ehrensvärd, Martin, 83, 97, 101
Eskenazi, Tamara Cohn, 11, 12, 16, 21, 31, 32, 82, 100, 103, 117, 120, 140, 143, 149, 150, 155, 156, 157, 169, 180, 183, 187
Exum, J. Cheryl, 35, 36, 98, 121

Fentress-Williams, Judy, 5, 41, 155
Fewell, Danna Nolan, 24, 25, 26, 30, 31, 32, 35, 37, 38, 49, 97, 115, 139, 156
Fisch, Harold, 5, 42
Fischer, Irmtraud, 17, 19, 38, 49, 186, 187
Foster, Jeannette H., 36
Frevel, Christian, 80
Frymer-Kensky, Tikva, 11, 12, 16, 21, 31, 32, 82, 100, 103, 105, 117, 120, 140, 143, 149, 150, 155, 156, 157, 169, 180, 183, 187
Fuchs, Esther, 49, 50

Garsiel, Moshe, 8, 9, 82, 87, 113, 167
Gerleman, Gillis, 4, 19, 30, 80, 87, 134, 135, 183, 186
Glanzman, G., 19
Glover, Neil, 104
Glueck, Nelson, 32, 134
Goitein, Shlomo Dov, 19, 115
Gordis, Robert, 19
Gottwald, Norman K., 45, 112

Goulder, Michael D., 41
Gow, Murray D., 5, 19, 20, 22
Gray, John, 158, 186
Greenstein, Edward L., 21, 108
Gunkel, Hermann, 16, 17, 42
Gunn, David M., 24, 25, 26, 30, 31, 32, 35, 37, 38, 49, 97, 115, 139, 156

Hackett, Jo Ann, 51, 110, 145
Hals, Ronald M., 5, 21, 22, 30, 31, 35, 117, 160
Havrelock, Rachel S., 102
Hertzberg, Hans Wilhelm, 30, 36, 91, 186
Hiebert, Paula S., 47
Holmstedt, Robert D., 11, 21, 79, 80, 81, 83, 85, 92, 93, 94, 95, 97, 100, 106, 108, 109, 113, 114, 117, 121, 123, 125, 133, 135, 136, 141, 143, 148, 151, 163, 165, 168, 179
Honig, Bonnie, 49
Hopkins, David C., 153
Hornsby, Teresa J., 37
Hubbard, Robert L., 5, 16, 19, 20, 30, 31, 34, 35, 36, 80, 81, 82, 83, 84, 85, 93, 103, 107, 109, 113, 117, 118, 120, 121, 126, 127, 137, 145, 156, 163, 164, 166, 171, 175, 186
Humbert, Paul, 21, 30, 121, 127
Humphreys, W., 17
Hurvitz, Avi, 20, 120, 168
Hutton, Jeremy M., 101
Hyman, Robert T., 35

Irwin, Brian P., 142

Jackson, Bernard S., 105
Jackson, Melissa A., 5, 42
Jobling, David, 12, 102
Joüon, Paul, 80, 82, 83, 84, 93, 107, 120, 123, 124, 125, 126, 127, 148, 151, 169, 179, 186
Junior, Nyasha, 49

Karlin-Neumann, Patricia, 5
Kates, Judith A., 49

Kawashima, Robert, 118
Kidd, José E. Ramirez, 80
Kim, Dong-Hyuk, 83, 101, 106
Knoppers, Gary N., 19, 40, 46, 176
Köhlmoos, Melanie, 19, 20, 38, 158
Koosed, Jennifer L., 32, 36, 38, 50, 98, 117, 154
Korpel, Marjo C. A., 5, 19, 30, 38, 80, 91
Kruger, Paul A., 149
Krutzsch, Brett A., 37

Labuschange, C. J., 171
LaCocque, André, 5, 16, 19, 22, 30, 32, 36, 38, 88, 183
Landy, Francis, 154
Lapsley, Jacqueline E., 17, 32, 110
Lau, Peter H., 19, 20, 21, 32, 46
Lee, Eunny P., 43
Lemaire, André, 84
Lemche, Niels Peter 45, 112
Lemos, T. M., 167
Leuchter, Mark, 177
Levine, Amy-Jill, 50, 183
Levine, Baruch A., 9, 174
Levinson, Bernard M., 17, 168
Lim, Timothy H., 92, 121, 122, 136
Linafelt, Tod, 5, 11, 21, 26, 27, 30, 35, 81, 88, 97, 99, 100, 104, 107, 117, 144, 156, 164, 175, 187
Lys, Daniel, 120

Marsman, H. J., 104
Martín-Contreras, Elvira, 144
Matthews, Victor A., 5, 21
McNutt, Paula, 44, 45, 83
Melcher, Sarah, 34
Meyers, Carol, 19, 47, 50, 91, 102, 128, 153, 173
Miles, Jack, 19
Milgrom, Jacob, 29, 47, 85, 133, 135, 137, 176
Miller, Cynthia L., 118
Moore, Michael S., 11, 81, 108, 109, 120, 135, 142
Moss, Candida R., 33, 34

Myers, Jacob M., 26, 83, 91, 95, 97, 121, 125, 141, 142

Nadar, Sarojini, 51
Newsom, Carol A., 17
Niditch, Susan, 22
Nielsen, Kirsten, 5, 12, 16, 19, 20, 21, 23, 30, 41, 80, 110, 117, 143, 180, 186, 187
Novick, Tzvi, 130

Ostriker, Alicia, 110

Pa, Anna May Say, 51
Pardes, Ilana, 43
Parker, Simon B., 18, 33
Parsons, Mikael, 34
Pfau, Julie, 143, 157
Polzin, Robert, 20, 108
Porten, Bezalel, 5, 9, 42, 82, 167
Pressler, Carolyn, 5, 16, 21
Propp, William, 186
Pui-lan, Kwok, 49
Putman, Ruth Anna, 49

Qimron, Elisha, 96, 108
Quast, Udo, 3, 158

Rendsburg, Gary A., 21, 84, 92, 108, 120, 123, 165
Revell, E. J., 108
Rezetko, Robert, 83, 97, 101
Roberts, J. J. M., 97
Rudolph, Wilhelm, 30, 80, 82, 94, 120, 125, 158, 165, 169, 186

Sakenfeld, Katharine Doob, 5, 12, 30, 31, 32, 34, 113, 117, 134
Sanders, James A., 3
Sarna, Nahum N., 172
Sasson, Jack M., 5, 7, 9, 16, 20, 22, 34, 36, 40, 49, 80, 81, 82, 93, 95, 96, 98, 105, 109, 112, 113, 114, 117, 121, 124, 125, 127, 136, 137, 141, 148, 149, 164, 165, 166, 167, 168, 171, 180, 186, 187

Saxegaard, Kristin M., 8, 26, 37, 50, 104, 105, 186, 187
Schipper, Jeremy, 17, 18, 34, 86, 91, 93, 97, 103, 133
Schloen, J. David, 44, 45
Schmitt, Rüdiger, 102, 103
Shade, Aaron, 84
Sharp, Carolyn J., 26
Sievers, Eduard, 26
Siquans, Agnethe, 87, 174
Smith, Jonathan Z., 14
Smith, Mark S., 94, 100, 104, 105
Sommer, Benjamin D., 22
Stackert, Jeffrey, 15, 49
Stanton, Elizabeth Cady, 49
Steinberg, Naomi, 12, 47
Sternberg, Meir, 24, 118
Stone, Ken, 36, 37
Stone, Timothy, 176
Strawn, Brent A., 13, 91, 103
Sutskover, Talia, 126, 176

Talmon, Shemaryahu, 109, 127
Tov, Emanuel, 11, 111
Trible, Phyllis, 5, 30, 32, 49, 88, 103, 104, 115, 117, 118, 138, 142, 160, 184
Tropper, Josef, 92
Twersky, Reimer, 30, 49

van der Toorn, Karel, 45, 99
Van Dijk-Hemmes, Fokkelien, 19

Vesco, Jean-Luc, 20
von Rad, Gerhard, 21, 22
von Wolde, Ellen, 20, 38

Weems, Renita J., 49
Weisberg, Dvora E., 45, 103, 128, 167, 173
Weiss, David W., 167
Wells, Bruce, 47, 48
West, Mona, 36, 98
Westbrook, Raymond, 15, 128, 164, 166, 172, 173, 174
Whitman, Ruth, 25
Wilson, Robert R., 187
Witzenrath, Hagia Hildegard, 16, 109
Wojcik, Jan, 153, 160
Würthwein, E., 17, 84, 186

Yavin, Zipora, 20
Yee, Gale, 49
Yong, Amos, 34
Young, Ian, 83, 97, 101

Zakovitch, Yair, 5, 17, 20, 38, 41, 187
Zenger, Erich, 5, 16, 17, 19, 40, 134, 164, 186
Zevit, Ziony, 21, 22, 96, 165, 168, 172, 178
Zvi, Ron, 187

Index of Ancient Sources

Hebrew Bible

GENESIS

2:4	187	11:30	34
2:24	14, 98, 100	11:26–12:5	42
3:1	186	Chapter 12	14
4:1	144, 179	12:1	48
4:17	144	12:4–5	48
4:19	83	12:10	14, 80, 87
4:20–21	81	12:11	35
4:25	33, 144	12:13	40
4:26	181	12:14	35
5:1	187	Chapter 13	5, 41
5:3–32	187	13:1	41
6:2	83	13:9	41, 42
6:8	114	13:11	41, 42
6:9	187	13:14	41
6:22	147	14:1	79
7:5	147	14:12	41
10:1	187	14:16	41
10:21	181	16:2	14, 34
10:25	81, 181	16:2–3	149
11:3	152	16:3	34, 104
11:4	152	17:1–2	108
11:7	152	18:15	94
11:10–26	187	18:27	122
11:26	42	Chapters 18–19	5
11:27	41, 95	Chapter 19	41
11:29	83	19:2	94
		19:14–16	41
		19:30	41

GENESIS (*continued*)

19:30–35	40	Chapter 26	14
19:30–38	41, 157	26:1	14, 80, 87
19:30–38b	41	26:1–16	81
19:31	41	26:3	80, 87
19:32	41	26:8	87
19:32–35	157	26:12	142
19:33	41	27:4	27
19:33–35	41	27:18–19	158
19:34	41, 152	27:20	117
19:37	41	27:32–33	148
19:38	42	27:43	48
20:17–18	34	27:46	91
20:17	35	27:46–28:4	104
Chapters 20–21	81	28:3	108
21:1–2	34	28:9	82
21:2	179	28:10	48
21:21	104	28:11	136, 143
22:21	81	28:18	143
22:23	42	29:5	42, 48
23:4	85	29:10	42
23:10–11	164	29:11	94
23:13	164	29:14	14, 48, 85, 98, 133
Chapter 24	42	29:15	48, 130
24:2–4	104	29:17b	35
24:7	20, 33	29:18a	36
24:11	119	29:21	152
24:12	42, 117	29:21–30	48
24:13	119	29:23	182
24:15	42, 163	29:24	130
24:16	35	29:25	14, 48, 85, 133
24:23	158	29:28	104
24:24	42	29:29	130
24:27	134	29:30	14, 48, 85, 133
24:28	42, 91	29:31	33, 34, 48, 178
24:32–58	104	29:32	179
24:35	130	29:33	33, 179
24:38	44, 91	29:30–35	37
24:40	44	29:35	42
24:41	44	29:38	48
24:47	42, 158	29:30–30:24	14
24:50–59	47	30:3	14, 42, 149
24:53	91	30:4	104, 149, 182
24:60	18, 33, 42, 102	30:9	104, 149
24:60–67	45	30:16	144
25:10	166	30:22	33, 34, 178
25:19	95	31:2	124
25:21	33, 34, 179	31:5	124

31:7	48, 130	38:8–9	144
31:9	91	38:11	9, 42, 45, 86, 91, 104, 159, 166
31:15	167		
31:16	94	38:12–30	41
31:26–31	102	38:25	118
31:30	99	38:28	181
31:31	14	38:28–30	183
31:38	14, 85, 133	38:29	42
31:41	38, 130	39:1	16
31:42	161	39:4	114
32:1 (Eng. 31:55)	102	40:5	167
32:2	136	40:8	167
32:5	14, 48	41:5–7	113
32:18 (Eng. 32:17)	118, 158	41:11	167
32:20	152	41:15	167
33:1–6	149	41:22–24	113
33:4	94	41:34	91
33:15	14	41:35	125
33:17	172	41:49	125
34:3	97, 98	41:50	181
34:9	98	41:50–51	81
34:10–11	104	41:54	80
34:27	82	43:6	109
35:11	107	44:4	122
35:16–19	42	44:5	186
35:17	181	44:15	186
35:19	42, 45, 83, 172	45:41	25
35:23	42	45:15	94
35:26	181	46:8–12	187
36:26	81	46:12	40, 186
36:35	81	46:19–22	181
37:2a	187	46:21	81
37:4	25	46:22	181
37:4–11	87	46:27	171, 181
37:5	25, 167	46:34	120
37:8	25	47:16	152
37:9	167	47:23	166
37:11	25	48:3–4	107
Chapter 38	5, 9, 14, 40, 42, 99, 128, 166, 167, 175, 187	48:5–6	172
		48:7	42, 83, 172
		48:14	122
38:1–11	103	48:16	135, 172
38:2	40, 182	49:17	93, 186
38:4–10	128	49:25	107, 108
38:5–6	40	49:29	105
38:6–10	33, 87	50:1	94
38:6–11	104	50:25	167
38:8	98		

EXODUS

Chapter 1	14
1:15–21	181
1:21	91
2:6–10	84
2:7	180
2:16–21	104
3:3	113
3:5	168
3:22	91
4:3	186
4:18	113
5:7	124
5:8	124
6:3	108
6:9	100
6:19	82
6:23	186
9:3	97
9:18	120
9:31–32	137
11:2	84
13:13	84
15:1–18	6
18:3–4	81
18:26	121
19:16	148
19:18	148
20:6	103
20:10	45
20:16	109
20:26	143
21:2	166
21:2–3	47
21:5	105, 183
21:6	99
21:7–10	149
21:22	84
21:29	124
21:36	124
23:25–26	88
23:26	33, 34
23:27	84
28:9	92
28:11	92
28:14	92
28:26	92
28:27	92
30:4	92
31:2	81
32:4	99
32:10	82
32:11	82
32:24	118
32:32	27, 93
33:12	114
33:17	114
33:19	172
34:7	103
34:16	104
34:20	84
34:22–23	11
34:28	83
39:7	92
39:18	92
39:20	92
39:32	147
39:42	147
40:16	147

LEVITICUS

2:13	182
7:23	100
11:4	100
11:43	168
14:40	168
16:5	165
Chapter 18	41
18:6	41
18:6–19	143
19:9–10	15, 114, 115, 120, 122
19:9	15
19:10	15
19:25	186
20:11	143
20:17–21	143
20:18	143
20:20	143
21:2	135
21:3	95
21:14	45
22:11	166
22:12	95
22:13	45, 86, 91, 166
23:15–16	137
23:22	15, 114, 115, 120, 122

24:10–23	16	1:54	147
24:10	18	2:3	186
24:22	18	2:34	147
Chapter 25	9, 15, 48, 140, 164, 166	3:20	82
		5:8	135, 174
25:6	85, 138	7:12	186
25:14	166	7:17	186
25:14–15	165, 169	8:20	147
25:23	85, 138	9:5	147
25:23–55	14, 47, 85, 174	9:6–14	16
25:24	85	9:14	18
25:24–34	169	10:14	186
25:25	85, 135, 164, 173, 174	11:4	167
25:25–26	85	11:12	180
25:25–28	135	11:18	151
25:25–55	110	11:20	107
25:26	85	14:18–19	103
25:27	164	15:32–37	16
25:29	85	16:21	82
25:30	85	21:6	186
25:31	85	21:11–20	41, 87
25:32	85	21:20	81
25:33	85	21:22	101
25:35	48, 140	21:29	99
25:35–36	85, 138	22:9	158
25:39–41	85, 138	22:28	34
25:40	133	23:6–7	41
25:44	129, 166	24:4	108
25:47	47, 85, 138	24:17	41
25:47–55	135	24:18	171
25:48–49	112	25:1–5	38
25:49	86	25:2	99
25:50	85, 138	25:6	118
25:53	85, 138	26:29	95
26:4–5	88	26:33	82
26:9–10	88	26:52–56	45, 112
26:12	100	Chapter 27	9
26:19	171	27:1–11	16, 17, 18
26:44	82	27:11	17, 112, 135, 174
27:10	8, 168, 169	30:7	95
27:33	8, 169	32:3	39
30:22	100	32:36	39
31:33	100	32:42	125
32:38	100	33:54	45, 112
		35:8	165
NUMBERS		35:12	135
1:2	112	35:19	135
1:7	186	35:21	135

NUMBERS (*continued*)

35:24	135
35:25	135
35:27	135
Chapter 36	9
36:6	91, 104, 155

DEUTERONOMY

1:11	12
1:13	152
1:16	80
1:16–17	12
2:9	41
2:10	168
2:12	168
2:19	41, 42
2:20	168
2:27	101
2:28–29	41, 87
3:25	113
4:2	180
4:3–4	97
4:40	141
4:42	124
5:10	103
6:1	80
6:3	141, 142
6:10–12	12
7:1	12
7:3	104
7:6	88
7:9	103
7:12–15	88
7:13	33
7:13–14	12
7:13–15	88
7:14	34, 35
8:8	137
8:10	12
8:17	112
8:17–18	115
8:18	112
10:20	97
11:11–15	88
11:22	97
11:31–32	12
12:1	80
12:7	12
12:18	45
14:2	88
14:29	12
15:4	80
15:12	14, 85, 133
15:13–14	161
15:16	14, 85, 105, 183
15:18	85
Chapter 16	137
16:9	137
16:9–10	11
16:11	45, 137
16:14	45, 137
16:15	12
16:16	11
16:18	12, 150
17:9	12
17:12	12
18:10	186
19:4	124
19:5	168
19:6	124, 135
19:12	12, 135
19:14	80
19:17–18	12
21:2	12
21:3	12
21:4	12
21:6	12, 84
21:19	12, 170
21:20	12
22:15	12
22:15–16	12, 104, 150
22:17	12
22:18	12
22:25–27	137
23:1 (Eng. 22:30)	143, 149
23:4–5 (Eng. 23:3–4)	41, 87
23:4–7 (Eng. 23:3–6)	38, 41, 163
23:11 (Eng. 23:10)	35
24:1	114
24:1–4	17
24:2	95
24:19	12, 15, 114, 115, 120, 122
24:20	127

Chapter 25	9, 98, 166, 167	18:4	80
25:1–10	103	18:20	45
25:2	12, 39	18:28	45
25:5	9, 12, 166, 174	19:8	45
25:5–10	15, 128, 166, 167, 175	19:15	80, 82
		19:23	45
25:7	9, 12, 98, 150, 167	19:31	45
25:7–8	128	19:39	45
25:7–10	173	19:48	45
25:8	12	20:3	135
25:9	98, 168, 169	20:4	12
25:10	168	20:5	124, 135
26:15	12	20:9	135
26:18–19	88	21:45	159
27:20	143, 149	22:5	97
28:1–12	88	22:7	136
28:3–5	12	23:12	98
28:11	33	23:14	159
28:54	180	23:21	114
28:65	82	24:20	114
29:12	167	24:21	94
30:20	97	24:22	171
32:3	172	24:32	45, 167
JOSHUA		**JUDGES**	
2:12	91	1:10	168
3:4	124	1:11	168
3:9	125	1:23	168
4:18	124	2:16–18	12
5:15	168	3:2	168
7:14	112	3:12–30	38
7:26	172	4:4–5	12
8:31	20	4:11	142
9:16	114	4:21	148
10:13	10	4:22	118
12:1–5	101	5:1–30	6
13:23	45	5:2	12
13:27	39	5:9	12
13:28	45	5:24	12
14:15	168	6:11	127
15:3	39	6:23	125
15:15	168	6:25	83
15:16–17	104	7:13	142
15:20	45	8:16	12
15:44	40	Chapter 9	81
15:53	39	9:1	44, 91
16:8	45	9:2	98
17:3	82	9:18	91

JUDGES (continued)

11:17–18	38
11:24	99
11:30	123
11:38	113
12:5	82
12:8	39
12:9	39
13:2–3	34
13:3	179
13:27	12
14:2	83
14:3	104
14:10	104
15:12	137
16:1	182
16:3	92, 153
16:20	152
16:29	148
Chapters 17–21	11
17:1	80
17:2	11, 12, 134
17:5	99
17:6	81
17:7	14, 80
17:7–9	11
17:8	14, 80
17:9	14, 80
17:10	85
18:1	81
18:19	112
18:20	148
18:24	99
18:25	136
Chapters 19–21	11
19:1	14, 80, 81
19:6	148
19:13	119
19:21	81
19:22	144, 148
19:23	11
19:24	92
20:13	144
21:19b	93
21:21	47
21:23	21, 83
21:25	81

I SAMUEL

1:1	80, 82
1:5	183
1:5–6	34
1:6	148
1:8	180
1:17	103
1:18	124
1:19	144
1:20	179
1:23	159
2:5	34
2:21	85
3:17	100
3:18	91
4:5	107
5:6	97
5:9	97
6:9	117
8:1–2	12
8:8	123
8:16	37
8:19	94
9:1	112
9:2	37
9:9	168
9:12	45
9:12–13	120
9:15	164
11:5	118
12:3	109, 158
12:12	94
14:38	125
14:44	91, 100
15:13	12, 134
15:18	82
16:4	12
16:18	39, 112, 115
16:22	114
17:12	11, 14, 39, 83, 87
17:17	127
17:20	132
17:55	158
17:56	158
17:58	158
18:11	152

18:22	148	2:5–6	91
18:27	104	2:5–6a	103
20:2	164	2:20	181
20:6	39	2:26	107
20:12–13	164	3:3	39
20:13	91	3:9	100
20:23	100	3:12	118
20:26	117	3:15	14
20:41	94	3:17	124
21:2	81	3:35	100
21:3	163	3:37	133
21:6 (Eng. 21:5)	124	3:39b	124
21:7	81	4:3	83
21:9	81	4:4	180
22:3–4	39, 87	5:1	98
22:8	164	5:13–8:18	5
22:15	91	5:20	172
22:17	164	6:20	143
22:18	136–137	6:23	34
23:21	12, 134	7:10–11	12
24:4 (Eng. 24:3)	143	7:27	164
24:5	148	8:2	38
Chapter 25	82	8:3	144
25:22	91, 100	11:21	81
25:23	129	Chapters 11–12	157
25:27	124	12:3	180
25:27–28	124	12:5	94
25:36	148	12:8	180
25:40	83	12:9	83
25:41	129	12:15	84
26:7	143	12:18–19	84
26:11	143	12:24	182
26:12	143	Chapter 13	157
26:16	143	13:11	152
27:1	136	13:28	148
28:5	148	13:33	150
28:13	99	13:38	83
28:21	124	14:1–20	153
28:22	124	14:2	19
30:13	118, 158	14:4	129
31:8	82	14:5	170
		14:5–7	110
2 SAMUEL		14:5b–7	16
1:5	136	14:7	124
1:16	109	14:9	91
1:18	10	14:11	135
2:5	12, 134, 183	14:12	124

2 SAMUEL (continued)
14:14   124
14:16   99
14:17   124
14:19   124
15:7   113
15:21   150
15:25   114
16:4   124, 129
16:5   44
16:23   144
17:12   80
17:19   84
17:25   144
17:28   137
18:3   136
18:5   148
18:20   144
19:13–14 (Eng. 19:12–13)   98
19:14 (Eng. 19:13)   100
19:34 (Eng. 19:33)   85
19:36 (Eng. 19:35)   159
19:43 (Eng. 19:42)   112
20:2   97
20:16   19
21:18   84
22:9   81
22:11   81
22:16   81
22:41   84
23:16   132
23:36   166
24:21   166
24:22–23   164
24:24   94

I KINGS
1:4   144
1:16   129
1:42   112
1:45   107
1:52   112
2:23   91, 100
2:25   137
2:30   94
2:31   129
2:33   124
2:34   137
2:46   137
3:1   39, 83
3:9   101
3:22   94
4:15   83
7:21   113
7:46   83
8:1–2   87
8:56   159
8:66   148
9:26   142
10:9   133
11:1   123
11:1–2   38, 39
11:2   97
11:4   181
11:8   123
11:9b   93
11:15   82
11:17   99
11:19   114
11:22   85
11:26   82, 83
11:28   112
11:33   99
11:41   10
13:1   118
13:6   82
13:24–25   118
14:12   84
14:19   20
14:21   39
14:29   20
14:31   39
15:4   167
16:1–4   23
16:3   171
16:11   135
16:12   23
17:15   91
17:21–23   84
18:13   123
18:30   125
19:2   100
19:6   143

208   INDEX OF ANCIENT SOURCES

20:10	100	24:2	38
20:36	122	24:14	112
21:7	148		
22:4	105	**ISAIAH**	
23:8	142	1:8	153
		1:15	136
2 KINGS		3:9	109
Chapter 3	14	5:1	113
3:4–27	38	7:1	79
3:7	105	7:11	124
4:1	84	7:17	91
4:6	120	8:6	148
4:8–37	102	8:19	99
4:13	45	8:19–20	99
4:14	34, 35	9:5	181
4:27	97	9:7 (Eng. 9:8)	159
4:29	118	10:22	82
4:37	129	13:6	107
5:18	150	15:1–16:14	38
5:23–24	132	17:5	113, 119
6:8	163	17:11	9
6:31	100	19:17	107
7:8	132	20:2	168
Chapter 8	14	22:2	107
8:1–2	14	27:12	127
8:1–6	91, 102	27:29–30	136
9:10	23	30:16	94
9:25	132	34:17	148
9:26	132	38:18	96
9:36	23	39:8	152
10:1	180	40:11	180
10:5	180	41:14	135
10:10	159	43:14	135
10:11	111, 112	44:6	135
10:15	118	44:24	135
11:9	147	47:3	143
13:4	82	47:4	135
13:5	124	48:17	135
13:20	38	49:6	167
15:20	112	49:7	135
16:16	147	49:23	180
18:6	97	49:26	135
19:31	144	54:1	34
19:37	144	54:4–5	135
20:19	152	54:4	135
21:6	186	54:8	135
23:13	99	59:12	109

ISAIAH (*continued*)

59:20	135
60:16	135
63:16	135
66:9	34

JEREMIAH

1:3	79
2:27	84
2:33	142
3:1	95
7:16	100
8:3	112
9:17	97
13:22	143
14:7	109
20:14	133
20:15	181
26:19	82
27:18	100
29:6	104
31:14	84
31:16–17	130
31:38	144
Chapter 32	9, 15, 164
32:6–8	174
32:6–15	15
32:7	169
32:7–8	164, 168, 169, 173
32:8	169
32:25	169
32:33	84
35:18	147
36:8	147
36:25	100
38:16	150
39:7–8	168
39:12	150
40:4	164
41:8	137
42:6	141
42:14	94
44:26	172
44:28	158
48:1–47	38
48:39	84
48:46	99
49:24	148
50:29	144
50:34	135
51:3	150

EZEKIEL

1:24	107
4:14	120
10:5	107
10:7	132
16:8	149
16:18	142
16:36	143
16:37	143
22:10	143
23:6	37
23:8–10	143
23:10	143
23:12	37
23:18	143
23:23	37
23:29	143
23:45	92
23:46	92
23:47	92
27:30	107
28:18	133
31:21	142
36:28	100
37:27	100
40:1	114
44:25	95
45:13	137
47:22–23	17
48:16	150

HOSEA

2:7 (Eng. 2:5)	156
2:12 (Eng. 2:10)	143
2:14 (Eng. 2:12)	92
3:2	167
3:3	95
5:5	109
6:2	133
8:10	136
9:11	178
9:16	136

JOEL
1:11	137
1:15	107

AMOS
2:1–3	38
3:1	112
4:2	94
4:7	80
6:5	181
7:2	158
7:5	158
8:11	87
9:11	181

JONAH
4:11	101

MICAH
1:9	150
2:3	112
5:1 (Eng. 5:2)	83
7:6	47, 86

NAHUM
3:5	143

HABAKKUK 97

ZEPHANIAH
2:9	38, 41

ZECHARIAH
5:8–9	92
5:11	125
6:10	165
11:14	101
12:10	97

MALACHI
2:14	101
3:18	101

PSALMS
3:8	136
14:5	167
19:8 (Eng. 19:7)	179
19:15 (Eng. 19:14)	135
23:4	136
30:12	82
31:12 (Eng. 31:11)	111
34:1	81
45:11	91
51:2 (Eng. 51:1)	144
55:14 (Eng. 55:13)	111
62:13 (Eng. 62:12)	103
68:15 (Eng. 68:14)	107
68:22	125
78:20	133
78:35	135
83:6–9	38
83:9 (Eng. 83:8)	41
88:9 (Eng. 88:8)	111
88:19 (Eng. 88:18)	111
102:26 (Eng. 102:25)	168
103:4	135
104:27	96
105:41	34
106:28	38, 99
107:9	133
115:5	134
115:15	12
118:15	171
118:16	171
119:116	96
119:166	96
121:2	124
127:2	107
127:3	33, 130
132:6	83, 172
141:4	114
141:4b	113
145:15	96
146:5	96

PROVERBS
2:16	123, 154
5:4	107
5:18	133
5:20	123, 154
6:24	123, 154
7:4	111
7:5	123, 154

PROVERBS (*continued*)
7:22	56
9:7	148
12:4	13, 150
14:1	91
14:3	121
18:24	98
22:6	136
23:10–11	135
23:27	123, 154
25:12	82
25:13	179
25:20	125
26:16	180
27:22	84
Chapter 31	13
31:10	13, 150, 154
31:16	173
31:21	13, 91
31:26	150
31:27	13, 91

JOB
1:1	80
1:2	180, 183
6:8	148
12:2	150
15:6	109
15:31	168
16:18	170
19:14	111
20:18	168
21:25	107
24:21	34
24:24	113
27:2	97, 108
27:13b–14	108
28:17	168
31:40	137
32:2	185
33:16	164
42:13	180, 183

SONG OF SONGS
1:13	107, 157
3:4	13, 42, 91
7:2	82
7:12	157
8:2	13, 42, 91
8:10	107

RUTH
Chapter 1	41
1:1	7, 11, 14, 28, 39, 44, 79, 80–81, 83, 87, 88, 89, 109, 114, 119, 121, 122, 164
1:1b	14, 89
1:1–2	39, 44, 45, 83, 114
1:1–3	44, 85
1:1–5	25
1:1–7a	39, 79–89, 183
1:1–7	182
1:1–15	11
1:2	8, 11, 39, 40, 46, 80, 81–83, 87, 88, 97, 107, 109, 113, 164, 166, 167, 169, 172
1:2–3	86
1:2–4	114
1:2–5	25
1:3	24, 28, 44, 49, 81, 83, 85, 88, 170
1:3–5	47, 89, 139, 184
1:4	21, 23, 24, 25, 34, 35, 38, 39, 44, 45, 48, 81, 83–84, 86, 87, 112, 113, 126, 128, 130, 138, 159, 181
1:4–5	8, 41, 82, 187
1:5	9, 24, 35, 44, 82, 83, 84–85, 88, 89, 143, 149, 156, 169, 170, 171, 180, 182
1:5b	28
1:5b–7a	28
1:6	5, 24, 27, 28, 29, 30, 31, 32, 39, 45, 83, 85, 86, 87, 88, 89, 91, 105, 138, 146, 154, 155, 164, 171
1:6a	80, 85
1:6b	28, 80, 89, 134

1:6–8	44, 47, 179	1:13	9, 10, 11, 42, 44, 88, 91, 92, 94, 95, 96–97, 101, 104, 107, 108, 110, 124, 155, 183
1:7	8, 14, 42, 83, 85, 86, 88, 95, 101, 109, 170		
1:7a	14, 41, 48, 85–86, 91, 95, 109, 110, 133, 134, 138, 146, 176	1:14	14, 27, 45, 47, 83, 93, 94, 95, 97–98, 100, 103, 121, 122, 123, 170
1:7b	91, 105		
1:7b–19a	89, 90–105, 139, 145, 176, 183	1:14b	95
		1:14–15	84
1:8	8, 10, 13, 31, 32, 42, 43, 44, 82, 85, 87, 88, 91–93, 94, 95, 96, 99, 102, 109, 111, 112, 123, 134, 138, 139, 165, 170, 171	1:15	25, 45, 47, 84, 86, 88, 97, 98–99, 100, 103, 104, 114, 136, 170
		1:15–16	179
		1:16	8, 10, 15, 25, 45, 48, 86, 88, 99, 104, 105, 113, 123, 137, 139, 151, 157
1:8b	33, 85, 93		
1:8–9	12, 18, 30, 45, 47, 102, 103, 104, 135, 138, 145, 160, 176, 182, 183		
		1:16b	94, 101, 124
		1:16–17	25, 26, 27, 36, 99, 100, 101, 105, 109, 110, 144, 155, 166
1:8–14	146		
1:8–15	87		
1:8–17	88		
1:9	10, 18, 26, 27, 44, 50, 80, 91, 92, 93–94, 97, 102, 103, 104, 114, 121, 129, 135, 141, 144, 159, 170, 171	1:16b–17a	99
		1:16b–17	99, 101, 107
		1:16–18	176
		1:17	42, 43, 91, 101, 151, 170
		1:17a	105, 170
1:9a	103	1:17b	18, 27, 42, 100, 105
1:9aβ	103	1:17–18	45
1:9–10	27	1:18	18, 27, 28, 85, 88, 101, 105, 110, 146, 155, 160
1:9–14	80		
1:10	25, 45, 85, 86, 88, 93, 94, 124, 136, 144, 150, 155, 166		
		1:19	8, 24, 42, 87, 91, 92, 106, 107, 110, 114, 138
1:10–12	179		
1:11	14, 86, 88, 91, 92, 94, 95, 98, 108, 134	1:19a	101, 105
		1:19b	101, 106–107, 109, 115
1:11a	95		
1:11–12	44	1:19–21	80
1:11–13	44, 48, 93, 94, 98, 103, 115, 160	1:19b–22a	106–110, 173
		1:20	8, 10, 80, 81, 94, 97, 101, 107–108, 110, 124, 181
1:12	44, 80, 88, 92, 94, 95–96, 101, 104, 124, 170, 182		
		1:20b	107

RUTH (continued)		2:6	14, 24, 38, 43, 50, 80, 86, 92, 93, 109, 119, 134, 179
1:20–21	26, 27, 31, 88, 99, 103, 107, 108, 110, 115, 135, 139		
1:20–21a	170	2:7	15, 44, 45, 93, 94, 114, 115, 119–121, 122, 126, 129, 153, 168
1:21	10, 97, 107, 108–109, 110, 122, 159, 160, 179, 181, 182, 183		
1:21b	8, 170	2:7a	26, 119, 120
1:21–22	179	2:7b	119, 129
1:22	14, 38, 42, 43, 44, 47, 80, 86, 91, 92, 93, 94, 95, 102, 119, 128, 129, 134, 164, 166	2:7–8	119
		2:8	15, 44, 48, 50, 85, 97, 113, 115, 119, 121–122, 123, 129, 133, 136, 139, 144, 151, 159
1:22a	109, 110, 114		
1:22b	95, 111, 114, 138	2:8–9	133, 139, 141
1:22b–2:2	111–115, 153, 157	2:9	3, 50, 94, 119, 121, 122, 124, 126, 153, 156, 168
2:1	7, 15, 32, 43, 44, 46, 47, 81, 87, 110, 111–113, 114, 115, 124, 130, 135, 139, 142, 150, 171, 176, 181, 186		
		2:10	7, 37, 43, 100, 108, 114, 115, 122–123, 124, 129, 130, 138, 149, 151, 152, 154, 156, 165
2:2	8, 15, 38, 44, 48, 110, 113–114, 115, 117, 119, 122, 124, 125, 129, 130, 136, 139, 146, 158	2:11	8, 10, 14, 15, 24, 25, 26, 44, 45, 47, 48, 86, 100, 110, 113, 115, 123–124, 125, 129, 130, 139, 144, 145
2:2a	43		
2:2b	43	2:11b	98
2:3	9, 15, 30, 42, 44, 45, 80, 81, 110, 112, 117–118, 119, 124, 128, 135, 158, 164, 172	2:11–12	25
		2:12	10, 23, 30, 48, 85, 93, 99, 102, 124, 130, 149, 154, 161
		2:13	7, 25, 30, 43, 47, 97, 108, 114, 124–125, 129, 130, 149, 151, 160
2:3–17	116–131		
2:4	12, 31, 85, 89, 97, 102, 113, 113, 128, 148, 156, 163		
		2:14	4, 8, 84, 94, 125–126, 127, 130, 132, 153, 168
2:4–7	80		
2:5	25, 50, 80, 110, 118–119, 123, 128, 138, 154, 158, 160	2:15	15, 50, 80, 97, 126, 129, 136, 151, 156
		2:15–16	130
2:5–6	46	2:15–19	119
2:5–7	27		

214 INDEX OF ANCIENT SOURCES

2:16	8, 10, 15, 94, 100, 113, 125, 126–127, 130, 139, 151, 156	3:1	44, 47, 48, 87, 93, 103, 104, 115, 122, 125, 137, 140, 141–142, 145, 158, 159, 160, 183
2:17	7, 15, 120, 127–128, 131, 132, 133, 138		
2:17–18	87, 156	3:1–2	95, 98, 104
2:18	8, 15, 84, 126, 132–133, 134, 138, 160	3:1–4	135, 146
		3:1–5	139, 131–146, 151, 154, 168, 169
2:18–19	47		
2:18–20	125	3:2	44, 50, 111, 142, 143, 161
2:18–23	132–140, 145, 157, 173		
		3:2–4	145, 146, 173
2:19	7, 12, 14, 15, 86, 102, 114, 123, 127, 133–134, 138, 139, 140, 152, 154, 156, 160	3:3	21, 44, 47, 80, 94, 142–143, 144, 149, 156, 161, 166, 182
		3:3–4	153, 156, 174
		3:4	8, 94, 106, 121, 142, 143–144, 152, 153, 154, 156, 164, 166, 168, 170, 182
2:19bα	138		
2:19bβ	138		
2:19–20	8		
2:19b–20a	113	3:5	144, 146, 149, 150, 153, 154, 159
2:20	7, 8, 10, 12, 15, 17, 18, 20, 30, 31, 32, 33, 42, 44, 45, 46, 47, 80, 82, 86, 87, 88, 100, 102, 110, 112, 114, 115, 124, 126, 134–136, 138, 139, 144, 145, 149, 151, 155, 163, 167, 168, 173, 174, 179	3:6	47, 97, 127, 142, 161
		3:6–7	153
		3:6–15	25, 37, 144, 147–157, 169, 174, 175
		3:7	8, 25, 28, 143, 148, 152, 153, 156, 164
		3:7–8	41
		3:8	80, 106, 143, 148, 152, 153, 155, 156, 157
		3:9	3, 10, 23, 30, 43, 47, 80, 94, 108, 110, 112, 129, 130, 135, 137, 138, 148–149, 154, 155, 156, 158, 160, 161, 166
2:20b	130		
2:20–23	44, 47		
2:21	38, 43, 50, 85, 97, 121, 123, 133, 136, 137, 139, 140		
2:22	44, 48, 50, 85, 99, 115, 129, 136–137, 158	3:10	10, 12, 30, 32, 33, 41, 49, 89, 102, 103, 134, 138, 149, 156
2:22–23	146		
2:23	15, 47, 50, 97, 98, 115, 119, 121, 123, 137–138, 140, 141, 142, 145, 146, 159, 166	3:10–11	44, 48, 115
		3:11	12, 13, 32, 41, 80, 85, 112, 143, 144, 149–150, 151, 154, 156, 170, 171, 172, 176, 181
2:23b	48, 119		

RUTH (*continued*)

3:12	17, 44, 80, 86, 94, 108, 112, 114, 115, 130, 135, 150–151, 154, 163, 165	4:4	3, 8, 80, 83, 85, 108, 164–165, 166, 170, 171, 175
3:12b	108	4:4a	108, 173
3:13	10, 18, 37, 41, 94, 97, 105, 106, 108, 112, 136, 143, 150, 151–152, 155, 156, 157, 163, 164, 172, 174, 175, 176	4:4b	108, 174, 175
		4:4b–5a	175
		4:5	3, 8, 12, 38, 41, 43, 44, 45, 48, 82, 93, 94, 112, 142, 145, 165–167, 169, 170, 173, 174, 175, 176, 177, 179
3:13a	155	4:5b	168, 175
3:13b	155	4:5–6	128
3:14	3, 4, 18, 28, 80, 85, 143, 152, 155, 156, 161	4:6	8, 45, 80, 85, 135, 139, 151, 164, 167–168, 169, 174
3:14a	25, 28	4:7	8, 19, 39, 85, 94, 119, 163, 168–169, 175, 177
3:15	128, 152–153, 156, 159, 160, 168		
3:16	4, 25, 44, 48, 97, 110, 115, 125, 138, 154, 156, 158–159, 160	4:8	8, 14, 15, 80, 85, 164, 169, 174
		4:9	81, 82, 85, 164, 166, 169–170, 171
3:16b	160	4:9–10	175
3:16–17	47	4:10	8, 9, 12, 25, 37, 38, 41, 43, 44, 45, 82, 85, 99, 112, 145, 154, 161, 165, 166, 167, 169, 170, 172, 174, 175, 176, 179
3:16–18	156, 157, 158–161		
3:17	3, 10, 26, 110, 129, 139, 144, 153, 156, 159, 160, 179		
3:17b	173		
3:18	44, 47, 48, 94, 115, 121, 143, 145, 156, 159–160, 172	4:10–11	12
		4:11	14, 18, 33, 35, 37, 40, 43, 44, 46, 83, 91, 92, 102, 121, 150,170–172, 175, 176, 179, 181, 183, 187
Chapter 4	15		
4:1	8, 12, 80, 85, 94, 95, 135, 142, 148, 150, 151, 163–164		
4:1–8	115		
4:1–12	99, 104, 145, 162–177, 182	4:11–12	12, 13, 19, 30, 33, 40, 42, 46, 87, 102, 103, 184, 187, 188
4:2	163, 164, 170, 172		
4:3	14, 15, 26, 44, 45, 48, 80, 81, 85, 92, 93, 109, 112, 128, 135, 139, 145, 160, 164, 169, 170, 172, 179	4:11–14	31
		4:11–22	87
		4:12	8, 40, 41, 42, 44, 46, 168, 171, 172, 175, 183, 186

4:13	5, 8, 29, 30, 31, 32, 33, 34, 37, 44, 88, 112, 125, 157, 171, 176, 178–179, 182, 187	**ESTHER**	
		1:1	79
		1:10	148
		1:19	84, 151
		2:7	180
4:13–17	178–184	2:8	106
4:14	12, 30, 33, 80, 85, 102, 107, 134, 135, 138, 172, 179, 181, 182, 183	2:15	114
		2:17	114
		2:28	114
		3:4	106
4:14–15	50, 87, 104, 145, 182	5:2	106
4:15	36, 44, 47, 97, 110, 159, 179–180, 181, 182, 187	5:8	114
		6:10	159
		DANIEL	
4:16	9, 84, 88, 97, 179, 180, 183, 185	2:3	167
		2:6	96
4:17	5, 11, 44, 50, 80, 81, 83, 102, 119, 172, 178, 180–181, 183, 184, 186	2:9	96
		2:11	96
		2:30	96
		3:28	96
4:17b	172	4:24	96
4:17c	184, 186, 188	6:6 (Eng. 6:5)	96
4:17–22	26, 40, 45, 176	6:8 (Eng. 6:7)	96
4:17b–22	18, 19	6:13 (Eng. 6:12)	96
4:18	13, 111, 185	8:2	106
4:18–19	12	8:13	163
4:18–22	4, 5, 19, 42, 44, 83, 94, 95, 178, 182, 185	8:15	106
		9:13	82
4:19	185–186, 187	10:6	143
4:20	185, 186	10:11	108
4:21	40, 128, 186	11:41	38
4:22	11, 39, 40, 81, 83, 181, 186	**EZRA**	
		8:18	82
LAMENTATIONS		9:1–2	38, 39
3:8	107	9:2	83
3:12	107	9:11	144
4:5	180	9:12	83
		10:2	123
ECCLESIASTES		10:10–11	123
2:7	166	10:14	12, 123
2:14	117	10:17–18	123
3:20	170	10:26	81
7:3	148	10:44	83, 123
7:19	180		
9:7	148		

NEHEMIAH		2:37–38	181
1:4	106	2:46	40
1:6	108	2:48–49	40
2:13	96	2:50–55	40
2:15	96	2:51	83, 186
3:32	101	2:54	186
8:8	17	2:1–4:23	40
12:10–11	95	3:1–2	39
13:1	17, 20	3:19	22
13:1–2	38, 39, 41, 163	3:22	166
		4:4	40
13:3	106	4:5	40
13:4	112	4:7	40
13:5	168	4:9	40
13:25	83, 104	4:18–19	40
13:26	123	4:22	38, 39, 181
13:26–27	123	4:22b	39, 175
		5:1	171
I CHRONICLES		5:3	171
1:19	81, 181	6:4 (Eng. 6:19)	82
1:34	171, 187, 188	6:7 (Eng. 6:22)	186
1:46	81	6:14 (Eng. 6:29)	82
2:1	171, 188	6:23	171
2:1–11	187	6:32 (Eng. 6:47)	82
2:3	188	7:18	82
2:3–4	40	7:29	171
2:4	40	8:8	81
2:5	40, 185, 186	9:13	112
2:9	185	9:20	168
2:9–12	40, 111, 185, 186	9:34–44	95
2:10	185, 186	11:2	124
2:10–11	186	11:26	181
2:11	128, 186	11:46	39, 81
2:12	181	11:47	181
2:15	40, 181, 185, 186	12:40	83
		13:2	151
2:16–18	40	15:10	186
2:17	39	17:1	108
2:19	40	17:9–10	12
2:21	40	17:25	164
2:24	40	18:2	38
2:25	185	21:16	101
2:26	40	23:21	82
2:27	185	23:23	82
2:29	40	24:26	82
2:34	40	24:28	82
2:34–35	40, 104	24:30	82

26:6	112, 181
26:7	181
26:31	112

2 CHRONICLES
2:10	137
2:11–12	113
2:15	113
3:17	113
4:17	83, 101
7:10	148
9:8	133
11:18	82
11:21	83
12:1	106
12:13	39–40
13:2	101
13:3	112
13:21	83
17:13–14	112
17:16–17	112
18:3	105
19:5–6	12
21:13	91
22:8	106
23:1	181
23:8	147
24:3	83
25:6	112
25:14	106
25:16	106
26:5	106
27:5	137
29:31	125
32:21	112
33:12	82

Apocrypha and Pseudepigrapha
BEN SIRA
7:23	83

TOBIT
7:13	102
7:14–17	91

JUDITH
	16

JUBILEES
16:7–9	41
28:9–24	14

Christian Scriptures
MATTHEW
1:3	185
1:5	40, 113
22:23–33	103
26:18	163

LUKE
3:32	113, 186
3:33	185

Qumran Literature
2QRuth[a]	4, 125, 126, 127, 132, 133, 134, 135, 136, 137, 142, 143, 144, 147, 148
2QRuth[b]	4, 151, 152, 153, 158
4QRuth[a]	4, 80, 83, 84, 93, 94, 99
4QRuth[b]	4, 80, 96, 97, 99

Mishna
YEBAMOT 6.6	34

Babylonian Talmud
BAVA BATRA
14b	11
14b–15a	19
91a	37, 39, 87

BAVA QAMMA 103B	32
BAVA METZI'A 47A	169
KETUBBOT 7B	172
MEGILLAH 23B	172

SANHEDRIN 93A	160	**Other Rabbinic Sources**	
SHABBAT 113B	142	MAIMONIDES	32
SOTAH 42B	84	**Inscriptions**	
		ARAD	
		16.2–3	118, 134
Jerusalem Talmud		21.3–4	118, 134
		21.4	124
YEBAMOT 8:3	119	40.3	134
Aggadic Literature		ELAMITE TOMB INSCRIPTION	149
AVOT OF RABBI NATHAN		HAZOR 6	81
5:2–3	187	KHIRBET EL-QÔM 3.2	134
GENESIS RABBAH		KUNTILLET 'AJRÛD	
41:10	42	9	134
		19A.5–6	134
RUTH RABBAH		MESAD HASHAVYAHU	
1:4	87	lines 2–3	120
1:4–5	87		
1:19	37		
2:1	152	MESHA INSCRIPTION	38
2:9	38, 84		
2:10	87, 110	Line 3	99
2:14	32	5	99
4:3	119	8	99
4:6	35	12	84, 99
5	137	13	99
5:12	142	14	99
6:2	36	17	99
6:3	151	18	99
6:4	157	19	99
7:1	152, 157	32	99
7:4	159	33	99
7:7	163		
7:14	34	SILOAM	
		Line 4	97
RUTH ZUTA			
1:1	11	SILWAN I	149
1:4	84		

| YAVNEH-YAM | 109, 127 | ENKI AND NINMAH | 33 |
| Lines 4–5 | 119 | | |

Other Ancient Near Eastern Texts

| | | GEZER CALENDAR | 137 |
| EPIC OF ATRA-HASIS | 33 | KIRTA | 18, 33, 81, 183 |